Christina L

Paul Seligson

with Anna Lowy
Rachel Godfrey
Beatriz Martín García
Kate Mellersh

ENGLISH FILE

Pre-intermediate Teacher's Book

Paul Seligson and Clive Oxenden are the original co-authors of *English File 1* and *English File 2*

Great Clarendon Street, Oxford, OX2 6DP, United Kingdom

Oxford University Press is a department of the University of Oxford. It furthers the University's objective of excellence in research, scholarship, and education by publishing worldwide. Oxford is a registered trade mark of Oxford University Press in the UK and in certain other countries

First published in 2012
2016 2015 2014 2013 2012
10 9 8 7 6 5 4 3 2 1

ISBN: 978 0 19 459825 5 Book
ISBN: 978 0 19 459808 8 Test and Assessment CD-ROM
ISBN: 978 0 19 459875 0 Pack

Printed in Spain by Orymu S. A.

This book is printed on paper from certified and well-managed sources

ACKNOWLEDGEMENTS

The publisher would like to thank the following for their kind permission to reproduce photographs and other copyright material: Alamy Images pp.162 (TV interview/ Captured Sight), 248 (Man with long moustache/Wesley Roberts), 248 (Man laughing/UpperCut Images), 248 (Portrait of man/Steven Frame), 255 (Musee du Louvre/Didier ZYLBERYNG), 255 (St. Paul's Cathedral/nobleIMAGES), 255 (Brighton Beach/scenicireland.com/Christopher Hill Photographic); Corbis pp.234 (Obama/ Kevin Dietsch), 234 (Justin Timberlake/Peter Andrews), 234 (Orlando Bloom/ Joe Stevens), 234 (Madonna/Kurt Krieger); Getty Images pp.213 (Loch Ness Monster/Hulton Archive), 234 (Jennifer Aniston/Steve Granitz/), 234 (Nicole Kidman/Pascal Le Segretain), 270 (Nightclub/Nicholas Monu/Photodisc); Kobal Collection p.272 (*The Spy Who Loved Me* movie poster/Eon Productions); Oxford University Press p.255 (Statue of Liberty/Thinkstock); Rex Features pp.235 (Jerry Hall), 235 (Elizabeth Jagger/David Fisher); 213 (Great white breaching/Charles Maxwell) 213 (HH-60G Pave Hawk Helicopter/Lance Cheung)

Illustrations by: Emma Brownjon pp.168, 189, 193, 260; Mark Duffin pp.162, 215, 227, 229; Joy Gosney pp.171, 183, 186, 232, 273, 278, 279; Ben Hasler pp.194, 196, 237; Javier Joaquim p.269; Sophie Joyce pp.274, 276; Joanna Kerr pp.170, 174, 192, 217, 239; Jerome Mirault p.231; Roger Penwill pp.163, 165, 167, 172, 176, 178, 184, 187, 195, 259; Lucy Truman pp.268, 275; Kath Walker pp.164, 166, 173, 188, 190, 191, 220, 240, 250, 271, 277

Although every effort has been made to trace and contact copyright holders before publication, this has not been possible in some cases. We apologise for any apparent infringement of copyright and, if notified, the publisher will be pleased to rectify any errors or omissions at the earliest possible opportunity.

Contents

Syllabus checklist

		Grammar	Vocabulary
	1		
4	**A Where are you from?**	word order in questions	common verb phrases, spelling and numbers
6	**B Charlotte's choice**	present simple	describing people: appearance and personality
8	**C Mr and Mrs Clark and Percy**	present continuous	clothes, prepositions of place
10	**PRACTICAL ENGLISH** Episode 1 Hotel problems		
	2		
12	**A Right place, wrong person**	past simple: regular and irregular verbs	holidays
14	**B The story behind the photo**	past continuous	prepositions of time and place: *at*, *in*, *on*
16	**C One dark October evening**	time sequencers and connectors	verb phrases
18	**REVISE AND CHECK 1&2**		
	3		
20	**A Plans and dreams**	*be going to* (plans and predictions)	airports
22	**B Let's meet again**	present continuous (future arrangements)	verbs + prepositions e.g. *arrive in*
24	**C What's the word?**	defining relative clauses	expressions for paraphrasing: *like*, *for, example*, etc.
26	**PRACTICAL ENGLISH** Episode 2 Restaurant problems		
	4		
28	**A Parents and teenagers**	present perfect + *yet*, *just*, *already*	housework, *make* or *do*?
30	**B Fashion and shopping**	present perfect or past simple? (1)	shopping
32	**C Lost weekend**	*something*, *anything*, *nothing*, etc.	adjectives ending *-ed* and *-ing*
34	**REVISE AND CHECK 3&4**		
	5		
36	**A No time for anything**	comparative adjectives and adverbs, *as... as*	time expressions: *spend time*, etc.
38	**B Superlative cities**	superlatives (+ *ever* + present perfect)	describing a town or city
40	**C How much is too much?**	quantifiers, *too*, *not enough*	health and the body
42	**PRACTICAL ENGLISH** Episode 3 The wrong shoes		
	6		
44	**A Are you a pessimist?**	*will / won't* (predictions)	opposite verbs
46	**B I'll never forget you**	*will / won't* (decisions, offers, promises)	verb + *back*
48	**C The meaning of dreaming**	review of verb forms: present, past, and future	adjectives + prepositions
50	**REVISE AND CHECK 5&6**		

Pronunciation	Speaking	Listening	Reading
vowel sounds, the alphabet	Common verb phrases: home and family, job / studies, free time		
final *-s* / *-es*	Do you have a friend who is looking for a partner?	Charlotte's two dates	Who knows you better – your mother or your best friend?
/ə/ and /ɜː/	Describing a picture	David Hockney's *Mr and Mrs Clark and Percy*	
regular verbs: *-ed* endings	Your last holiday	Mia and Linda	The place is perfect, the weather is wonderful
sentence stress	Talking about photographs	*The image that cost a fortune*	A moment in history
word stress	The story of Hannah and Jamie	When Hannah met Jamie	
			We were there!
sentence stress and fast speech		Three travel plans	Top airports in the world
sounding friendly		Facebook friends	Flight details
pronunciation in a dictionary	*What's the word?*	TV game show	900 new words in 3 months
/j/ and /dʒ/		Teenage carers	Teenagers have annoying habits – but so do their parents
c and *ch*	Present perfect questionnaire	*Have you ever bought something that you've never worn?*	The style interview
/e/, /əʊ/, and /ʌ/	Last weekend	*Sven's weekend*	What did you really do at the weekend?
			Shoe shops discover matching crimes
sentence stress	Spending time	Expert advice	We're living faster, but are we living better?
word and sentence stress	All capital cities are unfriendly – or are they?	Three tests in London	All capital cities are unfriendly – or are they?
/ʌ/, /uː/, /aɪ/, and /e/	Diet and lifestyle questionnaire	Radio programme – *Lifestyle*	Everything bad is good for you
'll, won't	Are you a positive thinker?	Radio programme – *Positive thinking*	A pessimist plays a pessimist
word stress: two-syllable verbs	I'll never forget you		I'll never forget you
the letters *ow*	Revision questionnaire	Understanding your dreams	Dreams
			Can music really make you run faster?

			Grammar	Vocabulary
7				
52	**A**	**How to...**	uses of the infinitive with *to*	verbs + infinitive: *try to, forget to*, etc.
54	**B**	**Being happy**	uses of the gerund (verb + *-ing*)	verbs + gerund
56	**C**	**Learn a language in a month!**	*have to, don't have to, must, mustn't*	modifiers: *a bit, really*, etc.
58		**PRACTICAL ENGLISH** Episode 4 At the pharmacy		
8				
60	**A**	**I don't know what to do!**	*should*	*get*
62	**B**	**If something can go wrong,...**	*if* + present, *will* + infinitive (first conditional)	confusing verbs
64	**C**	**You must be mine**	possessive pronouns	adverbs of manner
66		**REVISE AND CHECK 7&8**		
9				
68	**A**	**What would you do?**	*if* + past, *would* + infinitive (second conditional)	animals
70	**B**	**I've been afraid of it for years**	present perfect + *for* and *since*	phobias and words related to fear
72	**C**	**Born to sing**	present perfect or past simple? (2)	biographies
74		**PRACTICAL ENGLISH** Episode 5 Getting around		
10				
76	**A**	**The mothers of invention**	passive	verbs: *invent, discover*, etc.
78	**B**	**Could do better**	*used to*	school subjects
80	**C**	**Mr Indecisive**	*might*	word building: noun formation
82		**REVISE AND CHECK 9&10**		
11				
84	**A**	**Bad losers**	expressing movement	sports, expressing movement
86	**B**	**Are you a morning person?**	word order of phrasal verbs	phrasal verbs
88	**C**	**What a coincidence!**	*so, neither* + auxiliaries	similarities
90		**PRACTICAL ENGLISH** Episode 6 Time to go home		
12				
92	**A**	**Strange but true!**	past perfect	verb phrases
94	**B**	**Gossip is good for you**	reported speech	*say* or *tell*?
96	**C**	**The *English File* quiz**	questions without auxiliaries	revision
98		**REVISE AND CHECK 11&12**		

100 **Communication**
111 **Writing**
118 **Listening**
126 **Grammar Bank**
150 **Vocabulary Bank**
164 **Irregular verbs**
166 **Sound Bank**

Pronunciation	Speaking	Listening	Reading
weak form of *to*, linking		Nigel's first meeting	How to Survive Meeting Your Girlfriend's Parents for the First Time
the letter *i*	Singing and being happy	Singing school	
must, mustn't	Have you ever...?	Language tests	I will survive (in Spanish) ...or will I?
/ʊ/ and /uː/, sentence stress	What's the problem?	Radio programme – *What's the problem?*	Too macho to talk?
linking		Holiday couple survive seven natural disasters	It always happens
sentence rhythm		*Girl* continued	*Girl* by O.Henry
			Why are the British so bad at learning languages?
word stress	What would you do...?		Would you know what to do?
sentence stress	Questionnaire revising tenses	Three phobias	Scared of spiders. Take this pill.
word stress, /ɔː/	Talking about an older person	*Top Sounds*	Like father like son
/ʃ/, *-ed*, sentence stress	Passives quiz	Radio programme – *Inventions*	Did you know...?
used to / didn't use to	Did you use to...?	Memories of school	
diphthongs	Are you indecisive?		Is too much choice making us unhappy?
			Dolphins save swimmers from a shark attack
sports	Sport – you love it or you hate it		Bad losers?
linking	Phrasal verb questionnaire		Early bird!
sentence stress, /ð/ and /θ/	True sentences	Facebook coincidence	
contractions: *had / hadn't*		And finally ...	News round the world
double consonants	An anecdote	Rosemary and Iris	Here's a secret: Gossip might be good for you
revision	General knowledge quiz		
			Heart couple's amazing coincidence

Our aim with *English File third edition* has been to make every lesson better and more student- and teacher-friendly. As well as the main A, B, C Student's Books lessons, there is a range of material which can be used according to your students' needs and the time available. Don't forget:

- the Practical English video and exercises (also available on class audio)
- the Revise & Check pages, with video (also available on class audio)
- Photocopiable Grammar, Vocabulary, Communicative, and Song activities

STUDY LINK iTutor, Workbook (print or online) iChecker, Online skills, Pronunciation app, and the Student's website provide multimedia review, support, and practice for students outside the classroom.

The Teacher's Book also suggests different ways of exploiting many of the Student's Book activities depending on the level of your class. We very much hope you enjoy using *English File*.

What do Pre-intermediate students need?

Pre-intermediate students are at a crucial stage in their learning. Students at this level need material that maintains their enthusiasm and confidence. They need to know how much they are learning and what they can now achieve. At the same time they need the encouragement to push themselves to use the new language that they are learning.

Grammar, Vocabulary, and Pronunciation

At any level the tools students need to speak English with confidence are Grammar, Vocabulary, and Pronunciation (G, V, P). In *English File third edition* all three elements are given equal importance. Each lesson has clearly stated grammar, vocabulary, and pronunciation aims. This keeps lessons focused and gives students concrete learning objectives and a sense of progress.

Grammar

Pre-intermediate students need

- clear and memorable presentations of new structures
- regular and motivating practice
- student-friendly reference material.

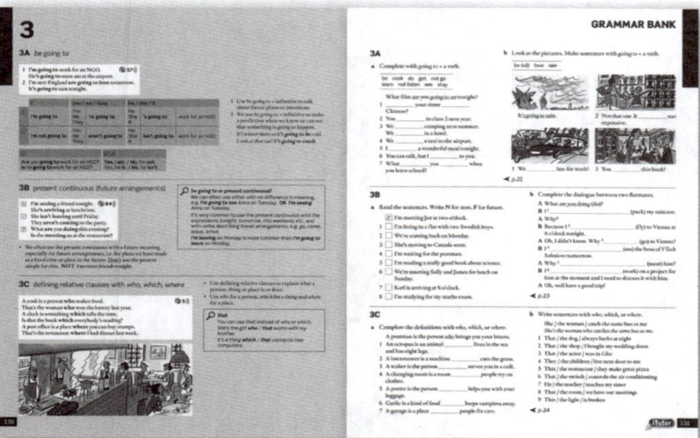
3

3A be going to

GRAMMAR BANK

3B present continuous (future arrangements)

3C defining relative clauses with who, which, where

English File third edition Pre-intermediate provides contexts for new language that will engage students, using real-life stories and situations, humour, and suspense. The **Grammar Banks** give students a single, easy-to-access grammar reference section, with clear rules, example sentences with audio, and common errors. There are at least two practice exercises for each grammar point.

Vocabulary

Pre-intermediate students need

- to revise and reactivate previously learnt vocabulary
- to increase their knowledge of high-frequency words and phrases
- tasks which encourage them to use new vocabulary
- accessible reference material

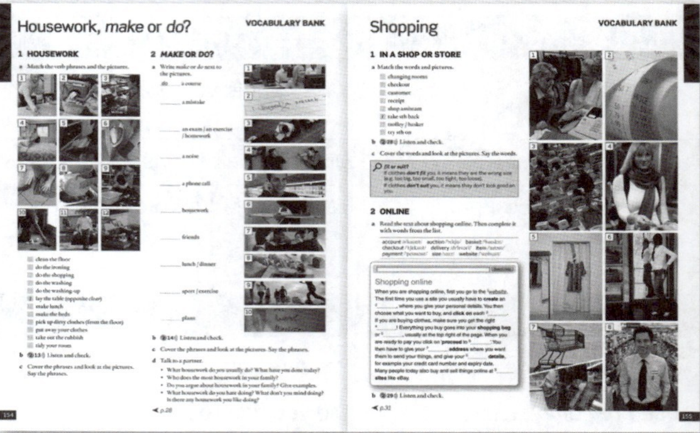
Housework, *make* or *do*?

VOCABULARY BANK

1 HOUSEWORK

2 MAKE OR DO?

Shopping

VOCABULARY BANK

1 IN A SHOP OR STORE

2 ONLINE

Every lesson focuses on high frequency vocabulary and common lexical areas, but keeps the load realistic. Many lessons are linked to the **Vocabulary Banks** which help present and practise the vocabulary in class, give an audio model of each word, and provide a clear reference so students can revise and test themselves in their own time.

Pronunciation

Pre-intermediate students need

- a solid foundation in the sounds of English.
- targeted pronunciation development.
- to see where there are rules and patterns.

or	sport door	water four
al	talk small	bought thought
aw	saw draw	

With new language come fresh pronunciation challenges for pre-intermediate learners, particularly sound-spelling relationships, silent letters, and weak forms. Students who studied with *English File 3rd edition Elementary* will already be familiar with English File's unique system of sound pictures, which give clear example words to help identify and produce sounds. *English File Pre-intermediate* continues with a pronunciation focus in every lesson, which integrates improving students' pronunciation into grammar and vocabulary practice.

Speaking

Pre-intermediate students need

- topics that will inspire their interest.
- tasks that push them to incorporate new language
- a sense of progress in their ability to speak

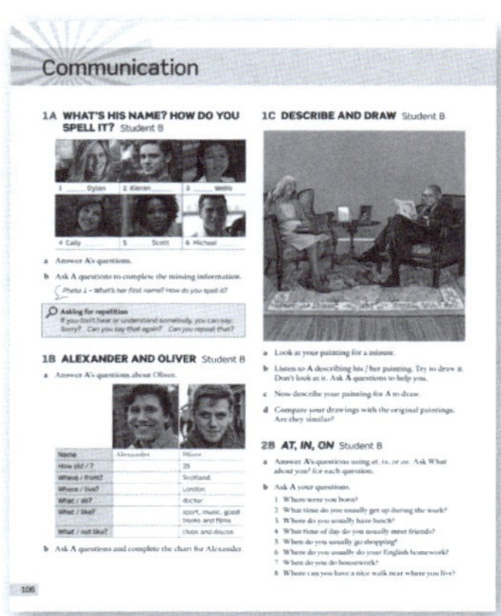
Communication

The ultimate aim of most students is to be able to communicate orally in English. Every lesson in *English File Pre-intermediate* has a speaking activity which activates grammar, vocabulary, and pronunciation. The tasks are designed to help students to feel a sense of progress and to show that the number of situations in which they can communicate effectively is growing.

Listening

Pre-intermediate students need

- confidence-building achievable tasks
- to practise getting gist and listening for detail
- to make sense of connected speech.
- a reason to listen

At pre-intermediate level students need confidence-building tasks which are progressively more challenging in terms of speed, length, and language difficulty, but are always achievable. They also need a variety of listening tasks which practise listening for gist and for specific details. We have chosen material we hope students will want to listen to.

Reading

Pre-intermediate students need

- engaging topics and stimulating texts.
- manageable tasks that help students to read.

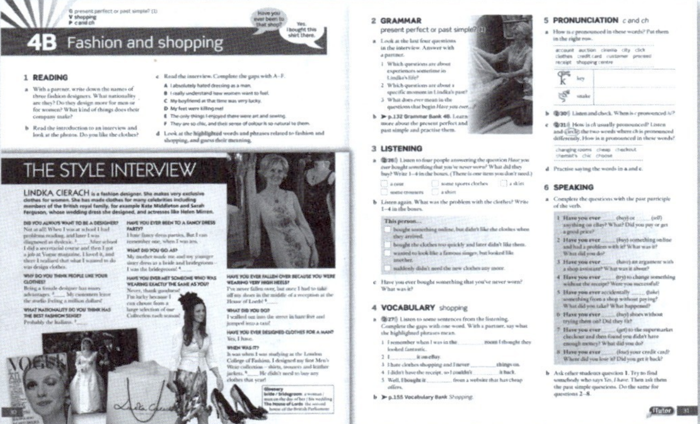
4B Fashion and shopping

THE STYLE INTERVIEW

Many students need to read in English for their work or studies, and reading is also important in helping to build vocabulary and to consolidate grammar. The key to encouraging students to read is to give them motivating but accessible material and tasks they can do. In *English File Pre-intermediate* reading texts have been adapted from a variety of real sources (the press, magazines, news websites) and have been chosen for their intrinsic interest.

Writing

Pre-intermediate students need

- clear models.
- an awareness of register, structure, and fixed phrases.

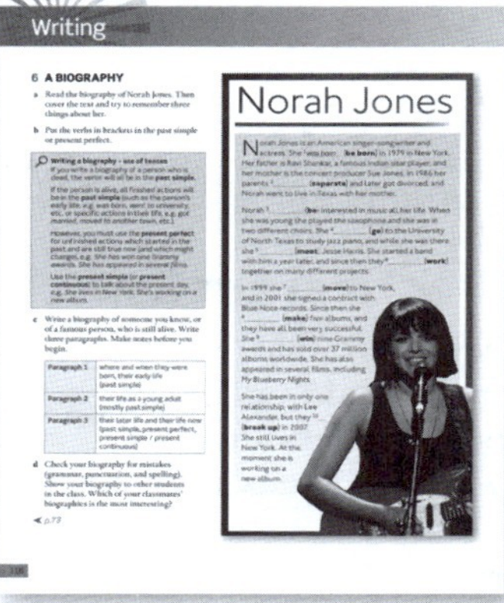
Writing

Norah Jones

The growth of the Internet and email means that people worldwide are writing in English more than ever before both for business and personal communication. There are guided writing tasks in each File.

Practical English

Pre-intermediate students need

- to understand high-frequency phrases that they will hear
- to know what to say in typical situations
- to know how to overcome typical travel problems

The six *Practical English* lessons give students practice in key language for situations such as explaining that there are problems in a hotel or in a restaurant, or taking something back to a shop. To make these everyday situations come alive there is a story line involving two main characters, Jenny (from New York) and Rob (from London). The story line carries on from where it left off in *English File Elementary*, but it is self-standing, so can be used equally with students who did not use this level. The **You hear / You say** feature makes a clear distinction between what students will *hear* and need to understand, for example *How can I help you?* and what they need to say, for example *There's a problem with the air-conditioning*. The lessons also highlight other key 'Social English' phrases such as *Here you are. Time to go*. The Practical English lessons are on the ***English File Pre-intermediate DVD***, and ***iTools***. Teachers can also use the Practical English Student's Book exercises with the class audio-CD. Using the video will provide a change of focus and give the lessons a clear visual context. The video will make the lessons more enjoyable and will also help students to roleplay the situations. Students can watch and listen to the Practical English video on their ***iTutor***.

Revision

Pre-intermediate students need

- regular review.
- a sense of progress.

Students will usually only assimilate and *remember* new language if they have the chance to see it and use it several times. Grammar, Vocabulary, and Pronunciation are recycled throughout the course. After every two Files there is a two-page Revise & Check section. The left-hand page revises the grammar, vocabulary, and pronunciation of each File. The right-hand page provides a series of skills-based challenges, including video interviews, and helps students to measure their progress in terms of competence. These pages are designed to be used flexibly according to the needs of your students. There is also a separate short film on video for students to watch and enjoy.

Student's Book Files 1–12

The Student's Book has twelve Files. Each File is organized like this:

A, B, and C lessons

Each file contains three two-page lessons which present and practise **Grammar**, **Vocabulary**, and **Pronunciation** with a balance of reading and listening activities, and lots of opportunities for speaking. These lessons have clear references > to the Grammar Bank, Vocabulary Bank, and Sound Bank at the back of the book.

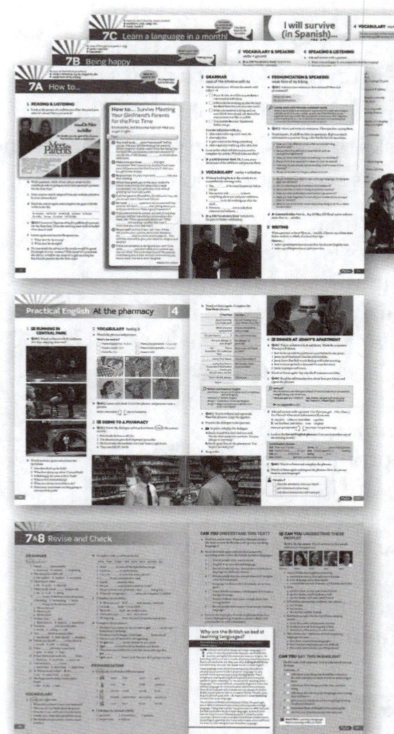

Practical English

Every two Files (starting from File 1), there is a two-page lesson which teaches functional 'survival English' (for example langauge for checking into a hotel or ordering a meal) and also social English (useful phrases like *Nice to meet you, Let's go.*). The lessons have a story line and link with the *English File Pre-intermediate Video.*

Revise & Check

Every two Files (starting from File 2) there is a two-page section revising **Grammar**, **Vocabulary**, and **Pronunciation** of each File and providing **Reading**, **Listening**, and **Speaking** '*Can you...?*' challenges to show students what they can achieve.

The back of the Student's Book

The lessons contain references to these sections: Communication, Writing, Listening, Grammar Bank, Vocabulary Bank, and Sound Bank.

STUDY LINK

iTutor

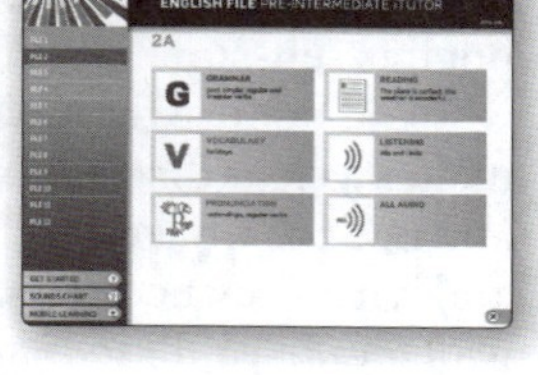

For students to review after class, or catch up on a class they have missed.

- All the Grammar, Vocabulary, and Pronunciation
- Readings (with audio)
- Listenings (with tapescripts)
- All the video for Practical English, In the Street, and Short films
- Revise and Check readings and dictations
- All video and audio can be transferred to mobile devices.
- iTutor does not contain the songs or the surprise endings to stories or lessons.

Workbook

For practice after class

- All the Grammar, Vocabulary, and Pronunciation, and Practical English
- Extra reading
- A listening exercise for every lesson
- Pronunciation exercises with audio
- Useful Words and Phrases
- Audio for Pronunciation and Listening exercises (on iChecker)
- Available with or without key

Online workbook

- All the Workbook content, with instant answers
- Hints and tips
- 'Speak and record'
- Audio for all the Reading texts and Useful Words and Phrases

Online skills

For students to develop and practice their skills

- Reading and Listening with exercises for every File
- Writing and Speaking models and tasks for every File

iChecker

For students to check their progress and challenge themselves

- Progress Check, with 30 multiple choice questions on Grammar, Vocabulary, and Practical English for each File
- Challenge, where students build a text using the language they have learnt from the File
- Audio Bank, with all the audio for the Workbook listening and pronunciation

Pronunciation app

For students to learn and practise the sounds of English

- Individual sounds
- Sounds in useful phrases
- Speak and record

Student's website

www.oup.com/elt/englishfile

- Extra practice of Grammar, Vocabulary, Pronunciation and Practical English
- Learning resources
- **Games and puzzles**

For teachers

Teacher's Book

Detailed lesson plans for all the lessons including:

- an optional 'books-closed' lead-in for every lesson
- **Extra idea** suggestions for optional extra activities
- **Extra challenge** suggestions for ways of exploiting the Student's Book material in a more challenging way if you have a stronger class
- **Extra support** suggestions for ways of adapting activities or exercises to make them work with weaker students

Extra activities are colour coded so you can see at a glance what is core material and what is extra when you are planning and teaching your classes.

All lesson plans include keys and complete audio scripts.

Over 100 pages of photocopiable activities in the Teacher's Book

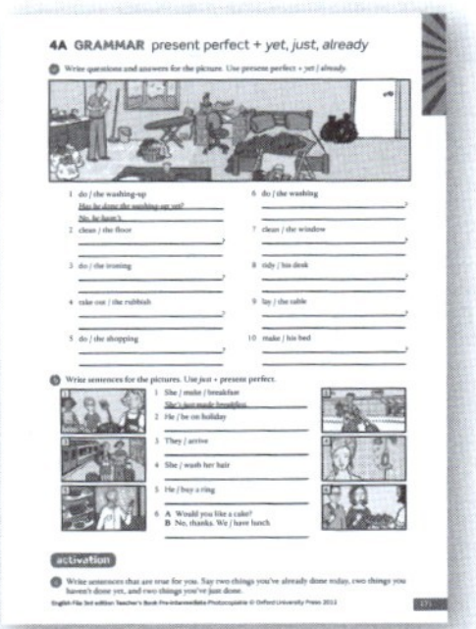

Grammar

see *pp. 162–197*

- An activity for every Grammar Bank, which can be used in class or for self-study extra practice
- An Activation section, to encourage students to use the new language in class

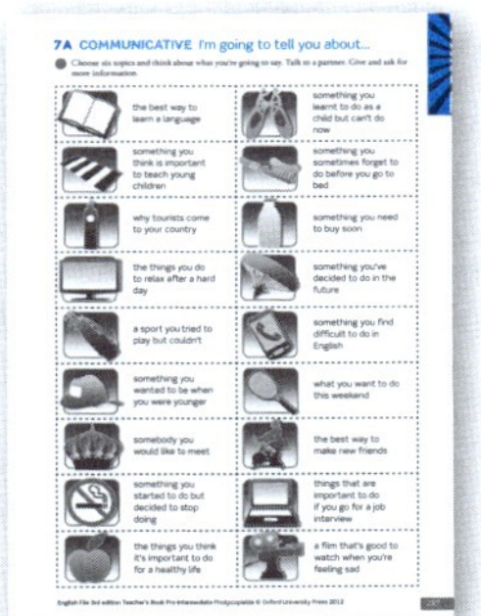

Communicative

see *pp.209–244*

- Extra speaking practice for every A, B, C lesson
- 'No cut' alternatives to reduce preparation time

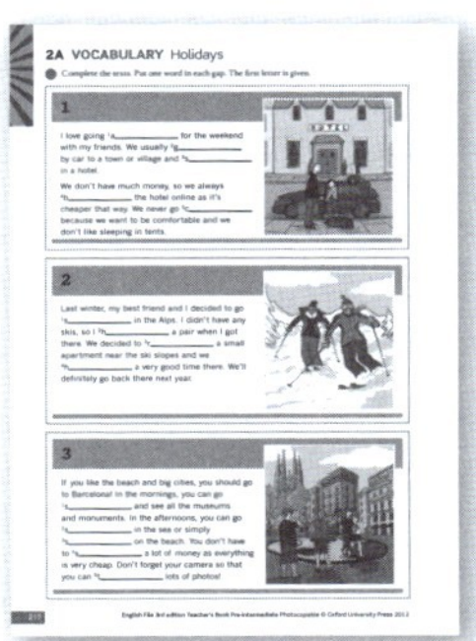

Vocabulary

see *pp.248–262*

- Extra practice of new vocabulary, for every Vocabulary Bank

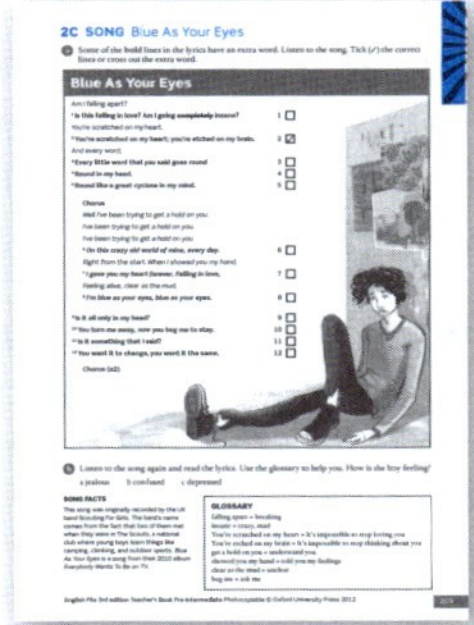

Song

see *pp.268–279*

- A song for every File
- provides the lyrics of the song, with tasks to do before, during, or after listening.

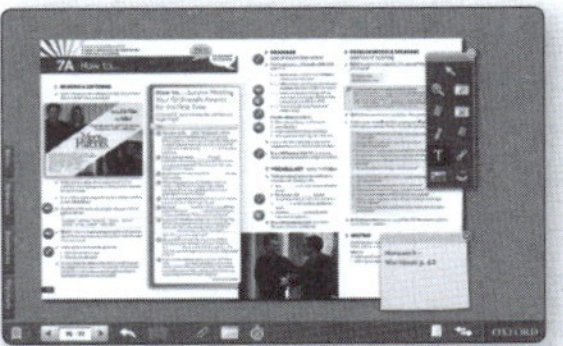

iTools

- The complete Student's Book, Workbook and Teacher's Book (photocopiables) onscreen
- Interactive activities for all Grammar and Vocabulary Banks
- All class audio (including songs) and video, with interactive scripts
- 'Click and reveal' answer keys for Student's Book, Workbook, and Teacher's Book
- Resources including, Grammar Bank PowerPoints and Vocabulary flashcard

Test and Assessment CD-ROM

- A Quick Test for every File
- An End-of-File test for every File
- Entry Tests, Progress Tests, and an End-of-course Test
- A and B versions of all the main Tests
- Audio for all the Listening tests

Class audio CDs

- All the listening materials for the Student's Book

DVD

Practical English

- A unique teaching video that goes with the Practical English lessons in the Student's Book

In the street

- Short interviews filmed in London, New York, and Oxford University Press to accompany the Revise and Check section

Short film

- Short documentary film for students to watch for pleasure after the Revise and Check section

Teacher's website

www.oup.com/elt/teacher/englishfile

- Extra digital ideas, teaching resources, and support

G word order in questions
V common verb phrases, spelling and numbers
P vowel sounds, the alphabet

1A Where are you from?

Lesson plan

This first lesson has three main objectives: to help you and the Sts to get to know each other, to give you a clear idea of the level of your class, and to provide some quick, efficient revision of some elementary language points.
The first exercise provides the context for revising an important grammar point: the order of words in questions. The vocabulary focus is on common verb phrases. Sts use these to complete the questions, which they then ask each other. They then focus on the word order and practise it in the Grammar Bank. The alphabet is revised, and the listening activity gives you the chance to quickly revise spelling and numbers. Sts then bring all the language together by interviewing each other and completing a form.

There is an Entry Test on the *Test and Assessment CD-ROM*, which you can give the Sts before starting the course.

STUDY LINK

- **Workbook** 1A
- **iTutor**
- **www.oup.com/elt/englishfile**

Extra photocopiable activities

- **Grammar** Word order in questions *p.162*
- **Communicative** Student profile *p.209* (instructions *p.198*)
- **www.oup.com/elt/teacher/englishfile**

Optional lead-in (books closed)

- Before the class choose some party music. You could use one of the songs from the book, e.g. *I Heard It Through the Grapevine* (CD 5 Track 26).
- Introduce yourself to the class. Say *Hello, I'm…* .
- Tell Sts to stand up. Divide the class into two groups, **A** and **B**. Ask both groups to make a circle, **A** inside **B**. Tell them to imagine that they're at a party. When you play the music, tell them to walk round in their circle, one clockwise and the other anticlockwise. Each time you stop the music, tell them to introduce themselves to the person standing opposite them. Elicit that they can say *Hello* or *Hi, I'm…* or *My name's…* and should respond *Nice to meet you.*

1 VOCABULARY & SPEAKING

common verb phrases

a If you didn't do the **Optional lead-in**, and your Sts don't know each other, set a time limit of for example two minutes, and tell Sts to stand up and move round the room introducing themselves to other Sts. Tell them to say *Hello / Hi, I'm…*; *Nice to meet you*, and to try to remember other Sts' names.

Books open. Focus on the pictures and the questions. Elicit the verbs for the first three questions under **1 Home and Family** (*are, were, live*).

Put Sts in pairs and tell them to complete the other questions with the correct verbs. Point out that in the **Job / Studies** section there are two possible conversations depending on whether the person has a job or is a student.

! You may have Sts who are neither at school / university nor working, e.g. they are unemployed or at home with children. If so, point out that if in section 2 somebody answers the question *What do you do?* with for example *I'm unemployed / looking for a job*, they should think of a follow-up question if they can, and then go to the question *Can you speak any other languages?*

Check answers, making sure that Sts understand the whole question, not just the missing verb.

1 **HOME AND FAMILY** are, were, live, live, have, have
2 **JOB / STUDIES** do / study
work / like — go / are
speak
study / learn
3 **FREE TIME** listen, play, watch / like, do, read, go, do

b  Focus on the **Sentence stress** box and go through it with Sts.

Tell Sts to listen to the rhythm in the seven questions in **Free Time**. Play the audio once for Sts just to listen.

1 2))
What kind of music do you listen to?
Do you play a musical instrument? Which?
What TV programmes do you watch?
Do you do any sport or exercise? What?
What kind of books or magazines do you read?
How often do you go to the cinema?
What did you do last weekend?

Now play it again, stopping after each question for Sts to repeat. Then repeat the activity eliciting responses from individual Sts.

c Focus on the instructions and the example. Demonstrate the activity by getting Sts to ask you questions first. Use full answers, giving extra information.

Extra challenge

- Encourage Sts to ask follow-up questions, e.g.:
  A *Do you have any brothers and sisters?*
  B *I have one brother.*
  A *How old is he? / What's his name? / What does he do?*

Put Sts in pairs. Give them at least five minutes to ask and answer all the questions. Monitor their conversations, to give you an idea of their oral level.

Get feedback from several pairs to see what they have in common.

At this point you could teach them the word *both* and its position (before all verbs except *be* and modals verbs like *can*), e.g. *We both live in the city centre. We're both doctors. We can both speak German.*

2 GRAMMAR word order in questions

a Focus on the instructions. Do the first one together. Give Sts a minute to do the other three and check answers.

1 Where were your parents born?
2 Where is our teacher from?
3 How do you spell your name?
4 Did you go out last night?

Extra idea

- Put Sts in pairs and get them to ask and answer the four questions.

b 1.3 1.4 Tell Sts to go to **Grammar Bank 1A** on *p.126*. Explain that all the grammar rules and exercises are in this part of the book.

Focus on the example sentences and play the audio for Sts to listen and repeat. Encourage them to copy the rhythm. Then go through the rules with the class.

Additional grammar notes

- In questions with the auxiliaries *do, does, did* Sts might leave out the auxiliary or get the word order wrong. Typical mistakes: ~~*You live with your parents?*~~ ~~*Why she didn't like the film?*~~
- The memory aids **ASI** (**A**uxiliary **S**ubject **I**nfinitive) and **QUASI** (**Qu**estion word **A**uxiliary **S**ubject **I**nfinitive) may help Sts here.
- In questions with *be* Sts sometimes forget to invert the subject and verb. Typical mistakes: *Ana's a student? Where they are from?*
  If a verb is followed by a question (e.g. *talk about, listen to*), the preposition goes at the end of the question: *What did you talk about?*

Focus on the exercises for **1A** on *p.127*. Sts do the exercises individually or in pairs.

Check answers, getting Sts to read the full sentences.

a 1 Where do you come from?
2 Where is the train station?
3 How often do you read magazines?
4 Where are your friends from?
5 Why didn't you write to me?
6 Do you often go to the cinema?
7 What does this word mean?
8 What time did your friends arrive?
9 Does the class finish at 8.00?
10 Where were you born?

b 1 Do you have a car?
2 Is your brother older than you?
3 How often does he write to you?
4 What time does this class start?
5 Is your friend from Brazil?
6 How many languages do you speak?
7 Where was she born?
8 Where did you go last summer?
9 Is your father a doctor?
10 Did you come to school by bus?

Tell Sts to go back to the main lesson **1A**.

Extra support

- If you think Sts need more practice, you may want to give them the Grammar photocopiable activity at this point.

c In this activity Sts move from *yes / no* questions to questions beginning with question words. Focus on the instructions, the example, and the questions. Demonstrate the activity by asking the first question (*Do you drink a lot of tea or coffee?*) until someone answers *Yes, I do.* Then ask the follow-up question (*How many cups do you drink?*).

Give Sts a few minutes to work out how to form the questions and how to answer them.

Extra support

- Put Sts in pairs and get them to write the questions. Check the questions with the class before asking Sts to stand up and mingle.

Ask Sts to stand up and move around the class asking each other the questions. If it's difficult to move around the class, do this in pairs.

Get some feedback from the class.

3 PRONUNCIATION vowel sounds, the alphabet

Pronunciation notes

- Emphasize the importance of being able to spell in English, particularly your name. Point out that it is very useful to be able to recognize and write down letters correctly when people spell words to you.
- If your Sts didn't use *English File* Elementary, this will be the first time that they have seen the sound pictures (*train, tree,* etc.). Explain that the pictures will give Sts a clear example of the target sound and that they will help them remember the pronunciation of the phonetic symbol. This is very important if they want to check the pronunciation of a word in the dictionary.
- Tell Sts that the two dots in /iː/, /uː/, and /ɑː/ mean that they are long sounds.

a 1.5 Focus on the sound pictures and instructions.

Give Sts a few minutes, in pairs, to write the words.

Play the audio for Sts to listen and check answers.

! If Sts haven't seen the *English File* sound pictures before, you may want to play the audio and pause after each word for Sts to write them down.

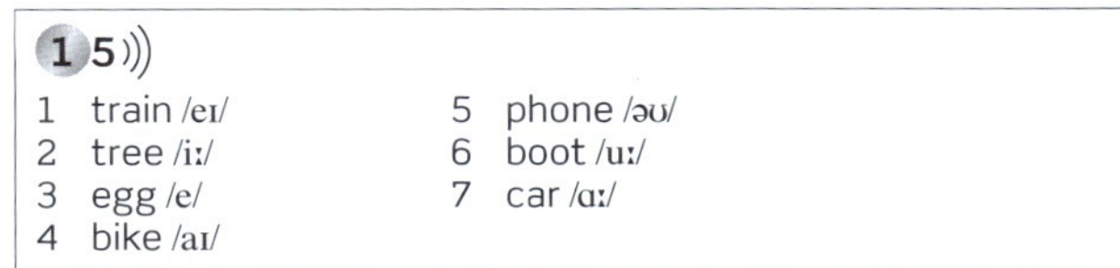
1.5

1 train /eɪ/
2 tree /iː/
3 egg /e/
4 bike /aɪ/
5 phone /əʊ/
6 boot /uː/
7 car /ɑː/

Now play it again, pausing after each word for Sts to repeat.

b Tell Sts to go to the **Sound Bank** on *p.166*. If your Sts didn't use *English File* Elementary, explain that this is a reference section of the book, where they can check the symbols and see common sound-spelling patterns.

Look at the spelling rules for the seven sounds. Model and drill the example words for the vowels and elicit / explain their meaning.

Tell Sts to go back to the main lesson **1A**.

STUDY LINK Sts can practise these sounds on the *iTutor* and on the *English File* Pre-intermediate website.

c Now focus on the letters in the list, but don't elicit their pronunciation yet. Tell Sts, in pairs, to write the letters in the right circle according to their sound.

d **1.6** Play the audio for Sts to listen and check. Then play it again for them to listen and repeat.

1.6

train	AHJK	phone	**O**
tree	BCD**EG**PTV	boot	QU**W**
egg	FL**M**NS**XZ**	car	**R**
bike	**IY**		

Ask Sts which letters are difficult for them. Highlight the difference between pairs and groups of letters which are often confused, e.g. *a / e / i*, *g / j*, *k / q*, etc.

In pairs, Sts practise saying the letters in each circle.

e Focus on the questions, all of which include words which use letters of the alphabet, e.g. email, iPod, etc. Elicit from the class how to say the questions, and the meaning of *to get in touch with somebody*.

Get Sts to ask you the questions. Then in pairs, Sts ask and answer the questions.

Get some feedback from various pairs.

4 SPELLING & NUMBERS

a **1.7** Focus on the instructions. Tell Sts they are going to listen to six people spelling their names and they must write them down. Elicit the question you ask someone when you don't know how to spell something (*How do you spell it?*) and write it on the board.

Play the audio for Sts to listen and write the names. Play again if necessary.

Check answers by getting Sts to spell the names and write them on the board.

1.7

1 "What's your name?" "George." "How do you spell it?" "G-E-O-R-G-E."
2 "What's your name?" "Celia." "That's a pretty name. How do you spell it?" "C-E-L-I-A."
3 "What's your name?" "Wayne Roberts." "How do you spell your first name?" "W-A-Y-N-E."
4 "What's your name?" "Katie." "Is that K-A-T-Y?" "No, it's K-A-T-I-E."
5 "What's your name?" "Hannah." "Sorry, Hannah or Anna?" "H-A-N-N-A-H, with an H."
6 "What's your name?" "Christopher." "How do you spell it?" "C-H-R-I-S-T-O-P-H-E-R."

b Put Sts in pairs, **A** and **B**, and tell them to go to **Communication *What's his name? How do you spell it?***, **A** on *p.100*, **B** on *p.106*.

Go through the instructions with them, and focus on the example questions in the speech bubbles. Tell Sts to ask these questions for each of their six people (using *first name* or *surname* depending on what the gap is) and write the answers in the spaces. Now go through the **Asking for repetition** box.

Sit **A** and **B** face-to-face. **A** asks his / her questions to **B** and writes the first name or surname.

B now asks **A** his / her questions.

When they have finished, get them to compare books to check their answers.

Extra support

- Before Sts start the activity, elicit the question you would ask for a woman *What's her first name?* Then explain / elicit the difference between *first name* and *surname*. Some Sts might be more familiar with the term *family name*.

Tell Sts to go back to the main lesson **1A**.

c In pairs, get Sts to say the numbers in the list.

Check answers by eliciting the numbers from different Sts. Remind Sts of the difference between thirTEEN / THIRty, fourTEEN / FORty, etc. Remind them also:

– of the use of the hyphen, e.g. *twenty-one*

– of the use of *and*, e.g. *a hundred and twenty*

– that you can say *a hundred* or *one hundred*

– that you don't put an *s* on hundred or thousand, e.g. *two hundred, three thousand*

13 = thirteen
30 = thirty
76 = seventy-six
100 = one hundred / a hundred
150 = a hundred and fifty
375 = three hundred and seventy-five
600 = six hundred
1,500 = one thousand five hundred
2,000 = two thousand
10,500 = ten thousand five hundred

Extra support

- Count to 30 round the class. Write random numbers between 20 and 1,000 on the board for Sts to say.

d **1.8** Tell Sts they are going to listen to five situations and must write down the five numbers they hear. You could warn them that one of them is a phone number.

Play the audio, pausing after each number to give Sts time to write it down.

Get Sts to compare with a partner, and then check answers.

1 Gate **40**	3 Tel: **0792 9618 847**	5 **£6.15**
2 **181** miles	4 Population: **2,500**	

1 8)))

1 Passengers on the British Airways flight to Barbados please go to gate number 40, where this flight is ready to board.

2 **A** How far is it from London to Manchester?
B I'm not sure. Let's google it. It says here 181 miles.

3 **A** Hello.
B It's Ben. I'm at the station. Do you have Nicola's mobile number?
A Yes. Just a moment.
B OK.
A It's 0792 9618 847.
B 0792 9618 847?
A That's right.

4 **A** Where do you live in Ireland?
B I live in a village near Dublin.
A How big is it?
B It's quite small. The population is only about 2,500 people.

5 **A** Can I have two Cokes and a mineral water, please?
B Two Cokes?
A Yes, and a mineral water. How much is that?
B £6.15.
A Sorry? 50 or 15?
B 15. £6.15.

e Focus on the instructions and the form.

Put Sts in pairs and get them to interview each other. If Sts do not want to give their real address and phone number, tell them to invent one. Remind Sts that when we say phone numbers in English we say the individual digits, and that 0 can be *oh* or *zero*. You might also want to check that Sts know how to say an email address, e.g. that @ = *at* and . = *dot*.

When they have finished, get Sts to show each other their forms to check the information.

Get some feedback.

G present simple
V describing people: appearance and personality
P final *-s* / *-es*

1B Charlotte's choice

Lesson plan

In this lesson the present simple (all forms) is revised in detail through a British magazine article *Who knows you better?* A family member and a friend both try to choose a suitable partner for Charlotte, a single woman. The lesson begins with vocabulary. Basic language for physical description is revised and in the Vocabulary Bank new language is presented, and adjectives of personality are introduced. Sts then read the article about Charlotte, and focus on the grammar of the present simple. They then listen to Charlotte describing her two dates. This is followed by a pronunciation focus on the 3rd person *-s* ending, and the lesson ends with Sts describing a member of their family in detail, and writing a short description.

STUDY LINK
- **Workbook** 1B
- **iTutor**
- **www.oup.com/elt/englishfile**

Extra photocopiable activities

- **Grammar** Present simple *p.163*
- **Communicative** Ask me a question *p.210* (instructions *p.198*)
- **Vocabulary** Describing people *p.248* (instructions on *p.245*)
- **Song** *Ugly p.268* (instructions *p.263*)
- **www.oup.com/elt/teacher/englishfile**

Optional lead-in (books closed)

- Write on the board:

DIRECT FAMILY	*mother*
OTHER RELATIVES	*grandmother*
HUSBAND / WIFE'S FAMILY	*mother-in-law*

- Put Sts in pairs. Give them a minute to add more words to each category. Get feedback and write the words on the board.
- Remind Sts of the pronunciation of difficult words like *daughter*.

1 VOCABULARY describing people

a 1 9))) Books open. Focus on the instructions and the three pictures. Tell Sts they are going to listen to Luke, who is describing his girlfriend. Play the audio for Sts to listen and choose the best picture.

Check answers, eliciting the words and phrases which helped Sts to identify the girl, e.g. *short dark hair.* Elicit / teach the meaning of *curly.*

Picture 1

1 9)))
F = friend, L = Luke
F Tell me about Molly. What does she look like?
L She's quite tall and she has short dark hair. It's very curly. And she has brown eyes and a beautiful smile.
F And what's she like?
L She's really nice – very friendly and extrovert. She's got lots of friends. I'm sure you're going to like her.

b Play the audio again. This time Sts must listen for the two questions asked by the friend and Luke's response to the second question.

Get Sts to compare with a partner, and then check answers.

The two questions are: What does she look like? What's she like?
Luke answers 'She's really nice.'

Now go through the ***What does she look like? What is she like?*** box with the class.

c Tell Sts to go to **Vocabulary Bank *Describing people*** on *p.150*. Focus on **1 Appearance** and get Sts to do **a** individually or in pairs.

1 10))) Now do **b**. Play the audio for Sts to check answers. Make sure Sts understand the individual words in the descriptions, and give further practice of any words your Sts find difficult to pronounce, e.g. *beard, height*, etc.

1 10)))
Appearance
2 She has curly red hair.
3 She has long straight hair.
1 She has big blue eyes.
6 She has dark wavy hair.
5 He has a beard and a moustache.
4 He's bald.
7 He's very tall and thin.
9 He's quite short and a bit overweight.
8 He's medium height and quite slim.

Now go through the information box with the class about ***thin* or *slim*? *fat* or *overweight*?** and **Using two adjectives together**.

You might also want to elicit from Sts different typical colours for hair, i.e. *fair / blond(e), red, grey, light / dark brown, black, white.*

Focus on **2 Personality** and get Sts to do **a** individually or in pairs.

Check the answers to **a** before moving on to **b**.

2 talkative	4 kind	6 funny	8 shy
3 generous	5 lazy	7 clever	

Now Sts do **b** by putting the adjectives from the list into the **Opposite** column in **a**.

1 11 Now do **c**. Play the audio for Sts to check answers. Play again pausing for Sts to repeat the words. Give further practice of any words your Sts find difficult to pronounce.

1 11

Personality

1 friendly, unfriendly	5 lazy, hard-working
2 talkative, quiet	6 funny, serious
3 generous, mean	7 clever, stupid
4 kind, unkind	8 shy, extrovert

You might want to teach Sts *silly* as a softer version of *stupid*.

Focus on the ***nice*; *funny* or *fun*?** box and go through it with the class.

Finally, for **d**, put Sts in pairs and get them to ask and answer questions about a member of their family and a good friend. Get some feedback from the class.

Tell Sts to go back to the main lesson **1B**.

Extra support

- If you think Sts need more practice, you may want to give them the Vocabulary photocopiable activity at this point.

2 READING

a Do this as an open-class question and elicit Sts' opinions. Tell them what you think too.

b Focus on the magazine article and the photo. Ask Sts *What does Charlotte look like?*, etc. to revise physical descriptions.

Give Sts a minute to read the introduction and first paragraph and answer questions 1–4 in pairs.

Check answers. Remind Sts of the *'s* in 3 *Alice is Charlotte's mother.*

1 Single people ask their mother and best friend to find them a partner.
2 Charlotte is a single, 25-year-old web designer, who is looking for a partner.
3 Alice is Charlotte's mother and Katie is Charlotte's best friend.
4 Alice and Katie have to choose a man for Charlotte. Then Charlotte goes on a date with each man.

c Focus on the rest of the article (what Charlotte says). Remind Sts of the importance of guessing words from context when they are reading.

Tell Sts to read what she says, and as they read try to guess the meaning of the highlighted words and phrases. Set a time limit.

Then get Sts to compare their guesses with a partner.

Check answers, by miming or translating into Sts' L1 if you prefer. Alternatively, Sts could check in their dictionaries.

Deal with any other new vocabulary.

d Put Sts in pairs. Get them to cover the text and answer the four questions.

Check answers, eliciting as much information as possible.

1 She likes going to the cinema and reading.
2 She's friendly, sociable, and has a good sense of humour.
3 She likes interesting men who can make her laugh. She likes men who are taller than her and have a nice smile. She likes men who are into literature, art, and classical music.
She doesn't like men with beards.
4 She doesn't know who is going to choose better. Katie might choose a man who is physically right for her, but Charlotte's mother has known her for longer.

Extra idea

- Get Sts to close their books and write the four questions on the board.

3 GRAMMAR present simple

a Focus on the instructions. Give Sts a few minutes to complete the gaps.

Check answers.

1 doesn't	3 does	5 don't
2 goes	4 do	

b Put Sts in pairs and tell them to answer the three questions.

Check answers.

1 You add the letter *s*.
2 watches / studies / goes / has
3 **a** Do, don't **b** Does, doesn't

c 1 12 1 13 Tell Sts to go to **Grammar Bank 1B** on *p.126*. Focus on the example sentences and play the audio for Sts to listen and repeat. Encourage them to copy the rhythm. Then go through the rules with the class.

Additional grammar notes

Present simple

- Remind Sts:
  – of the difference in pronunciation between *do* /duː/, *don't* /dəʊnt/, and *does* /dʌz/.
  – of the pronunciation of *goes* /gəʊz/ and *has* /hæz/.
  – that the contracted forms *don't* and *doesn't* are always used in conversation.

Adverbs and expressions of frequency

- You may want to point out that *usually* / *normally* and *sometimes* can also be used at the beginning of a present simple sentence, e.g. *Sometimes I get up late on Saturday.*
- Other common *every* expressions of frequency are *every week, every month, every year.*
- In expressions like *once a month, twice a day*, etc. remind Sts that *once* and *twice* are irregular (NOT ~~*one time, two times*~~). 'times' is used with all other numbers, e.g. *ten times, thirty times* (a year).

Focus on the exercises for **1B** on *p.127*. Sts do the exercises individually or in pairs.

Check answers, getting Sts to read the full sentences.

a 1 Does Anna like music?
2 My sister has a lot of hobbies.
3 I don't get on very well with my parents.
4 My brother studies at university.
5 My neighbours don't have any children.
6 When does the film start?
7 He goes out twice a week.
8 We don't often talk about politics.
9 How often do you email your brother?
10 I don't go on Facebook very often.

b 1 I always go to bed before 11.00.
2 Kate hardly ever sees her family.
3 We never go shopping on Saturdays.
4 I go to the dentist's twice a year.
5 They sometimes have breakfast in the garden. / Sometimes they have breakfast in the garden.
6 We usually listen to the radio in the morning.
7 Alan runs in the park every day.
8 I never drink coffee after 4.00.
9 John doesn't often go to the cinema.
10 I visit my mum once a month.

Tell Sts to go back to the main lesson **1B**.

Extra support

- If you think Sts need more practice, you may want to give them the Grammar photocopiable activity at this point.

d Get Sts to cover the text or close their books. Put them in pairs. Give them a minute to write down as many things as they can remember about the men Charlotte likes and doesn't like.

Check answers and then let Sts look back at the text.

e Focus on the photos of Alexander and Oliver. Elicit some adjectives to describe them.

Put Sts in pairs, **A** and **B**, and get them to sit face-to-face if possible. Tell them to go to **Communication *Alexander and Oliver***, **A** on *p.100*, **B** on *p.106*.

Go through the instructions carefully with them and make sure they know what they have to do.

Extra support

- Elicit the questions from the class first.

A asks his / her questions to **B** about Oliver.

B then asks **A** his / her questions about Alexander.

When they have finished, get them to compare books to check their answers.

Tell Sts to go back to the main lesson **1B**.

f Do this as an open-class question and elicit Sts' opinions. Tell them what you think too.

4 LISTENING

a **1 14** Tell Sts they are going to listen to Charlotte talking about when she met Alexander for the first time. Focus on the two questions. You could write the two questions on the board and get Sts to close their books.

Play the audio once the whole way through.

Get Sts to compare with a partner and play the audio again if necessary.

Check answers.

Extra support

- Read through the scripts and decide if you need to pre-teach any new lexis before Sts listen.

She really liked him, but physically he wasn't her type – there wasn't any chemistry between them.
Yes, as a friend, to go to a concert or the theatre.

1 14
(script in Student's Book on *p.118*)
My first impression of Alexander was that he was much older than me. In fact he was 32, but I thought he was older. But when we started talking I really liked him. He was extrovert and funny and he had a very good sense of humour. He works for a TV company and he told me a lot of good stories about his work. He was also interested in the same things as me – art and music and we talked a lot about that. Physically he wasn't really my type. It's difficult to say why. He was tall and dark and quite good-looking and he had a nice smile, but there just wasn't any chemistry between us. I could imagine going to a concert or theatre with him, but as a friend. Sorry Mum, but no.

b Play the audio again for Sts to write down adjectives or expressions that Charlotte uses to describe Alexander's appearance and personality.

Get Sts to compare with a partner, and then check answers.

Appearance: tall, slim, quite good-looking, nice smile
Personality: extrovert, funny, a very good sense of humour

c **1 15** Sts now listen to Charlotte talking about when she met Oliver for the first time. Focus on the two questions in **a**. Play the audio once the whole way through.

Get Sts to compare with a partner and play the audio again if necessary.

Check answers.

She thought he was attractive (more than Alexander), friendly, and generous.
No, because he smokes.

1 15
(script in Student's Book on *p.118*)
When I first saw Oliver I thought he looked warm and friendly, and more attractive than Alexander. He was quite tall with short, blond hair and he had lovely blue eyes, a bit like the actor Jude Law. He was a bit shy and quiet at first, but when we started chatting he relaxed and we found we had a lot of things in common – we both like books, and the cinema. He was generous too – he wanted to pay for everything. I really enjoyed the evening. When it was time to go he asked for my phone number and said he wanted to meet again.

We walked out of the restaurant and went to look for a taxi. And then something happened, and I knew that it was impossible for me to go out with him. He said 'At last!' and took out a packet of cigarettes. That was it, I'm afraid. I could never have a boyfriend who was a smoker. I think perhaps for my next date I'm going to choose the man myself. I don't think another person can really choose a partner for you.

Extra idea

- When you play the audio the first time, pause after 'And then something happened, and I knew that it was impossible for me to go out with him.' Ask Sts what they think happened. Then play the rest of the audio to see if they predicted correctly.

Now play the audio again for Sts to write down adjectives or expressions that Charlotte uses to describe Oliver's appearance and personality.

Get Sts to compare with a partner, and then check answers.

Appearance: attractive, quite tall, short blond hair, lovely blue eyes
Personality: warm, friendly, a bit shy, quiet, generous

Extra support

- If there's time, you could get Sts to listen again to both parts of the audio with the scripts on *p.118*, so they can see exactly what they understood / didn't understand. Translate / explain any new words or phrases.

d Do this as an open-class and elicit that Charlotte is going to choose her next date herself.

Then ask for Sts' opinions. Tell them what you think too.

You may like to tell Sts that the text and listening were based on a real magazine experiment. Several single people took part in the experiment and in 75% of the cases, the family member chose best.

5 PRONUNCIATION final *-s* / *-es*

Pronunciation notes

- The pronunciation rules for adding an *-s* (or *-es*) to verbs (e.g. *smokes*) and nouns (e.g. *books*) are the same.
- The difference between the /s/ and /z/ sounds is very small and only occasionally causes communication problems. The most important thing is for Sts to learn when to pronounce *-es* as /ɪz/.
- You may want to give Sts these rules:
  - the final *s* is pronounced /ɪz/ in verbs and nouns which end in /tʃ/ (*churches*), /s/ (*dresses*), /ʃ/ (*washes*), and /dʒ/ (*bridges*).
  - the *s* is pronounced /s/ after these unvoiced* sounds /k/, /p/, /f/, and /t/, e.g. *walks, stops, laughs, eats*.
  - in all other cases the final *s* is voiced and pronounced /z/, e.g. *plays, parties*, etc.

*** Voiced and unvoiced consonants**

- Voiced consonant sounds are made in the throat by vibrating the vocal chords, e.g. /b/, /l/, /m/, /v/, etc. Unvoiced consonant sounds are made in the mouth without vibration in the vocal chords, e.g. /k/, /p/, /t/, /s/, etc.
- You can demonstrate this to Sts by getting them to hold their hands against their throats. For voiced sounds they should feel a vibration in their throat, but not for unvoiced sounds.

a 1 16))) Explain that the final *-s* in the third person of the present simple and in plurals can be pronounced in three different ways.

Focus on the sound pictures. Elicit and drill the words and sounds: *snake* /s/, *zebra* /z/, and /ɪz/.

! Sts may have problems distinguishing between the /s/ and /z/ sounds. Tell them that the /s/ is like the sound made by a snake and the /z/ is a bee or fly.

Play the audio once for Sts just to listen.

1 16)))
See sentences in Student's Book on *p.7*

Then play it again, pausing for Sts to listen and repeat.

Now go through the **Pronunciation of the final *-s* / *-es*** box with the class.

b 1 17))) Write the three phonetic symbols, /s/, /z/, and /ɪz/ on the board. Elicit the third person pronunciation of the first verb in the list (*chooses*) and ask Sts which group it belongs to (group 3). Write it on the board under the correct heading. Get Sts to continue with the other verbs.

Then tell them to do the same thing with the plural form of the nouns.

Play the audio once the whole way through for Sts to listen and check their answers.

	/s/	/z/	/ɪz/
verbs:	cooks	goes	chooses
	stops	lives	teaches
	/s/	/z/	/ɪz/
nouns:	dates	boys	classes
	parents	friends	languages

1 17)))
chooses, cooks, goes, lives, stops, teaches, boys, classes, dates, friends, languages, parents

Highlight that the most important thing to get right is that *lives* and *dates* are pronounced /lɪvz/ and /deɪts/, NOT ~~/lɪvɪz/~~ and ~~/deɪtɪz/~~, but that in *chooses, teaches, languages*, and *classes* the *-es* is pronounced /ɪz/.

Now play the audio, pausing after each word and sound for Sts to repeat.

Then repeat the activity eliciting responses from individual Sts.

6 SPEAKING & WRITING describing a person

a Give Sts five minutes to make a few notes about a person they know well who is single and looking for a partner. Monitor and help with vocabulary.

Extra support

- Tell Sts to make notes about their person in the form.

b Put Sts in pairs, **A** and **B**. Remind Sts of the meaning of *compatible* and tell them to think of people who are possibilities for each other, e.g. if **A** has thought of a man, **B** should try to think of a woman.

A describes his / her person and **B** listens and asks for more information.

Sts swap roles and **B** describes his / her person to **A**. Are the two people compatible?

c This is the first time Sts are sent to the **Writing** at the back of the Student's Book. In this section Sts will find model texts, with exercises, and language notes, and then a writing task. We suggest that you go through the model and do the exercise(s) in class, but set the actual writing (the last activity) for homework.

Tell Sts to go to **Writing *Describing a person*** on *p.111*.

Focus on **a** and get Sts to read Charlie's email and correct the ten mistakes.

Get Sts to compare with a partner, and then check answers.

1	I am 21 years old.	6	can be
2	studying	7	don't
3	photo	8	much
4	brown	9	because
5	friends	10	English

Now do **b** and tell Sts to read the email again and then to cover it and answer questions 1–7.

Check answers.

1 He's from Barcelona.
2 Carlos.
3 His parents and his dog.
4 He's at university. / He's a student.
5 He has black hair and brown eyes.
6 He's positive and funny.
7 Watching TV and playing computer games.

Now focus on the chart in **c** and get Sts to write their own emails on a piece of paper.

In **d** Sts check their work for mistakes before giving it in.

Tell Sts to go back to the main lesson **1B**.

7 1 18 SONG *Ugly* ♫

This song was originally made famous by the Sugababes in 2005. For copyright reasons this is a cover version. If you want to do this song in class, use the photocopiable activity on *p.268*.

1 18

Ugly
When I was seven they said I was strange
I noticed that my eyes and hair weren't the same
I asked my parents if I was OK
They said you're more beautiful and that's the way
They show that they wish that they had your smile
So my confidence was up for a while
I got real comfortable with my own style
I knew that they were only jealous 'cause

Chorus
People are all the same
And we only get judged by what we do
Personality reflects name
And if I'm ugly then so are you, so are you

There was a time when I felt like I cared
That I was shorter than everyone there
People made me feel like life was unfair
And I did things that made me ashamed
'Cause I didn't know my body would change
I grew taller than them in more ways
But there will always be the one who will say
Something bad to make them feel great

Chorus x2

Everybody talks bad about somebody and
Never realize how it affects somebody and
You bet it won't be forgotten
Envy is the only thing it could be

Chorus x2

G present continuous
V clothes: boots, skirt, etc., prepositions of place: *under, next to*, etc.
P /ə/ and /ɜː/

1C Mr and Mrs Clark and Percy

Lesson plan

In this lesson Sts learn vocabulary for clothes and revise prepositions of place and the present continuous in the context of a famous painting by David Hockney, which has an interesting story behind it. The lesson begins with clothes vocabulary, and a pronunciation focus on two common vowel sounds /ə/ and /ɜː/. Focussing on the painting then leads them to the Grammar Bank, where they look at using the present continuous for things that are happening now, around now, and for describing what is happening in a picture. The present continuous is also contrasted with the present simple for habitual or permanent actions. Sts then have a listening activity where they hear about the story behind the painting. They then revise prepositions of place, and all the language of the lesson is pulled together in a final speaking activity, where Sts describe paintings to each other.

STUDY LINK

- **Workbook** 1C
- **iTutor**
- **iChecker**
- **www.oup.com/elt/englishfile**

Extra photocopiable activities

- **Grammar** Present simple or present continuous? *p.164*
- **Communicative** At an art gallery *p.211* (instructions *p.198*)
- **Vocabulary** Things to wear *p.249* (instructions *p.245*)
- **www.oup.com/elt/teacher/englishfile**

Optional lead-in (books closed)

- Write the word CLOTHES on the board (or play *Hangman* with it). Then ask Sts how to pronounce it (/kləʊðz/) and if it is singular or plural (plural). Explain that there is no singular form, and that if they want to talk about an item of clothing, they should refer to it by name, e.g. *a sweater*. Now draw a line before CLOTHES on the board, e.g. _______ CLOTHES, and ask Sts what verbs they can use with *clothes*. They should be able to produce *wear, buy, try on*, and possibly *put on* and *take off*.

1 VOCABULARY clothes

a Books open. Focus on the pictures of the models and ask Sts to match the items of clothing and the words.

Check answers.

1 top	3 skirt	5 boots
2 shirt	4 trousers	6 shoes

b Tell Sts to go to **Vocabulary Bank *Things you wear*** on *p.151*. Focus on the four sections (clothes, footwear, accessories, and jewellery) and make sure Sts know what they mean and how to pronounce them.

Now get Sts to do **a** individually or in pairs.

1 19))) Now do **b**. Play the audio for Sts to check answers. Play it again, pausing after each word for Sts to repeat. Give further practice of words your Sts find difficult to pronounce.

1 19)))

Things you wear

Clothes	Footwear	Jewellery
12 cardigan	18 boots	30 bracelet
3 coat	19 flip-flops	29 earrings
2 dress	16 sandals	32 necklace
9 jacket	17 shoes	31 ring
5 jeans	15 trainers	
8 shirt	**Accessories**	
1 shorts	21 belt	
6 skirt	25 cap	
7 suit	27 hat	
14 sweater	26 leggings	
4 top	23 gloves	
10 tracksuit	24 scarf	
11 trousers	28 socks	
13 T-shirt	22 tie	
	20 tights	

Highlight that plural clothes cannot be used with *a*, e.g. NOT ~~a trousers~~. If Sts want to use an indefinite article, they should use *some*, e.g. *I bought some trousers* / *some shoes*.

Extra challenge

- You could also teach *a pair of* which is often used with plural clothes words.

Focus on **c**. Give Sts a minute to cover the words and test themselves or each other.

Finally, go through the ***wear, carry,* or *dress?*** box with the class.

Tell Sts to go back to the main lesson **1C**.

Extra support

- If you think Sts need more practice, you may want to give them the Vocabulary photocopiable activity at this point.

2 PRONUNCIATION /ə/ and /ɜː/

Pronunciation notes

- /ə/ is the most common sound in English. It is a short sound, and always occurs in an unstressed syllable, e.g. doctor /'dɒktə/, address /ə'dres/.
- You may want to point out to Sts that unstressed *-er* or *-or* at the end of a word are always pronounced /ə/, e.g. *teacher, better*, etc. and that *-tion* is always pronounced /ʃən/.
- /ɜː/ is a similar sound, but it is a long sound and is always a stressed syllable, e.g. nurse /nɜːs/, worker /'wɜːkə/.

a 1 20 Tell Sts to listen to the words in the two groups. Play the audio once for Sts just to listen.

> 1 20
> See words in Student's Book on *p.8*

Then play it again, pausing after each word for Sts to repeat.

Finally, repeat the activity eliciting responses from individual Sts.

b Put Sts in pairs. Give them a few minutes to underline the stress in the words in the list and then to decide if the highlighted sounds belong to 1 or 2 in **a**.

c 1 21 Play the audio for Sts to check their answers.

> 1 21
> actor, cinema, first, painter, third, arrive, fashion, world, university, picture, working, prefer

Play the audio again, stopping after each word or group for Sts to repeat.

> 1 /ə/ actor, cinema, painter, arrive, fashion, picture
> 2 /ɜː/ first, third, world, university, working, prefer

d Tell Sts to go to the **Sound Bank** on *p.166*. Go through the spellings for /ə/ and /ɜː/.

Tell Sts to go back to the main lesson **1C**.

STUDY LINK Sts can practise these sounds on the *iTutor* and on the *English File* Pre-intermediate website.

e Put Sts in pairs and get them to answer the questions.

Get some feedback from the class.

3 GRAMMAR present continuous

a Focus on the painting on *p.9* by David Hockney and ask Sts if they like it.

Give Sts a few minutes to answer the questions in pairs, either orally or in writing.

Get feedback, accepting all reasonable suggestions.

> 1 The woman has curly blonde hair and she is medium height. The man has long dark hair and is slim.
> 2 The woman is wearing a long black and red dress. The man is wearing a shirt, a blue jumper, and trousers. He isn't wearing shoes.
> 3 The woman is standing by the window. The man is sitting on a chair, and a white cat is sitting on his knee. They are looking at the painter.

b Focus on the sentences and give Sts a minute to choose the right form and discuss in pairs why the other is wrong.

Check answers.

> 1 isn't wearing (because we are describing a painting and saying what is happening at that moment)
> 2 wear (because it's something that happens habitually / frequently)
> 3 is sitting (because we are saying what is happening at the moment, now)
> 4 sits (because it's something that habitually happens)

c 1 22 1 23 Tell Sts to go to **Grammar Bank 1C** on *p.126*. Focus on the example sentences and play the audio for Sts to listen and repeat. Encourage them to copy the rhythm. Then go through the rules with the class.

Additional grammar notes

- Some languages do not have an equivalent to the present continuous and may always use the present simple. Typical mistake: *The man in the picture wears a hat. We live with friends at the moment because builders work on our house.*
- The present continuous is used to describe what is happening in a painting because it is as if we were looking at a scene through a window.
- The future use of the present continuous (*I'm leaving tomorrow.*) is presented in **3B**.

Focus on the exercises for **1C** on *p.127*. Sts do the exercises individually or in pairs.

Check answers, getting Sts to read the full sentences.

> a 1 John is wearing a shirt today!
> 2 It's hot. Why are you wearing a coat?
> 3 Anna isn't sitting next to Jane today.
> 4 Hey! You're standing on my foot!
> 5 What book are you reading?
> 6 We are thinking of you at the moment.
> 7 Is she wearing make-up?
> 8 They are making a big mistake.
> 9 Is your mother shopping in town?
> 10 She isn't living with her parents at the moment.
>
> b 1 doesn't bite
> 2 are ... wearing, 's raining
> 3 'm not listening
> 4 need, don't have
> 5 's putting
> 6 Do ... cook, eat
> 7 are ... doing, 'm waiting
> 8 want
> 9 works
> 10 live, 're staying

Tell Sts to go back to the main lesson **1C**.

Extra support

- If you think Sts need more practice, you may want to give them the Grammar photocopiable activity at this point.

d Tell Sts to look at the pictures on *p.4*, and to answer the two questions.

Extra support

- Give Sts some time to write three sentences about each picture.

Get some feedback from the class.

> On the left there's a man. He's wearing a suit, and he's carrying a case. He's running. In front of him there's a woman. She's wearing a pink dress and a scarf. She's walking, etc.

4 LISTENING

a  Tell Sts that they are going to find out more about the painting on *p.9*. Focus on the title, and ask them who they think Percy is (the cat).

Play the audio once the whole way through.

Ask Sts to tell you anything they can remember about the painting.

Extra support

- Read through the script and decide if you need to pre-teach any new lexis before Sts listen.

1 24

(script in Student's Book on *p.118*)

Mr and Mrs Clark and Percy is by the British artist David Hockney, and it's considered to be one of the greatest British paintings of the 20th century.

It was painted in 1971 and it's a portrait of two of his friends, Ozzie Clark and his wife Celia, and their cat Percy. Ozzie Clark and Celia were fashion designers and they had a very successful clothes shop in London. In the 1960s they dressed a lot of the famous pop stars of the time including The Rolling Stones and Eric Clapton.

Hockney painted Ozzie and Cecilia a few months after they got married in their flat at Notting Hill in London. He painted them in their bedroom, because he liked the light there, and on the wall on the left of the window you can see one of his own paintings.

Mr and Mrs Clark and Percy is a very big painting, approximately three metres wide and two metres high. The couple are wearing typical clothes of the late 1960s. Celia is wearing a long dress, and in fact she was expecting a baby at that time. Her husband isn't wearing any shoes, and he is putting his feet into the carpet. This was because Hockney had a lot of problems painting his feet. He just couldn't get them right. Hockney said that his aim with this painting was to paint the relationship between the two people. Traditionally when a painter paints a married couple, the woman is sitting down and the man is standing up. In this painting the man is sitting and woman is standing. Usually in a painting the married couple are close together, but in this painting they are separated by a big open window, which symbolizes the distance between them. The white cat, sitting on Mr Clark, is a symbol of infidelity. It seems that Hockney didn't think that their marriage was going to be very happy and in fact the couple got divorced four years later.

Celia often posed as a model for Hockney, but she says that this painting, his most famous picture of her, is not her favourite. She said 'It's a wonderful painting, but it makes me look too heavy.'

In 1996, 25 years after this picture was painted, Ozzie Clark died. He was murdered by his lover in his Kensington flat.

b Give Sts a few minutes to read sentences 1–12.

Play the audio once the whole way through for Sts to mark the sentences T (true) or F (false).

Then play it again, pausing if necessary, for Sts to make notes.

Get Sts to compare with a partner, and then check answers , making sure (where relevant) Sts say why an answer is true or false.

1 T
2 T (They dressed a lot of the famous pop stars.)
3 F (He painted them in their bedroom.)
4 F (The painting is very big.)
5 T (She was expecting a baby.)
6 F (Hockney had problems painting his feet.)
7 T (Usually in a painting a married couple are close together.)
8 F (It symbolizes the distance between them.)
9 T
10 T
11 F (She says it is wonderful, but not her favourite.)
12 F (He died in 1996.)

Extra support

- Pause the audio after each paragraph to give Sts time to take in the information.

Extra support

- If there's time, you could get Sts to listen again with the script on *p.118*, so they can see exactly what they understood / didn't understand. Translate / explain any new words or phrases.

Finally, tell Sts that in 2005 this painting was voted one of the top ten greatest paintings in Britain, the only one in the top ten by a living artist.

5 VOCABULARY prepositions of place

a Tell Sts that when you are describing a picture it's important to use the right prepositions to say where things are. Focus on the prepositions and phrases in the list and give Sts a few minutes to complete the gaps.

Get Sts to compare with a partner.

Extra support

- If Sts don't remember the prepositions very well, you could spend a bit more time recycling them using things in the classroom, e.g. *Where's the TV? It's on a shelf behind the table*, etc.

b  Play the audio for Sts to listen and check answers.

Check answers.

See prepositions in **bold** in script 1.25

1 25

1 There are two people **in** the room.
2 The woman is standing **on the left**, and the man is sitting **on the right**.
3 **In the middle** of the painting, **between** the man and the woman, there's an open window.
4 A white cat is sitting **on** the man.
5 There's a carpet **under** the man's chair.
6 There's a telephone **on** the floor **behind** the man's chair.
7 **Next to** the telephone there's a lamp.
8 **In front of** the woman there's a table, and a vase with flowers **in** it.

Now put Sts in pairs. Get them to cover the sentences in **a** and to describe the painting, saying where the things and people are.

Get some feedback from the class.

Extra idea

- Write the following on the board as prompts for Sts to say where they are:
  THE CAT, MRS CLARK, THE CARPET, THE TELEPHONE, THE LAMP, THE TABLE, THE VASE, THE FLOWERS

6 SPEAKING

a Focus on the **Describing a picture** box and go through it with the class.

Put Sts in pairs, **A** and **B**, and get them to sit face-to-face if possible. Then tell them to go to **Communication *Describe and draw***, **A** on *p.100*, **B** on *p.106*.

Go through the instructions with them carefully and make sure Sts are clear what they have to do. Stress that they have to sketch the figures, objects, etc., according to their partner's description.

Give Sts a few minutes to look at their paintings and think about how they are going to describe them. Remind them to use the present continuous to say what the people are doing.

When Sts have finished, they can compare their drawing with their partner's painting to check they followed the instructions correctly.

Tell Sts to go back to the main lesson **1C**.

Extra idea

- You could do this activity using postcards of paintings from an art gallery.

b Put Sts into groups of four to ask and answer the questions. You could first answer the questions yourself to give Sts more listening practice and to model how they might answer.

Get feedback from a few groups.

Function Language describing problems; asking for help
There's a problem with... It isn't working, I'm sorry to bother you, etc.

PRACTICAL ENGLISH

Episode 1 Hotel problems

Lesson plan

This is the first in a series of six Practical English lessons (one every other File) which teach Sts functional language to help them 'survive' in English in travel and social situations.

There is a storyline based on two characters, Jenny Zielinski, an American journalist who works in the NY office of a magazine called *NewYork24seven* and Rob Walker, a British journalist who works in London for the same magazine, but who is now in New York for a month. If your Sts did *English File* Elementary, they will already be familiar with the characters. If your Sts didn't do *English File* Elementary, you might want to point out that in the You Say section of the lessons, they will be listening and then repeating what the people say. If the speaker is Jenny, they will be listening to an American accent, but they do not need to copy the accent when they repeat her phrases. The main focus of this lesson is on describing problems and asking for help.

These lessons can be used with *Class DVD*, *iTools*, or *Class Audio* (audio only).

Sts can find all the video content and activities on the *iTutor*.

STUDY LINK

- **Workbook** Hotel problems
- **iTutor**
- **www.oup.com/elt/englishfile**

Test and Assessment CD-ROM

- **Quick Test 1**
- **File 1 Test**
- **www.oup.com/elt/teacher/englishfile**

Optional lead-in (books closed)

- If your Sts did *English File* Elementary, elicit anything they can remember about Rob and Jenny, and write it on the board in columns under their names. Leave it on the board, so when Sts do exercise **c**, they can see if Jenny mentions any of the points on the board.
- If your Sts didn't do *English File* Elementary, introduce this lesson by giving the information in the Lesson plan.

1 INTRODUCTION

a Focus on the first two photos at the top of the page and tell Sts that the woman is Jenny and the man is Rob, and that they are the main characters in these lessons.

Get Sts to describe them, using language that they learned in **1B**, e.g. *Jenny is blonde. She has long straight hair*, etc.

b **1 26**)) Focus on the instructions and the six photos. Make sure Sts understand the meaning of *mention*. Give Sts a few minutes to think about which order to put them in.

Now play the audio once the whole way through for Sts just to listen.

Then play it again and get Sts to number them 1–6 in the order in which Jenny mentions them.

Get Sts to compare with a partner, and then check answers.

A 1	C 5	E 2
B 3	D 6	F 4

1 26))
(script in Student's Book on *p.118*)
My name's Jenny Zielinski. I live and work in New York. I'm the assistant editor of a magazine called *New York24seven*.
A few months ago, I visited our office in London to learn more about the company. I met the manager, Daniel O'Connor. I had lots of meetings with him, of course. And a working dinner on my birthday... But I spent more time with Rob Walker. He's one of the writers on the London magazine. We had coffees together. We went sightseeing.
I even helped Rob buy a shirt! He was fun to be with. I liked him a lot. I think he liked me too. Rob isn't the most punctual person in the world, but he is a great writer. We invited him to work for the New York magazine for a month... and he agreed! So now Rob's coming to New York. I know he's really excited about it. It's going to be great to see him again.

c Focus on questions 1–7 and give Sts time to read them.

Play the audio again, so Sts can listen a second time and answer the questions.

Get Sts to compare with a partner, and then check answers. Make sure Sts understand the meaning of *punctual*. Model and drill the pronunciation /ˈpʌŋktʃuəl/.

1 She works for a magazine. / She is the assistant editor of a magazine.
2 She went to London.
3 Rob is one of the writer's for the magazine.
4 They had coffee, went sightseeing and shopping.
5 She likes him a lot. He was fun.
6 He isn't very punctual.
7 He is going to be in New York for a month.

Extra support

- If there's time, you could get Sts to listen again with the script on *p.118*, so they can see exactly what they understood / didn't understand. Translate / explain any new words or phrases.

2 CALLING RECEPTION

a **1 27**)) Focus on the photo and ask Sts *Where is Rob?* (In his hotel room) *What is he doing?* (Making a phone call).

Now either tell Sts to close their books and write the questions on the board, or get Sts to focus on the two questions and cover the dialogue.

Play the audio once the whole way through and then check answers.

Rob calls reception because he has some problems in his room.

1 27))) 1 28)))

Re = **receptionist**, **R** = **Rob**

Re Hello, reception.
R Hello. This is room 613. (*repeat*)
Re How can I **help** you?
R There's a problem with the air conditioning. (*repeat*) It isn't working, and it's very hot in my room. (*repeat*)
Re I'm sorry, sir. I'll **send** somebody up to look at it right now.
R Thank you. (*repeat*)
***
Re Good **evening**, reception.
R Hello. I'm sorry to bother you again. This is room 613. (*repeat*)
Re How can I help you?
R I have a problem with the Wi-fi. (*repeat*) I can't get a signal. (*repeat*)
Re I'm sorry sir. I'll **put** you through to IT.
R Thanks. (*repeat*)

b Now focus on the dialogue in the chart. Ask Sts *Who says the **You Hear** sentences?* and elicit that it is the receptionist. Ask *What nationality is he?* (American) Then ask *Who says the **You Say** sentences?* and elicit that here it is Rob. These phrases will be useful for Sts if they have a problem in a hotel.

Give Sts a minute to read through the dialogue and think what the missing words might be. Then play the audio again, and get Sts to complete the gaps. Play again if necessary.

Get Sts to compare with a partner, and then check answers.

See words in **bold** in script 1.27

You might want to model and drill the pronunciation of *Wi-fi* /ˈwaɪ faɪ/ and *signal* /ˈsɪɡnəl/. Elicit / explain what *to put someone through* means and that *IT* stands for Information Technology, so here the people responsible for Wi-fi.

Go through the dialogue line by line with Sts, helping them with any words or expressions they don't understand.

c 1 28))) Now focus on the **You Say** phrases and tell Sts they're going to hear the dialogue again. They should repeat the **You Say** phrases when they hear the beep. Encourage them to copy the rhythm and intonation.

Play the audio, pausing if necessary for Sts to repeat the phrases.

d Focus on the ***I'll*** information box and go through it with the class.

Put Sts in pairs, **A** and **B**. **A** is the receptionist. Get Sts to read the dialogue aloud, and then swap roles.

e Put Sts in pairs, **A** and **B**. Tell Sts to read their instructions, and help them to understand exactly what they have to do.

A is the receptionist and has his / her book open. He / she reads the **You Hear** part with the new information. Elicit that he / she may need to change *Sir* to *Madam* if **B** is a woman.

B has his / her book closed. He / she should quickly read the **You Say** phrases again before starting.

Sts now roleplay the dialogue. **A** starts. Monitor and help.

Extra idea

- Before Sts start the roleplay, elicit some other things they could have in a hotel room, e.g. a TV, a towel, a chair, etc., and write them on the board. Then elicit some problems they might have with these things in the room, e.g. The TV doesn't work, there's no towel, the chair is broken, etc.

f When Sts have finished, they should swap roles.

You could get a few pairs to perform in front of the class.

3 JENNY AND ROB MEET AGAIN

a 1 29))) Focus on the photo and ask Sts where they are and how Rob looks.

Focus on the instructions and on sentences 1–7. Go through them with Sts and make sure they understand them.

Now play the audio once the whole way through, and get Sts to mark the sentences T (true) or F (false). Make it clear that they don't need to correct the false sentences yet.

Get Sts to compare with a partner, and then check answers.

1 F	3 T	5 F	7 F
2 F	4 F	6 T	

1 29)))

(script in Student's Book on *p.118*)

J = **Jenny**, **R** = **Rob**

J So, here you are in New York at last.
R Yeah, it's great to be here. It's really exciting.
J And how's your hotel?
R It's fine. My room is really... nice.
J Do you have a good view from your room?
R I can see lots of other buildings.
J Tomorrow I'm going to show you around the office and introduce you to the team. Barbara's looking forward to meeting you... You remember, Barbara, my boss?
R Oh... yeah, sorry.
J And then you can start thinking about your blog and the column. Have you got any ideas yet, Rob? ... Rob?
R What? Sorry, Jenny.
J You must be really tired.
R Yes, I am a bit. What time is it now?
J It's nine o'clock.
R Nine o'clock? That's two o'clock in the morning for me.
J Let's finish our drinks. You need to go to bed.
R I guess you're right.
J So, I'll see you in the office at eleven in the morning.
R At eleven?
J Is that OK?
R It's perfect. Thanks, Jenny.
J There's just one thing.
R What's that?
J Don't be late.
R By the way, it's great to see you again.
J Yeah. It's great to see you, too.

b Play the audio again, so Sts can listen a second time and correct the false sentences.

Get Sts to compare with a partner, and then check answers.

1 Rob says the hotel is **fine**.
2 Jenny is going to show him round the **office** tomorrow.
4 Rob is **tired**.
5 It's **two** in the morning for Rob.
7 Jenny thinks that Rob is going to **be late**.

Extra support

- If there's time, you could get Sts to listen again with the script on *p.118*, so they can see exactly what they understood / didn't understand. Translate / explain any new words or phrases.

c Focus on the **Social English phrases**. In pairs, get Sts to think about what the missing words could be.

Extra challenge

- In pairs, get Sts to complete the phrases before they listen.

d **1 30**))) Play the audio for Sts to listen and complete the phrases.

Check answers.

1 30)))

Jenny	Here you **are** at last.
Rob	It's **great** to be here.
Jenny	Do you have a **good** view?
Jenny	Barbara's **looking** forward to meeting you.
Jenny	You **must** be really tired.
Rob	I guess you're **right**.
Rob	By the **way**...
Jenny	It's **great** to see you too.

e Now play the audio again, pausing after each phrase for Sts to listen and repeat.

If you know your Sts' L1, you could get them to translate the phrases. If not, get Sts to have a look at the phrases again in context in the script on *p.118*.

Finally, focus on the **Can you...?** questions and ask Sts if they feel confident they can now do these things. If they feel that they need more practice, tell them to watch the episode again and practise the language on their *iTutor*.

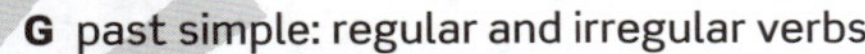

G past simple: regular and irregular verbs
V holidays
P regular verbs: *-ed* endings

2A Right place, wrong person

Lesson plan

The past simple (regular and irregular verbs) is revised in detail in this lesson through the context of holidays, and an article about holidays where things go wrong because of not being with the right people. Sts begin by learning new holiday vocabulary, which is recycled through a short questionnaire. They then do a split reading, and tell each other about the holiday in their article. This is followed by a listening which gives the other side of the two stories. Sts then thoroughly revise the past simple of both regular and irregular verbs. There is a pronunciation focus which revises *-ed* endings in regular verbs, and finally Sts interview each other about their last holiday.

STUDY LINK
- **Workbook** 2A
- **iTutor**
- **www.oup.com/elt/englishfile**

Extra photocopiable activities

- **Grammar** Past simple: regular and irregular *p.165*
- **Communicative** Bingo *p.212* (instructions *p.199*)
- **Vocabulary** Holidays *p.250* (instructions *p.245*)
- **www.oup.com/elt/teacher/englishfile**

Optional lead-in (books closed)

- Write MY LAST HOLIDAY on the board and tell Sts they have two minutes to find out from you as much as possible about your last holiday. Elicit questions in the past simple, e.g. *Where did you go?*, etc.

1 VOCABULARY holidays

a Books open. Focus on the instructions and the examples. Highlight that the verbs are in the *-ing* form because they are things you like doing.

Give Sts a minute to write five things, then get them to compare their list with a partner.

Elicit some of the verb phrases Sts have used and write them on the board, e.g. *swimming*, *going to restaurants*, *seeing new places*, etc.

Extra idea

- Tell Sts to decide which activity on the board is their favourite and take a vote with a show of hands.

b Tell Sts to go to **Vocabulary Bank** ***Holidays*** on *p.152*. Focus on **1 Phrases with** ***go*** and get Sts to do **a** individually or in pairs. Some of these phrases should already be familiar to them.

1 31 Now do **b**. Play the audio for Sts to check answers. Play it again, pausing after each phrase for Sts to repeat. Give further practice of words and phrases your Sts find difficult to pronounce.

Highlight the difference between *go out* (at night) = leave your house, e.g. go to a restaurant, a club, etc. and *go away* (for the weekend) = leave your town, e.g. go to the country, to another town, etc.

1 31
Phrases with *go*
10 go abroad
1 go away for the weekend
6 go by bus / go by car / go by plane / go by train
2 go camping
4 go for a walk
3 go on holiday
8 go out at night
5 go sightseeing
7 go skiing / go walking / go cycling
9 go swimming / go sailing / go surfing

Focus on **c** and get Sts to cover the phrases and look at the pictures. They can test themselves or their partner.

Focus on **2 Other holiday activities** and get Sts to do **a** individually or in pairs.

1 32 Now do **b**. Play the audio for Sts to check answers. Give further practice of any phrases your Sts find difficult to pronounce.

1 32
Other holiday activities
stay in a hotel / **stay** at a campsite / **stay** with friends
take photos
buy souvenirs
sunbathe on the beach
have a good time
spend money / spend time
rent an apartment
hire a bicycle / hire skis
book flights / book hotels online

Focus on the ***rent* or *hire?*** box and go through it with the class.

Now focus on **c**. Get Sts to test themselves by covering the verbs and remembering the phrases.

Focus on **3 Adjectives**. Elicit the meaning of the *What was the…like?* questions. Then give Sts a minute to match the questions and answers.

1 33 Now do **b**. Play the audio for Sts to check answers. Give further practice of any words or phrases your Sts find difficult to pronounce.

1 33
Adjectives
1 What was the weather like?
It was warm. It was sunny.
It was very windy. It was foggy. It was cloudy.
2 What was the hotel like?
It was comfortable. It was luxurious.
It was basic. It was dirty. It was uncomfortable.
3 What was the town like?
It was beautiful. It was lovely.
It was noisy. It was crowded.
4 What were the people like?
They were friendly. They were helpful.
They were unfriendly. They were unhelpful.

5 What was the food like?
It was delicious.
It was nothing special. It was disgusting.

Finally, go through the **General positive and negative adjectives** box with the class.

Tell Sts to go back to the main lesson **2A**.

Extra support

- If you think Sts need more practice, you may want to give them the Vocabulary photocopiable activity at this point.

c In pairs, Sts interview each other using the holiday questionnaire. Remind them to always ask for extra information.

Get some feedback from various pairs.

Extra support

- You could get Sts to interview you first. Make sure they ask you *Why?* and then give as much information as you can.

2 READING & SPEAKING

a Focus on the title of the lesson and the photos, and ask Sts what they think the title means (that somebody went to a nice place, but didn't enjoy it because of the person they were with). You could point out to Sts that the stories are based on real people, although their names have been changed.

Put Sts in pairs, **A** and **B**. Focus on the text. Tell all the **A**s to read about Joe and the **B**s about Laura. Remind them to try to guess new words from context as they read. They should all find the answers to questions 1–5 and either underline them in the text or make notes. Set a time limit for Sts to read their part.

b Tell Sts to stop reading and if possible, sit face-to-face with their partner. They then tell each other about the text they read, using the answers to questions 1–5 to help them remember the important details.

c Now get Sts to read the text they didn't read earlier. In pairs, they should try to guess the meaning of the highlighted words and phrases.

Check answers, either explaining in English, translating into Sts' L1, or getting Sts to check in their dictionaries.

Deal with any other new vocabulary. Model and drill the pronunciation of any tricky words.

Do the question as an open-class activity.

d In pairs or small groups, get Sts to discuss the question. Tell the class if you have ever had a holiday you didn't enjoy.

Finally, get some feedback and find out if any Sts have ever been on holiday 'in the right place, but with the wrong person'.

3 LISTENING

a **1 34** Now tell Sts they are going to listen to Mia and Linda talking about the same holidays. Ask *Who is Mia?* to elicit *Joe's ex-girlfriend*, and *Who is Linda?* to elicit *Laura's friend*.

! If you are not doing this listening in the same class as the reading, get Sts to read the text again quickly and elicit what the problems were.

Tell Sts that they will hear Mia first and they should just listen to find out if she agrees with Joe about the holiday. Play the audio once the whole way through and check the answer.

Extra support

- Read through the scripts and decide if you need to pre-teach any new lexis before Sts listen.

Yes, Mia agrees with Joe about the holiday.

1 34
(script in Student's Book on *p.118*)
Mia
It was a really terrible holiday. It was my fault, I mean I wanted to go to Thailand, but I knew before I went that I didn't really want to have a serious relationship with Joe. And the holiday just showed how different we are. He irritated me all the time. He wanted to stay in some really cheap hostels, because he thought the hotels were too expensive. I didn't want five-star luxury, but when I go on holiday I want to be comfortable. The places where Joe wanted to stay were very basic and had very small rooms. There's nothing worse than being in a very small room with someone when you're not getting on very well. Another thing I didn't like was that Joe got very jealous. When you're travelling, part of the fun is talking to other travellers, but he hated it if I talked to other people, especially other men.
And then he kept taking photos! Hundreds of them. Every time we saw a monument he said, 'Go and stand over there, so I can take a photo.' I hate being in photos. I just wanted to enjoy the sights. The holiday was all a big mistake. Never go on holiday with a boyfriend if you're not sure about the relationship. It's sure to be a disaster!

b Now focus on the questions. Play the audio again and get Sts to answer the questions.

Get Sts to compare with a partner, and then check answers.

1 She didn't want to have a serious relationship with Joe.
2 She didn't like them. She prefers more comfortable hotels.
3 Mia liked talking to other travellers, but Joe was very jealous.
4 Joe took hundreds of photos. She didn't like this as she hates being in photos.
5 Only go on holiday with a boyfriend if you are sure about the relationship.

c **1 35** Now repeat the process for Linda by playing the audio.

Elicit her opinion of the holiday.

Linda doesn't agree that the holiday was a disaster. She loved it.

> 1 35
> (script in Student's Book on *p.118*)
> **Linda**
> Oh, it was a wonderful holiday. I loved every moment! Venice is just a paradise. We did everything – we went on a gondola, we saw all the museums, and we had some fantastic meals. And you know, everyone says that Venice is expensive, but I didn't think it was – it wasn't an expensive holiday at all. I thought it was quite reasonable. We all got on very well. I think I'm going to suggest to Isabelle and Laura that we go on holiday together again next year...

Focus on the questions. Play the audio and get Sts to answer the questions.

Get Sts to compare with a partner, and then check answers.

1 Venice is paradise and not expensive.
2 They went on a gondola, saw museums, and had fantastic food.
3 It wasn't expensive.
4 She wants to go somewhere with Isabelle and Laura.

Extra support

- If there's time, you could get Sts to listen again to both parts of the audio with the scripts on *p.118*, so they can see exactly what they understood / didn't understand. Translate / explain any new words or phrases.

d Make sure Sts understand *sympathize* and ask them to discuss the questions in small groups or as an open class. You could finish by telling them what you think.

Get some feedback from the class.

4 GRAMMAR past simple: regular and irregular verbs

a Focus on the verbs and tell Sts they are a mixture of regular and irregular verbs. Make sure Sts know what they mean, but don't spend too much time on the pronunciation, as Sts will be focussing on this later. Elicit the past simple of the first one (*went*) and then give Sts a minute to do the others in pairs. Encourage Sts to do as many as they can without looking back at the text and then check their answers in Joe's text.

Check answers as a class.

go – went	begin – began
spend – spent	leave – left
want – wanted	be – was, were
stay – stayed	think – thought
know – knew	argue – argued
sunbathe – sunbathed	take – took

b Focus on the instructions and tell Sts to find and underline the positive past simple verbs in Laura's text. Tell Sts that some verbs are repeated, but they only need to underline them once.

Check answers and then elicit the infinitives.

booked – book	cost – cost
rented – rent	complained – complain
asked – ask	wanted – want
could – can	bought – buy
felt – feel	ate – eat
had – have	invited – invite
said – say	chose – choose
was – be	paid – pay
went – go	

c Put Sts in pairs. Tell them to find and underline two negative past simple verbs. Give them a minute to remember how to make negatives and questions.

Check answers.

Joe's text: didn't show   Laura's text: didn't want

normal verbs:
[–] = *didn't* + infinitive, e.g. *I didn't show them, I didn't want it.*
[?] = *Did* (you, etc.) + infinitive?, e.g. *Did you go...?*
was / were:
[–] = *wasn't* or *weren't*, e.g. *It wasn't cold.*
[?] = *Were* (you, etc.)?, *Was* (he, etc.)?, e.g. *Was it nice?*
could:
[–] = *couldn't*, e.g. *We couldn't stay very long.*
[?] = *Could* (I, you, etc.)?, e.g. *Could you swim there?*

d 1 36 Tell Sts to go to **Grammar Bank 2A** on *p.128*. Focus on the example sentences and play the audio for Sts to listen and repeat. Encourage them to copy the rhythm. Then go through the rules with the class.

Additional grammar notes

- You may also want to remind Sts:
  – that irregular forms (*went*, *had*, etc.) are only used in [+] sentences.
  – that the vast majority of verbs are regular. The irregular verbs need to be learnt, but Sts already know the most common ones.
- Tell Sts to go to **Irregular verbs** on *p.164* and explain that this is their reference list. Get Sts to go through the list quickly in pairs, checking that they know what the verbs mean. Encourage them to highlight verbs they didn't know or had forgotten the past form of. Let Sts test each other or test round the class. You could use audio 5.29 to drill the pronunciation of the irregular verbs.

Focus on the exercises for **2A** on *p.129*. Sts do the exercises individually or in pairs.

Check answers, getting Sts to read the full sentences.

a 1 drove 2 broke 3 spent 4 got 5 couldn't 6 were 7 didn't know 8 found 9 stayed 10 saw 11 went 12 bought 13 wanted 14 didn't have 15 was 16 wasn't 17 started 18 left

b 1 Did you have a good time?
2 Who did you go with?
3 Where did you stay?
4 How much did the plane ticket cost?
5 What was the weather like?
6 What did you do at night?

Tell Sts to go back to the main lesson **2A**.

Extra idea

- Remind Sts that a very good way of learning irregular verbs is through reading stories. Show them a few Graded Readers if you can, and if you have a class library, encourage them to take out a book to read at home.

Extra support

- If you think Sts need more practice, you may want to give them the Grammar photocopiable activity at this point.

5 PRONUNCIATION regular verbs: *-ed* endings

Pronunciation notes

- The regular past simple ending *-ed* can be pronounced in three different ways:

  1 *-ed* is pronounced /t/ after verbs ending in these unvoiced sounds: /k/, /p/, /f/, /s/, /ʃ/, and /tʃ/, e.g. *looked, hoped, laughed, passed, washed, watched.*

  2 After voiced* endings *-ed* is pronounced /d/, e.g. *arrived, changed, showed.* This group is the largest.

  3 After verbs ending in /t/ or /d/ the pronunciation of *-ed* is /ɪd/, e.g. *hated, decided.*

- The difference between 1 and 2 is very small and only occasionally causes communication problems. The most important thing is for Sts to be clear about rule 3.

***Voiced and unvoiced consonants**

- Voiced consonant sounds are made in the throat by vibrating the vocal chords, e.g. /b/, /l/, /m/, /v/, etc. Unvoiced consonant sounds are made in the mouth without vibration in the vocal chords, e.g. /k/, /p/, /t/, /s/, etc.
- You can demonstrate this to Sts by getting them to hold their hands against their throats. For voiced sounds they should feel a vibration in their throat, but not for unvoiced sounds.

a 1 37 Remind Sts of the three different pronunciations of the *-ed* ending (see **Pronunciation notes**).

Focus on the three groups of sentences. Play the audio once for Sts just to listen.

1 37

See sentences in Student's Book on *p.13*

Then play it again for Sts to listen and repeat.

b Put Sts in pairs. Give them a minute to practise saying the verbs in the list in the past.

c 1 38 Play the audio for Sts to listen and check.

ended, invited, needed, started

Elicit that you only pronounce the *e* in *-ed* endings when verbs finish in a /t/ or /d/ sound, and then the *-ed* ending is pronounced /ɪd/.

1 38

arrived loved
asked needed
ended parked
invited started
liked stayed

Extra challenge

- Draw three columns on the board for the sounds. Get Sts to write the verbs in the right column. Then play the audio for them to listen and check.

Finally, go through the **Regular past simple verbs** box with the class.

6 SPEAKING

a Focus on the questions and elicit what the missing words are (*did you* in most questions and *was* / *were* in others).

Add *did you* to all the questions except 5 and 6 where it is *was* (*What was the food like? What was the weather like?*).

Drill the complete questions quickly round the class.

b Give Sts time to think about their answers to the questions. Tell them that they can talk about another holiday they remember well, not necessarily their last holiday or they could talk about a holiday where they were in the right place with the wrong person.

Extra support

- Give Sts enough time to make notes or write full answers to the questions.

c Focus on the **Useful language for showing interest** box and go through it with the class. Model and drill the expressions and encourage Sts to use appropriate intonation.

Put Sts in pairs, **A** and **B**. **A**s answer **B**s questions. **B**s must try to show interest and ask for more information. Monitor and correct.

Sts swap roles.

Get some feedback from the class.

G past continuous
V prepositions of time and place: *at, in, on*
P sentence stress

2B The story behind the photo

Lesson plan

This lesson is based on two photos by well-known newspaper photographers, both of which show large groups of people living a historic moment. The first photo, which shows people of all races in the USA waiting to see if the first black president will be elected on 4 November 2008, provides the context for the presentation of a new structure, the past continuous. Sts then focus on vocabulary, the correct use of the prepositions *at*, *in*, and *on*, both for time (revision) and place. This is then linked to the past continuous in a pronunciation exercise, where the focus is on sentence stress and weak forms, and Sts ask each other where they were and what they were doing at different times on the previous day. The second photo, which shows students demonstrating in Paris in the famous May '68 revolt, gives Sts a chance to speculate about what was happening when it was taken, and leads into a listening, where Sts discover why this photo resulted in the girl in it losing a fortune. The lesson ends with Sts talking about their own favourite photos, and then writing about one of them.

STUDY LINK
- **Workbook** 2B
- **iTutor**
- **www.oup.com/elt/englishfile**

Extra photocopiable activities

- **Grammar** Past continuous *p.166*
- **Communicative** Fake or real? *p.213* (instructions *p.199*)
- **Vocabulary** Prepositions *in, at, on p.251* (instructions *p.245*)
- **www.oup.com/elt/teacher/englishfile**

Optional lead-in (books closed)

- Write PHOTO on the board. Ask Sts what it is short for (*photograph*) and elicit the verb we use with it (*take*). Elicit / teach the words for a person who takes photos (*photographer*) and the subject (*photography*). Write them on the board and model the pronunciation. Ask Sts how the syllable stress changes and underline it on the board.
  photograph photographer photography

1 READING

a Books open. Focus on the photo on *p.14*. Get Sts to cover the text and discuss the question with the whole class. Elicit answers / ideas and write them on the board, but do not tell Sts if they are right or not yet.

b Get Sts to read the text and check their answer to **a** (People are looking at a screen in Chicago to see if Barack Obama has won the elections on 4 November 2008). Point out to Sts that the text is in American English, so some words are spelt differently, e.g. *center*.

Deal with any new vocabulary that is causing problems, e.g. *a press pass, screen, hold hands, go mad*, etc.

c Focus on the instructions and get Sts to answer questions 1–7.

Get Sts to compare with a partner, and then check answers.

1 To photograph Obama and his family at the Convention Center.
2 He didn't have his press pass.
3 It was warm.
4 In the park outside the Convention Center.
5 On TV screens.
6 No.
7 Everyone went mad.

d Do this as an open-class question. You could then tell the class what you think and why.

2 GRAMMAR past continuous

a Focus on the highlighted verbs in the extract. Elicit / explain that the verbs describe actions that were in progress at the same time as he took the photo.

b

Extra idea

- Draw a time line on the board to help Sts to understand the concept:

He took the photo.
↓
---------------------------X----------
Everybody was looking at the TV screens.

b 1 39))) 1 40))) Tell Sts to go to **Grammar Bank 2B** on *p.128*. Focus on the example sentences and play the audio for Sts to listen and repeat. Encourage them to copy the rhythm. Then go through the rules with the class.

Additional grammar notes

- If Sts have an equivalent of the past continuous in their L1, then it doesn't normally cause problems. If they don't, it's important to make the use very clear.
- We often use the past continuous at the beginning of a story to set the scene and to say what was happening, e.g. *On April 1st I was staying with some friends in the country. It was a sunny day and we were sunbathing in the garden.*
- Very often these 'actions in progress' (past continuous) are 'interrupted' by a short, completed action (past simple), e.g. *We were having lunch in the garden when suddenly it started to rain.*
- Highlight the similarity in form with the present continuous. It is identical except for using *was / were* instead of *am / is / are*.
- You may also want to remind Sts of the spelling rules for the *-ing* form (see **Grammar Bank 1C**).

Focus on the exercises for **2B** on *p.129*. Sts do the exercises individually or in pairs.

Check answers, getting Sts to read the full sentences.

a	1 was working	5 was shining
	2 was living	6 were ... doing
	3 weren't waiting	7 wasn't listening
	4 Was ... wearing	8 weren't watching
b	1 broke, was playing	5 called, was talking
	2 Were ... driving, stopped	6 were studying, met
	3 was snowing, left	7 Were ... living, had
	4 didn't see, was working	

Tell Sts to go back to the main lesson **2B**.

Extra support

- If you think Sts need more practice, you may want to give them the Grammar photocopiable activity at this point.

c **1 41** Focus on the instructions and the example. Make sure Sts understand they are only going to hear sound effects and that they must write a sentence using the past continuous and the past simple. Put Sts in pairs. Play the audio, pausing after each sound effect to give Sts time to discuss what they think was happening and to write a sentence.

Check answers and write the sentences on the board.

Possible answers
1 They were playing tennis when it started to rain.
2 She was driving when somebody called her.
3 They were having a party when the police came.
4 He was having a shower when somebody knocked on the door.
5 They were sleeping when the baby started crying.
6 She was walking her dog when she met a friend.

Sound effects to illustrate the following:
1 They were playing tennis when it started to rain.
2 She was driving when somebody called her.
3 They were having a party when the police came.
4 He was having a shower when somebody knocked at the door.
5 They were sleeping when the baby started crying.
6 She was walking her dog when she met a friend.

3 VOCABULARY *at, in, on*

a Focus on the instructions and give Sts time to answer the questions.

b Get Sts to compare their answers to **a** with a partner, and then check in the text.

Finally, check together.

1 on	2 at	3 in	4 in

Now focus on the questions in **b** and give Sts time to answer them.

Check answers. Point out that we don't use an article with *at home, at work, at school*.

1 in	2 at	3 at

c Tell Sts to go to **Vocabulary Bank *Prepositions*** on *p.153* and do part **1 *at* / *in* / *on***.

Focus on **a** and get Sts to complete the left-hand column of the chart.

1 42 Now do **b**. Play the audio for Sts to check answers.

! Years from 2000 to 2010 are usually *two thousand and one*, etc. From 2011 onwards we normally say *twenty eleven*, *twenty twelve*, etc.

1 42

at / in / on

1 in
in France, in Paris
in the kitchen
in a shop, in a museum
in a park, in a garden, in a car

in February, in June
in winter
in 2011
in the morning, in the afternoon, in the evening

2 on
on a bike, on a bus, on a train, on a plane, on a ship
on the floor, on a table, on a shelf, on the balcony, on the roof, on the wall

on the first of March
on Tuesday, on New Year's Day, on Valentine's Day

3 at
at school, at home, at work, at university
at the airport, at the station, at a bus stop
at a party, at the door

at 6 o'clock, at half past two, at 7.45
at Christmas, at Easter
at night
at the weekend

! With shops and buildings, e.g. the supermarket, the cinema, you can use *at* or *in* when you answer the question *Where were you?* With *airport* and *station* we normally use *at*.

Focus on **c**. Put Sts in pairs, **A** and **B**. **A** (book open) tests **B** (book closed) for two minutes. Then they swap roles. Allow at least five minutes for Sts to test each other. Then get Sts to close their books and test them round the class, saying a word, e.g. *home*, for Sts to say the preposition *at*.

Tell Sts to go back to the main lesson **2B**.

Extra support

- If you think Sts need more practice, you may want to give them the Vocabulary photocopiable activity at this point.

d Put Sts in pairs, **A** and **B**, and tell them to go to **Communication at, *in*, *on***, **A** on *p.100*, **B** on *p.106*.

Go through the instructions with them carefully.

Sit **A** and **B** face-to-face. **A** asks his / her questions to **B**, who replies using a preposition and then asks *What about you?*

B then asks **A** his / her questions.

When they have finished, get some feedback from the class.

Tell Sts to go back to the main lesson **2B**.

4 PRONUNCIATION sentence stress

Pronunciation notes

- Remind Sts that information words are the ones which are usually stressed in a sentence. These are the words which you hear more clearly when somebody speaks to you. The unstressed words are heard much less clearly or sometimes hardly at all.

! Short prepositions (*up*, *for*, *in*, etc.) are not normally stressed except when they occur at the end of a sentence. Compare *Where are you from?* (*from* is stressed) and *I'm from Munich* (*from* is unstressed).

a 1 43 Play the audio once for Sts just to listen.

1 43
See dialogue in Student's Book on *p.15*

Now play it again, pausing after each line for Sts to listen and repeat, copying the stress. Encourage Sts to say the unstressed words as fast as they can.

b Focus on the instructions and speech bubbles. Explain that Sts are going to practise the dialogue in **a** with different times. First, focus on the times and elicit that where they see 'a.m.' they should say *in the morning*, and where they see 'p.m.' they should say *in the afternoon* or *at night* for 10.00p.m.

Put Sts in pairs, **A** and **B**. **A** asks the questions for the first time (6.30 a.m.), and then **B** asks the questions for 11.00 a.m., etc.

When Sts have finished, get some feedback from the class.

Extra support

- Get Sts to ask you the questions first, and correct any pronunciation errors. Answer the questions, giving more information where you can as a model for Sts when they answer themselves.

5 LISTENING

a Focus on the instructions and the photo. Elicit some opinions from the class. You may want to teach (*to be / go on*) *a demonstration*. Highlight that this is a true story.

b Tell Sts to read the beginning of the article and answer the question. Elicit that the title could mean either that the photo was very expensive or that it cost the woman a lot of money, i.e. that she lost a lot of money because of it.

Tell Sts they will find out exactly what the title means when they listen to the woman. Do not tell Sts the answer yet.

c 1 44 Tell Sts to focus on the photo and to listen to the woman in the photo talking about it. Play the audio once the whole way through.

Check answers to **b**.

Extra support

- Read through the script and decide if you need to pre-teach any new lexis before Sts listen.

It is called 'The image that cost a fortune' because the woman's grandfather saw the photo on the cover of a magazine and then decided not to leave her any money when he died.

1 44
(script in Student's Book on *p.118*)
En mai 1968 je suis rentré à Paris.
In May 1968, I came back to Paris. It was a very exciting time. There were a lot of demonstrations, and fighting between students and the police. I wasn't really interested in politics – I wasn't a communist or an anarchist. But I loved the atmosphere. All the students were fighting for freedom, for revolution, and the French police were everywhere. On May the 15th I was with thousands of other young people. We were walking towards the Place de la Bastille. I was tired, so a friend picked me up and I sat on his shoulders. Another boy who was walking next to us was carrying a Vietnamese flag (it was the time of the Vietnam War) and he said to me, 'Hey, could you carry the flag for me?' and I said, 'OK.' There was so much happening that I didn't notice all the photographers. The next day the photo was on the cover of magazines all over the world. When my grandfather saw it, he immediately ordered me to come to his house. He was furious – really really angry. He said, 'That's it! You are a communist! I'm not going to leave you anything. Not a penny!' I walked out of the room and I never saw him again. Six months later he died, and I didn't get any money from him. Nothing.

d Focus on the multiple choice sentences and give Sts a few moments to read them before you play the audio again.

Play the audio again if necessary.

Get Sts to compare with a partner, and then check answers.

1 a 2 c 3 a 4 b 5 c

Extra support

- If there's time, you could get Sts to listen again with the script on *p.118*, so they can see exactly what they understood / didn't understand. Translate / explain any new words or phrases.

e Do this as an open-class question. You could tell Sts that according to the press she would have inherited £7.5 million, but she says that she has no regrets, and has had a very happy life.

6 SPEAKING & WRITING My favourite photo

a Focus on the questions. Make sure Sts understand all the vocabulary, e.g. *to upload a photo*, *a screen saver*, *admire sby*, etc. Demonstrate the activity by getting Sts to ask you the questions. Then get Sts to discuss the questions in pairs. Encourage them to give more information if they can.

Get feedback from a few pairs.

Extra idea

- You could ask Sts to bring one or two favourite photos to the next class to show other Sts and talk about them, or to show each other photos they have on their phone.

b Tell Sts to go to **Writing *My favourite photo*** on *p.112*.

Focus on the information at the top of the image and establish that this is for a photo competition on the internet.

Now focus on **a** and get Sts to match the questions with paragraphs 1–5. Tell them not to worry about the gaps.

Check answers.

1 What's your favourite photo?
2 Who took it? When? Where?
3 What was happening when you took the photo?
4 Why do you like it?
5 Where do you keep it?

Now focus on **b** and get Sts to complete the gaps with *in*, *of*, *on*, or *round*.

Get Sts to compare with a partner, and then check answers.

2 in, on, in
3 on, round
5 on, on, of

Focus on the **You can keep a photo** box and go through it with the class.

Set the writing in **c** in class or for homework and ask Sts to include a photo. Tell Sts to answer the questions in **a** in the right order and not as they appear on the page, so the first question they write about is *What's your favourite photo?*

In **d** Sts first check their writing for mistakes and attach the photo if they have one. Then Sts swap their descriptions and see if their photos are similar or not.

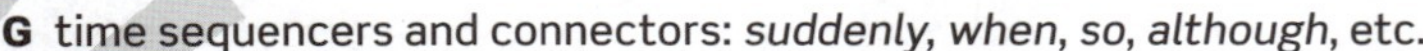

G time sequencers and connectors: *suddenly, when, so, although*, etc.
V verb phrases
P word stress

2C One dark October evening

Lesson plan

In this lesson Sts learn to use time sequencers, e.g. *after that*, *later*, etc. and the connectors *so*, *because*, *but*, and *although*. They also revise the past simple and continuous. The context is a short story with a twist. After Sts have read most of the story, and worked on the grammar, they have a pronunciation focus on word stress in two-syllable words, and then in Vocabulary expand their knowledge of verb phrases. The language is then pulled together in the speaking activity, where they use picture prompts to retell the story so far. They then decide as a class whether they want to hear a happy or a sad ending to the story, and then listen to the one they have chosen, and the lesson ends with the song mentioned in the story, *Blue As Your Eyes*.

STUDY LINK

- **Workbook** 2C
- **iTutor**
- **iChecker**
- **www.oup.com/elt/englishfile**

Extra photocopiable activities

- **Grammar** Time sequences and connectors *p.167*
- **Communicative** Sentence race *p.214* (instructions *p.199*)
- **Song** *Blue As Your Eyes p.268* (instructions *p.263*)
- **www.oup.com/elt/teacher/englishfile**

Optional lead-in (books closed)

- Elicit song titles with colours in them and write them on the board, for example *Yellow* by Coldplay, *White Flag* by Dido, *Blue Eyes* by Elton John, *Purple Rain* by Prince, etc.
- Then tell Sts that they are going to read a short story where a song with a colour plays a part.

1 GRAMMAR time sequencers and connectors

a 1 45))) Books open. Focus on the text and tell Sts that they are going to listen to a story, but that first they have to read it and complete the gaps. Tell them that the end of the story is on audio, so the last paragraph here is not the end of the story.

Give Sts five minutes to read the paragraphs.

Get them to compare with a partner, and then play the audio for Sts to listen to the story and check answers.

2 When
3 Next day
4 After that
5 One evening in October
6 Suddenly

1 45)))

Hannah met Jamie in the summer of 2010. It was Hannah's 21st birthday and she and her friends went to a club. They wanted to dance, but they didn't like the music, so Hannah went to speak to the DJ. 'This music is awful,' she said. 'Could you play something else?' The DJ looked at her and said, 'Don't worry, I have the perfect song for you.'

Two minutes later he said, 'The next song is by Scouting For Girls. It's called *Blue As Your Eyes* and it's for a beautiful girl who's dancing over there.' Hannah knew that the song was for her.

When Hannah and her friends left the club, the DJ was waiting for her at the door. 'Hi, I'm Jamie,' he said to Hannah. 'Can I see you again?' So Hannah gave him her phone number.

Next day Jamie phoned Hannah and invited her to dinner. He took her to a very romantic French restaurant and they talked all evening. Although the food wasn't very good, they had a wonderful time. After that Jamie and Hannah saw each other every day. Every evening when Hannah finished work they met at 5.30 in a coffee bar in the high street. They were madly in love.

One evening in October, Hannah was at work. As usual she was going to meet Jamie at 5.30. It was dark and it was raining. She looked at her watch. It was 5.20! She was going to be late! She ran to her car and got in. At 5.25 she was driving along the high street. She was going very fast because she was in a hurry. Suddenly, a man ran across the road. He was wearing a dark coat, so Hannah didn't see him at first. Quickly she put her foot on the brake...

b Tell Sts to read the story again if necessary and answer questions 1–8. They can answer orally in pairs, or in writing.

Check answers.

1 Because she didn't like the music.
2 Because Hannah has blue eyes.
3 Jamie was waiting at the door and asked to see Hannah again.
4 It was very romantic, but the food wasn't very good.
5 To a coffee bar in the high street.
6 It was dark and raining.
7 Because she was in a hurry.
8 Because he was wearing a dark coat.

Extra challenge

- Get Sts to answer the questions in pairs before they read the story again. They then reread the story to check.

c Focus on the three sentences. Tell Sts not to look back at the story, but to try and complete the sentences from memory.

Check answers and elicit / explain the meaning of the missing words or ask Sts how to say them in their L1. Model and drill the pronunciation of *so*, *because*, and *although*. Write them on the board and underline the stressed syllable, or write them up in phonetics (/səʊ/, /bɪ'kɒz/, and /ɔːl'ðəʊ/).

1 because
2 Although
3 so

d 1.46, 1.47 and 1.48 Tell Sts to go to **Grammar Bank 2C** on *p.128*. Focus on the example sentences and play the audio for Sts to listen and repeat. Encourage them to copy the rhythm. Then go through the rules with the class.

Additional grammar notes

- We usually put a comma before *so*, *although*, and *but*, e.g. *She was tired, so she went to bed.*
- Sts may also ask you about *though*, which is a colloquial, abbreviated form of *although*. *Though* is not usually used at the beginning of a sentence. It is probably best at this level if Sts just learn *although*.

! *So* has another completely different meaning which is to intensify adjectives, e.g. *He was so tired that he went to bed at 9.00.* You may want to point out this meaning too in case Sts get confused.

Now focus on the exercises for **2C** on *p.129*. Sts do the exercises individually or in pairs.

Check answers, getting Sts to read the full sentences.

a	2 g	4 e	6 f	8 d
	3 b	5 a	7 h	
b	1 Although	4 Although	7 but	
	2 because	5 so	8 so	
	3 but	6 because	9 Although	

Tell Sts to go back to the main lesson **2C**.

Extra support

- If you think Sts need more practice, you may want to give them the Grammar photocopiable activity at this point.

e Tell Sts to look at the six sentences and to complete them with their own ideas.

When Sts have finished, get them to swap pieces of paper with a partner.

Get some feedback from the class. You could write some of the sentences on the board.

2 PRONUNCIATION word stress

a Focus on the **Stress in two-syllable words** box and go through it with the class.

Now focus on the task and give Sts time, in pairs, to underline the stressed syllable.

b 1.49 Play the audio for Sts to listen and check.

Pause the audio after each word, elicit the answer, and write the word on the board with the stressed syllable underlined.

1.49

a<u>cross</u>, <u>af</u>ter, a<u>gain</u>, a<u>long</u>, al<u>though</u>, <u>aw</u>ful, be<u>cause</u>, <u>birth</u>day, <u>eve</u>ning, in<u>vite</u>, <u>per</u>fect, <u>se</u>cond

Play the audio again, pausing after each word for Sts to repeat.

3 VOCABULARY verb phrases

a Focus on the two boxes and the example. Tell Sts that by combining a verb from **1** with a phrase from **2**, they will make verb phrases from the story.

Put Sts in pairs and give them a few minutes to match the verbs and phrases. Tell them that sometimes two verbs may be possible with a phrase, but to try to remember the phrases from the story.

Check answers.

have a wonderful evening
drive along the high street (also in a hurry)
meet in a coffee bar
give somebody your email address / phone number
take somebody to a restaurant
wait for somebody (also in a coffee bar)
be in a hurry
play a song
leave the club very late (also in a hurry)
run across the road (also along the high street)

b Get Sts to test themselves by covering box **1** and remembering the verbs for each phrase.

4 SPEAKING & LISTENING

a Re-telling a story gives Sts the opportunity for some extended oral practice, and in this case to recycle the tenses and connectors they have been studying.

Focus on the pictures and tell Sts they are going to re-tell the story of Hannah and Jamie. Give them a few minutes to re-read the story on *p.16*.

b Put Sts in pairs, **A** and **B**. Get **A**s to cover the text and focus on the pictures. Tell them to tell as much of the story as they can for pictures 1, 2, and 3 while **B** looks at the story on *p.16* to prompt / correct. They then swap roles for pictures 4 and 5.

Get individual Sts to tell the class about each picture.

c Tell Sts they are now going to hear the end of the story. First, Sts have to vote with a show of hands on whether they want to hear a happy ending or a sad ending.

If Sts vote for the happy ending, play audio 1.50. If they vote for the sad ending, play audio 1.51.

d 1.50 or 1.51 Before playing the ending chosen by Sts, elicit ideas from the class about what they think happened, but don't tell them if they are right or wrong to help build suspense.

Play the audio once the whole way through for Sts to listen.

Extra support

- Read through the script and decide if you need to pre-teach any new lexis before Sts listen.

1 50

(script in Student's Book on *pp.118–119*)

Happy ending

N = Narrator, H = Hannah, J = Jamie, W = waiter

N Suddenly, a man ran across the road. He was wearing a dark coat, so Hannah didn't see him at first. Quickly she put her foot on the brake. She stopped just in time. She got out of her car and shouted at the man.
H Don't you usually look before you cross the road? I nearly hit you. I didn't see you until the last moment.
J Sorry! Hey, Hannah it's me. It's Jamie.
H Jamie! What are you doing here? I nearly killed you!
J I was buying something. I was in a hurry and I crossed the road without looking.
H Come on. Get in!
N Hannah and Jamie drove to the coffee bar. They sat down in their usual seats and ordered two cups of coffee.
W Here you are. Two cappuccinos.
H and J Thanks.
H What an evening! I nearly killed you.
J Well, you didn't kill me, so what's the problem?
H But what were you doing in the high street? I thought you were here, in the café, waiting for me.
J I went to the theatre to buy these tickets for the Scouting For Girls concert. I know you wanted to go. And it's on the 15th of October – next Saturday. Our anniversary.
H Our anniversary?
J Yes. Three months since we first met. We met on Saturday the 15th of July. Remember?
H Gosh, Jamie. I can't believe you remember the exact day! What a romantic! It's lucky I didn't hit you in the street...

1 51

(script in Student's Book on *p.119*)

Sad ending

N = Narrator, H = Hannah, P = policewoman

N Suddenly, a man ran across the road. He was wearing a dark coat, so Hannah didn't see him at first. Quickly she put her foot on the brake. Although Hannah tried to stop, she couldn't. She hit the man. Hannah panicked. She drove away as fast as she could. When she arrived at the coffee bar, Jamie wasn't there. She called him, but his mobile phone was turned off. She waited for ten minutes and then she went home.
Two hours later a car arrived at Hannah's house. A policewoman knocked at the door.
P Good evening, Madam. Are you Hannah Davis?
H Yes, I am.
P I'd like to speak to you. Can I come in?
N The policewoman came in and sat down on the sofa.
P Are you a friend of Jamie Dixon?
H Yes.
N said Hannah.
P Well, I'm afraid I have some bad news for you.
H What? What's happened?
P Jamie had an accident this evening.
H Oh no. What kind of accident?
P He was crossing the road and a car hit him.
H When... When did this happen? And where?
P This evening at twenty-five past five. He was crossing the road in the High Street by the theatre.
H Oh no! How is he?
P He's in hospital. He's got a bad injury to his head and two broken legs.
H But is he going to be OK?
P We don't know. He's in intensive care.
H Oh no. And the driver of the car?
P She didn't stop.
H She?
P Yes, it was a woman in a white car. Somebody saw the number of the car. You have a white car outside, don't you, Madam? Is your number plate XYZ 348S?
H Yes... yes it is.
P Can you tell me where you were at twenty-five past five this evening?

At the end of the story, get Sts to tell you what happened.

Extra support

- If there's time, you could get Sts to listen again with the script on *pp.118–119*, so they can see exactly what they understood / didn't understand. Translate / explain any new words or phrases.

e If Sts chose the happy ending (1.50), tell them to go to **Communication *Happy ending*** on *p.101*. If Sts chose the sad ending (1.51), tell them to go to **Communication *Sad ending*** on *p.109*.

Play the end of the story again. Set a time limit for Sts to answer questions 1–8 in pairs.

Check answers.

Happy ending
1 Because he was wearing a dark coat.
2 Jamie.
3 He was in a hurry.
4 To a coffee bar.
5 Two cappuccinos.
6 He was buying tickets for a concert.
7 It was the Scouting For Girls concert on 15th October.
8 15th October was their three-month anniversary.

Sad ending
1 Because he was wearing a dark coat.
2 She hit him.
3 She went to the coffee bar and called Jamie.
4 The police. / A policewoman.
5 That Jamie was in a car accident.
6 He has a bad injury to his head and two broken legs. / He's in intensive care.
7 The car was white and the driver a woman.
8 She asked Hannah about the number plate of her car and where she was at 6.25 p.m.

Tell Sts to go back to the main lesson **2C**.

5  **SONG** *Blue As Your Eyes* ♫

This song was originally made famous by the English band Scouting For Girls in 2010. For copyright reasons this is a cover version. If you want to do this song in class, use the photocopiable activity on *p.269*.

1 52

Blue As Your Eyes

Am I falling apart?
Is this falling in love? Am I going insane?
You're scratched on my heart.
You're scratched on my heart; you're etched on my brain.

And every word;
Every word that you said goes round
Round in my head
Round like a cyclone in my mind.

Chorus
I've been trying to get a hold on you.
I've been trying to get a hold on you.
I've been trying to get a hold on you.
On this crazy world of mine, everyday.
Right from the start. When I showed you my hand,
I gave you my heart. Falling in love,
Feeling alive, clear as the mud,
I'm blue as your eyes, blue as your eyes.

Is it all in my head?
You turn me away, you beg me to stay.
Is it something I said?
You want it to change, you want it the same.

Chorus

1 & 2 Revise and Check

There are two pages of revision and consolidation after every two Files. The first page revises the grammar, vocabulary, and pronunciation of the two Files. These exercises can be done individually or in pairs, in class or at home, depending on the needs of your Sts and the class time available. The second page presents Sts with a series of skills-based challenges. First, there is a reading text which is of a slightly higher level than those in the File, but which revises grammar and vocabulary Sts have already learned. Then Sts can watch or listen to five unscripted street interviews, where people are asked questions related to the topics in the File. You can find these on the *Class DVD*, *iTools*, and *Class Audio* (audio only). Finally, there is a speaking challenge, which measures Sts' ability to use the language of the File orally. We suggest that you use some or all of these activities according to the needs of your class.

In addition, there is a short documentary film available on the *Class DVD*, and *iTools* on a subject related to one of the topics of the Files. This is aimed at giving Sts enjoyable extra listening practice and showing them how much they are now able to understand. Sts can find all the video content and activities on the *iTutor*.

STUDY LINK
- **iTutor**

Test and Assessment CD-ROM
- **Quick Test 2**
- **File 2 Test**

GRAMMAR

1 c
2 b
3 a
4 c
5 a
6 c
7 c
8 b
9 b
10 c
11 a
12 c
13 a
14 b
15 c

VOCABULARY

a 1 do
2 look
3 wear
4 take
5 stay
6 book
7 invite
8 drive
9 play
10 leave

b 1 on
2 in
3 in
4 on
5 at
6 at
7 on

c 1 beard (the others are about hair)
2 lazy (the others are positive adjectives)
3 friendly (the others are negative adjectives)
4 tie (the others are normally worn by women)
5 gloves (the others are worn on your feet)
6 scarf (the others are pieces of jewellery)
7 dirty (the others are about the weather)
8 luxurious (the others are negative)

PRONUNCIATION

a 1 J
2 shorts
3 lives
4 weight
5 university

b 1 talkative
2 moustache
3 prefer
4 disgusting
5 comfortable

CAN YOU UNDERSTAND THIS TEXT?

a A bad thing.

b 1 T
2 T
3 T
4 F
5 F
6 T

CAN YOU UNDERSTAND THESE PEOPLE?

1 53)))

1 b 2 c 3 c 4 b 5 c

1 53)))

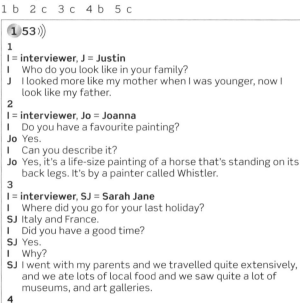

1
I = interviewer, J = Justin
I Who do you look like in your family?
J I looked more like my mother when I was younger, now I look like my father.

2
I = interviewer, Jo = Joanna
I Do you have a favourite painting?
Jo Yes.
I Can you describe it?
Jo Yes, it's a life-size painting of a horse that's standing on its back legs. It's by a painter called Whistler.

3
I = interviewer, SJ = Sarah Jane
I Where did you go for your last holiday?
SJ Italy and France.
I Did you have a good time?
SJ Yes.
I Why?
SJ I went with my parents and we travelled quite extensively, and we ate lots of local food and we saw quite a lot of museums, and art galleries.

4
I = interviewer, D = David
I Do you take a lot of photos?
D I don't, but my wife does.
I What does she take photos of?
D Mostly buildings and some of me. She doesn't like to be in photos herself, so I have to do all the modelling.

5
I = interviewer, A = Andy
I Do you prefer films with a happy or a sad ending?
A I quite like ones with sad endings actually.
I Why?
A I have no particular reason why, it's just in general the films I like tend to have sad endings.

G *be going to* (plans and predictions)
V airports
P sentence stress and fast speech

3A Plans and dreams

Lesson plan

In this lesson Sts revise *going to*, which they learnt at Elementary level to talk about plans and predictions. The context is a listening based on interviews with people at Heathrow airport in London, who are all questioned about their plans. The lesson begins with vocabulary, and Sts learn useful vocabulary related to airports. They then listen to the interviews, which leads them into the grammar, which is revised and practised. The pronunciation focus is on sentence stress and fast speech, which helps Sts to recognize the contraction of *going to* (*gonna*), and Sts then ask and answer questions about their plans. The lesson ends with an article about the world's top airports, and what makes them special.

STUDY LINK
- **Workbook** 3A
- **iTutor**
- **www.oup.com/elt/englishfile**

Extra photocopiable activities

- **Grammar** *be going to* (plans and predictions) *p.168*
- **Communicative** Find a partner *p.215* (instructions *p.200*)
- **Song** *This is the Life p.270* (instructions *p.263*)

www.oup.com/elt/teacher/englishfile

Optional lead-in (books closed)

- Write AIRPORT on the board. Put Sts in pairs and give them two minutes to think of five things people do at an airport, e.g. *catch a plane, leave, arrive, meet somebody, check in, board, fly*, etc. Elicit answers and write some of their suggestions on the board.

1 VOCABULARY airports

a Books open. Focus on the questions. Sts can answer them in pairs or do them as an open class.

b Focus on the instructions and tell Sts to look at the 12 signs and to match them with the words and phrases.

Get Sts to compare their answers with a partner.

c  Play the audio for Sts to listen and check.

1 54
3 Arrivals
7 Baggage drop-off
1 Baggage reclaim
9 Check-in
8 Customs
2 Departures
11 Gates
5 Lifts
10 Passport Control
4 Terminal
12 Toilets
6 Trolley

Then tell Sts to cover the words and look at the symbols, and try to remember the words.

2 LISTENING

a Focus on the three people in the picture and the caption. Make sure the term NGO (non-governmental organization) is clear; you might want to tell Sts that NGOs are non-profit voluntary organizations, which often have humanitarian aims.

Elicit some opinions to the question and get Sts to say why, but do not tell them the answer.

b  Now play the audio for Sts to check their answer to **a**.

Extra support

- Read through the script and decide if you need to pre-teach any new lexis before Sts listen.

Olivia is going to work abroad for an NGO.
Matthew is going to do a photo shoot.
Lily is going to see an ex-partner.

1 55
(script in Student's Book on *p.119*)
I = Interviewer, O = Olivia, M = Matthew, L = Lily

Olivia
I Excuse me, do you have a moment?
O Yes, sure.
I Where are you going?
O To Nicaragua.
I For a holiday?
O No, I'm going to do voluntary work. I'm going to teach English to young children.
I Where exactly in Nicaragua are you going?
O To a town called Estelí. It's about 150 kilometres from Managua.
I How long are you going to be there for?
O I'm going to be in Estelí for six weeks and after that I'm going to travel round Nicaragua for a month.
I That sounds amazing.
O Yes, I'm really looking forward to it.
I Are you feeling nervous at all?
O A bit, because I don't speak much Spanish. But they're going to give us a 40-hour language course when we arrive so I hope that's enough to start with.
I Well, good luck and have a great time.
O Thanks. I'm sure it's going to be a fantastic experience.

Matthew
I Excuse me, do you have a moment?
M Yeah, OK.
I Where are you going?
M To Australia.
I That's a long flight. Are you going to stop on the way?
M No, I'm going direct to Melbourne.
I Why Melbourne?
M I'm going to work there. I'm a model and we're going to do a photo shoot for a magazine.
I That sounds exciting. What kind of clothes are you going to model?
M Winter clothes, for next season. It's winter in Australia now so it's going to be quite cold. That's why we're going there.
I Of course, it's their winter. How cold do you think it's going to be?
M I'm not quite sure. About eight or nine degrees during the day and colder at night, I suppose.
I Well, have a good trip, and I hope the photos are fabulous!
M Thanks.

Lily
I Excuse me, do you have a moment?
O OK, sure.
I Where are you going?
L To Budapest.
I Why are you going there?
L I'm going to a conference.
I So it's a work trip.
L Yes. But I'm also going to see an old friend there. Actually, an old boyfriend. Someone I went out with a long time ago.
I When did you decide to meet up again?
L Well, I knew he was working at Budapest University, so when the conference came up about a month ago I got in touch with him on Facebook.
I Is he going to meet you at the airport?
L I don't think so! But who knows?
I How do you feel about it?
L Quite excited. It's going to be strange meeting again after all these years.
I Well, good luck. I'm sure you're going to have a great time. And enjoy the conference, too.
L Thanks very much.

Now play the audio again and get Sts to complete the chart on a piece of paper. Pause the audio after each section to give Sts time to write.

Get Sts to compare with a partner, and then check answers.

Olivia	Nicaragua. To teach English to children / To do voluntary work. She is going to travel for a month.
Matthew	Australia. To do a photo shoot for a magazine. He is going to model winter clothes.
Lily	Budapest. To go to a conference. She is going to meet her ex-boyfriend from university.

Extra support

- If there's time, you could get Sts to listen again with the script on *p.119*, so they can see exactly what they understood / didn't understand. Translate / explain any new words or phrases.

3 GRAMMAR *be going to* (plans and predictions)

a  **1 56** Focus on the instructions and give Sts time to complete the gaps with the correct form of *be going to*.

Get Sts to compare with a partner, then play the audio for them to check their answers.

1 56
1 **I'm going to teach** English to young children.
2 How long **are you going to be** there for?
3 It's winter in Australia now, so **it's going to be** quite cold.
4 **Is he going to meet** you at the airport?
5 I'm sure **you're going to have** a great time.

b First, make sure that Sts are clear about what the difference is between a plan (something you intend to do) and a prediction (something that you think will happen).

Now, in pairs, Sts focus on whether sentences 1–5 in a are plans (PL) or predictions (PR).

Check answers.

1 PL 2 PL 3 PR 4 PL 5 PR

c **1 57** Tell Sts to go to **Grammar Bank 3A** on *p.130*. Focus on the example sentences and play the audio for Sts to listen and repeat. Encourage them to copy the rhythm. Then go through the rules with the class.

Additional grammar notes

- *Be going to* is revised here with its two main uses: plans (*I'm going to stay for six months.*) and predictions (*It's going to be a big surprise for him.*).

Focus on the exercises for **3A** on *p.131*. Sts do the exercises individually or in pairs.

Check answers, getting Sts to read the full sentences.

a 1 Is ... going to learn
2 're going to be
3 aren't going to go, 're going to stay
4 're going to get
5 'm going to cook
6 'm not going to listen
7 are ... going to do

b 1 're going to be
2 's going to be
3 're going to love

Tell Sts to go back to the main lesson **3A**.

Extra support

- If you think Sts need more practice, you may want to give them the Grammar photocopiable activity at this point.

4 PRONUNCIATION & SPEAKING

sentence stress and fast speech

Pronunciation notes

- The first exercise gives Sts more practice in sentence stress, and shows them which words are normally stressed in sentences with *be going to*. In the second exercise the focus is on how native speakers often pronounce *going to*, i.e. as *gonna*. Point out to Sts that they need practice in understanding *gonna*, but that it is probably not a good idea for them to pronounce it in this way, as it will not sound natural unless they speak very fast, which they will probably not be able to do yet.

a **1 58** Remind Sts that in English we stress (pronounce more strongly) the words in a sentence which are the most important for communication, i.e. the information words, and say the other words more lightly.

Focus attention on the first question and ask Sts to tell you which words are the most important for communication. (*What*, *going*, *do*, and *tonight*), and highlight that these are the four words you have to stress in the question.

Play the audio once for Sts just to listen.

 **1 58**
See sentences in Student's Book on *p.21*

Now play it again, pausing after each line for Sts to listen and repeat.

b  Focus on the **Fast speech: *gonna*** box and go through it with the class.

This dictation is for recognition (not production) of *gonna*. Tell Sts they are going to listen to six sentences or questions read at normal speed and they must write them down. Play the audio, pausing after each one to give Sts time to write.

Get Sts to compare with a partner, and then check answers.

1 59

1 It's going to be difficult.
2 What are we going to do now?
3 Is it going to rain?
4 Where are we going to go?
5 They aren't going to come.
6 What's going to happen?

c Tell Sts to go to **Communication *What are your plans?*, A** on *p.101*, **B** on *p.107*. Go through the instructions with them carefully, and elicit the words missing from the question prompts (*are* and *going to*).

Sit **A** and **B** face-to-face. **A** asks **B** his / her questions.

B now asks **A** his / her questions.

Monitor and help, correcting any errors they make with *going to*.

When they have finished, get feedback from some pairs.

Tell Sts to go back to the main lesson **3A**.

5 READING

a Focus on the questions and elicit answers from the class.

b Now focus on the article and the photo. Read the introduction aloud (or get a student to read it) and establish that the rest of the article describes the facilities at various top airports around the world. Look at the names of the cities and establish which country they are in (Singapore, Hong Kong – China, Seoul – South Korea, Munich – Germany, Osaka – Japan, Zurich – Switzerland).

Give Sts two minutes to read the whole article and answer questions 1–7.

Get Sts to compare with a partner, and then check answers.

1 Osaka	4 Osaka	7 Singapore
2 Munich	5 Hong Kong	
3 Seoul	6 Zurich	

c Now get Sts to read the article again, and work with a partner to decide what the highlighted words and phrases mean. Encourage Sts to use the context, and any part of the sentence that they know to help them.

Check answers, either explaining in English, translating into Sts' L1, or getting Sts to check in their dictionaries.

Deal with any other new vocabulary.

Extra support

- To check comprehension, ask some more questions on each text, e.g. *Which is the best airport for people who like flowers?* (Singapore) *Which airport offers free drinks?* (Munich), etc.

d Focus on the instructions and set the scene. Put Sts in pairs and give them time to do the roleplay. Monitor and help, encouraging Sts to use *be going to*.

You could get some pairs to roleplay in front of the class.

6  SONG *This is the Life* ♫

This song was originally made famous by Scottish singer Amy Macdonald in 2007. For copyright reasons this is a cover version. If you want to do this song in class, use the photocopiable activity on *p.270*.

1 60

This is the Life

Oh the wind whistles down
The cold dark street tonight
And the people they were dancing
To the music vibe
And the boys chase the girls with the curls in their hair
While the shy tormented youth sit way over there
And the songs they get louder each one better than before

Chorus

And And you're singing the songs, thinking this is the life
And you wake up in the morning and you're head feels twice the size
Where you gonna go? Where you gonna go? Where you gonna sleep tonight?

So you're heading down the road in your taxi for four
And you're waiting outside Jimmy's front door
But nobody's in and nobody's home till four
So you're sitting there with nothing to do
Talking about Robert Riger and his motley crew
And where you're gonna go and where you're gonna sleep tonight

Chorus

G present continuous (future arrangements)
V verbs + prepositions, e.g. *arrive in*
P sounding friendly

3B Let's meet again

Lesson plan

In this lesson Sts learn a new use of the present continuous: to talk about fixed plans and arrangements. The context is the continuation of the story of Lily, one of the people they listened to in **3A**, who was going to a conference and hoping to meet up with an ex-boyfriend. They begin this lesson reading messages between her and Ben, the ex-boyfriend, in which they make contact, and they then listen to her leaving him a voicemail about her travel arrangements. After focussing on the grammar, they get more practice through a listening where Lily and Ben arrange to see each other, and finally they hear what happens when they actually meet. The lesson continues with a pronunciation focus on friendly intonation, and Sts then complete a diary and try to make arrangements to go out with other Sts in the class. The lesson ends with a vocabulary focus on verbs which are normally followed by prepositions, and Sts then use both the grammar and the vocabulary to write an email about travel arrangements.

STUDY LINK
- **Workbook** 3B
- **iTutor**
- **www.oup.com/elt/englishfile**

Extra photocopiable activities

- **Grammar** Present continuous (future arrangements) *p.169*
- **Communicative** Come fly with me! *p.216* (instructions *p.200*)
- **Vocabulary** What's the preposition? *p.252* (instructions *p.245*)
- **www.oup.com/elt/teacher/englishfile**

Optional lead-in (books closed)

- Quickly revise months. Write SPRING, SUMMER, AUTUMN, and WINTER on the board and tell Sts, in pairs, to write three months in each season. Check answers and model and drill the pronunciation of any which Sts find difficult, e.g. *February* /ˈfebruəri/, *July* /dʒuˈlaɪ/, etc.

1 READING & LISTENING

a 1 61))) Focus on the dates and elicit the first one from the class (the third of May). Then put Sts in pairs, and get them to practise saying the other dates.

Play the audio for them to listen and check.

> 1 61)))
> the third of May
> the twelfth of August twenty twelve
> the thirty-first of December
> the twenty-second of June
> the fifth of February
> the twentieth of July nineteen ninety-eight

Remind Sts that we use ordinal numbers to say the date, and that we say *the* before the ordinal and *of* before the month. Now play the audio again, pausing after each date for Sts to listen and repeat.

Extra support

- Get Sts to count round the class using ordinal numbers from 1st to 31st.

b Focus on the instructions. Ask Sts if they recognize Lily (she is the woman from the Listening in **3A**). Elicit what Sts can remember about her (She is going to Budapest for a conference. She is going to meet an old friend, who works at Budapest University.)

Show Sts that the first message has been numbered for them and ask them to continue putting them in order.

Get Sts to compare with a partner, and then check answers.

> 2 Lily! Great to hear from you...
> 3 It's from 3rd to 7th May...
> 4 It depends on the day...
> 5 Great. I'm going to book...
> 6 OK. Why don't you...
> 7 Fantastic...

c Get Sts to read the messages again in the right order and to answer the two questions.

Get Sts to compare with a partner, and then check answers.

> She wants to see him when she is in Budapest.
> They are planning to meet for dinner in a restaurant that Ben knows.

Extra idea

- Put Sts in pairs, **A** and **B**. Assign them a role each, **A** is Lily and **B** is Ben. They should read the messages out loud in the correct order. Then they answer the questions.

Extra support

- To check comprehension, ask some more questions on the messages, e.g. *Does Ben like Budapest?* (Yes, he says it is a wonderful city.) *How long is Lily's conference?* (Five days.) *How long is Ben going to stay in Vienna?* (One day.), etc.

d Focus on the task and get Sts to match the highlighted words and phrases in the messages to meanings 1–6.

Check answers.

1 for ages	3 I'm still	5 both
2 arrangements	4 perhaps	6 fix a day

Deal with any other new vocabulary.

e **1 62** Ask Sts *What does Lily say in her last message to Ben on Facebook?* (She is going to book her tickets and then let Ben know the flight times). Now focus on the instructions and make sure Sts understand the expression *leave a message*.

Play the audio for Sts to listen and complete the flight details. Play again if necessary.

Get them to compare with a partner, and then check answers.

Going out:
Date: (Sunday) **2nd May**
Arrive Budapest at **14.40**
Going back:
Date: (Saturday) **8th May**
Depart: Budapest at **16.35**
Hotel reservations: Six nights at Hotel **Gellert**

1 62
(script in Student's Book on *p.119*)
Ben Hi. This is Ben West. Sorry I can't take your call. Please leave a message.
Lily Hi, Ben. It's me, Lily. Hope you're OK. I've booked my flight and hotel. I'm coming on Sunday the 2nd of May – I couldn't get a flight on the first. I'm flying from Gatwick with easyJet and I'm arriving at Budapest Airport at 14.40. I'm going back on Saturday the 8th leaving at 16.35. I'm staying at a lovely old hotel, quite a famous one I think. It's called the Hotel Gellert or Jellert – I'm not sure how you pronounce it, but it's G-E-double L-E-R-T. I'm sure you know it. I'll call you on Sunday night when I get there. See you soon – I'm really looking forward to seeing you again.

Extra support

- If there's time, you could get Sts to listen again with the script on *p.119*, so they can see exactly what they understood / didn't understand. Translate / explain any new words or phrases.

2 GRAMMAR present continuous (future arrangements)

a Tell Sts to look back at the Facebook messages in **1** and, in pairs, to underline five present continuous verbs. Then they should answer the two questions.

Check answers.

1 Are you still working at Budapest University?
2 I'm going to Vienna.
3 I'm coming back the same day.
4 What are you doing that week?
5 ...it's going very well...

'Are you still working...?' and '...it's going very well...' are about now.
The other three refer to the future.

Explain briefly that the present continuous has two main uses:

1 To talk about temporary actions happening now and around now (e.g. *It's raining*). Sts revised this use in **1C**.

2 To talk about future actions (*I'm leaving tomorrow*).

b **1 63** Now Sts focus on three sentences from the message Lily left Ben and complete the three gaps.

Get Sts to compare with a partner, and then play the audio for them to check their answers.

1 flying 2 arriving 3 staying

1 63
1 I'm flying from Gatwick with easyJet.
2 I'm arriving at Budapest Airport at 14.40.
3 I'm staying at a lovely old hotel.

c **1 64** Tell Sts to go to **Grammar Bank 3B** on *p.130*. Focus on the example sentences and play the audio for Sts to listen and repeat. Encourage them to copy the rhythm. Then go through the rules with the class.

Additional grammar notes

- Sts already know how to use the present continuous to talk about things happening now, but may find this future use (*What are you doing this evening?*) quite strange. They may find it more natural to use the present simple tense for this. Typical mistake: *What do you do this evening? I go to the cinema.*
- The difference between using *be going to* and the present continuous is quite subtle, so it is probably worth stressing that they can often be used as alternative forms when we talk about plans and arrangements, e.g. *What are you going to do tonight? / What are you doing tonight?*
- You may want to point out that whereas it is very common to use the present continuous with verbs such as *leave, arrive, go, come* because these often refer to previously made travel arrangements, *be going to* is more common with actions for which you don't often make special arrangements, e.g. *I'm going to wash my hair tonight* is more common than *I'm washing my hair tonight*.
- It is also important to highlight that the present continuous is not used for predictions, e.g. *I'm sure you're going to find a job.* NOT ~~I'm sure you're finding a job.~~

Focus on the exercises for **3B** on *p.131*. Sts do the exercises individually or in pairs.

Check answers, getting Sts to read the full sentences.

a 1 N
2 F
3 F
4 N
5 N
6 F
7 F
8 N

b 1 'm packing
2 'm flying
3 are you going
4 'm seeing
5 are you meeting
6 'm working

Tell Sts to go back to the main lesson **3B**.

Extra support

- If you think Sts need more practice, you may want to give them the Grammar photocopiable activity at this point.

d **1 65** Focus on the instructions. You could ask Sts *What day of the week is it when Lily phones?* (Sunday) *What's the date?* (2nd May).

Now play the audio for Sts to listen to Lily and Ben's conversation. They must answer the question *What day do they arrange to meet?*

Check the answer.

Thursday

1 65

B = Ben, L = Lily

B Hello.
L Hi, Ben, it's me.
B Lily! How are you? How was your flight?
L Oh, fine. No problems at all.
B Are you at the hotel?
L Yes, and it's wonderful. It's got these amazing baths.
B Yes, I know, I've been there.
L So when can we meet?
B Let's see – well, tonight's impossible, I'm seeing Paul, a Hungarian friend. He invited me to dinner ages ago.
L That's fine – I'm a bit tired anyway.
B How about tomorrow? I'm meeting students during the day, but I'm free in the evening.
L I've got a conference dinner tomorrow night. Are you doing anything on Tuesday night?
B Sorry, but I'm playing tennis with three of my friends. We always play on Tuesday nights, so I can't cancel it. And I'm going to Vienna on Wednesday, like I told you, and I don't get back till very late, so Wednesday's out. What about Thursday night?
L Thursday's fine. Are you going to take me to that restaurant you mentioned?
B Restaurant – yes, yes of course.
L And then perhaps you can show me round a bit on Friday? I'm free in the afternoon – the conference finishes at lunchtime.
B Sorry, Friday afternoon's no good. I'm going to the dentist at four.
L Oh, poor you!
B But maybe after dinner on Thursday we can go for a walk and you can see Budapest at night.
L Great!
B I can pick you up at the hotel at about 7.30. Is that OK?
L Perfect, see you there. Looking forward to it. It's ages since I last saw you. Bye.

e Focus on Ben's diary and elicit / teach *diary*. Highlight how Ben has made the first entry, i.e. that he has left out *I am* before *seeing*, and just written the *-ing* form of the verb. Then tell Sts they are going to listen to the telephone conversation again and they need to complete Ben's diary for the other days in the same way.

Play the audio once or twice if necessary.

Check answers and copy his diary onto the board.

Monday	meeting students (during the day)
Tuesday	playing tennis (with three friends)
Wednesday	going to Vienna
Thursday	meeting Lily
Friday	going to dentist (at 4 p.m.)

f Focus on the instructions and the example.

Then get Sts to cover the diary (and rub the answers off the board). In pairs, Sts test each other on what Ben is doing each day.

g **1 66** Focus on the task. You could ask Sts to predict if they think the meeting is going to be a success, what they think is going to happen, etc.

Play the audio once the whole way through.

Check answers.

Ben arrives to take Lily to the restaurant, and Lily is very pleased to see him. But Ben is not alone, he is with his girlfriend, Erika.

1 66

B Hi, Lily.
L Hi, Ben. How are you?
B I'm fine. And you? Not too tired from the conference?
L No, I'm fine. You look really well. Just the same as always.
B Thanks, you too.
L Right. Where are we going?
B A restaurant called Tigris . It's really good.
L Wonderful. Let's go then.
B My car's outside. That one there. The blue Fiat.
L Who's that?
B Er, that's er, Erika. She's my...
Erika Hello, Lily. So nice to meet you. Ben has told me a lot about you.
L Hi, Erika.
B Come on then girls, get in. Let's go!

3 PRONUNCIATION & SPEAKING

sounding friendly

a **1 67** Tell Sts that sounding friendly often depends on intonation (the tone and movement of our voice up and own) and not always the words used. Emphasize that even if you use the right words, you may sound unfriendly or bored if your voice is too flat or monotone.

Focus on the dialogue and play the audio once for Sts just to listen.

1 67

See dialogue in Student's Book on *p.23*

Now play the audio again, pausing after each sentence for Sts to listen and repeat. Encourage Sts to pay particular attention to copying the intonation and to try to use a wide voice range.

b In pairs, Sts practise the dialogue in **a**. Monitor and help with intonation.

c Focus on the instructions. Get Sts to complete three evenings in their diary with activities. Encourage them just to write the *-ing* form of the verb, as in Ben's diary.

Extra support

- Elicit a list of different activities they might be doing in the evening and write them on the board, e.g. going to the cinema, meeting friends, having dinner with…, going to a concert, studying for an exam, etc.

d Focus on the instructions and the example. Tell Sts they need to find another student who is free the same evening as them and do an activity together. When they agree, they both write it in their diaries. They then continue talking to other Sts to try to fill all their free evenings.

Demonstrate the activity by asking individual Sts *Are you free on Wednesday night?* Elicit either *Sorry, I'm…* or *Yes, I am.* If they are free, invite them to do something.

Tell Sts to stand up and talk to other Sts.

When they have finished, get some feedback from the class.

Extra support

- Write on the board ways of making suggestions / inviting to remind Sts, e.g. *Would you like to…?, Let's…, Why don't we…?*

4 VOCABULARY verbs + prepositions

a Focus on the three extracts from Lily and Ben's conversations and elicit that in each sentence there is a preposition missing. Highlight the fact that certain verbs are often followed by a particular preposition, e.g. *It depends **on** the weather.*

In pairs, get Sts to complete the sentences and then check answers.

1 on 2 in 3 to

b Tell Sts to go to **Vocabulary Bank *Prepositions*** on *p.153* and do part **2 Verbs + prepositions**.

Focus on **a** and get Sts to complete the **Prepositions** column, individually or in pairs.

1 68 Now do **b**. Play the audio for Sts to check answers.

1 68

Verbs + prepositions

1 I arrived **in** Paris on Friday night.
2 I was very tired when I arrived **at** the hotel.
3 I hate waiting **for** people who are late.
4 **A** What are you going to do **at** the weekend?
B I don't know. It depends **on** the weather.
5 I'm sorry, but I really don't agree **with** you.
6 I asked **for** a chicken sandwich, but this is tuna!
7 Let's invite Debbie and Tim **to** the party.
8 Who's going to pay **for** the meal?
9 I need to speak **to** Martin **about** the meeting.
10 I don't spend much money **on** food.
11 Are you going to write **to** him soon?
12 Don't worry **about** the exam. It isn't very hard.
13 She fell **in** love **with** a man she met on the internet.
14 You're not listening! What are you thinking **about**?
15 **A** What do you think **of** Shakira?
B I really like her. I think she's great.

Focus on **c** and get Sts to cover the **Prepositions** column and test themselves or each other.

Finally, go through the ***arrive in* or *arrive at*?** box with the class.

Tell Sts to go back to the main lesson **3B**.

Extra support

- If you think Sts need more practice, you may want to give them the Vocabulary photocopiable activity at this point.

c Get Sts to complete the questions with a preposition, and check answers.

1 for 2 for 3 to, about 4 on, on 5 in, with

Now put Sts in pairs and get them to ask and answer the questions.

Finally, get some feedback from the class.

5 WRITING an informal email

Tell Sts to go to **Writing *An informal email*** on *p.113*.

a Focus on the instructions. Get Sts to read the email and help them with any vocabulary, e.g. *your own room, to share a room, attaching*, etc.

Then focus on the expressions in the list and give Sts a few minutes in pairs to complete the gaps.

Check answers. Make sure Sts understand the meaning of the expressions.

1 Dear Goran
2 Looking forward to hearing from you
3 Best wishes
4 PS

b Now get Sts to read the email again and answer questions 1–7.

Get Sts to compare with a partner, and then check answers.

1 In the summer.
2 By plane.
3 The Barnes family.
4 No.
5 a
6 b
7 So he can recognize them at the airport.

c Now focus on the instructions and tell Sts they are going to write an email to Mrs Barnes. Go through the layout of the email with the class, pointing out the three different paragraphs.

Set the writing in class or for homework.

d Make sure Sts check their emails for mistakes before handing them in.

G defining relative clauses (*a person who…, a thing which…*)
V expressions for paraphrasing: *like, for example*, etc.
P pronunciation in a dictionary

3C What's the word?

Lesson plan

The topic of this lesson is words. First, Sts are introduced to simple, defining relative clauses through the context of a TV game show, where contestants have to define words to each other. This context shows Sts that relative clauses can help them with the essential language skill of paraphrasing. After practising the grammar, they go on to learn other useful phrases which will help them keep going in a conversation when they don't know the exact word for something. Sts then read an article about new words which come into the language each year, and finally, Sts see how a dictionary can help them pronounce new words correctly.

STUDY LINK

- **Workbook** 3C
- **iTutor**
- **iChecker**
- **www.oup.com/elt/englishfile**

Extra photocopiable activities

- **Grammar** Defining relative clauses *p.170*
- **Communicative** Can you explain the word? *p.217* (instructions on *p.200*)
- **www.oup.com/elt/teacher/englishfile**

Optional lead-in (books closed)

- Tell Sts you are going to play a word game.
- Play *Hangman* with the word DICTIONARY.

! If you don't know how to play *Hangman*, see Elementary Teacher's Book *p.23*.

- Tell Sts that the first part of the lesson is going to be about word games.

1 LISTENING

a Books open. Focus on the questions. Do the first one in pairs or as an open-class question.

Now give Sts, in pairs, three minutes to find as many words of four letters or more as possible.

Get some possible answers.

BRING, GREAT, DISH, CLEAN, SHINE, BLOND, etc.

Extra challenge

- You could play other words games with these letters, e.g. give Sts three minutes to try to make the longest word they can, and the highest scoring word they can (the numbers on each letter are the number of points the letters score, so e.g. BET scores 5).

b 2 2 Focus on the instructions and the question.

Play the audio for Sts to listen to the rules of the game.

Get Sts to compare with a partner and then play the audio again.

Elicit the rules of the game show by asking these questions:

1 *How many contestants are there?* (two – Lola and Martin)
2 *How many words can Martin see on the TV screen?* (six)
3 *Who is going to give definitions, the presenter or Martin?* (Martin)
4 *Who is going to guess the words?* (Lola / the contestant)
5 *Which words can't Martin use?* (the words on the TV screen)

To make the rules absolutely clear demonstrate the game to the class by drawing a card on the board and writing TAXI DRIVER on it. Explain that Martin can't use *taxi* or *driver* (or *drive*) in his definition. Elicit a possible definition, e.g. *A person who is in a car every day. He takes you to places and you pay him.*

Extra support

- Read through the scripts and decide if you need to pre-teach any new lexis before Sts listen.

2 2

(script in Student's Book on *p.119*)
P = presenter, L = Lola
P Good evening ladies and gentlemen, and welcome to *What's the word?* And our first contestants tonight are Martin and Lola. Hello to you both. Are you nervous?
L Just a bit.
P Well, just try and relax and play *What's the word?* with us. If you're watching the show for the first time, here's how we play the game. As you can see Martin has a TV screen in front of him and six words are going to appear on the screen. Martin has two minutes to describe the words to Lola so that she can guess what they are. But he can't use any part of the words on the screen. So, for example, if the word is *taxi driver*, he can't use the word *taxi* or *driver*, or *drive*.
Martin, Lola, are you ready?

c 2 3 Sts now listen to the rest of the show. Tell them that they have to listen to Martin's definitions. They will not hear Lola's answers, so they have to guess the six words on the TV screen.

Tell Sts you are going to play the audio twice. Explain that the first time you are going to play all the show and Sts should try to write down some of the words. Tell Sts not to call out the answers. Tell Sts that the second time you are going to pause the audio to give them time to write down each word.

Play the audio.

Get Sts to compare with a partner, but do <u>not</u> check answers yet.

> **2 3**
> (script in Student's Book on *p.119*)
> **P = presenter, L = Lola, M = Martin**
> **P** Martin, Lola, are you ready?
> **M and L** Yes.
> **P** OK, Martin, you have two minutes to describe your six words, starting now!
> **M** OK, word number one. It's a person. It's somebody who works in a hospital.
> **L** A doctor.
> **M** No, no, no, it's the person who helps the doctor and looks after the patients.
> **L** Oh, a (bleep).
> **M** That's right. Word number two. It's a place. It's somewhere where people go when they want to buy things.
> **L** A shop.
> **M** Not exactly. It's bigger and you can buy all kinds of different things there, especially food.
> **L** A (bleep)?
> **M** Yes, well done. OK, word number three. It's a thing... mmm. It's something which we use for everything nowadays. For the internet, for talking to people, for taking photos... It's a kind of gadget. Everyone has one.
> **L** A (bleep)?
> **M** That's it! Word number four. It's an adjective. It's the opposite of dark.
> **L** Light?
> **M** It's like light, but you only use it to describe hair.
> **L** (bleep)?
> **M** Yes! Word number five. It's an adjective again. Er... You use it to describe a person who's... er, who's quick at learning things.
> **L** Intelligent?
> **M** No, but it's similar to intelligent. It's the opposite of stupid.
> **L** (bleep)!
> **M** Yes, brilliant. And word number six, the last one. OK. It's a verb. For example, you do this to the TV.
> **L** Watch?
> **M** No... It's what you do when you finish watching TV at night.
> **L** Er...go to bed?
> **M** No! Come on! You do it <u>to</u> the TV <u>before</u> you go to bed.
> **L** Oh, (bleep)?
> **M** Yes!

d **2 4** Tell Sts that they are going to listen to Lola and Martin again, but this time they will hear Lola's answers. They must compare their answers to Lola's.

Play the audio the whole way through for Sts to compare their answers.

Check answers.

1 a nurse	3 a mobile	5 clever
2 a supermarket	4 blond(e)	6 turn off

> **P** Martin, Lola, are you ready?
> **M and L** Yes.
> **P** OK, Martin, you have two minutes to describe your six words, starting now!
> **M** OK, word number one. It's a person. It's somebody who works in a hospital.
> **L** A doctor.
> **M** No, no, no, it's the person who helps the doctor and looks after the patients.
> **L** Oh, a nurse.
> **M** That's right. Word number two. It's a place. It's somewhere where people go when they want to buy things.
> **L** A shop.
> **M** Not exactly. It's bigger and you can buy all kinds of different things there, especially food.
> **L** A supermarket?
> **M** Yes, well done. OK, word number three. It's a thing... mmm. It's something which we use for everything nowadays. For the internet, for talking to people, for taking photos... It's a kind of gadget. Everyone has one.
> **L** A mobile?
> **M** That's it! Word number four. It's an adjective. It's the opposite of dark.
> **L** Light?
> **M** It's like light, but you only use it to describe hair.
> **L** Blond?
> **M** Yes! Word number five. It's an adjective again. Er...You use it to describe a person who's... er, who's quick at learning things.
> **L** Intelligent?
> **M** No, but it's similar to intelligent. It's the opposite of stupid.
> **L** Clever!
> **M** Yes, brilliant. And word number six, the last one. OK. It's a verb. For example, you do this to the TV.
> **L** Watch?
> **M** No... It's what you do when you finish watching TV at night.
> **L** Er...go to bed?
> **M** No! Come on! You do it <u>to</u> the TV <u>before</u> you go to bed.
> **L** Oh, turn off?
> **M** Yes!

Extra support

- If there's time, you could get Sts to listen again to all three parts of the audio with the scripts on *p.119*, so they can see exactly what they understood / didn't understand. Translate / explain any new words or phrases.

2 GRAMMAR defining relative clauses

a Focus on the three sentences from the script of *What's the word?* and get Sts to complete the gaps.

Check answers and elicit what they refer to.

> 1 which 2 where 3 who
> 1 = a mobile, 2 = a supermarket, 3 = a nurse

b Get Sts to focus on the three sentences in **a** and to look at when the words *who*, *which*, and *where* are used.

Get feedback.

> We use *who* with people, *which* with things, and *where* with places.

c **2 5** Tell Sts to go to **Grammar Bank 3C** on *p.130*. Focus on the example sentences and play the audio for Sts to listen and repeat. Encourage them to copy the rhythm. Then go through the rules with the class.

Additional grammar notes

- You may want to point out that in conversation and informal writing native speakers often use *that* instead of *who* and *which*, e.g. *A waiter is somebody that works in a restaurant.*

! The relative pronoun can be omitted in sentences like *This is the book I told you about*, where the subject of the relative clause changes, but this is not focussed on at this level.

Focus on the exercises for **3C** on *p.131*. Sts do the exercises individually or in pairs.

Check answers, getting Sts to read the full sentences.

a	1 which	3 who	5 who	7 where
	2 which	4 where	6 which	

b
1 That's the dog which always barks at night.
2 That's the shop where I bought my wedding dress.
3 That's the actor who was in *Glee*.
4 They're the children who live next door to me.
5 This is the restaurant where they make great pizza.
6 That's the switch which controls the air conditioning.
7 He's the teacher who teaches my sister.
8 That's the room where we have our meetings.
9 This is the light which is broken.

Tell Sts to go back to the main lesson **3C**.

Extra support

- If you think Sts need more practice, you may want to give them the Grammar photocopiable activity at this point.

3 VOCABULARY paraphrasing

a Focus on the question and go through the possible answers a–c making sure Sts understand them.

Elicit answers and try to get a mini discussion going about the relative merits of each one.

You may want to point out to Sts that the word to describe option **c** is *paraphrasing* (the subheading of this section).

b 2 6)) Tell Sts that they are going to learn some useful expressions to help them explain words they don't know. In pairs, Sts complete the eight expressions using the words in the list.

Play the audio for Sts to listen and check.

2 6))

1 It's **somebody** who works in a hospital.
2 It's **something** which we use for everything nowadays.
3 It's **somewhere** where people go when they want to buy something.
4 It's a **kind** of gadget.
5 It's the **opposite** of dark.
6 It's **like** light, but you use it to describe hair.
7 It's **similar** to intelligent.
8 For **example**, you do this to the TV.

Extra idea

- Play the audio again, pausing after each sentence, and elicit the word being defined – they are all from **1 Listening**.

c Focus on the six words and make sure Sts know what they mean.

In pairs, Sts write definitions for the words.

Elicit some of their answers onto the board.

Possible answers
1 It's somebody who plays music on the radio or in a club.
2 It's somewhere where you see paintings.
3 It's something which you use to take photos.
4 It's a kind of machine which you use to go from one floor of a building to another.
5 For example, you do this when you are on the beach.
6 It's the opposite of *straight*.

4 SPEAKING

Put Sts in pairs, **A** and **B**, and get them to sit face-to-face. Tell them to go to **Communication *What's the word?***, **A** on *p.101*, **B** on *p.107*.

Go through the instructions with them carefully and make sure Sts are clear what they have to do.

! If Sts don't know what any of their words mean, they should put up their hand for you to go and help them.

A starts by defining his / her first word and **B** guesses and writes it down. When **A** has finished defining all six words, they swap roles.

When Sts have finished, they show each other their guesses to make sure they have the right answers.

Tell Sts to go back to the main lesson **3C**.

5 READING

a Focus on the article and the title. Ask Sts if they can think of a new word that has come into their language recently, and say what it means. Then ask them if they can think of an English word which has come into use in the last five years.

Now focus on the two questions. Tell Sts to read the article to find the answers.

Get Sts to compare with a partner, and then check answers.

The article mentions four ways of creating new words:
1 by combining two words
2 by changing nouns into verbs
3 by adopting foreign words
4 from the names of brands or companies.

b Now focus on the highlighted words. Tell Sts, in pairs, to look at them in context and try to guess what they mean, and then to match them to definitions 1–6.

Check answers.

1 toy boy	3 barista	5 latte
2 to text	4 road rage	6 gastropub

c Finally, focus on the words in the list. Model and drill the pronunciation. Tell Sts to be careful with *iPod* /ˈaɪpɒd/ and *Wi-fi* /ˈwaɪ faɪ/ as they may be pronounced with a different vowel sound in their language.

Put Sts in pairs and give them two minutes to think of good definitions.

Check answers and pronunciation of these words. Accept any suggestions that define the words well.

Possible answers

emoticon	– a symbol which expresses or shows a feeling, e.g. happy or sad
to tweet	– to write something on *Twitter*
iPod	– something people use to listen to music which they download from the internet
to google	– to look for information on the internet using Google
Wi-fi	– a way of getting the internet without cables
ringtone	– the sound a mobile makes when it rings
smartphone	– a mobile phone which also has internet

3C

6 PRONUNCIATION pronunciation in a dictionary

Pronunciation notes

- Although many Sts will still be using a bilingual dictionary, many also with audio on their phone, it is also useful for them to be able to recognize phonetic symbols so that they can work out the pronunciation of words in their dictionary.
- Encourage Sts to use their dictionaries to check pronunciation of new words.

a Focus on the two dictionary extracts and establish what abbreviations 1–4 mean. You might want to tell Sts that the first extract is from a monolingual dictionary and the second one is from a French–English dictionary.

1 verb 2 adjective 3 somebody 4 something

b Focus on the phonetic transcription of the two words in **a** (*search* and *busy*) and elicit the pronunciation. Ask *Why doesn't 'search' have a stress mark in it?* (because it only has one syllable). For *busy* show the correct stress by writing it on the board with the stressed syllable underlined (*busy*).

c 2 7))) Focus on the **Checking pronunciation in a dictionary** box and go through it with the class.

Then put Sts in pairs and give them a couple of minutes to decide how the six words are pronounced, using the **Sound Bank** on *pp.166–167* to help them with phonetic symbols.

Now play the audio for Sts to listen and check. Also check Sts know what the words mean.

Then play it again, pausing after each word for Sts to repeat.

See words in Student's Book on *p.27*

Vocabulary restaurants: *menu, bill*, etc.
Function ordering food and a drink; explaining when there is a problem
Language *I'm sorry, but...*, etc.

PRACTICAL ENGLISH

Episode 2 Restaurant problems

Lesson plan

In this lesson Sts practise ordering food and then explaining that there is a problem. The Rob and Jenny story develops. Jenny shows Rob around the New York office, and introduces him to Barbara, the boss. Jenny and Rob go out for lunch and Holly, Jenny's colleague, joins them and takes over the conversation!

STUDY LINK

- **Workbook** Restaurant problems
- **iTutor**
- **www.oup.com/elt/englishfile**

Test and Assessment CD-ROM

- **Quick Test 3**
- **File 3 Test**

www.oup.com/elt/teacher/englishfile

Optional lead-in (books closed)

- Before starting Episode 2 elicit what Sts can remember about Episode 1. Ask *Who's Rob?, Where does he work / live?, Who's Jenny?, Where is she from?*, etc.
- Alternatively, you could play the last scene of Episode 1.

1 IN THE NEW YORK OFFICE

a **2 8** Focus on the photo and ask Sts to guess where Rob is and who the people are.

Now focus on the instructions and on sentences 1–6. Go through them with Sts and make sure they understand them.

Now play the audio once the whole way through, and get Sts to mark the sentences T (true) or F (false). Make it clear that they don't need to correct the false sentences yet.

Get Sts to compare with a partner, and then check answers.

1 F	3 F	5 T
2 F	4 F	6 F

2 8
(script in Student's Book on *pp.119–120*)
J = **Jenny**, **R** = **Rob**, **B** = **Barbara**, **H** = **Holly**
J Well, I think that's everything. What do you think of the office?
R It's brilliant. And much bigger than our place in London.
J Oh, here's Barbara. Rob, this is Barbara, the editor of the magazine.
B It's good to finally meet you, Rob.
R It's great to be here.
B Is this your first time in New York?
R No, I came here when I was 18. But only for a few days.
B Well, I hope you get to know New York much better this time!
J Barbara, I'm going to take Rob out for lunch. Would you like to come with us?
B I'd love to, but unfortunately I have a meeting at one. So, I'll see you later. We're meeting at three, I think.
J That's right.
B Have a nice lunch.
***
H Hey, are you Rob Walker?
R Yes.
H Hi, I'm Holly. Holly Tyler.
R Hello, Holly.
H We're going to be working together.
J Really?
H Didn't Barbara tell you? I'm going to be Rob's photographer!
J Oh, well... We're just going for lunch.
H Cool! I can come with you. I mean, I had a sandwich earlier, so I don't need to eat, but Rob and I can talk. Is that OK?
J Sure.
H So, let's go.

b Play the audio again, so Sts can listen a second time and correct the false sentences.

Get Sts to compare with a partner, and then check answers.

1 The New York office is **much bigger**.
2 Barbara is the **editor** of the magazine.
3 Rob **has been** to New York before.
4 **Holly** is going to have lunch with Rob and Jenny.
6 Holly wants to go to the restaurant because she wants **to talk to Rob**.

Extra support

- If there's time, you could get Sts to listen again with the script on *pp.119–120*, so they can see exactly what they understood / didn't understand. Translate / explain any new words or phrases.

2 VOCABULARY restaurants

Put Sts in pairs and tell them to answer the questions in the restaurant quiz.

Check answers.

What do you call...?
1 the menu
2 courses
3 a waiter / waitress
4 the bill
5 the tip
What do you say...?
1 A table for four, please.
2 Can / Could I have the...? / I'll have the... / I'd like the...
3 Can / Could we have the bill, please?

Extra idea

- You could do the quiz as a competition. Set a time limit and the pair with the most correct answers are the winners.

3 AT THE RESTAURANT

a 2 9 Focus on the photo and ask Sts *Where are they?* (At the restaurant), *Who are the three people?* (Rob, the waitress, and Jenny).

Now either tell Sts to close their books and write the questions on the board, or get Sts to focus on the two questions.

Play the audio once the whole way through and then check answers. You might want to point out that the waitress has an Australian accent.

1 Jenny orders tuna and a green salad. Rob orders steak and fries. Holly doesn't order anything.
2 The waitress gives Jenny fries instead of a salad and Rob's steak is rare, not well done.

2 9 2 10

W = waitress, J = Jenny, R = Rob, H = Holly
W Are you ready to **order**?
J Yes, please. *(repeat)*
W Can I get you something to **start** with?
J No, thank you. *(repeat)* I'd like the tuna with a green salad. *(repeat)*
W And for you, sir?
R I'll have the steak, please. *(repeat)*
W Would you like that with fries or a baked **potato**?
R Fries, please. *(repeat)*
W How would you like your steak? Rare, **medium**, or well done?
R Well done. *(repeat)*
H Nothing for me. *(repeat)*
W OK. And to **drink**?
J Water, please. *(repeat)*
W **Still** or sparkling?
J Sparkling. *(repeat)*
***
W The tuna for you ma'am, and the steak for you, **sir**.
J I'm sorry, but I asked for a green salad, not fries. *(repeat)*
W No problem. I'll **change** it.
R Excuse me. *(repeat)*
W Yes, sir?
R Sorry, I asked for my steak well done and this is rare. *(repeat)*
W I'm really sorry. I'll **take** it back to the kitchen.

b Focus on the dialogue in the chart. Elicit who says the **You Hear** phrases (the waitress) and who says the **You Say** phrases (the customer or here Jenny, Rob, and Holly). These phrases will be useful for Sts if they need to order food / a drink and if they then have problems. Point out the **British and American English** box on the page. You might also want to point out the difference between 'madam' in British English, which Sts will have seen if they did Elementary, and 'ma'am' in American English.

Give Sts a minute to read through the dialogue and to think about what the missing words might be. Then play the audio again, and get Sts to complete the gaps. Play again if necessary.

Get Sts to compare with a partner, and then check answers.

See words in **bold** in script 2.9

Go through the dialogue line by line with Sts, helping them with any words or expressions they don't understand. Make sure Sts understand that *rare*, *medium*, and *well done* refer to the different ways a steak can be cooked. Also remind Sts of the two kinds of mineral water, *still* (= no gas) and *sparkling* (= with gas).

c 2 10 Now focus on the **You Say** phrases and tell Sts they're going to hear the dialogue again. They should repeat the **You Say** phrases when they hear the beep. Elicit / explain the two ways of ordering, e.g. *I'd like* (I would like) *the tuna with a green salad* or *I'll have the steak, please.* Elicit what Holly says (*Nothing for me.*) and ask Sts why she says that (She had a sandwich earlier).

Play the audio, pausing if necessary for Sts to repeat the phrases. Encourage them to copy the rhythm and intonation, but probably not to try to copy Jenny and Holly's American accents. When Jenny pronounces *water* as /ˈwɔːdər/ Sts should use the British English pronunciation of *water* /ˈwɔːtə/.

d Put Sts in pairs, **A** and **B**. **A** is Jenny, Rob, and Holly, and **B** is the waiter / waitress. Get Sts to read the dialogue aloud, and then swap roles.

e Focus on the instructions. **B** (book open) is the waiter / waitress. **A** (book closed) should decide what to eat and then respond when **B** starts with *Are you ready to order?*

Sts now roleplay the dialogue.

f When they have finished, they should swap roles.

You could get a few groups to perform in front of the class.

4 HOLLY AND ROB MAKE FRIENDS

a 2 11 Focus on the photo and the question.

Play the audio once the whole way through and then check answers.

Rob and Holly enjoy the lunch, but Jenny doesn't.

2 11

(script in Student's Book on *p.120*)
H = Holly, R = Rob, J = Jenny, W = waitress
H So tell me, Rob, what are you going to write about?
R Well, to start with, my first impressions of New York. You know, the nightlife, the music, things like that.
H Are you planning to do any interviews?
R I'd like to. Do you have any suggestions?
H Well, I know some great musicians.
R Musicians?
H You know, guys in bands. And I also have some contacts in the theatre and dance.
R That would be great.
H Maybe we could go to a show, and after you could talk to the actors.
R I really like that idea.
W Can I bring you anything else?
J Could we have the check, please?
W Yes, ma'am.
***
W Here's your check.
J Thanks.
***
J Excuse me. I think there's a mistake. We had two bottles of water, not three.
W You're right. I'm really sorry. It's not my day today! I'll get you a new check.
J Thank you.
H We're going to have a fun month, Rob.
R Yeah, I think it's going to be fantastic.
J OK, time to go. You have your meeting with Barbara at three.
R Oh yeah, right.

b Focus on questions 1–6 and give Sts time to read them.

Before playing the audio again, focus on the **British and American English** box and go through it with the class.

Now play the audio again, so Sts can listen a second time and answer the questions.

Get Sts to compare with a partner, and then check answers.

1 He's going to write about his first impressions of New York, the nightlife, and music.
2 Holly says she can introduce him to musicians, and she also knows people in the theatre and dance.
3 She says they could go to a show.
4 It says three bottles of water, but they only had two.
5 Because Rob has a meeting with Barbara (and maybe because she is getting tired of Holly).
6 No, she wanted to be alone with Rob.

Extra support

- If there's time, you could get Sts to listen again with the script on *p.120*, so they can see exactly what they understood / didn't understand. Translate / explain any new words or phrases.

c Focus on the **Social English phrases**. In pairs, get Sts to think about what the missing words could be.

Extra challenge

- In pairs, get Sts to complete the phrases before they listen.

d **2 12** Play the audio for Sts to listen and complete the phrases.

Check answers.

2 12

Holly	**So** tell me, Rob...
Rob	Well, to **start** with...
Rob	Do you have any **suggestions**?
Rob	That would **be** great.
Jenny	**Could** we have the check, please?
Jenny	Excuse me, I think there's a **mistake**.
Jenny	OK, **time** to go.

If you know your Sts' L1, you could get them to translate the phrases. If not, get Sts to have a look at the phrases again in context in the script on *p.120*.

e Now play the audio again, pausing after each phrase for Sts to listen and repeat.

Finally, focus on the **Can you...?** questions and ask Sts if they feel confident they can now do these things. If they feel that they need more practice, tell them to watch the episode again and practise the language on their *iTutor*.

G present perfect + *yet, just, already*
V housework, *make* or *do*?
P /j/ and /dʒ/

4A Parents and teenagers

Lesson plan

This lesson presents the present perfect to talk about the recent past, and Sts also learn to use it with *yet, just,* and *already*. Sts who completed *English File Elementary* will have already seen the present perfect (though not *yet, just,* and *already*), but for other Sts this will be completely new. The context is problems between teenagers and parents, from both points of view. Sts begin with an article to read, where they have to decide whether the problems referred to are teenagers talking about their parents, or vice versa. There is then a vocabulary focus on common verb phrases for housework, and collocations with *make* and *do*. The grammar is then presented through four short dialogues. This is followed by a pronunciation focus on two consonant sounds /j/ and /dʒ/, and the lesson ends with a listening about teenagers who look after their parents.

STUDY LINK
- Workbook 4A
- iTutor
- www.oup.com/elt/englishfile

Extra photocopiable activities
- **Grammar** Present perfect + *yet, just, already p.171*
- **Communicative** Find the response *p.218* (instructions *p.200*)
- **Vocabulary** Housework, *make* and *do p.253* (instructions *p.246*)
- **www.oup.com/elt/teacher/englishfile**

Optional lead-in (books closed)
- Write MY FAMILY'S ANNOYING HABITS on the board and establish the meaning of *annoying habits*. Give examples to help, e.g. *My sister spends hours in the bathroom in the morning. My father changes TV channels all the time.*
- Elicit some annoying habits that your Sts' families have and write them on the board.

1 READING

a Books open. Focus on the definition of *teenager*. Elicit its pronunciation, and then model and drill. Elicit a similar word in Sts' L1 if there is one. Find out how many teenagers there are in your class and if you have adults, how many of them have teenage children.

b Focus on the title of the article and, if you didn't do the **Optional lead-in**, elicit / explain the meaning of *annoying habits* (= things people do regularly that others don't like). Then focus on the task and make sure Sts are clear that they have to write P if they think the sentence is a parent complaining about a teenager, and T if it is a teenager complaining about his / her parents. Set a time limit for them to read the article and do the task.

c Get Sts to compare their guesses with a partner, and see if they agree with each other.

Check answers. Although this is who was speaking in the original article, Sts (especially teenagers) may argue that some of them could refer to either, e.g. 1 and 3.

1 T	3 T	5 P	7 T
2 P	4 P	6 T	8 P

d Now focus on the highlighted verbs and verb phrases and get Sts in pairs to try to guess their meaning from the context.

Check answers, either explaining in English, translating into Sts' L1, or getting Sts to check in their dictionaries.

Deal with any other new vocabulary.

e Do this as an open-class activity and elicit opinions and ideas about what annoys your Sts, and tell the class what you think.

2 VOCABULARY housework, *make* or *do*?

a Tell Sts to look back at the highlighted verb phrases in the article and to find three connected with housework.

Check answers.

1 to tidy 2 pick up dirty clothes 3 do the washing-up

b Tell Sts to go to **Vocabulary Bank *Housework, make or do?*** on *p.154*. Focus on **1 Housework** and get Sts to match the verb phrases and pictures in **a**.

2 13 Now do **b**. Play the audio for Sts to check answers. Play it again, pausing after each phrase for Sts to repeat. Give further practice of words and phrases your Sts find difficult to pronounce.

You may want to point out that *wash* and *wash up* are used as normal verbs, (e.g. *I'm going to wash my hair*, etc.), but that when we refer to the housework activity of washing clothes or washing up plates, etc. it is more common to use the phrases *do the washing* and *do the washing-up*.

2 13
Housework
7 clean the floor
6 do the ironing
3 do the shopping
2 do the washing
8 do the washing-up
1 lay the table
12 make lunch
4 make the beds
10 pick up dirty clothes
5 put away your clothes
11 take out the rubbish
9 tidy your room

Finally, do **c** and get Sts to cover the phrases and look at the pictures. They can test themselves or a partner.

Now focus on 2 ***Make* or *do?*** and get Sts to do **a**.

2 14 Now do **b**. Play the audio for Sts to check answers. Then play it again, pausing after each phrase for Sts to repeat. Give further practice of any words your Sts find difficult to pronounce.

2 14

Make* or *do?
1 **do** a course
2 **make** a mistake
3 **do** an exam / **do** an exercise / **do** homework
4 **make** a noise
5 **make** a phone call
6 **do** housework
7 **make** friends
8 **make** lunch / **make** dinner
9 **do** sport / **do** exercise
10 **make** plans

Suggest that when Sts aren't sure whether to use *make* or *do*, to bear in mind that *make* often has the meaning of 'creating' something which wasn't there before, e.g. *make dinner, make a noise, make a cake*, etc. whereas *do* has the meaning of fulfilling a task which already exists, e.g. *do an exercise, do housework, do a course*, etc. This rule of thumb is generally true, although there are a few exceptions, e.g. *make the bed*.

Finally, do **c** and get Sts to cover the phrases and look at the pictures. They can test themselves or a partner.

Focus on **d** and make sure Sts understand the questions. Then in pairs, get Sts to discuss them.

Get some feedback from the class.

Tell Sts to go back to the main lesson **4A**.

Extra support

- If you think Sts need more practice, you may want to give them the Vocabulary photocopiable activity at this point.

3 GRAMMAR present perfect + *yet, just, already*

a **2 15** Get Sts to cover the dialogues in **b** and focus on the pictures. Remind Sts of the meaning of *argue* and model and drill pronunciation. Ask them to discuss what they think the people are arguing about.

Elicit some ideas, but do not tell Sts if they are right.

Now play the audio once for Sts to check their guesses.

Check answers.

1 The daughter borrowed her mother's jumper.
2 The father thinks the son hasn't done his homework.
3 The father thinks his daughter is spending too long in the bathroom.
4 The boy is making a mess with his sandwich.

2 15

1 **A** Have you seen my yellow jumper? I can't find it.
B No, I haven't. Have you looked in your wardrobe?
A Of course, I have. What's that under your bed?
B Oh, yes. I remember now. I borrowed it.
2 **A** Why aren't you doing your homework?
B I've already done it.
A Really? When?
B I did it on the bus this evening.
3 **A** Have you finished yet?
B Nearly.
A I need the bathroom now.
B But I haven't dried my hair yet.
A Well, hurry up then.
4 **A** Can you get a plate for that sandwich? I've just cleaned the floor.
B OK. Oops – too late. Sorry!

b Focus on the dialogues and the list of verbs. Explain that these are past participles. Give Sts time to complete the four dialogues.

Then play the audio again for Sts to listen and check.

Check answers and elicit the infinitive of each verb.

1 looked (look) 2 done (do) 3 finished (finish), dried (dry) 4 cleaned (clean)

c Focus on the instructions. Give Sts time to look at the questions.

Check answers. Elicit / explain that the verbs are in the present perfect.

b

d Give Sts time to underline *just, yet*, and *already* in dialogues 2–4.

Check answers.

If you know your Sts' L1, you could elicit the translation of *just, yet*, and *already*.

just (in this context) = a very short time ago
yet = until now
already = earlier than expected

! *Just* has other meanings in other contexts, e.g. *only*.

e **2 16** **2 17** Tell Sts to go to **Grammar Bank 4A** on *p.132*. Focus on the example sentences and play the audio for Sts to listen and repeat. Encourage them to copy the rhythm. Then go through the rules with the class.

If your Sts are new to the present perfect, when you go to the **Irregular verbs** list on *p.164*, get them to underline or highlight the verbs where the past participle is different from the past simple, e.g. *be, become*, etc.

Additional grammar notes

- For some Sts the present perfect may be new. They may have something similar in their L1 or they may not, and the use is likely to be different. It takes time for Sts to learn and use the present perfect correctly, but this use (for things that have happened recently with no time mentioned) is probably the simplest to understand, and Sts will probably already be used to you asking them, e.g. *Have you finished?*, etc.
- *Yet / already* may not have an exact equivalent in Sts' L1, and the meaning is not that easy to explain, as they are words which simply add emphasis. There is not much difference between *I haven't finished* and *I haven't finished yet*, but adding *yet* implies that you are going to finish.

- *just* + present perfect: This use may be difficult for Sts to assimilate as it may be expressed in a completely different way in Sts' L1, i.e. with another verb followed by the infinitive. Sts may also have previously met *just* with a different meaning, e.g. *only*. Tell them that the meaning is usually clear from the context.
- Lesson **4B** focusses on the present perfect for past experience with *ever* / *never*, and contrasts it with the past simple. Later in the course (**9B**) Sts are introduced to the present perfect with *for* and *since* for unfinished actions, and this is again contrasted with the past simple in **9C**.

Focus on the exercises for **4A** on *p.133*. Sts do the exercises individually or in pairs.

Check answers, getting Sts to read the full sentences.

a
1 She's bought a new jacket.
2 He hasn't found a job yet.
3 Have you spoken to Mr Jackson?
4 We've found a fantastic hotel.
5 They haven't finished eating.
6 Have you seen Peter this morning?
7 Have you done your homework this week?
8 We haven't replied to Mr Jones's email yet.

b
1 I've just had breakfast.
2 Have you finished your homework yet?
3 The film has already started.
4 I haven't met his girlfriend yet.
5 They've just got married.
6 He's already gone home.
7 Have you spoken to him yet?
8 I haven't read his new book yet.

Tell Sts to go back to the main lesson **4A**.

Extra support

- If you think Sts need more practice, you may want to give them the Grammar photocopiable activity at this point.

f 2 18 Focus on the instructions and examples. Play the audio, pausing after each sentence for Sts to make the appropriate change.

Get Sts to repeat the 'new' sentence when they have heard it.

2 18
1 I've finished. (*pause*) I haven't finished.
2 It hasn't rained. (*pause*) It's rained.
3 You haven't changed. (*pause*) You've changed.
4 He's arrived. (*pause*) He hasn't arrived.
5 We haven't argued. (*pause*) We've argued.
6 It's started. (*pause*) It hasn't started.
7 They haven't landed. (*pause*) They've landed.
8 She hasn't passed. (*pause*) She's passed.
9 I haven't studied a lot. (*pause*). I've studied a lot.
10 It hasn't stopped raining. (*pause*) It's stopped raining.

Then repeat the activity eliciting responses from individual Sts.

4 PRONUNCIATION & SPEAKING /j/ and /dʒ/

Pronunciation notes

- Remind Sts that:
  - *y* at the beginning of a word is always pronounced /j/.
  - many words with *u* have a hidden /j/, e.g. *use, music, student*.
  - the letter *j* is always pronounced /dʒ/.
  - *g* before *i* or *e* is also often pronounced /dʒ/, e.g. *manager, general, giraffe, German*, etc.

a 2 19 Focus on the sound pictures and elicit the words and sounds: *yacht* /j/ and *jazz* /dʒ/.

Then play the audio once for Sts just to listen.

2 19
yacht /j/ jazz /dʒ/

Play the audio again, pausing after each word and sound for Sts to repeat.

b 2 20 Get Sts to look at the list of words and put them in the right column. Remind Sts that this kind of exercise is easier if they say the words aloud to themselves.

Get Sts to compare with a partner, and then play the audio to check answers.

2 20
yacht yet, yellow, new, uniform, year, student, beautiful, young, argue
jazz just, jumper, change, teenager, enjoy, jacket, bridge

Now play the audio again for Sts to listen and repeat the words.

c Read the two sentences out loud for Sts. Then read the first and get Sts to repeat it. Do the same with the second.

Get Sts to practise saying the sentences in pairs.

Get some feedback.

d Tell Sts to go to **Communication *Has he done it yet?*** on *p.101*. Give Sts one minute to look at and remember the picture.

Now tell Sts to go to *p.102*. Go through the instructions. They should write their nine sentences with either *yet* or *already*.

When Sts have written their sentences, put them into pairs. They read their sentences aloud to each other, to see if they have written the same. Monitor to check they are forming the present perfect correctly and are putting *yet* and *already* in the right place.

Finally, Sts check with the picture to see how many of their sentences were right.

Get feedback.

Things Max has already done
1 He has already made the bed.
2 He has already taken the dog for a walk.
3 He has already had a shower.
4 He has already had breakfast.

Things Max hasn't done yet
1 He hasn't washed up his coffee cups yet.
2 He hasn't tidied his desk yet.
3 He hasn't picked up his towel yet.
4 He hasn't turned off his computer yet.
5 He hasn't put his clothes in the cupboard yet.

Tell Sts to go back to the main lesson **4A**.

e 2 21 Tell Sts they are going to hear some sound effects of things that have just happened. Put Sts in pairs and tell them first to listen and make notes only. Play the audio once.

Then play the audio again, pausing after each sound effect for Sts to write a sentence with *just* and the present perfect.

Check answers. Accept all correct and possible sentences.

2 21
Sound effects to illustrate the following sentences:
1 She's just broken a glass.
2 They've just got married.
3 He's just taken a photo.
4 She's just seen a mouse.
5 The film has just finished.
6 A dog has just seen a cat.

5 LISTENING

a 2 22 Focus on the instructions and elicit / explain that *teenage carers* = teenagers who have to look after family members. Sts should listen and answer questions 1–3. Make sure they understand *reputation* (= what people think or say about sby or sth).

Play the introduction to the programme.

Get Sts to compare with a partner, and then check answers.

Play the audio again if necessary.

Extra support

- Read through the scripts and decide if you need to pre-teach any new lexis before Sts listen.

1 They have a bad reputation, e.g. for being lazy, untidy, etc.
2 They have to look after a member of their family.
3 Between 25 and 50.

2 22
(script in Student's Book on *p.120*)
P = **presenter**
P Teenagers today have a bad reputation. People say that they are lazy and untidy, and that they do very little to help their parents in the house. But there are some teenagers for whom this description is just not true at all. It is estimated that there are more than 200,000 teenagers in the UK who have to look after a member of their family, their mother or father or brother or sister. In many cases these young helpers, or 'carers' as they are called, have to do between 25 and 50 hours work helping in their house, as well as doing their school work.

b 2 23 Now tell Sts they are going to listen to the rest of the programme, which is an interview with two teenagers. The first time they listen, they should answer the two questions.

Play the audio once the whole way though.

Check answers.

They both take care of their mothers and do housework. They feel positive.

2 23
(script in Student's Book on *p.120*)
P = **presenter**, **A** = **Alice**, **D** = **Daniel**
P I'd like to welcome to the programme two of these teenagers, Alice and Daniel, who are 17 years old, and who both look after members of their family. Hello, Alice, hello, Daniel.
A and D Hi.
P Who do you look after?
A I look after my mum. She has ME – it's an illness which means that she feels tired all the time and she can't walk very well. And I also look after my younger brother and sister. He's six and she's four.
D I look after my mum too. She had a bad car accident seven years ago and she can't walk. I also look after my little sister.
P You both do a lot of housework. What exactly do you do?
A On a normal day I get up early and I clean the house and I do the ironing. After school, I sometimes take my mum to the shops in her wheelchair. In the evening, my dad makes the dinner – I'm not very good at cooking! But I make sure my brother and sister eat their dinner and then I put them to bed.
D My day's quite similar. I clean the house and iron, but I also do the cooking, and the shopping. My dad left home four years ago so we're on our own. I take my sister to school and make sure that my mum is OK. I need to give her massages every evening.
P How do you feel about the way you live?
A I don't really mind looking after my mum. She's ill and she needs my help. But sometimes I feel a bit sad when I can't go out because there are things to do in the house. And I sometimes get angry with my school friends. They don't really understand the problems I have at home. All they think about are clothes, boys, and going out.
D I enjoy what I do because I'm helping my mum and I'm helping my sister at the same time. Of course, it's true that I can't go out much, because I need to spend most of my time at home. I sometimes go out with my friends, but I don't like leaving my mum on her own. I always make sure that I have my mobile. If my mum needs anything, she calls me and I go back home. It's not a problem for me. It's just part of my life.
P You're both doing a great job, thanks very much for coming on the programme…

c Now tell Sts they are going to listen to the interview again and they need to decide who 1–8 refer to and write the appropriate initial next to each one. Give Sts a minute to read 1–8 and then play the audio.

Get Sts to compare with a partner and play the audio again if necessary.

Check answers.

1 B	3 B	5 D	7 A
2 A	4 A	6 D	8 D

Extra support

- If there's time, you could get Sts to listen again with the scripts on *p.120*, so they can see exactly what they understood / didn't understand. Translate / explain any new words or phrases.

d Do this as an open class and answer the questions yourself if you know any teenagers who are carers.

G present perfect or past simple? (1)
V shopping
P *c* and *ch*

4B Fashion and shopping

Lesson plan

In this lesson Sts look at the present perfect for past experience with *ever / never*, and contrast it with the past simple. Again, for Sts who completed *English File* Elementary this will be revision. The context of the lesson is fashion and shopping. Sts begin by reading an interview (especially given to *English File*) with a designer who designs clothes for celebrities, and through this the grammar is presented. Sts then listen to four different people answering the question *Have you ever bought something that you've never worn?* The vocabulary focus is on shopping, and the pronunciation on different ways of pronouncing the letters *c* and *ch*. Finally, Sts have a mingle activity where they ask other Sts some shopping-related *Have you ever...?* questions, which they then follow up with past simple questions.

STUDY LINK

- **Workbook** 4B
- **iTutor**
- **www.oup.com/elt/englishfile**

Extra photocopiable activities

- **Grammar** Present perfect or past simple? *p.172*
- **Communicative** Have you ever...? *p.219* (instructions *p.201*)
- **Vocabulary** Shopping *p.254* (instructions *p.246*)
- **www.oup.com/elt/teacher/englishfile**

Optional lead-in (books closed)

- Quickly revise vocabulary for clothes. Tell Sts to test each other using the **Vocabulary Bank** on *p.151*.

1 READING

a Books open. Focus on the questions and get Sts to answer them in pairs.

Get some feedback.

> **Some possible answers**
> Coco Chanel: French, designs for women; clothes, perfume, and bags, sunglasses, etc.
> Giorgio Armani: Italian designer of clothes for men and women. Also perfume, sunglasses, etc.
> Donna Karan: American, designs for women; clothes, and perfume

b Focus on the introduction and the photos. In pairs or as a class, Sts say whether they like the clothes in the photos. You could tell the class what you think too.

Extra idea

- If Sts know who Sarah Ferguson and Kate Middleton (now the Duchess of Cambridge) are, ask them if they like the way they dress.

c Focus on the instructions and the **Glossary**. Before Sts read the interview, you might also want to check they understand all the lexis in sentences A–F, e.g. *sewing* and *chic*. You might also want to model and drill their pronunciation, /ˈsəʊɪŋ/ and /ʃiːk/.

Then give Sts time to read the interview and complete gaps 1–6 with sentences A–F.

Get Sts to compare with a partner, and then check answers.

> 1 E 2 B 3 F 4 A 5 D 6 C

d Tell Sts to read the interview again and look at the highlighted words and phrases. They should try to guess their meaning from context. Remind them that all the words and phrases are related to fashion and shopping.

In pairs, Sts should compare their guesses.

Check answers, either explaining in English, translating into Sts' L1, or getting Sts to check in their dictionaries.

Deal with any other new vocabulary.

2 GRAMMAR present perfect or past simple? (1)

a Tell Sts to look back at the last four questions in the interview, and, in pairs, to answer questions 1–3.

Check answers.

> 1 Have you ever fallen over because you were wearing very high heels? Have you ever designed clothes for a man?
> 2 What did you do? When was it?
> 3 at any time

b 2 24)) 2 25)) Tell Sts to go to **Grammar Bank 4B** on *p.132*. Focus on the example sentences and play the audio for Sts to listen and repeat. Encourage them to copy the rhythm. Then go through the rules with the class.

Additional grammar notes

- This use of the present perfect, to talk about past experiences when we don't mention a time, is usually quite easy for Sts to understand. However, they may have problems with the switch to the past simple to talk about the specific experience / time, as in some Sts' L1 they may be able to continue with the present perfect.
- If this is your Sts' first exposure to the contrast, don't expect too much oral accuracy yet. The contrast between present perfect and past simple for unfinished and finished actions is also studied in **9C**.

Focus on the exercises for **4B** on *p.133*. Sts do the exercises individually or in pairs.

Check answers, getting Sts to read the full sentences.

a	1	Have ... bought	6	've gone
	2	've ... wanted	7	hasn't flown
	3	haven't read	8	hasn't met
	4	haven't been	9	Have ... eaten
	5	Has ... lived	10	has gone
b	1	did you see	4	saw
	2	went	5	Did you enjoy
	3	haven't been	6	loved

c 1 gone 3 been 5 been
2 been 4 gone

Tell Sts to go back to the main lesson **4B**.

Extra support

- If you think Sts need more practice, you may want to give them the Grammar photocopiable activity at this point.

3 LISTENING

a **2 26** Tell Sts that they're going to hear four people being asked the same question, *Have you ever bought something that you've never worn?* Tell them just to listen for the items of clothing and to number them in the list.

Play the audio once the whole way through.

Check answers.

Extra support

- Read through the script and decide if you need to pre-teach any new lexis before Sts listen.

1 some trousers	3 a shirt
2 some sports clothes	4 a coat

2 26
(script in Student's Book on *p.120*)
I = **interviewer**, **M** = **man**, **W** = **woman**

1 **I** Have you ever bought something that you've never worn?
M1 Yes – hasn't everyone? I remember some trousers I bought that I never wore.
I What was the problem with them?
M1 They were very tight, black leather trousers that I bought from a second-hand shop near Portobello Road, when I was about 20 years old. I remember when I was in the changing room I thought they looked fantastic. I thought I looked like Jim Morrison from The Doors. But when I got home, in the cold light of day, I realized that I looked more like one of the women from Abba! That's why I never wore them.

2 **I** Have you ever bought something that you've never worn?
W1 Yes, a karate suit. I decided that I wanted to do karate, and I signed up for a course and bought the suit and the orange belt, but then I changed my mind and decided not to do the course.
I Why not?
W1 I was worried that someone would knock my teeth out.
I Do you still have the suit?
W1 No, I sold it on eBay.

3 **I** Have you ever bought something that you've never worn?
M2 Sadly it happens to me quite often, because I hate clothes shopping, and I never try things on. For example, I have a shirt in my wardrobe now that I've never worn.
I Why not?
M2 Well, I bought it in a hurry a few months ago and then I put it away in my wardrobe. A few weeks later I took it out and looked at it and I thought 'Why did I buy this?' It's horrible – pink and purple stripes. And of course I didn't have the receipt, so I couldn't take it back.

4 **I** Have you ever bought something that you've never worn?
W2 Lots of things, I'm afraid. The last one was a brown leather coat.
I What was wrong with it?
W2 Well, I bought it online from a website that has cheap offers, but when it arrived it looked completely different from what it looked like on screen and I decided I didn't like it. So it's in my wardrobe. I'm sure I'm never going to wear it, but perhaps I'll give it to someone as a present.

b Before playing the audio again, get Sts, in pairs, to talk about what they understood from the first listening, and to see if they already know what the problem was with each item.

Play the audio again. Stop after each speaker to give Sts time to number the right answer. Play again if necessary.

Get Sts to compare with a partner, and then check answers.

1 wanted to look like a famous singer...
2 suddenly didn't need the new clothes any more.
3 bought the clothes too quickly...
4 bought something online...

Extra support

- If there's time, you could get Sts to listen again with the script on *p.120*, so they can see exactly what they understood / didn't understand. Translate / explain any new words or phrases.

c You could answer the questions yourself first and then put Sts in pairs or small groups.

Get some feedback from the class.

4 VOCABULARY shopping

a **2 27** Tell Sts they are going to hear five sentences from the listening and that they need to complete the gaps.

Play the audio, pausing after each sentence to give Sts time to write.

Check answers.

1 changing	3 try	5 online
2 sold	4 take	

2 27
1 I remember when I was in the changing room I thought they looked fantastic.
2 I sold it on eBay.
3 I hate clothes shopping and I never try things on.
4 I didn't have the receipt, so I couldn't take it back.
5 Well, I bought it online from a website that has cheap offers.

Extra challenge

- Get Sts to complete the gaps first and then play the audio for them to listen and check their answers.

In pairs, Sts try to guess the meaning of the highlighted phrases.

Check answers, either explaining in English, translating into Sts' L1, or getting Sts to check in their dictionaries.

b Tell Sts to go to **Vocabulary Bank *Shopping*** on *p.155* and do **1 In a shop or store**. Elicit / explain that *store* is American English for *shop*, but now in the UK people use both *shop* and *store*.

Focus on **a** and get Sts to match the words and pictures.

2 28 Now do **b**. Play the audio for Sts to check answers. Play it again, pausing after each phrase for Sts to repeat. Point out to Sts that the *p* in *receipt* is silent. Give further practice of words and phrases your Sts find difficult to pronounce.

2 28

In a shop or store
5 changing rooms
3 checkout
4 customer
2 receipt
8 shop assistant
1 take something back
7 trolley / basket
6 try something on

Focus on **c** and get Sts to cover the words and look at the pictures. They can test themselves or each other.

Finally, go through the ***fit* or *suit*?** box with the class. Model and drill the pronunciation of *suit* /suːt/.

Now do **2 Online**, focus on **a** and get Sts to complete the gaps.

2 29 Now do **b**. Play the audio for Sts to check their answers. Give further practice of any words your Sts find difficult to pronounce.

2 account	5 basket	8 payment
3 item	6 checkout	9 auction
4 size	7 delivery	

2 29

Shopping online
When you are shopping online, first you go to the website. The first time you use a site you usually have to create an account, where you give your personal details. You then choose what you want to buy, and click on each item. If you are buying clothes, make sure you get the right size! Everything you buy goes into your shopping bag or basket, usually at the top right of the page. When you are ready to pay you click on 'proceed to checkout'. You then have to give your delivery address where you want them to send your things, and give your payment details, for example your your credit card number and expiry date. Many people today also buy and sell things online at auction sites like *eBay*.

Tell Sts to go back to the main lesson **4B**.

Extra support

- If you think Sts need more practice, you may want to give them the Vocabulary photocopiable activity at this point.

5 PRONUNCIATION *c and ch*

a Write on the board CUT and CENT and elicit their pronunciations. Highlight that *c* can be pronounced /k/ or /s/.

Focus on the two sound pictures and elicit the words and sounds: *key* /k/ and *snake* /s/. Give Sts a few minutes to put the words in the right rows. Encourage them to say the words aloud as they do this.

b **2 30** Get Sts to compare with a partner.

Now play the audio for them to listen and check.

2 30

key /k/	account, auction, click, clothes, credit card, customer
snake /s/	cinema, city, proceed, receipt, shopping centre

Play the audio again, pausing after each word for Sts to repeat.

Then focus on the question and check the answer.

c is usually /s/ before *e* and *i*, e.g. *city*, *centre*, etc.

c **2 31** Focus on the first question and elicit the answer.

The letters *ch* are usually pronounced /tʃ/.

Now play the audio for Sts to listen to the words and circle the two that are pronounced differently.

Check answers.

chemist's and *chic* are pronounced differently.
In *chemist's* the letters *ch* are pronounced /k/ and in *chic* they are pronounced /ʃ/.

2 31
changing rooms, cheap, checkout, chemist's, chic, choose

Extra challenge

- Elicit some more words where *ch* is pronounced /k/ or /ʃ/. They should know, e.g. *architect*, *mechanic*, *Christmas* (*ch* = /k/), and *machine*, *chef* (*ch* = /ʃ/).

d Get Sts to practise saying all the words in **a** and **c**.

Get some feedback.

6 SPEAKING

a Focus on the instructions. Do question 1 with the whole class and elicit the missing past participles (*bought* and *sold*). Sts should complete questions 2–8 with the missing participles.

Check answers.

2 bought	4 tried	6 bought	8 lost
3 had	5 taken	7 got	

b Focus on the follow-up question(s) after each present perfect question in **a** and point out that they are in the past simple.

Get Sts to interview you with the first three or four questions.

Finally, get Sts to stand up and move round the class. When somebody answers *Yes, I have* to the present perfect question, Sts should ask the follow-up questions.

Get some feedback from the class.

4C Lost weekend

Lesson plan

In this lesson Sts learn how to use *something, anything, nothing*, etc. These words will be familiar to Sts by this stage, but here they are focussed on in detail. The context is a (true) story about a man who spent the weekend trapped in a lift, and an article about the fact that many people today invent what they did at the weekend in order to make it sound more exciting.

After listening to the story and focussing on the grammar, Sts focus on some vowel sounds in order to be able to pronounce the key grammar expressions correctly. They read the article, and then talk about their own weekends. Finally, in Vocabulary Sts focus on the contrast between *-ed* and *-ing* adjectives.

STUDY LINK

- **Workbook** *pp.28–29*
- **iTutor**
- **iChecker**
- **www.oup.com/elt/englishfile**

Extra photocopiable activities

- **Grammar** *something, anything, nothing, etc. p.173*
- **Communicative** The same or different? *p.220* (instructions *p.201*)
- **Song** *If You Love Somebody, Set Them Free p.271* (instructions *p.264*)
- **www.oup.com/elt/teacher/englishfile**

Optional lead-in (books closed)

- Write the following sentence on the board, completing the start and finish times for you.
  MY ______ STARTS ON FRIDAY AT (time) AND FINISHES ON SUNDAY AT (time).
- Elicit the missing word (*weekend*) and explain why it starts and finishes at these times for you, e.g. because you finish work on Friday evening and start again on Monday morning.
- Then put Sts in pairs to tell each other when their weekends start and finish, and why. Get feedback to see who has the longest / shortest weekend.

1 LISTENING

a 2 32 Books open. Here Sts listen to a true story about a man who was stuck in a lift for a whole weekend. The story introduces some of the words from the new grammar.

Focus on the photo and ask Sts *What do you think the story is about?*

Now play the audio once the whole way through.

Get Sts to compare with a partner, and then check the answer.

Extra support

- Read through the script and decide if you need to pre-teach any new lexis before Sts listen, e.g. *lift, press the button, alarm*, etc.

He spent the weekend in a lift at his office. He was there from Friday evening to Monday morning.

2 32
(script in Student's Book on *p.120*)
N = newsreader, S = Sven, Si = Silvia

N Last Friday Sven, a lawyer from Stockholm, was looking forward to a relaxing two days in the mountains. He and his wife had a reservation in a luxury hotel at a skiing resort, so they could spend the weekend skiing. But the weekend didn't work out exactly as they were expecting. Sven worked until late on Friday evening. His office was on the 12th floor. When he finished, at 8 o'clock, he locked his office and got into the lift... and he didn't get out again until Monday morning!

S I pressed the button for the ground floor and the lift started going down, but then it stopped. I pressed the button again, but nothing happened. I pressed the alarm and shouted, but nobody heard me. Most people had already gone home. I tried to phone my wife, but my mobile didn't work in the lift... I couldn't do anything. I just sat on the floor and hoped maybe somebody would realize what had happened. But on Saturday and Sunday I knew nobody would be there. I slept most of the time to forget how hungry I was.

N Meanwhile Sven's wife, Silvia, was waiting for her husband to come home.

Si I was very worried when he didn't come home on Friday evening and I couldn't understand why his mobile wasn't working. I phoned the police and they looked for him but they couldn't find him anywhere. I thought maybe he was with another woman.

N So Sven was in the lift the whole weekend from Friday evening until Monday morning. At eight o'clock, when the office workers arrived, they phoned the emergency number and somebody came and repaired the lift.

S I was very happy to get out. I hadn't eaten since Friday afternoon and I was very hungry. It's lucky that I am not claustrophobic because the lift was very small. The first thing I did was to phone my wife to say that I was OK.

N Sven will soon be the fittest man in his office – from now on he's going to take the stairs every day – even though it's 12 floors.

b Give Sts time to read questions 1–7.

Now play the audio again. Then get Sts to compare with a partner, and check answers.

1 Sven is a lawyer.
2 His office was on 12th floor.
3 The lift started going down, and then stopped.
4 He pressed the alarm. He shouted. He tried to call his wife.
5 She thought perhaps he was with another woman.
6 Office workers phoned the emergency number, so somebody came and repaired the lift. He was very happy and hungry.
7 He is going to walk up the stairs.

Extra support

- If there's time, you could get Sts to listen again with the script on *p.120*, so they can see exactly what they understood / didn't understand. Translate / explain any new words or phrases.

c Do this as an open-class activity and elicit any stories.

2 GRAMMAR *something, anything, nothing, etc.*

a  Focus on the instructions and give Sts time to try to complete the sentences.

Then play the audio for Sts to listen and check. Tell Sts that for number 3 both *somebody* and *someone* are possible.

> **2 33**
> 1 I pressed the button again, but **nothing** happened.
> 2 The police couldn't find him **anywhere**.
> 3 They phoned the emergency number and **somebody** came and repaired the lift.

b Focus on the instructions and give Sts a few moments to complete the rules in pairs.

Check answers.

1 things 2 people 3 places

c **2 34** Tell Sts to go to **Grammar Bank 4C** on *p.132*. Focus on the example sentences and play the audio for Sts to listen and repeat. Encourage them to copy the rhythm. Then go through the rules with the class.

Additional grammar notes

- Sts may have problems with the negative form. The typical mistakes are:

  1 using *nobody* / *nothing* / *nowhere* with a negative verb, e.g. *I didn't see nobody*. Highlight that you cannot use a 'double negative' in English.

  2 using *anybody* / *anything* / *anywhere* in one word answers to convey a negative meaning, e.g. *Who did you see? Anybody*.

- To talk about people there are two alternative forms: *-body* and *-one*, e.g. *somebody* / *someone*. They are identical in meaning.

! *something* (like *some*) is also used in questions to make an offer or request, e.g. *Would you like something to drink? Could you go somewhere for me this afternoon?* To avoid overloading Sts it may be best to focus on this rule only if Sts bring it up.

Focus on the exercises for **4C** on *p.133*. Sts do them individually or in pairs.

Check answers, getting Sts to read the full sentences.

a 1 anybody 6 somewhere
2 Somebody 7 something
3 somewhere 8 nobody
4 nothing 9 anything
5 anybody 10 nowhere
b 1 Nothing. 2 Nowhere. 3 Nobody.
c 1 I didn't do anything.
2 I didn't go anywhere.
3 I didn't see anybody.

Tell Sts to go back to the main lesson **4C**.

Extra support

- If you think Sts need more practice, you may want to give them the Grammar photocopiable activity at this point.

3 PRONUNCIATION /e/, /əʊ/, and /ʌ/

a Focus on the three sound pictures and elicit the words and sounds: *egg* /e/, *phone* /əʊ/, and *up* /ʌ/.

Focus on sentences 1–6 and the pink letters. Give Sts, in pairs, a few minutes to say them out loud to each other and decide which sound they are (a, b, or c).

b **2 35** Play the audio for Sts to listen and check.

Check answers.

1 b 2 c 3 a 4 c 5 a 6 b

> **2 35**
> 1b Nobody knows where he goes.
> 2c Somebody's coming to lunch.
> 3a I never said anything.
> 4c I've done nothing since Sunday.
> 5a Don't tell anybody about the message.
> 6b There's nowhere to go except home.

Play the audio again, pausing after each sentence for Sts to listen and repeat.

Give Sts time to practise saying the sentences.

Finally, get individual Sts to say them out loud.

c **2 36** Focus on the example and tell Sts they are going to hear a question and they must answer it first with a one word negative answer, and then with a full sentence using a negative verb. You might want to stress that this is a drill, so Sts must always answer in the negative and not think about themselves.

Play the audio, pausing after each question to give Sts time to respond.

> **2 36**
> 1 What did you buy? (*pause*) Nothing. I didn't buy anything.
> 2 Where did you go? (*pause*) Nowhere. I didn't go anywhere.
> 3 Who did you see? (*pause*) Nobody. I didn't see anybody.
> 4 What did you eat? (*pause*) Nothing. I didn't eat anything.
> 5 Who did you speak to? (*pause*) Nobody. I didn't speak to anybody.
> 6 Where did you walk? (*pause*) Nowhere. I didn't walk anywhere.
> 7 Who did you meet? (*pause*) Nobody. I didn't meet anybody.
> 8 What did you say? (*pause*) Nothing. I didn't say anything.

Then repeat the activity eliciting responses from individual Sts.

Extra support

- Write *Nothing, Nobody, Nowhere*, and *I didn't…any-* on the board to give Sts something to focus on and to help elicit the response.

4 READING

a Focus on the instructions and make sure Sts understand the word *summary* as well as the three options.

Tell Sts to read the article quickly and say what the best summary is.

Check answers.

The best summary is c.

b Focus on the article and tell Sts to read it again and answer the multiple choice questions.

Get Sts to compare with a partner, and then check answers.

1 b 2 a 3 a 4 b

Extra support

- Before Sts read the article a second time, you could pre-teach some vocabulary, e.g. *a colleague*, *jealous*, *invent something*, *a survey*, *lie* (here not tell the truth), etc.

c Do this as an open-class question and elicit opinions.

5 SPEAKING

a Tell Sts to look at all the questions in **b** about last weekend. Sts must think about their answers; they must tell the truth when answering all the questions except for one. This 'lie' must make their day sound very exciting.

b Now put Sts in pairs and get them to interview each other. Monitor and help, when necessary. Before Sts swap roles, the student asking the questions should try to guess the lie.

Get feedback from the class.

6 VOCABULARY adjectives ending *-ed* and *-ing*

a Several common adjectives in English have two forms which have different meanings, e.g. *tired* and *tiring*. The *-ed* form has a passive meaning, that is it describes a person who feels this way. The *-ing* form has an active meaning, and describes the person or thing that produces the feeling.

Focus on the two sentences in the text and elicit the answers to the questions.

tired = describes how you feel
tiring = describes people, things, and situations

Highlight that we use the *-ed* adjectives mainly for people, because they refer to feelings, e.g. *I'm bored*. We use the *-ing* adjectives for things (and sometimes people), which produce the feeling, e.g. *This book is boring*.

! Not all adjectives that end in *-ed* also exist ending in *-ing*, e.g. *I'm feeling stressed. My job is very stressful.* NOT ~~*My job is very stressing.*~~

b 2 37 Get Sts to read questions 1–10 and circle the right adjective.

Play the audio for Sts to listen and check their answers, making sure that Sts understand the meaning of all the adjectives.

! Be careful with *excited* / *exciting*. It is a false friend in some languages.

1 boring	6 relaxed
2 bored	7 interesting
3 depressed	8 interested
4 depressing	9 excited
5 relaxing	10 exciting

2 37

1 Do you think Sundays are usually boring?
2 Are you bored with your job or studies?
3 What kind of weather makes you feel depressed?
4 Why do you think the news is often depressing?
5 What activity do you find most relaxing?
6 Do you usually feel relaxed at the end of the weekend? Why (not)?
7 What is the most interesting book you've read recently?
8 What sports are you interested in?
9 Are you excited about your next holiday?
10 What's the most exciting sports match you've ever watched?

Drill the pronunciation of the adjectives. Remind Sts that the *-ed* is pronounced in the same way as regular past verbs, i.e. /t/, /d/, or /ɪd/.

Extra challenge

- You could elicit / teach some more *-ed* / *-ing* adjectives, e.g. *surprised* / *surprising*, *frightened* / *frightening*, etc.

c Now put Sts in pairs and get them to ask and answer the ten questions. They should give extra information when possible.

Get some feedback from the class.

7 2 38 SONG *If You Love Somebody, Set Them Free* ♫

This song was originally made famous by the English singer Sting in 1985. For copyright reasons this is a cover version. If you want to do this song in class, use the photocopiable activity on *p.271*.

2 38

If You Love Somebody, Set Them Free

If you need somebody, call my name
If you want someone, you can do the same
If you want to keep something precious
You got to lock it up and throw away the key
If you want to hold onto your possessions,
Don't even think about me

Chorus
If you love somebody
If you love someone
If you love somebody
If you love someone
Set them free

If it's a mirror you want, just look into my eyes
Or a whipping boy, someone to despise
Or a prisoner in the dark
Tied up in chains you just can't see
Or a beast in a gilded cage
That's all some people ever want to be

Chorus

You can't control an independent heart
Can't tear the one you love apart
Forever conditioned to believe that we can't live
We can't live here and be happy with less
So many riches, so many souls
Everything we see that we want to possess

If you need somebody, call my name
If you want someone, you can do the same
If you want to keep something precious
You got to lock it up and throw away the key
If you want to hold onto your possession,
Don't even think about me

If you love somebody, set them free

3 & 4 Revise and Check

For instructions on how to use these pages see *p.38*.

STUDY LINK
- **iTutor**

Test and Assessment CD-ROM
- **Quick Test 4**
- **File 4 Test**

GRAMMAR

1 b	6 a	11 a
2 c	7 b	12 c
3 a	8 a	13 b
4 b	9 a	14 b
5 c	10 c	15 b

VOCABULARY

a 1 in 2 for 3 for 4 on 5 for

b 1 do 2 make 3 do 4 do 5 make

c 1 lay 2 washing 3 try on 4 receipt 5 fit 6 Gate 7 trolley 8 check-in 9 Terminal 10 lifts

d 1 boring 2 relaxed 3 exciting 4 depressed 5 interested

PRONUNCIATION

a 1 trolley 2 worry 3 chemist's 4 customer 5 yet

b 1 Arrivals 2 opposite 3 teenager 4 delivery 5 arrangement

CAN YOU UNDERSTAND THIS TEXT?

a a) expensive designer shoes (only the left ones)
b) expensive designer shoes (only the right ones)

1 Malmö.
2 Two men. They stole expensive designer shoes shoes – the left ones only.
3 Shop assistants.
4 30 minutes.
5 Because in Sweden shops display left shoes and in Denmark shops display right shoes.
6 Yes, they did.
7 Because many stores have fewer shop assistants.
8 Because the thieves will then go to Germany.

CAN YOU UNDERSTAND THESE PEOPLE?

2 39

1 a 2 c 3 c 4 a 5 c

2 39

1
I = interviewer, P = Paul
I When was the last time you were at an airport?
P Two weeks ago.
I Were you going somewhere or meeting someone?
P I flew in from Frankfurt to London Heathrow.

2
I = interviewer, G = Gurjot
I Do you have any plans for tonight?
G Yes, I'm meeting an old friend who I haven't seen in a while and we're having Domino's Pizza.

3
I = interviewer, E = Ellie
I What housework do you hate doing?
E Cleaning the bathroom.
I Is there anything you don't mind doing?
E I like ironing.

4
I = interviewer, A = Alise
I Have you ever bought something online and had a problem?
A Yes, I just bought a pair of shoes online and they didn't fit and they were the wrong colour.

5
I = interviewer, An = Anya
I Did you do anything nice last weekend?
An Last weekend I spent some time with my friends and I did some shopping for a friend's birthday.

G comparative adjectives and adverbs, *as...as*
V time expressions: *spend time*, etc.
P sentence stress

5A No time for anything

Lesson plan

In this lesson Sts revise comparative adjectives, and learn to use comparative adverbs and the structure (*not*) *as...as* to compare things. The context is some pieces of information based on recent research which shows how the pace of life has increased in recent years. Sts start by doing a questionnaire and then reading the article, which has a vocabulary focus on expressions with *time*, e.g. *waste time*. This leads them to the grammar, and after it has been presented and practised there is a pronunciation focus on the /ə/ sound in unstressed syllables and words. Sts then compare their lives today to their lives five years ago, to see if they are living faster, and the lesson ends with a listening where a lifestyle expert gives advice on how to slow down.

STUDY LINK
- **Workbook** 5A
- **iTutor**
- **www.oup.com/elt/englishfile**

Extra photocopiable activities

- **Grammar** Comparative adjectives and adverbs, *as...as p.174*
- **Communicative** Which do you prefer? Why? *p.221* (instructions *p.221*)
- **www.oup.com/elt/teacher/englishfile**

Optional lead-in (books closed)

- Write on the board WORKING / STUDYING, EATING, SLEEPING, RELAXING.
  Sts, in pairs, say how long they spend doing these things in a typical day.
  Get feedback and ask Sts if they think they have enough free time.

1 READING & VOCABULARY
time expressions

a Books open. Focus on the article and headings, and check Sts know who Snow White (from the fairytale *Snow White and the Seven Dwarfs*) and Van Gogh (Dutch painter) are. Now tell Sts to read the article and match the headings to the paragraphs.

Get Sts to compare with a partner, and then check answers.

1 No time to stop	4 No time to write
2 No time for Snow White	5 No time for Van Gogh
3 No time to wait	6 More time on the road

b Focus on the task and tell Sts to read the article again and see if they can find the one piece of invented information.

Elicit some opinions and then tell Sts what it is.

Paragraph 4 (there is no such new networking site)

Ask Sts if they were surprised by any of the information.

c Now focus on the highlighted 'time' expressions and get Sts, in pairs, to try to guess their meaning from the context.

Check answers, either explaining in English, translating into Sts' L1, or getting Sts to check in their dictionaries.

Deal with any other new vocabulary.

d Put Sts in pairs and get them to look at the headings in **a**, or write the headings on the board in the right order. Sts try to remember what each paragraph was about.

Get some feedback from the class.

Extra support

- Put Sts in pairs, **A** and **B**. **A** talks about the first three headings and **B** helps by looking at the article. Then they swap roles and **B** looks at the next three headings whilst **A** helps.

Get Sts to answer the question in pairs or do it as an open class.

e Now focus on the instructions and the questionnaire. You might want to check that Sts understand *get impatient*, *feel frustrated*, and *get irritable*. Tell Sts that they should answer with *often*, *sometimes*, or *never* and then explain why or give examples.

Put Sts in pairs and get them to ask and answer the questions. Tell Sts they must make a note of their partner's answers as they will need them later.

Extra support

- Get Sts to interview you first, so you can model how you want them to answer.

f When Sts have answered the questions in **e**, tell them to go to **Communication** ***How fast is your life?*** on *p.101*.

Go through the instructions with them carefully. Sts should add up their partner's score and tell them what it is.

Sts then read their own results. While they read, go round monitoring and helping with any vocabulary problems, e.g. *lane*, *pace of life*, *rushing*, etc.

When they have finished, Sts should tell their partner if they agree with what they read.

Get feedback from some pairs.

Finally, with a show of hands find out how many people belong to each category (the slow lane, medium lane, and fast lane).

Tell Sts to go back to the main lesson **5A**.

Extra support

- Before telling Sts to go to **Communication**, you might want to pre-teach *slow lane* and *fast lane*.

2 GRAMMAR comparative adjectives and adverbs, *as...as*

a Tell Sts to look at the list of words from the text and decide if they are adjectives, adverbs, or both.

Check answers.

quickly = adverb	bad = adjective
fast = both	slowly = adverb
busy = adjective	stressed = adjective
patient = adjective	

b Focus on the instructions. Give Sts a few minutes to read sentences 1–6 and decide which form is correct.

Get Sts to compare with a partner, and then check answers.

1 faster	3 busier	5 ✓
2 worse	4 more stressed	6 as patient as

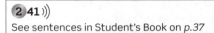

c 2 40 Tell Sts to go to **Grammar Bank 5A** on *p.134*. Focus on the example sentences and play the audio for Sts to listen and repeat. Encourage them to copy the rhythm. Then go through the rules with the class.

Additional grammar notes

- Although Pre-intermediate Sts will usually have studied comparative adjectives before, they will probably need reminding of the rules, especially for one-syllable adjectives. Typical mistakes: *more big, more easy*, etc.
- Point out that the rules for adverbs are very similar. The only difference is that two-syllable adverbs ending in *y*, e.g. *slowly*, form the comparative with *more*, e.g. *more slowly* NOT ~~*slowlier*~~.
- The structure *as...as* is more common in the negative, but can also be used in the affirmative, e.g. *She's as tall as I am*. It is also very common with *much* and *many*, e.g. *I don't eat as much as you*.
- You may also want to teach *the same as...*, e.g. *Your book is the same as mine*.

Focus on the exercises for **5A** on *p.135*. Sts do the exercises individually or in pairs.

Check answers, getting Sts to read the full sentences.

a 1 faster than
2 taller than
3 busier this week than
4 further from London than Leeds.
5 worse than
6 better than
7 harder than
8 more boring than
9 bigger than
10 more slowly than

b 1 Jerry isn't as short as Adam.
2 My bag isn't as nice as yours.
3 London isn't as big as Tokyo.
4 Cricket isn't as popular as tennis.
5 Adults don't learn languages as fast as children.
6 You don't work as hard as me.
7 France didn't play as well as England.

Tell Sts to go back to the main lesson **5A**.

Extra support

- If you think Sts need more practice, you may want to give them the Grammar photocopiable activity at this point.

3 PRONUNCIATION sentence stress

Pronunciation notes

- If you encourage Sts to get the stress right both in words and sentences, then you should find that they will start producing the /ə/ sound quite naturally.

a 2 41 Go through the /ə/ **sound** box with the class, and remind Sts that it is the most common sound in English.

Now focus on the sentences. Play the audio once for Sts just to listen.

Elicit that the pink letters are the /ə/ sound.

2 41
See sentences in Student's Book on *p.37*

Now play it again, pausing after each sentence for Sts to repeat and copy the rhythm.

Then repeat the activity eliciting responses from individual Sts.

b Focus on sentence 1 and say whether it is true for you or not, and give reasons.

Then put Sts in pairs or small groups and get them to say whether the sentences in **a** are true for them.

Get some feedback from the class.

4 SPEAKING

a Focus on the instructions and tell Sts to read the questionnaire all the way through. You could talk about some of the prompts in question 1 yourself to give Sts an example. Give Sts some time to think about their answers.

Extra support

- Get Sts to think first about their answers to question 1. They could make notes, e.g. write M (more) or L (less), or S (for the same) next to each thing.

b Put Sts in pairs and get them to answer the questionnaire together. Monitor and make sure Sts are forming the comparative correctly and using the expressions with time.

Get feedback from a few pairs and find out whose life has changed more.

5 LISTENING

a Focus on the task and give Sts some time to guess the missing words. Elicit some ideas, but do not tell Sts if they are right yet.

b 2 42 Play the audio once the whole way through for Sts to check their guesses. Tell them not to worry about the example yet.

Get Sts to compare with a partner, and then check answers.

Extra support

- Read through the script and decide if you need to pre-teach any new lexis before Sts listen.

1 slow down
2 most important
3 two things
4 nothing
5 water

2 42

(script in Student's Book on *pp.120–121*)
P = presenter, L = Laurel Reece

P Today we talk to Laurel Reece, who's writing a book about how to live more slowly. She's going to give us five useful tips.

L My first tip is something which is very simple to say, but more difficult to do in practice. Whatever you're doing, just try to slow down and enjoy it. If you are walking somewhere, try to walk more slowly; if you are driving, make yourself drive more slowly. It doesn't matter what you are doing, cooking, having a shower, exercising in the gym, just slow down and really enjoy the moment.
We all try to do too many things that we just don't have time for. So my second tip is: make a list of the three things which are most important for you, your priorities in life. Then when you've made your list, make sure that you spend time doing those things. Imagine, for example, that your three things are your family, reading, and playing sport. Then make sure that you spend enough time with your family, that you have space in your life for reading, and that you have time to do sports. And forget about trying to do other things that you haven't got time for.
Tip number three is: don't try to do two things at the same time. The worst thing you can do is to multitask. So, for example don't read your emails while you are talking to a friend on the phone. If you do that, you aren't really focussing on your emails or your friend, and you aren't going to feel very relaxed either.
Tip number four is very simple: once a day, every day, sit down and do nothing for half an hour. For example, go to a café and sit outside, or go to a park and sit on a bench. Turn off your phone, so that nobody can contact you, and then just sit and watch the world go by. This will really help you to slow down.
OK. My fifth and final tip. One of the most relaxing things you can do is to be near water or even better, to be on water. So if you live near a lake or river, go and sit by the river or go boating. If you live near the sea, go and sit on the beach. Relax and listen to the sound of the wind and the water. You will feel your body and mind slowing down as the minutes go past.

Now tell Sts they are going to listen again and they should not to try to write down everything the speaker says for the example, but just some key words. Then play the audio again, pausing after each tip to give Sts time to write the example.

Get Sts to compare with a partner, and then check answers.

Possible answers
1 Example: Try to walk or drive more slowly.
2 Example: Make sure that you spend enough time with your family, and have time for reading, and sport.
3 Example: Don't read your emails while you are talking to a friend on the phone.
4 Example: Go to a café or a park and sit down. Turn off your phone and watch the world go by (look around you).
5 Example: If you live near a lake or river, go and sit by the river or go boating. If you live near the sea, go and sit on the beach. Relax and listen to the sound of the wind and the water.

Extra support

- If there's time, you could get Sts to listen again with the script on *pp.120–121*, , so they can see exactly what they understood / didn't understand. Translate / explain any new words or phrases.

c Do this as an open-class question, or get Sts to discuss the tips with a partner and then get some feedback.

G superlatives (+ *ever* + present perfect)
V describing a town or city
P word and sentence stress

5B Superlative cities

Lesson plan

In this lesson Sts move from comparatives to superlatives. Sts who did not use Elementary may not have studied superlatives before, in which case you will probably need to spend more time on them. The context is a travel survey on European cities, and a light-hearted *Sunday Times* article in which a journalist went to four big cities, London, Rome, Paris, and New York to find out which was the friendliest towards tourists. The present perfect is also recycled in expressions like *the most beautiful place I've ever been to.* The lesson begins with the grammar presentation through the travel survey, which is followed by a pronunciation focus on word stress in superlative sentences. Sts then do a split reading on three of the cities the journalist visited, and then listen to his account of the fourth. There is then a vocabulary focus on language used to describe a city, which Sts use to write a description of the place where they live. The lesson ends with the song *Nobody Does It Better.*

STUDY LINK
- **Workbook** 5B
- **iTutor**
- **www.oup.com/elt/englishfile**

Extra photocopiable activities

- **Grammar** Superlatives (+ *ever* + present perfect) *p.175*
- **Communicative** Superlative questions *p.222* (instructions *p.201*)
- **Vocabulary** Describing a town or city *p.255* (instructions *p.246*)
- **Song** *Nobody Does It Better p.272* (instructions *p.264*)
- **www.oup.com/elt/teacher/englishfile**

Optional lead-in (books closed)

- Ask Sts *What are the biggest cities in your country?* and write them on the board.
- Then ask Sts *Which city do you think has the friendliest people?* and elicit opinions and reasons.

1 GRAMMAR superlatives (+ *ever* + present perfect)

a Books open. Focus on the photos and the list of cities and get Sts to match them.

1 Copenhagen (Denmark)	4 Dublin (Ireland)
2 Venice (Italy)	5 Paris (France)
3 Barcelona (Spain)	

Then do the questions as an open-class activity (or in pairs). You could then tell Sts what you know about these places, and if you've been to any of them.

b Before Sts read the article ask them if they know the website *TripAdvisor*, and if so, what they think of it.

Then focus on the article. Go through the first paragraph with Sts, and then get them to read the rest of the article and complete the gaps with a city from **a**.

Get Sts to compare with a partner, and then check answers.

1 Venice	3 Paris	5 Dublin
2 Copenhagen	4 Barcelona	

Go through the last paragraph (the quote) with them, and deal with any vocabulary problems.

If your Sts have been to any of these cities, including London, ask them if they agree with the survey.

c Tell Sts to look at 1–5 in **b** and think about their country / continent. Can they think of a city for each one?

In pairs or small groups, Sts tell each other their choices.

Get some feedback from the class, and tell them what you think.

d Focus on the instructions and get Sts to work out the rules.

Get Sts to compare with a partner, and then check answers.

1 Add *-est* to the adjective
2 Change the *y* to *i* and add *-est*
3 Add *the most* before the adjective
4 Change them to *the best* and *the worst*

e 2 43 Tell Sts to go to **Grammar Bank 5B** on *p.134*. Focus on the example sentences and play the audio for Sts to listen and repeat. Encourage them to copy the rhythm. Then go through the rules with the class.

Additional grammar notes

- Remind Sts that the rules for making superlatives are similar to comparatives, but adding *-est* instead of *-er*, or using *most* instead of *more*. Remind them to use *the* before superlatives.
- Sts sometimes use comparatives where they should use superlatives. Typical mistake: *the more expensive city in Europe*, etc.
- Highlight that Sts must always think if they are comparing two things (comparative), or more than two (superlative) when deciding which form to use, e.g. *The most beautiful city I've ever been to.*
- Some languages use *never* (not *ever*) in this structure. Typical mistake: *The most beautiful city I've never been to.*
- Adverbs can also be used in the superlative, e.g. *He drives the fastest.*

Focus on the exercises for **5B** on *p.135*. Sts do the exercises individually or in pairs.

Check answers, getting Sts to read the full sentences.

a 1 the most polite
2 the hottest
3 the worst
4 the friendliest
5 the most important
6 The best
7 the most polluted
8 The furthest
9 the funniest
10 the prettiest

b 1 It's the hottest country I've ever been to.
2 She's the most unfriendly person I've ever met.
3 It's the easiest exam he's ever done.
4 They're the most expensive trousers I've ever bought.
5 It's the longest film I've ever watched.
6 He's the most attractive man I've ever seen.
7 It's the worst meal I've ever eaten.
8 He's the most interesting teacher I've ever had.
9 It's the most exciting job we've ever done.

Tell Sts to go back to the main lesson **5B**.

Extra support

- If you think Sts need more practice, you may want to give them the Grammar photocopiable activity at this point.

2 PRONUNCIATION word and sentence stress

a Focus on the task and give Sts time, in pairs, to underline the stressed syllable in the adjectives in 1–8.

Get Sts to compare with a partner.

b 2 44 Play the audio for Sts to listen and check. Write the adjectives on the board with the stress underlined and drill pronunciation. Remind Sts of the silent syllable in interesting /ˈɪntrəstɪŋ/.

1 <u>beau</u>tiful
2 ex<u>pen</u>sive
3 im<u>pa</u>tient
4 <u>ge</u>nerous
5 <u>frigh</u>tening
6 ex<u>ci</u>ting
7 <u>in</u>teresting
8 ro<u>man</u>tic

2 44

1 <u>What's</u> the <u>most</u> <u>beautiful</u> <u>city</u> you've <u>ever</u> <u>been</u> <u>to</u>?
2 <u>What's</u> the <u>most</u> <u>expensive</u> <u>thing</u> you've <u>ever</u> <u>bought</u>?
3 <u>Who's</u> the <u>most</u> <u>impatient</u> <u>person</u> you <u>know</u>?
4 <u>Who's</u> the <u>most</u> <u>generous</u> <u>person</u> in your <u>family</u>?
5 <u>What's</u> the <u>most</u> <u>frightening</u> <u>film</u> you've <u>ever</u> <u>seen</u>?
6 <u>What's</u> the <u>most</u> <u>exciting</u> <u>sport</u> you've <u>ever</u> <u>done</u>?
7 <u>What's</u> the <u>most</u> <u>interesting</u> <u>book</u> you've <u>read</u> <u>recently</u>?
8 <u>What's</u> the <u>most</u> <u>romantic</u> <u>restaurant</u> you've <u>ever</u> <u>been</u> <u>to</u>?

Play the audio again for Sts to hear which words are stressed. Check answers. Highlight that the prepositions *to* and *at*, which are not normally stressed, are stressed here because of their end position.

See underlining in script 2.44

Finally, play the audio again, pausing after each question for Sts to copy the rhythm. Then repeat the activity eliciting responses from individual Sts.

c Focus on the instructions and speech bubbles. Do 1 yourself with Sts as an example, and elicit follow-up questions. Put Sts in pairs, **A** and **B**. Tell **A** to answer 1 with a full sentence, and **B** to ask extra questions. Then they swap roles, before moving on to 2.

Get some feedback from the class.

3 READING & SPEAKING

a Focus on the instructions and the three questions. Get Sts to read the article and answer 1–3 in pairs.

Check the answer to 1 and elicit ideas for 2 and 3.

1 A photo test, a shopping test, and an accident test.

Extra idea

- You could also ask Sts if there are any differences between people from the capital city and people from their town, or if they live in the capital, between them and people from small towns and villages.

b Put Sts into groups of three **A**, **B**, and **C**. If your class doesn't divide into threes, you may need to have one or two pairs. Get them to take the role of **A** and **B**, and then to read **C**'s text (Rome) together.

Tell Sts to go to **Communication *The friendliest city***, **A** on *p.102*, **B** on *p.107*, and **C** on *p.110*. Explain that all the **A**s are going to read about New York, the **B**s about Paris, and the **C**s about Rome.

Go through the instructions with them carefully.

When Sts have read their texts, put them back into their groups, so they can tell each other what happened in their city.

When they have finished, they should decide which city of the three is the friendliest.

When all the groups have finished, have a vote with a show of hands for their choice of friendliest city so far.

Tell Sts to go back to the main lesson **5B**.

4 LISTENING

a 2 45 Tell Sts they are going to listen to the journalist describe what happened in the fourth city, London. Ask Sts if anyone has been to London, and if they think it will be more or less friendly than the other three cities.

Focus on the question and tell Sts to just listen and not write the first time.

Check answers.

Extra support

- Read through the script and decide if you need to pre-teach any new lexis before Sts listen.

The photo test: not very well
The shopping test: very well
The accident test: not very well

2 45

(script in Student's Book on *p.121*)
First, I did the photo test. I was near Charing Cross station. I stopped a man who was walking quite slowly down the road and I said, 'Excuse me, could you take my photo?' The man said, 'No, no, no time for that,' and just continued walking. Then I asked a businessman in a grey suit who was walking towards the station. He took one photo, but when I asked him to take another one he walked away quickly.

Next, it was the shopping test. I went to a tourist shop in Oxford Street and I bought a key ring and a red bus. The red bus was very expensive. The total price was £40. I gave the man £100. He gave me £60 back.
Finally, it was time for the accident test. For this test I went down into the Tube, the London Underground. As I went down the stairs I fell over and sat on the floor. A man immediately stopped and looked down at me. I thought he was going to help me, but he didn't – he just said, 'Why don't you look where you are going?'.

b Before playing the audio again, give Sts some time to read questions 1–10.

Play the audio once the whole way through. Then play it again, pausing after each section for Sts to make notes.

Check answers.

1 A man.
2 'No, no, no time for that.'
3 A businessman. He took one photo (but no more).
4 In Oxford Street.
5 £40.
6 £100.
7 Yes.
8 In the Tube (the London Underground).
9 No.
10 'Why don't you look where you're going?'

Elicit now how London compared to the other three cities and elicit that it was the most unfriendly.

Extra support

- If there's time, you could get Sts to listen again with the script on *p.121*, so they can see exactly what they understood / didn't understand. Translate / explain any new words or phrases.

c In pairs or small groups, Sts discuss what they think would happen if they did the three tests in their nearest big city.

Get some feedback from pairs / groups.

5 VOCABULARY describing a town or city

a Focus on the task and give Sts time, in pairs, to answer the questions.

Get some feedback from a few pairs.

b Tell Sts to go to **Vocabulary Bank *Describing a town or city*** on *p.156*.

Focus on **1 Where is it? How big is it?**

In **a** tell Sts they are going to read about a town called Reading /redɪŋ/ and get them to circle the correct words or phrases.

2 46 Now do **b**. Play the audio for Sts to check their answers.

Where is it? How big is it?
Reading is a town in the **south** of England, on **the River Thames**. It is about 40 miles **west** of London. It is a **large** town and it has a population of about 250,000. It is famous for its music festival, which is one of the biggest in the UK.

Now do **2 What's it like?** and focus on **a**, where Sts match the adjectives and sentences.

Extra support

- Check Sts' answers to **a** before they match the opposites.

1 noisy	3 crowded	5 boring
2 polluted	4 modern	6 dangerous

Now do **b** and get Sts to match the adjectives in the list with their opposites in **a**.

2 47 Then do **c**. Play the audio for Sts to check answers to **a** and **b**. Play it again, pausing after each phrase for Sts to repeat. Give further practice of words and phrases your Sts find difficult to pronounce.

You may want to elicit / explain the difference between *crowded* and *full* (crowded = full of people), and *polluted* and *dirty* (polluted = dirty because of contamination).

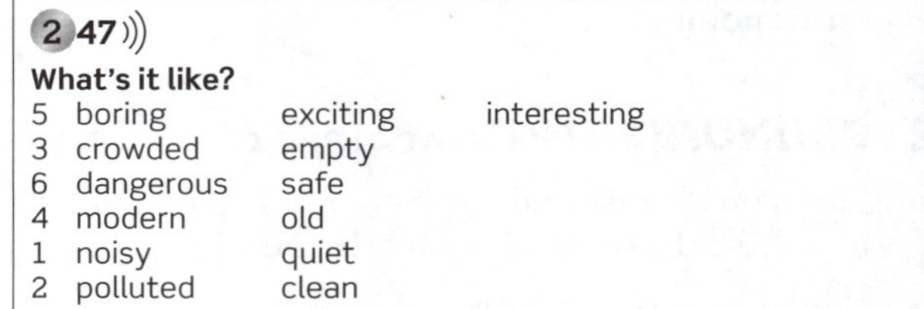

2 47
What's it like?

5 boring	exciting	interesting
3 crowded	empty	
6 dangerous	safe	
4 modern	old	
1 noisy	quiet	
2 polluted	clean	

Finally, do **d** and get Sts to cover the words and look at sentences 1–6. They can test themselves or each other.

Now do **3 What is there to see?** and tell Sts to look at the two photos and ask them what they can see. The photo on the left is the Guggenheim Museum in Bilbao and the photo on the right is the Castle de São Jorge in Lisbon.

Tell Sts to do **a** individually or in pairs.

2 48 Then do **b**. Play the audio for Sts to check answers. Play it again, pausing after each word or phrase for Sts to repeat. Give further practice of words and phrases your Sts find difficult to pronounce

What is there to see?
Religious buildings: cathedral, church, mosque, temple
Places where you can buy things: department store, market, shopping centre
Historic buildings and monuments: castle, museum, palace, statue, town hall

Extra challenge

- Elicit more words for each column, e.g. synagogue, mall, (clock) tower, etc.

Finally, do **c** in pairs or small groups. Then get some feedback from individual Sts.

Tell Sts to go back to the main lesson **5B**.

Extra support

- If you think Sts need more practice, you may want to give them the Vocabulary photocopiable activity at this point.

6 WRITING describing where you live

Tell Sts to go to **Writing *Describing where you live*** on *p.114*.

a Tell Sts to read the text and complete the gaps with the words in the list.

Check answers.

2 population	6 weather
3 area	7 food
4 historic	8 nature
5 modern	9 rivers

b Now tell Sts to match the questions with paragraphs 1–5.

Check answers.

1 Where do you live? Where is it? How big is it?
2 What's your hometown like? What is there to see there?
3 What's the weather like?
4 What's it famous for?
5 What's the best thing about it? Do you like living there?

c You may like to get Sts to do the writing in class or you could set it as homework. Get them to write a description of where they live, making sure they write five paragraphs by answering the questions in **b** in the right order.

d Sts should check for mistakes, and if they can, attach a photo or photos.

Sts should exchange their pieces of writing and decide which places they would like to visit.

Get some feedback.

Tell Sts to go back to the main lesson **5B**.

7 2 49 SONG *Nobody Does It Better* ♫

This song was originally made famous by the American singer Carly Simon in 1977. For copyright reasons this is a cover version. If you want to do this song in class, use the photocopiable activity on *p.272*.

2 49

Nobody Does It Better

Nobody does it better
Makes me feel sad for the rest
Nobody does it half as good as you
Baby, you're the best

I wasn't looking but somehow you found me
I tried to hide from your love light
But like heaven above me, the spy who loved me
Is keeping all my secrets safe tonight

And nobody does it better
Though sometimes I wish someone could
Nobody does it quite the way you do
Why do you have to be so good?

The way that you hold me
Whenever you hold me
There's some kind of magic inside you
That keeps me from running, but just keep it coming
How'd you learn to do the things you do?

And nobody does it better
Makes me feel sad for the rest
Nobody does it half as good as you
Baby, baby, darling, you're the best

Baby, you're the best
Darling, you're the best
Sweet thing, you're the best (x4)

G quantifiers, *too*, *not enough*
V health and the body
P /ʌ/, /uː/, /aɪ/, and /e/

5C How much is too much?

Lesson plan

In this lesson Sts revise quantifiers and learn to use *too much / many*, and *(not) enough*. The context is a magazine article about how some things commonly considered bad for you can, in the right quantities, be good for you. The lesson begins with a lifestyle questionnaire focussing on the five things (coffee, sun, video games, chocolate, and TV) which Sts will go on to read and listen about in the article *Everything bad is good for you*. In this article there is also a vocabulary focus on health and the body. Sts then work on the grammar, followed by a pronunciation focus on four vowel sounds which are often mispronounced in some of the quantifiers. The lesson ends with a speaking activity where Sts discuss more general lifestyle habits using the new quantifiers. Depending on the level of your class, you may want to do more or less revision of countability and basic quantifiers (see **Optional lead-in** and **Extra support**).

STUDY LINK
- **Workbook** 5C
- **iTutor**
- **iChecker**
- **www.oup.com/elt/englishfile**

Extra photocopiable activities

- **Grammar** Quantifiers, *too*, *not enough p.176*
- **Communicative** How old is your body? *p.223* (instructions *p.202*)
- **www.oup.com/elt/teacher/englishfile**

Optional lead-in (books closed)

- Revise countability. Write on the board in two columns:

1	2
COFFEE	VEGETABLES
BREAD	BISCUITS
CHOCOLATE	SWEETS

- Ask Sts *What's the difference between the words in columns 1 and 2?* and elicit that the words in column 1 are uncountable, and normally used in the singular, but the words in column 2 are countable and can be used in singular and plural. Elicit a few more words for each column, e.g. *water, rice, apples*, etc.
- Ask Sts *When do we use 'a', 'some', and 'any'?* and elicit that you use *a* with singular countable nouns and *some / any* with plural countable nouns and uncountable nouns, *some* in positive sentences and *any* in negatives and questions, e.g. *I ate a biscuit and some bread. I didn't eat any vegetables or any fruit.*

1 SPEAKING

a Books open. Focus on the questionnaire and its title. Go through the questions making sure Sts understand them, e.g. *sunscreen*.

Put Sts in pairs and give them time to answer the questions.

b In their pairs, Sts now discuss whether they think their habits are unhealthy.

Get some feedback from various pairs.

Extra support

- You could get Sts to ask you some of the questions from the questionnaire and then ask them if they think your habits are healthy or not.

2 READING & LISTENING

a Focus on the title of the article and ask Sts to predict what it's going to be about. Then set a time limit for Sts to read it once.

Focus on the question, and elicit answers from the class.

b Now get Sts to read the article again and to match the highlighted words to a picture or definition.

Get Sts to compare their answers with a partner.

c 2 50 Play the audio once for Sts to listen and check their answers to **b**.

2 50

1 bones	4 skin	7 anxious
2 face	5 prevent	
3 brain	6 illness	

Then play it again, pausing after each word for Sts to listen and repeat.

Finally, get Sts to practise saying the words.

Deal with any other new vocabulary in the three paragraphs.

d Focus on questions 1 and 2. Tell Sts to cover the text and, in pairs, to answer them.

Get some feedback.

Possible answers

1 Good about coffee: wakes you up, helps prevent some illnesses
Good about sunlight: helps produce vitamin D, good for bones and healthy immune system, makes you feel happier
Good about computer games: stimulate the brain, help learn important skills, e.g. solving problems and taking decisions

2 Bad about coffee: can make you feel anxious, or keep you awake at night
Bad about sunlight: too much can give skin cancer
Bad about computer games: can waste time

Extra idea

- Write the three headings from the article on the board. Put Sts into groups of three. **A** (book closed) says as much as he / she can remember about the first topic. **B** and **C** (books open) prompt and correct. They swap roles for the other topics.

e **2.51** Put Sts in pairs and get them to write a list of how chocolate and watching TV can be good for you.

Elicit some ideas and write them on the board.

Now tell Sts they are going to listen to a radio programme in which two experts talk about chocolate and TV. They must listen and check which answers on the board they hear. You might want to pre-teach *antioxidant* and *reality TV*.

Play the audio once the whole way through. Play again if necessary.

Check answers.

Extra support

- Read through the script and decide if you need to pre-teach any new lexis before Sts listen.

Chocolate: protects from illnesses and reduces bad cholesterol
Watching TV: makes us more intelligent and teaches us about group psychology

2.51

(script in Student's Book on *p.121*)

P = presenter, J = Jane, T = Tony

P Next in our list of things which you thought were bad for you is chocolate. Jane, our food expert, is going to tell us why actually it can be good for us.

J Well, there have been a lot of studies recently about chocolate. Remember, chocolate is something that we've been eating for hundreds of years, it's not a modern invention. And the studies show that chocolate, like red wine, contains antioxidants. In fact, chocolate has more antioxidants than wine. These antioxidants can protect us against illnesses like heart disease.

P Really?

J Yes, but, and this is very important, all the good antioxidants are only in dark chocolate. So don't eat milk chocolate or white chocolate – they aren't healthy at all. And of course you also need to remember that although dark chocolate is good for you, it contains quite a lot of calories, so if you are worried about your weight, don't eat too much. One or two pieces a day is enough.

P Great news for me because I love chocolate! And now to Tony, our TV journalist. Tony, newspaper articles are always telling us about studies which say that we watch too much TV, that we spend too much time sitting in front of the TV, and that as a result we don't do enough exercise. They also say that watching TV makes us stupid. Is this all true, Tony?

T Well, it's almost certainly true that we watch too much television, but it probably isn't true that watching TV makes us stupid. I've just finished reading a book by a science writer, Steven Johnson, called *Everything bad is good for you*. One thing he says in his book that modern TV series like *The Sopranos* or *House* or *Mad Men* are more intellectually stimulating than TV series were 20 years ago. He says that these shows are complicated and very clever and that they help to make us more intelligent.

P Well, I can believe that, but what about reality shows that are so popular on TV. I can't believe that these are good for us.

T Well, Steven Johnson says that we can even learn something from reality shows – he says this kind of programme can teach us about group psychology, about how people behave when they are in a group.

P Well, thank you, Tony and Jane. So, now you know what to do this evening. You can sit down in front of the TV with a box of dark chocolates...

f Tell Sts they are going to listen to the radio programme again and this time they must answer questions 1–4.

Play the audio, pausing when Jane has finished talking about chocolate to give Sts time to answer 1 and 2. Then play the rest of the audio.

Get Sts to compare with a partner, and then check answers.

1 It contains antioxidants.
2 Dark chocolate is good for you; milk and white chocolate aren't good for you.
3 They are complicated and very clever. They can help to makes us more intelligent.
4 How people behave in groups

Extra support

- If there's time, you could get Sts to listen again with the script on *p.121*, so they can see exactly what they understood / didn't understand. Translate / explain any new words or phrases.

g In pairs, small groups, or as an open-class activity Sts discuss the question.

3 GRAMMAR quantifiers, *too*, *not enough*

Extra support

- If you didn't do the **Optional lead-in**, you could do it here.

a This exercise revises what Sts should already know. Focus on the instructions. Stress that Sts, in pairs, must say why one is right and the other wrong while they are doing the exercise.

Check answers, and elicit the rules from them.

1	many	Use *many* with plural countable nouns.
2	much	Use *much* with uncountable nouns.
3	a lot of	Use *a lot of* + uncountable or countable nouns.
4	a little	Use *a little* + uncountable nouns.
5	a few	Use *a few* + countable nouns.
6	a lot	Use *a lot* after a verb when it's without a noun.

b Here the new language of the lesson is introduced. Focus on the instructions and get Sts, in pairs, to match the bold phrases with the meanings.

Check answers. You may want to elicit here that we use *too much* and *too many* with nouns, and *too* with adjectives.

1 B   2 A

c Tell Sts to look at the sentences in **b** and to focus on the position of the word *enough*.

Check answers.

a *enough* comes before a noun.
b *enough* comes after an adjective.

d **2.52** **2.53** Now tell Sts to go to **Grammar Bank 5C** on *p.134*. Focus on the example sentences and play the audio for Sts to listen and repeat. Encourage them to copy the rhythm. Then go through the rules with the class.

Additional grammar notes

too, too much | many

- Some Sts often use *too much* + adjective. Typical mistake: *It's too much big.*
- It is also important to highlight the difference between *too* and *very*:
  It's very big. (= a statement of fact, neither good nor bad)
  It's too big. (= more than it should be / than you want)

(not) enough

- The main problem here is the pronunciation of *enough* /ɪˈnʌf/ and the different positions: before nouns, but after adjectives. Some Sts may confuse *quite* and *enough* because of L1 interference.

Focus on the exercises for **5C** on *p.135*. Sts do them individually or in pairs.

Check answers, getting Sts to read the full sentences.

a	1	too much	5	too much
	2	too many	6	enough time
	3	enough water	7	go out enough
	4	too busy	8	too lazy
b	1	enough	5	enough
	2	too	6	too
	3	too many	7	too many
	4	too much	8	too much, enough

Tell Sts to go back to the main lesson **5C**.

Extra support

- If you think Sts need more practice, you may want to give them the Grammar photocopiable activity at this point.

4 PRONUNCIATION & SPEAKING /ʌ/, /uː/, /aɪ/, and /e/

a This exercise helps Sts with the pronunciation of some of the words from the lesson.

Focus on the sound pictures and elicit the words and sounds: *up* /ʌ/, *boot* /uː/, *bike* /aɪ/, and *egg* /e/.

Get Sts, in pairs, to say the words out loud to each other to identify the one with a different sound.

b 2 54)) Play the audio for Sts to listen and check.

1 busy	2 cups	3 little	4 water

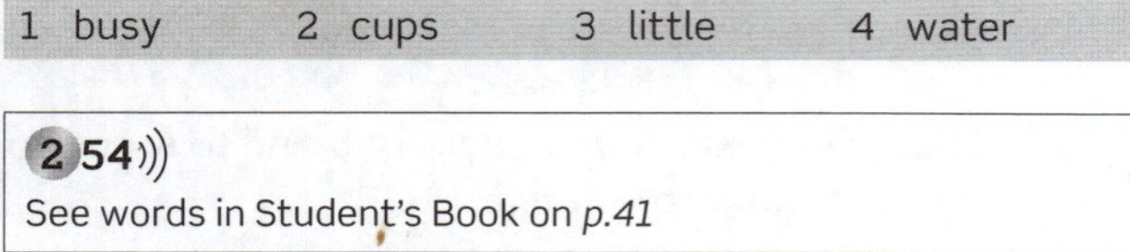

2 54))
See words in Student's Book on *p.41*

Play it again, pausing after each word for Sts to repeat.

Then get Sts to practise saying the words.

c Focus on the speech bubbles and then demonstrate the activity yourself by answering a couple of questions and explaining your reasons.

Now put Sts in pairs and get them to answer the questions giving their reasons too.

Get some feedback from various pairs.

Vocabulary shopping
Function making suggestions; taking something back to a shop; arranging when to meet
Language *Why don't you...? I'm afraid...*

PRACTICAL ENGLISH

Episode 3 The wrong shoes

Lesson plan

In this third Practical English lesson Sts revise some basic shopping vocabulary, and learn some key phrases for taking things back to a shop. The story develops: Rob decides that he is unfit and needs to do some exercise. Holly invites him to join her and some friends in a game of basketball. Rob accepts, but first needs to buy some trainers. He buys a pair, without trying them on, and then realizes they are too small. He takes them back to the shop and manages to exchange them. Later, he accepts an invitation to go running with Jenny very early in the morning in Central Park.

STUDY LINK

- **Workbook** The wrong shoes
- **iTutor**
- **www.oup.com/elt/englishfile**

Test and Assessment CD-ROM

- **Quick Test 5**
- **File 5 Test**
- **www.oup.com/elt/teacher/englishfile**

Optional lead-in (books closed)

- Before starting Episode 3 elicit what Sts can remember about Episode 2. Ask them *Who's Holly? Where does she work / live? Who's Barbara?*, etc.
- Alternatively, you could play the last scene of Episode 2.

1 ROB HAS A PROBLEM

a 2 55 Focus on the photos at the top of the page and elicit what is happening.

Now focus on questions 1–8 and give Sts time to read them. Sts may not know the expression *in shape* = in a good physical condition.

Play the audio once the whole way through. Play again if necessary.

Get Sts to compare with a partner, and then check answers.

1 He says he is eating too much.
2 Because he eats out all the time in New York and the portions are very big.
3 He cycles in London.
4 Because he doesn't have a bike (he lives near the office and is only going to stay for another three weeks).
5 She goes running before and after work.
6 Holly thinks running is very boring.
7 He could play basketball with Holly and her friends.
8 He needs to buy some trainers (*sneakers* in American English).

2 55
(script in Student's Book on *p.121*)
H = **Holly**, **R** = **Rob**
H Hey, Rob, come on. Keep up.
R Sorry. I'm a bit tired this morning.
H You aren't exactly in good shape, are you?
R I know, I know. I think I'm eating too much.
H Then eat less!
R It isn't easy. I eat out all the time. And the portions in American restaurants are enormous.
H You don't do enough exercise.
R I walk a lot.
H Walking isn't enough, Rob. Do you do *anything* to keep fit?
R I cycle when I'm in London...
H So why don't you get a bike here?
R I'm only here for another three weeks. Anyway, my hotel's near the office. I don't need a bike.
H You know, Jennifer goes running all the time. Before and after work. But I just think that running is just so boring. I mean, where's the fun?
R Yeah, I'm not very keen on running.
H So why don't you play basketball with me and my friends?
R OK. That's a great idea! But I don't have any trainers.
H Trainers? Sneakers! You can buy some.
R Is there a sports shop near here?
H Sure, there's one across the street.

Now focus on the **British and American English** box and go through it with the class.

Extra support

- If there's time, you could get Sts to listen again with the script on *p.121*, so they can see exactly what they understood / didn't understand. Translate / explain any new words or phrases.

b  Focus on the **Making suggestions with *Why don't you...?*** box and go through it with Sts.

Now play the audio and get Sts just to listen.

2 56
See Student's Book on *p.42*

Play the audio again, pausing after each phrase, and get Sts to repeat it.

c Put Sts in pairs and focus on the instructions. Make sure Sts understand the situation.

Tell **A**s to start.

When Sts have finished, ask a few **A**s what suggestions **B**s made and if they thought the suggestions were good or not.

d Sts stay in their pairs and focus on the new situation.

Tells **B**s to start.

When Sts have finished, ask a few **B**s what suggestions **A**s made and if they thought the suggestions were good or not.

Extra idea

- As a round-up ask Sts for good suggestions for both situations and write them on the board.

2 VOCABULARY shopping

Put Sts in pairs and tell them to answer the questions in the shopping quiz.

Check answers. For 1, you could also elicit XS and XXL.

1 S, M, L, and XL.
2 S = small, M = medium, L = large, XL = extra large
3 a changing room
4 a receipt
5 £25.99 = twenty-five pounds (and) ninety-nine p
75p = seventy-five p / pence
$45 = forty-five dollars
15c = fifteen cents
€12.50 = twelve euros (and) fifty (cents)

Extra idea

- You could do the quiz as a competition. Set a time limit and the pair with the most correct answers are the winners.

3 TAKING SOMETHING BACK TO A SHOP

a 2.57 Focus on the photo and ask Sts some questions, e.g. *Where is Rob? Who is he talking to?*, etc.

Now either tell Sts to close their books and write the two questions on the board, or get Sts to focus on the questions and cover the dialogue.

Play the audio once the whole way through and then check answers.

1 They are too small.
2 He changes them for another pair.

2.57 2.58

S = Sales assistant, R = Rob
S Can I help you, sir?
R Yes. Do you have these in an eight? (*repeat*)
S Just a **minute**, I'll go and check.
***
S Here you are, these are an eight. Do you want to **try** them on?
R No, thanks. I'm sure they'll be fine. (*repeat*) How much are they? (*repeat*)
S They're $83.94.
R Oh, it says $72.99. (*repeat*)
S Yes, but there's an added sales tax of **15%**.
R Oh, OK. Do you take MasterCard? (*repeat*)
S Sure.
***
S Can I help you?
R Yes, I bought these about half an hour ago. (*repeat*)
S Yes, I remember. Is there a **problem**?
R Yes, I'm afraid they're too small. (*repeat*)
S What **size** are they?
R They're an eight. (*repeat*) But I take a UK eight. (*repeat*)
S Oh right. Yes, a UK eight is a US nine.
R Do you have a pair? (*repeat*)
S I'll go and check. Just a minute.
***
S I'm **sorry**, but we don't have these in a nine. But we do have these and they're the **same** price. Or you can have a refund.
R Erm... I'll take this pair then, please. (*repeat*)
S No problem. Do you have the **receipt**?
R Yes, here you are. (*repeat*)
S Brilliant.

You might want to check Sts know what MasterCard is (same as Visa card) and that 'erm' is a sound we use to give ourselves time to think. Also check they understand *a refund*. Model and drill the pronunciation /'ri:fʌnd/.

b Focus on the dialogue in the chart. Elicit who says the **You Hear** phrases (the shop assistant) and who says the **You Say** phrases (the customer, here Rob). These phrases will be useful for Sts if they need to buy something and then take it back if they have a problem.

Give Sts a minute to read through the dialogue and think what the missing words might be. Then play the audio again, and get Sts to complete the gaps. Play again if necessary.

Get Sts to compare with a partner, and then check answers.

See words in **bold** in script 2.57

Go through the dialogue line by line with Sts, helping them with any words or expressions they don't understand. You may want to highlight the meaning of the phrasal verb *try on*.

Now focus on the **A pair** box and go through it with Sts.

c 2.58 Now focus on the **You Say** phrases and tell Sts they're going to hear the dialogue again. They should repeat the **You Say** phrases when they hear the beep. Encourage them to copy the rhythm and intonation.

Play the audio, pausing if necessary for Sts to repeat the phrases.

d Now put Sts in pairs, **A** and **B**. **A** is the shop assistant. Get Sts to read the dialogue aloud, and then swap roles.

e Focus on the instructions, **A** is the customer and **B** the shop assistant. Make sure Sts understand the situation. **B** keeps his / her book open and starts with *Can I help you, sir / madam?*

Sts now roleplay the dialogue. Monitor and help.

f Now focus on the new situation and make sure Sts know what *boots* are. **A**s are now the shop assistants.

Sts now roleplay the dialogue. Monitor and help.

You could get a few pairs to perform in front of the class.

4 ROB DECIDES TO DO SOME EXERCISE

a 2.59 Focus on the photos and ask Sts some questions, e.g. *Where's Jenny? What is she doing?*, etc.

Focus on sentences 1–7 and go through them with Sts. Then play the audio once the whole way through for Sts to just listen.

Now play again for Sts to circle the right answer.

Get Sts to compare with a partner, and then check answers.

1 Brooklyn	4 6.45	7 has
2 doesn't show	5 early	
3 morning	6 7.15	

2 59

(script in Student's Book on *p.121*)

R Hi, Jenny.
J Oh, hi.
R Have you had a good day?
J Oh, you know. Meetings! What about you?
R It was great. I went to Brooklyn and met some really interesting people.
J And you had time to go shopping, too.
R What? Oh yeah. I've just bought these.
J What are they?
R A pair of trainers – er, sneakers.
J Nice. Why did you buy sneakers?
R I think I need to get a bit fitter.
J Oh, I'm impressed. You know, I go running every morning in Central Park.
R Do you?
J It's so beautiful early in the morning. Why don't you come with me?
R Er... sure. Why not?
J Great! I'll come by your hotel tomorrow morning.
R OK. What time?
J Six forty-five?
R Six...?
J Forty-five.
R Can we make it a bit later? Say, seven forty-five?
J That's too late, Rob. Let's make it seven fifteen.
R OK.
J Excellent. See you later.
R Great.
H Basketball *and* running, Rob? You must have a lot of energy.
R Er... yeah.

Extra support

- If there's time, you could get Sts to listen again with the script on *p.121*, so they can see exactly what they understood / didn't understand. Translate / explain any new words or phrases.

b Focus on the **Social English phrases**. In pairs, get Sts to think about what the missing words could be.

Extra challenge

- In pairs, get Sts to complete the phrases before they listen.

c 2 60 Play the audio for Sts to listen and complete the phrases.

Check answers.

2 60

Rob	Have you **had** a good day?
Jenny	Oh, you **know**. Meetings!
Jenny	Why **don't** you come with me?
Rob	Can we **make** it a bit later?
Rob	**Say**, seven forty-five?
Jenny	**Let's** make it seven fifteen.

If you know your Sts' L1, you could get them to translate the phrases. If not, get Sts to have a look at the phrases again in context in the script on *p.121*.

d Now play the audio again, pausing after each phrase for Sts to listen and repeat.

Finally, focus on the **Can you...?** questions and ask Sts if they feel confident they can now do these things. If they feel that they need more practice, tell them to watch the episode again and practise the language on their *iTutor*.

G *will / won't* (predictions)
V opposite verbs: *pass – fail*, etc.
P *'ll, won't*

6A Are you a pessimist?

Lesson plan

In this lesson Sts are introduced to the future forms *will* and *won't* for the first time. They learn a specific use of these forms, which is to make predictions about the future, here particularly in response to what somebody says to you. The context of the lesson is pessimists and optimists. The lesson begins with a vocabulary focus on common opposite verbs, e.g. *pass – fail, buy – sell*. The grammar is then presented through a light-hearted pessimist's phrase book, i.e. the typical predictions a pessimist might make, e.g. *You won't like it, They'll be late*, etc. It is practised orally by making optimistic predictions. In Pronunciation Sts practise the contracted forms of *will / won't*. They then read an article about Hugh Laurie, a British actor who both plays the role of a very pessimistic person in the series *House M.D.* and is a pessimist himself. Finally, Sts listen to a radio programme about positive thinking and answer a questionnaire to find out how positive they are.

STUDY LINK

- **Workbook** 6A
- **iTutor**
- **www.oup.com/elt/englishfile**

Extra photocopiable activities

- **Grammar** *will / won't* (predictions) *p.177*
- **Vocabulary** Opposite verbs *p.256* (instructions *p.246*)
- **Communicative** The optimist's phrase book *p.224* (instructions *p.202*)
- **www.oup.com/elt/teacher/englishfile**

Optional lead-in (books closed)

- Draw a big glass on the board which is exactly half full of water. Underneath write THE GLASS IS HALF _____. Tell Sts to complete the sentence with one word, but they mustn't tell anybody which word they have written.
- Now elicit from the class how to finish the sentence (*full / empty*).

  Ask Sts who have written *empty* to put up their hands. Tell them that they are pessimists (explain / translate if necessary).

  Now ask who wrote *full* and tell these Sts that they are optimists.

1 VOCABULARY opposite verbs

a Books open. Focus on the list of verbs and give Sts a minute to write the opposite verbs.

Check answers.

win – lose
buy – sell
remember – forget
turn on – turn off
start – end / finish

b Tell Sts to go to **Vocabulary Bank *Opposite verbs*** on *p.157*.

Focus on **a** and get Sts to match the verbs and pictures.

Check answers, but don't drill pronunciation yet.

10	arrive	8	pass
6	break	1	push
4	buy	12	send
3	find	5	start
7	forget	11	teach
2	lend	9	turn on
14	miss	13	win

Then get Sts to do **b** by writing the verbs in the **Opposite** column in **a**.

3 2 Now do **c**. Play the audio for Sts to check answers to **b** and to drill the pronunciation of the verbs in **a** and **b**. Play it again, pausing after each pair of opposite verbs for Sts to repeat. Give further practice of verbs your Sts find difficult to pronounce.

3 2
Opposite verbs

10	arrive	leave
6	break	mend / repair
4	buy	sell
3	find	lose
7	forget	remember
2	lend	borrow
14	miss	catch
8	pass	fail
1	push	pull
12	send	get / receive
5	start	stop / finish
11	teach	learn
9	turn on	turn off
13	win	lose

Highlight the difference between *lend* and *borrow*, i.e. *I lend money to you / you borrow money from me.*

Focus on **d**. Get Sts to cover the verbs and look at the pictures. In pairs, they try to remember the verbs and their opposites.

Tell Sts to go back to the main lesson **6A**.

Extra support

- If you think Sts need more practice, you may want to give them the Vocabulary photocopiable activity at this point.

2 GRAMMAR *will / won't* (predictions)

a Focus on the cartoon and the questions. Elicit an answer to the first two questions (the fish with its head in the water is the optimist because it sees the glass as half full, whereas the other fish sees the glass as half empty). If you didn't do the **Optional lead-in**, get Sts to say whether they are an optimist or a pessimist.

b Focus on the phrase book, and explain that when it is completed, it is a list of typical things that a pessimist says.

Go through the **You Say** phrases with the class.

Now focus on the **A Pessimist Says** responses.

Then focus on the example in the phrase book and show how *It'll rain* is a pessimistic response to *We're having the party in the garden*. You may want to point out at this stage that *It'll* = *It will*. Then do the second one together (*You won't pass*) and elicit that *You won't* = *You will not*.

Tell Sts, in pairs, to write the pessimist's other responses in the phrase book.

c 3 3 Play the audio for Sts to listen and check.

3 You'll break your leg.
4 He won't pay you back.
5 You won't understand a word.
6 They'll lose.
7 They'll be late.
8 You won't find a parking space.

3 3

1 **A** We're having the party in the garden.
B It'll rain.
2 **A** I'm doing my driving test this afternoon.
B You won't pass.
3 **A** I'm having my first skiing lesson today.
B You'll break your leg.
4 **A** I've lent James some money.
B He won't pay you back.
5 **A** I'm going to see a film tonight in English.
B You won't understand a word.
6 **A** Our team are playing in the cup tonight.
B They'll lose.
7 **A** We're meeting Anna and Daniel at seven o'clock.
B They'll be late.
8 **A** We're going to drive to the city centre.
B You won't find a parking space.

Play the audio again and get Sts to repeat the pessimist's responses.

d Put Sts in pairs, **A** and **B**. Tell **A**s to keep their books open, **B**s to close theirs. Tell **B**s that they are pessimists. Tell **A**s to read the **You Say** phrases and **B**s to respond with **A Pessimist Says** phrases from memory. Then Sts swap roles.

e Focus on the responses in **A Pessimist Says** in the phrase book and elicit answers to the question.

the future

f 3 4 Tell Sts to go to **Grammar Bank 6A** on *p.136*. Focus on the example sentences and play the audio for Sts to listen and repeat. Encourage them to copy the rhythm. Then go through the rules with the class.

Additional grammar notes

- In Elementary Sts learnt that *be going to* can be used to make predictions, e.g. *You're going to be very happy*. This use was revised in **3A** (*It's going to be a surprise*).
- In this lesson Sts learn the future form *will* / *won't* + infinitive, and that it can also be used to make predictions. Sometimes both forms are possible, e.g. *I think the government will lose the election.* / *I think the government is going to lose the election.*

However, there is often a difference in usage: *will* / *won't* tends to be used more than *be going to* to make instant, on the spot predictions in reaction to what another person says, e.g.:
A *I'm going to see the new Tarantino film tonight.*
B *You won't like it.*

- At this level you may prefer to simplify things by telling Sts that both *be going to* and *will* / *won't* can be used to make predictions.
- Sts will learn other uses of the future (*will* / *won't*) in **6B** (promises, offers, and decisions) and will study the use of *will* / *won't* in conditional sentences with *if* in **8B**.

Focus on the exercises for **6A** on *p.137*. Sts do the exercises individually or in pairs.

Check answers, getting Sts to read the full sentences.

a 1 I think they'll lose the match.
2 Will the meeting be long?
3 She won't get the job.
4 Will you see him at work later?
5 It'll be impossible to park.
6 You won't like that book.
7 I think she'll love the present I bought her.
8 There won't be a lot of traffic in the morning.
9 You'll find a good job, I'm sure.
10 Everything will be OK, so there's no need to worry.

b 1 will be 3 will snow 5 will pass
2 will like 4 will get

Tell Sts to go back to the main lesson **6A**.

Extra support

- If you think Sts need more practice, you may want to give them the Grammar photocopiable activity at this point.

g Focus on the instructions and the example. Put Sts in pairs and tell them to now imagine they are optimists. They must look at the **You Say** sentences in the phrase book and write eight positive predictions.

Get some ideas from the class and write them on the board.

Extra support

- Elicit a more positive prediction for 1, e.g. *You'll have a wonderful time!*, *I'm sure it won't rain*, etc.

3 PRONUNCIATION *'ll, won't*

Pronunciation notes

- An important aspect of *will* / *won't* is the pronunciation of the contractions and Sts get some intensive practice here. Remind Sts that contractions are very common in conversation, but that it is not wrong to use the full uncontracted form.
- Sts often confuse the pronunciation of the contracted form of *will not* (*won't* /wəʊnt/) with the verb *want* /wɒnt/ when speaking and listening, so there is also a special focus on this.

a  3 5 Focus on **a** and play the audio for Sts just to listen.

> 3 5
> See Student's Book on *p.44*

Then play it again for them to listen and repeat. Encourage them to copy the rhythm. Sts often find the contracted form of *It will* (*It'll*) difficult to say.

b 3 6 Focus on the sound pictures and elicit the words and sounds: *clock* /ɒ/ and *phone* /əʊ/. Then explain that *want* and *won't* have the same consonants, but different vowel sounds.

Focus on the two sentences and play the audio, asking Sts to listen for the difference between *want* and *won't*.

> 3 6
> See Student's Book on *p.44*

Play the audio again and get Sts to listen and repeat.

c 3 7 Tell Sts that they are going to hear six sentences and that they have to write them down. Explain that they all include either *want* or *won't*. Tell Sts that they will hear each sentence twice.

Play the audio once the whole way through for Sts to listen.

Now play the audio again, pausing after each sentence to give Sts time to write down what they hear.

Then elicit answers and write them on the board.

> 3 7
> 1 I want to go with you.
> 2 They won't come tonight.
> 3 You won't find a job.
> 4 We want to learn.
> 5 They want to sell their house.
> 6 I won't win the match.

Extra idea

- Put Sts in pairs and get them to practise saying the sentences.

4 READING

a Focus on the article and the photo. Ask Sts who the actor is (Hugh Laurie) and what famous role he plays (Dr House in the series *House M.D.*). Then ask Sts what they think the title means and elicit ideas.

Give Sts time to read the article and find out which two things Hugh Laurie has in common with his character, Dr House.

Check answers.

> 1 They are both pessimists.
> 2 They are both talented musicians, passionate about the blues.

b Now tell Sts to read the article again and decide whether sentences 1–5 are true or false, and why.

Get Sts to compare with a partner, and then check answers.

> 1 T (He is a pessimist and says 'I am someone who is constantly expecting a plane to drop on my head.')
> 2 F (He says 'If we do a bad show next week, ... it'll just stop.')
> 3 T (He doesn't think people will like it.)
> 4 F (When he was asked on a TV show why he was so pessimistic, he said it was because he was Scottish.)
> 5 T (Complete strangers come up to him in the street and say 'Cheer up.')

c Do this as an open-class activity. If you have seen *House M.D.*, tell Sts what you think of it.

5 LISTENING & SPEAKING

a 3 8 Focus on the instructions and question. Tell Sts that the radio programme is a chat show, where one of the guests is an expert on positive thinking.

Play the audio once the whole way through.

Check answers.

Extra support

- Read through the scripts and decide if you need to pre-teach any new lexis before Sts listen.

> It helps you enjoy life more. Positive people are healthier and live longer.

> 3 8
> (script in Student's Book on *p.121*)
> **Presenter:**
> Today's topic is 'positive thinking'. We all know that people who are positive enjoy life more than people who are negative and pessimistic. But scientific studies show that positive people are also healthier. They get better more quickly when they are ill, and they live longer. A recent study has shown that people who are optimistic and think positively live, on average, nine years longer than pessimistic people. So, let's hear what you, the listeners, think. Do you have any idea to help us be more positive in our lives?

Extra challenge

- Before playing the audio, elicit some ideas from the class why positive thinking is good for you.

b Now explain that five people have called the radio programme to give some tips (useful suggestions) to help people be more positive.

Get Sts, in pairs, to try and guess what the missing words in the sentences could be. Tell them not to write them in the sentences, but on a separate piece of paper.

You could elicit some ideas, but do not check answers yet.

c 3 9 Play the audio once for Sts to check their guesses and complete the gaps.

Check answers.

> 1 Live in the **present**, not in the **past**.
> 2 Think **positive** thoughts, not negative ones.
> 3 Don't spend a lot of time reading the **papers** or watching the **news** on TV.
> 4 Every week make a list of all the **good things** that happened to you.
> 5 Try to use **positive language** when you speak to other people.

3 9

(script in Student's Book on *p.121*)
P = presenter, C = caller
P Our first caller this evening is Andy. Hi, Andy. What's your tip for being positive?
C1 Hello. Well, I think it's very important to live in the present and not in the past. Don't think about mistakes you made in the past. You can't change the past. The important thing is to think about how you can do things better now and in the future.
P Thank you, Andy. And now we have another caller. What's your name, please?
C2 Hi, my name's Julie. My tip is think positive thoughts, not negative ones. We all have negative thoughts sometimes, but when we start having them we need to stop and try to change them into positive ones. Like, if you have an exam tomorrow and you start thinking 'I'm sure I'll fail', then you'll fail the exam. So you need to change that negative thought to a positive thought. Just think to yourself 'I'll pass.' I do this and it usually works.
P Thank you, Julie. And our next caller is Martin. Hi, Martin.
C3 Hi. My tip is don't spend a lot of time reading the papers or watching the news on TV. It's always bad news and it just makes you feel depressed. Read a book or listen to your favourite music instead.
P Thanks, Martin. And our next caller is Miriam. Miriam?
C4 Hi.
P Hi, Miriam. What's your tip?
C4 My tip is every week make a list of all the good things that happened to you. Then keep the list with you, in your bag or in a pocket, and if you're feeling a bit sad or depressed, just take it out and read it. It'll make you feel better.
P Thanks, Miriam. And our last call is from Michael. Hi, Michael. We're listening.
C5 Hi. My tip is to try to use positive language when you speak to other people. You know, if your friend has a problem, don't say 'I'm sorry' or 'Oh poor you', say something positive like, 'Don't worry! Everything will be OK.' That way you'll make the other person think more positively about their problem.
P Thank you, Michael. Well that's all we've got time for. A big thank you to all our callers. Until next week then, goodbye.

d Play the audio again for Sts to write down extra information, e.g. a reason or an example. Get them to compare their answers in pairs and then play the audio again.

Check answers (see script 3.9).

Finally, in pairs, small groups or as an open class, answer the two questions. For the question *Which tips do you think are useful?* you could get Sts to vote for the best tip with a show of hands.

Extra support

- If there's time, you could get Sts to listen again with the scripts on *p.121*, so they can see exactly what they understood / didn't understand. Translate / explain any new words or phrases.

e Focus on the activity and on the seven questions.

Then go through the expressions in the **Responding to predictions** box with the class. Drill the pronunciation, making sure Sts do not over-stress the word *so* and are clear about the meaning. Point out that the word *so* in *I hope so*, etc. means *yes*, and that *maybe* and *perhaps* mean the same.

Sts take it in turns to ask and answer each question in pairs, giving reasons for their predictions. They should then decide if they are positive thinkers.

Finally, get some feedback, e.g. ask how many people in the class think they will pass their next English exam.

G *will / won't* (decisions, offers, promises)
V verb + *back*: *come back, call back*, etc.
P word stress: two-syllable verbs

6B I'll never forget you

Lesson plan

Sts continue their work on the uses of future *will*. In this lesson they learn that as well as for making predictions *will* can be used for making promises, offers, and decisions. The presentation context is three humorous cartoons. This is followed by a pronunciation focus on stress in two-syllable verbs, e.g. *promise, decide*. Sts then discuss a list of promises which are often not kept, e.g. *This won't hurt* and then read and listen to the true story of a couple whose promise to love each other was only kept after a chain of strange circumstances. The lesson ends with a vocabulary focus on using certain verbs with *back* (*come back, take back*, etc.), which Sts then put into practice with a final speaking activity.

STUDY LINK

- **Workbook** 6B
- **iTutor**
- **www.oup.com/elt/englishfile**

Extra photocopiable activities

- **Grammar** *will / won't* (promises, offers, decisions) *p.178*
- **Communicative** Guess my sentence *p.225* (instructions *p.202*)
- **Song** *Reach Out I'll Be There p.273* (instructions *p.264*)
- **www.oup.com/elt/teacher/englishfile**

Optional lead-in (books closed)

- Write the word PROMISES on the board and elicit its meaning. Teach / elicit that you can *make a promise* and then *keep* or *break a promise*.
- Ask Sts *What promises do people in love often make?* Try to elicit some and write them on the board, e.g. *I'll always love you / I'll never leave you / I'll marry you*, etc. Then ask Sts if they think people keep or break these promises.

1 GRAMMAR *will / won't* (decisions, offers, promises)

a Books open. Focus on the cartoons and the dialogues. Elicit / explain any new words or phrases (e.g. an ice cream sundae = a dessert with different kinds of ice cream, fruit, sauce, etc.). Now tell Sts to try to guess what the missing phrases are.

Extra support

- You could tell Sts that all the missing phrases begin with *I'll*.

Get feedback, and accept anything that makes sense in the context, but do not tell Sts if they are right yet.

b 3 10))) Play the audio for Sts to listen and complete the gaps.

Check answers.

1 I'll have a Diet Coke
2 I'll help you
3 I'll change

3 10)))
1 **A** That's two burgers, a double portion of chips, and two ice cream sundaes. Anything else?
B Yes, I'll have a Diet Coke, please.
2 **A** Do I want to go back to the previous version? Do I press Yes or No?
B I need to do my homework now. I'll help you when I finish.
3 **A** I'll change! I promise!
B Well, hurry up. I can't wait much longer.
A Just one more kiss...

c Focus on the instructions and make sure Sts understand *promise* and *offer*. Highlight that they should write the number of the cartoon.

Check answers.

promise to do something	3
decide to have something	1
offer to do something	2

d 3 11))) Tell Sts to go to **Grammar Bank 6B** on *p.136*. Focus on the example sentences and play the audio for Sts to listen and repeat. Encourage them to copy the rhythm. Then go through the rules with the class.

Additional grammar notes

- Sts shouldn't worry about being able to distinguish between an offer, a promise, or a decision. Depending on the context *I'll help you tomorrow* could be an offer, a promise, or a decision.
- In some languages the present tense is used for offers and decisions. Highlight that in English you say *I'll help you* NOT ~~*I help you.*~~
- *Shall I...?* is only used when an offer to do something is asked as a question, e.g. *Shall I make you a cup of coffee?* NOT ~~*Will I make you a cup of coffee?*~~
- In other future contexts *Will I...?* is used, e.g. *Will I need my passport?* NOT ~~*Shall I need my passport?*~~

! In the past *shall* was always used instead of *will* in the first person singular and plural. Today *will* is commonly used for all persons, and *shall* is mainly used in offers (*Shall I turn on the heating?*) and suggestions (*Shall we get a taxi?*).

Focus on the exercises for **6B** on *p.137*. Sts do the exercises individually or in pairs.

Check answers, getting Sts to read the full sentences.

a 1 I 2 H 3 A 4 B 5 C 6 D 7 F 8 E

b		
1 Shall I help	4 will ... pay	7 won't buy
2 won't tell	5 won't forget	8 'll get
3 'll call	6 Shall ... take	

Tell Sts to go back to the main lesson **6B**.

Extra support

- If you think Sts need more practice, you may want to give them the Grammar photocopiable activity at this point.

e Tell Sts to go to **Communication *I'll / Shall I? game*** on *p.102*. Put Sts into groups of three or four. Focus on the game board and explain the rules of the game.

S1 throws a coin: heads = move one square, tails = move two squares. When S1 lands on a square, he / she has to make a sentence with *will / won't* or *Shall I?* to fill the speech bubble. Sts 2, 3 (and 4) decide if the sentence is correct / appropriate. If it is, S1 stays on that square. If it is wrong / inappropriate, then S1 returns to the START square. S2 then throws the coin, etc.

Sts move around the board. If a student lands on a square where another student has already been, he / she must make a different sentence. The winner is the first student to reach the FINISH square and make a correct sentence.

The teacher is the referee in the case of any disagreement!

Some possible sentences
1 I'll have the steak.
2 I'll kill it. / I'll get it. / Shall I get it? / Shall I kill it?
3 I'll answer it. / Shall I answer it?
4 I'll go to the supermarket and buy some.
5 I'll help you. / Shall I help you? / I'll carry them. / Shall I carry them?
6 I won't be late. / I'll be home on time.
7 I'll have the green one.
8 I'll pick you up. / Shall I pick you up?
9 I'll turn on the light. / Shall I turn on the light?

Tell Sts to go back to the main lesson **6B**.

2 PRONUNCIATION word stress: two-syllable verbs

a Focus on the **Stress in two-syllable verbs** box and go through it with Sts.

Focus on the activity and give Sts, in pairs, time to put the verbs in the right column.

b 3 12 Play the audio for Sts to listen and check.

1st syllable: borrow, happen, offer, practise, promise, sunbathe
2nd syllable: agree, arrive, complain, decide, depend, forget, impress, invent, invite, prefer, receive, repair

First syllable
borrow, happen, offer, practise, promise, sunbathe
Second syllable
agree, arrive, complain, decide, depend, forget, impress, invent, invite, prefer, receive, repair

Play the audio again for Sts to practise saying the verbs, making sure they stress them clearly on either the first or second syllable.

Extra support

- Sts could use their dictionaries to help them check the pronunciation of the verbs in **a**. Remind them that the stressed syllable is the one which follows the stress mark ('), e.g. *borrow* /'bɒrəʊ/ and *forget* /fə'get/.

3 SPEAKING & LISTENING

a Focus on the two questions and seven sentences in the speech bubbles. Put Sts in pairs and get them to discuss each sentence.

Get some ideas from the class and elicit that what they have in common is that they are all promises that are often broken.

Possible answers for 1
I'll pay you back: When sb asks to borrow some money
This won't hurt: When a doctor or dentist is about to give you an injection
I'll come back and finish the job tomorrow: Builders and plumbers when they have started a job in your house
I'll text you when I get there: Teenagers just before they start a journey
I won't tell anyone: When sb tells you a secret
I'll do it later: When you ask sb to do sth they don't want to do at that moment, e.g. a teenager to tidy his / her room
We'll build new schools and hospitals: Politicians before an election

b Now tell Sts to look at the title of the article and do the question as an open-class activity.

c Tell Sts to read the article and answer questions 1–3.

Check answers.

1 Carmen was studying English and Steve was living there.
2 Because Carmen moved to France, and the long-distance relationship didn't work.
3 Because Carmen's mother didn't send it to her.

Extra support

- You might want to pre-teach some vocabulary, e.g. *get engaged*, *cool* (verb), *get in touch*, etc.

d 3 13 Focus on the task and tell Sts they are now going to find out what happened to Steve and Carmen. Now tell Sts to look at questions 1–5.

Play the audio for Sts to listen and answer the questions. Then play it again if necessary.

Get Sts to compare with a partner, and then check answers.

Extra support

- Read through the script and decide if you need to pre-teach any new lexis before Sts listen.

1 They gave it to Carmen's sister.
2 She rang Steve.
3 They arranged to meet in Paris.
4 They fell in love again.
5 They got married.

3 13

(script in Student's Book on *p.121*)
N = narrator, S = Steve, C = Carmen
N Earlier this year, ten years after Steve sent the letter, some builders were renovating the living room in Carmen's mother's house. When they took out the fireplace, they found Steve's letter, and gave it to Carmen's sister, and she sent the letter to Carmen in Paris. Carmen was now 42, and she was still single.
C When I got the letter, I didn't call Steve straight away because I was so nervous. I kept picking up the phone and putting it down again. I nearly didn't phone him at all. But I knew that I had to make the call.

N Carmen finally made the call and Steve answered the phone. He was also now 42 and also single.
S I couldn't believe it when she phoned. I've just moved house, but luckily I kept my old phone number.
N Steve and Carmen arranged to meet in Paris a few days later.
S When we met, it was like a film. We ran across the airport and into each other's arms. Within 30 seconds of seeing each other again we were kissing. We fell in love all over again.
N Last week the couple got married, 17 years after they first met.
C I never got married in all those years, but now I have married the man I always loved.
N So Steve and Carmen are together at last. But will they keep their promises?

Extra support

- If there's time, you could get Sts to listen again with the script on *p.121*, so they can see exactly what they understood / didn't understand. Translate / explain any new words or phrases.

4 VOCABULARY verb + *back*

a Here Sts learn / revise some common verbs with *back*, e.g. *come back*, *pay (somebody) back*. Focus on the question and elicit answers.

go = to move or travel from one place to another, e.g. go to the office
go back = to return to a place, e.g. go back to work (after lunch)

b Focus on the phrases in the list and highlight that *back* changes the meaning of the verb. Verb + *back* = to repeat an action or to return. Demonstrate *give back* by giving something to a student and then saying *Give it back, please*.

Give Sts a couple of minutes to read the dialogues and complete them with a phrase from the list.

c 3 14 Play the audio for Sts to listen and check.

Check answers.

1 take it back	4 Give it back
2 call you back	5 pay me back
3 come back	6 send it back

3 14
1 A The shirt you bought me is too small.
B Don't worry. I'll **take it back** to the shop and change it. I still have the receipt.
2 A Hi, Jack. It's me, Karen.
B I can't talk now, I'm driving – I'll **call you back** in 15 minutes.
3 A Could I see the manager?
B She's at lunch now. Could you **come back** in about half an hour?
4 A That's my pen you're using! **Give it back**!
B No, it's not. It's mine.
5 A Can you lend me 50 euros, Nick?
B It depends. When can you **pay me back**?
6 A I bought this jacket on the internet, but it's too big.
B Can't you **send it back**?

! You may want to point out that the object pronoun (*it*, *them*, etc.) goes between the verb and *back*. Word order with these kinds of verbs + prepositions / adverbs (phrasal verbs) is dealt with in detail in **11B**.

Get Sts to practise the dialogues in pairs.

d Focus on the task and make sure that Sts understand the questions. Put Sts into groups of three or four and get them to discuss 1–6.

Monitor and help while Sts are talking.

Get some feedback from the class.

Extra support

- Demonstrate the activity by answering a couple of questions yourself.

5 3 15 SONG *Reach Out I'll Be There* ♫

This song was originally made famous by the American quartet The Four Tops in 1966.

For copyright reasons this is a cover version. If you want to do this song in class, use the photocopiable activity on *p.273*.

3 15
Reach out I'll Be There

Now if you feel that you can't go on
Because all of your hope is gone
And your life is filled with much confusion
Until happiness is just an illusion
And your world around is tumbling down, darling
Reach out! Hang on, girl; reach on out for me
Reach out! Reach out, for me.

Chorus
I'll be there with a love that will shelter you
I'll be there with a love that will see you through

When you feel lost and about to give up
'Cause your best just ain't good enough
and you feel the world has grown cold
and you're drifting out all on your own
And you need a hand to hold, darling
Reach out! Hang on, girl; reach out for me
Reach out! Reach out, for me.

Chorus
I'll be there to love and comfort you
And I'll be there, to cherish and care for you
(I'll be there to always see you through)
(I'll be there to to love and comfort you)

I can tell the way you hang your head
You're without love now, now you're afraid
And through your tears you look around
But there's no peace of mind to be found
I know what you're thinking, you're alone now, no love of your own, but darling
Reach out! Come on, girl; reach out for me
Reach out! Reach out,

Just look over your shoulder
I'll be there to give you all the love you need.
And I'll be there, you can always depend on me.

G review of verb forms: present, past, and future
V adjectives + prepositions: *frightened of, good for*, etc.
P the letters *ow*

6C The meaning of dreaming

Lesson plan

The final lesson in File 6 provides a consolidation of the verb forms studied in this first half of the book. Present, past, and future are revised through the context of interpreting dreams. Although the lesson provides a light-hearted look at dreams, the symbols and their interpretations have been taken from serious sources. Sts begin by listening to a psychoanalyst interpreting a patient's dream. After focussing on and revising different forms which are used in the dialogue, they get the chance to interpret each other's dreams in a roleplay activity. In Pronunciation Sts look at the two possible pronunciations of the letters *ow*, and the lesson ends with a vocabulary focus on common verb + preposition combinations, e.g. *dream about*, *speak to*, etc.

STUDY LINK

- **Workbook** 6C
- **iTutor**
- **iChecker**
- **www.oup.com/elt/englishfile**

Extra photocopiable activities

- **Grammar** Review of tenses: present, past, and future *p.179*
- **Communicative** Talk about it *p.226* (instructions *p.203*)
- **www.oup.com/elt/teacher/englishfile**

Optional lead-in (books closed)

- Ask Sts if they dreamt last night. If they say *Yes*, elicit from three or four what they dreamt about (just the subject not the details), e.g. I dreamt I was falling / about my exams. Write the dreams on the board and quickly ask the class if they know what the dreams mean.

1 LISTENING & READING

a Books open. Do this in pairs or as an open-class activity.

b 3 16))) Focus on the instructions. Check Sts know the meaning of *psychoanalyst* and *patient*. Model and drill their pronunciation /saɪkəʊ'ænəlɪst/ and /'peɪʃnt/.

Focus on the pictures and ask Sts what they can see. Elicit that the pictures show an owl, champagne, a man playing the violin, feet, people at a party, and flowers.

Play the audio and get Sts to number the pictures 1–6 in the correct order.

Get Sts to compare with a partner, and then check answers.

Extra support

- Read through the scripts and decide if you need to pre-teach any new lexis before Sts listen.

party	1	flowers	3	owl	5
champagne	2	violin player	4	feet	6

3 16)))
Dr = Dr Allen, P = patient
Dr So, tell me, what did you dream about?
P I was at a party. There were a lot of people.
Dr What were they doing?
P They were drinking and talking.
Dr Were you drinking?
P Yes, I was drinking champagne.
Dr And then what happened?
P Then, suddenly I was in a garden. There were a lot of flowers...
Dr Flowers, yes... What kind of flowers?
P I couldn't really see – it was dark. And I could hear music – somebody was playing the violin.
Dr The violin? Go on.
P And then I saw an owl, a big owl in a tree...
Dr How did you feel? Were you frightened of it?
P No, not frightened really, no, but I remember I felt very cold. Especially my feet – they were freezing. And then I woke up.
Dr Your feet? Mmm, very interesting, very interesting indeed. Were you wearing any shoes?
P No, no, I wasn't.
Dr Tell me. Have you ever had this dream before?
P No, never. So, what does it mean, Doctor?

c Focus on the dialogue, and give Sts a few minutes to read it.

Play the audio again for Sts to complete the gaps. You may need to pause the audio to give Sts time to write the missing words.

Check answers.

1 doing	6 playing	11 wearing
2 talking	7 saw	12 had
3 drinking	8 feel	13 mean
4 were	9 remember	
5 couldn't	10 woke up	

Extra challenge

- Give Sts a minute to guess some of the missing words before they listen. Don't tell them whether their guesses are right or wrong.

d Tell Sts that they are going to try to understand the man's dream. In pairs, they must match the things in his dream in the **You dream...** column with interpretations 1–5 in **This means...**

e 3 17))) Focus on the task and play the audio for Sts to check their answers to **d**.

Check answers.

that you are at a party 1
that you are drinking champagne 5
about flowers 2
that somebody is playing the violin 3
about an owl 4

3 17

(script in Student's Book on *pp.121–122*)
P So what does it mean, Doctor?
Dr Well, first the party. A party is a group of people. This means that you're going to meet a lot of people. I think you're going to be very busy.
P At work?
Dr Yes, at work... You work in an office, I think?
P Yes, that's right.
Dr I think the party means you are going to have a lot of meetings.
P What about the champagne?
Dr Let me look at my notes again. Ah yes, you were drinking champagne. Champagne means a celebration. It's a symbol of success. So we have a meeting or meetings and then a celebration. Maybe in the future you'll have a meeting with your boss, about a possible promotion?
P Well, it's possible. I hope so... What about the garden and the flowers? Do they mean anything?
Dr Yes. Flowers are a positive symbol. So, the flowers mean that you are feeling positive about the future. So perhaps you already knew about this possible promotion?
P No, I didn't. But it's true, I am very happy at work and I feel very positive about my future. That's not where my problems are. My problems are with my love life. Does my dream tell you anything about that?
Dr Mm, yes it does. You're single, aren't you?
P Yes, well, divorced.
Dr Because the violin music tells me you want some romance in your life – you're looking for a partner, perhaps?
P Yes, yes, I am. In fact, I met a woman last month – I really like her... I think I'm in love with her. I'm meeting her tonight.
Dr In your dream you saw an owl in a tree?
P Yes, an owl... a big owl.
Dr The owl represents an older person. I think you'll need to ask this older person for help. Maybe this 'older person' is me? Maybe you need my help?
P Well, yes, what I really want to know is does this person, this woman... love me?

Extra support

- Play the audio again, pausing after each bit of interpretation, and elicit as much information as possible from the class.

f **3 18** Elicit a few ideas from Sts about the meaning of picture 6 (the feet). You could write some of the ideas on the board.

Now play the audio for Sts to listen.

Check the answer.

The woman doesn't love him.

3 18

(script in Student's Book on *p.122*)
P Well, yes, what I really want to know is does this person, this woman... love me?
Dr You remember the end of your dream? You were feeling cold?
P Yes, my feet were very cold.
Dr Well... I think perhaps you already know the answer to your question.
P You mean she doesn't love me.
Dr No, I don't think so. I think you will need to find another woman. I'm sorry. Perhaps you can find someone on the internet. I have heard of a very good website...

Extra support

- If there's time, you could get Sts to listen again to both parts with the scripts on *pp.121–122*, so they can see exactly what they understood / didn't understand. Translate / explain any new words or phrases.

2 GRAMMAR review of verb forms

a Look at the sentences and explain that they come from the listening, and are examples of the different tenses and forms Sts have studied so far.

Elicit which one is in the present perfect (8). Then give Sts, in pairs, time to determine what time the other sentences refer to.

Check answers.

1 P	3 P	5 F	7 F
2 F	4 PR	6 PR	8 PP

b **3 19** Tell Sts to go to **Grammar Bank 6C** on *p.136*. Focus on the example sentences and play the audio for Sts to listen and repeat. Encourage them to copy the rhythm. Then go through the rules with the class.

Additional grammar notes

- Sts should by now be reasonably confident with the present simple and continuous, the past simple, and *be going to*. With the new forms and tenses, how quickly they assimilate them will depend to a large extent on whether they have a similar form in their L1. Don't overcorrect mistakes, but encourage Sts to use them where appropriate and to get the form right.

Focus on the exercises for **6C** on *p.137*. Sts do the exercises individually or in pairs.

Check answers, getting Sts to read the full sentences.

a	1 Do	6 Was
	2 Did	7 didn't
	3 will	8 Have
	4 Does	9 Has
	5 are	
b	1 're having	6 was walking
	2 had	7 stopped
	3 want	8 saw
	4 Shall ... buy	9 're going to be / are
	5 have ... been	10 've already ordered

Tell Sts to go back to the main lesson **6C**.

Extra support

- If you think Sts need more practice, you may want to give them the Grammar photocopiable activity at this point.

3 SPEAKING

a Put Sts in pairs, **A** and **B**. Tell Sts to go to **Communication *Dreams***, **A** on *p.103*, **B** on *p.108*.

Go through the instructions with them carefully and make sure Sts know what they have to do.

Go through the **Useful language** box with the class.

Give them time to plan what happened in their dream.

A starts by telling **B** about his / her dream using the pictures as a guide. **B** listens and numbers the subjects in the box in the order **A** speaks about them. **B** then interprets **A**'s dream in the order in which the things were mentioned using the notes in the box.

Then they swap roles.

Monitor and help while Sts do the activity. Don't interrupt and correct (unless communication breaks down altogether), but make notes of any common errors and go through these on the board afterwards.

Tell Sts to go back to the main lesson **6C**.

b Focus on the revision questionnaire. Put Sts in pairs and get them to choose two questions from each group to ask their partner.

Give Sts time to interview each other, making sure they ask for more information.

Monitor and help while Sts are talking.

Get some feedback from the class.

4 PRONUNCIATION the letters *ow*

Pronunciation notes

- Like all combinations of letters which can be pronounced in different ways, *ow* is a problem for Sts. They should be encouraged to check pronunciation of new words which contain *ow*, and to learn by heart the pronunciation of common words with these letters.

a **3 20** Focus on the **Pronunciation of *ow*** box and go through it with the class.

Play the audio for Sts just to listen to the picture sounds and words.

3 20
See Student's Book on *p.49*

Then play it again for them to listen and repeat.

b Tell Sts to look at the words in the list and to put them in the right column depending on the sound of the letters *ow*. Remind Sts that this exercise is easier if they say the words aloud to themselves. Before Sts start, make sure they know the meaning of the words.

Get Sts to compare with a partner.

c **3 21** Play the audio for Sts to listen and check.

Check answers.

3 21

owl	brown, crowded, down, how, now, shower, towel, town
phone	blow, borrow, know, low, show, snow, throw

Play the audio again, pausing after each word for Sts to repeat.

d Put Sts in pairs and get them to practise saying the sentences.

Get some feedback from various Sts.

Extra support

- Before putting Sts in pairs, model the sentences for the class.

5 VOCABULARY adjectives + prepositions

a Focus on the **Adjectives + prepositions** box and go through it with the class.

Then focus on questions 1–10, and get Sts to complete the gaps with a preposition.

Get them to compare with a partner, and then check answers.

1 of	3 of	5 at	7 with, about	9 to
2 for	4 for	6 at	8 from	10 in

Extra support

- Write the possible prepositions on the board for Sts to choose from.

b Put Sts in pairs and get them to ask and answer the ten questions in **a**. Remind Sts to give extra details.

Monitor and help while Sts are talking.

Get some feedback from various pairs.

5 & 6 Revise and Check

For instructions on how to use these pages see *p.38*.

STUDY LINK
- **iTutor**

Test and Assessment CD-ROM
- **Quick Test 6**
- **File 6 Test**
- **Progress Test Files 1–6**

GRAMMAR

1 a 2 c 3 a 4 b 5 c 6 c 7 b 8 a 9 b 10 b 11 a 12 c 13 a 14 b 15 b

VOCABULARY

a 1 waste 2 spend 3 lend 4 coming back 5 teaching

b 1 sell 2 pull 3 forget 4 fail 5 learn

c 1 crowded 2 safe 3 noisy 4 south 5 museum 6 palace 7 mosque 8 bones 9 brain 10 skin

d 1 on 2 in 3 of 4 at 5 for

PRONUNCIATION

a 1 much 2 eat 3 won't 4 snow 5 receive

b 1 im<u>pa</u>tient 2 <u>in</u>teresting 3 in<u>vent</u> 4 <u>prac</u>tise 5 de<u>cide</u>

CAN YOU UNDERSTAND THIS TEXT?

a No, he doesn't.

b 1 F 2 T 3 T 4 T 5 F 6 T 7 F 8 F

CAN YOU UNDERSTAND THESE PEOPLE?

3 22

1 c 2 b 3 c 4 b 5 a

3 22

1
I = interviewer, Ia = Ian
I Have you got more free time than three years ago? Why?
Ia Yes, because I had a part-time job then, now I'm fully retired.

2
I = interviewer, Y = Yvonne
I What's the most beautiful city you have ever been to?
Y I think the most beautiful city I've been to is Rome in Italy.
I Why?
Y Because I think it has everything – beautiful buildings, lots of culture, a beach, mountains, and there's lots to see and do.

3
I = interviewer, B = Ben
I Do you think you have a healthy diet?
B I think I have quite a healthy diet, yes.
I Why?
B Well, I try to eat fruit and vegetables and I try not to eat too much sugar or fat.

4
I = interviewer, Jo = Joanna
I Are you an optimist or a pessimist?
Jo I don't know. My friends would probably say that I'm a pessimist, but I would like to think that I'm an optimist.

5
I = interviewer, A = Anya
I Do you often dream about the same thing? What?
A I have recurring dreams about being chased usually.
I Do you often have bad dreams?
A Depending on what's going on in my life, if I'm having a tough time at work, then I'll usually dream about bad things happening at work.

G uses of the infinitive with *to*
V verbs + infinitive: *try to, forget to*, etc.
P weak form of *to*, linking

7A How to...

Lesson plan

The context of this lesson is life skills and the material is based on information on a website called *wikiHow*, which gives help and advice (sent in by readers) on how to do thousands of different things. The lesson begins with Sts reading some humorous but useful advice on what to do and say (and not do and say) when you meet your boyfriend / girlfriend / partner's parents for the first time. They then listen to Nigel meeting his girlfriend's parents to see how he gets on. In Grammar, Sts learn when to use the infinitive form with *to* (after certain verbs, after adjectives, etc.). In Vocabulary, the focus is on some high frequency verbs which are followed by the infinitive form, and in Pronunciation Sts practise the weak form of *to* in phrases using an infinitive and linking. Finally, in Speaking Sts read and re-tell two more *How to...* texts (surviving a first date and surviving at a party where you don't know anybody) and then in Writing they write some tips of their own on a different subject.

STUDY LINK
- **Workbook** 7A
- **iTutor**
- **www.oup.com/elt/englishfile**

Extra photocopiable activities

- **Grammar** Uses of the infinitive with *to p.180*
- **Communicative** I'm going to tell you about... *p.227* (instructions *p.203*)
- **www.oup.com/elt/teacher/englishfile**

Optional lead-in (books closed)

- Write YOU'RE GOING TO MEET YOUR GIRLFRIEND / BOYFRIEND'S PARENTS FOR THE FIRST TIME TONIGHT on the board in big letters. Then ask Sts *What is it important to do* (*or not to do*)? and elicit ideas, e.g. *Don't be late, Dress well*, etc. Write Sts' ideas on the board. Continue until you have elicited five or six ideas.

1 READING & LISTENING

a Books open. Focus on the poster and ask Sts if they have seen the film. Elicit what it is about (meeting your girlfriend's parents for the first time). If some Sts have seen it, ask them what they thought of it.

b (If you did the **Optional lead-in**, go straight to **c**.) Put Sts in pairs and tell them to think of two pieces of advice they would give somebody who was going to meet their partner's parents for the first time.

Get some feedback from various pairs and write it on the board.

c Now tell Sts they are going to read an article from the website *wikiHow*. Ask if Sts have heard of it or used it. Explain that it is a website that anyone can add information to and it offers help and advice on how to do thousands of different things (anything from how to delete your Facebook account to how to make somebody fall in love with you). The first time Sts read they should just see if their advice is included in the article. Tell them not to worry about the gaps.

Check answers.

Extra support

- You could pre-teach some vocabulary, e.g. *punctual, ambition, controversial, tactic*, etc. or you may want to deal with it in context after Sts have read the text.

d Tell Sts to read the article again and this time to complete the gaps with a verb from the list.

Get Sts to compare with a partner, and then check answers.

1 to have	6 to answer, to know	9 to say
2 to make	7 to do, to show	
3 not to be	8 not to talk	

e 3 23))) Tell Sts they are now going to listen to Nigel meeting his girlfriend's parents for the first time. They must listen to see if the meeting starts well or not, and how it ends.

Play the audio once the whole way through.

Get Sts to compare with a partner, and then check answers.

Extra support

- Read through the script and decide if you need to pre-teach any new lexis before Sts listen.

The meeting starts badly, but ends well.

3 23)))
(script in Student's Book on *p.122*)
N = Nigel, S = Suzy, F = father, M = mother
N Hi, Suze. Sorry I'm a bit late. I was watching the match.
S Come on in then. Mum, this is Nigel. Nigel, this is my mum.
N Oh... hello.
M Nice to meet you, Nigel.
S And this is my dad.
F Hello, Nigel.
N Hello.
F Come on into the living room.
***
F Would you like a drink, Nigel? Orange juice, beer?
N Oh thanks, John. I'll have a beer, please.
***
M You are a vegetarian, aren't you, Nigel?
N Yes, I am. Personally, I think eating animals is totally wrong.
M Well, this is vegetable lasagne. I hope you like it. Suzy's Dad made it.
***

F Any more lasagne, Nigel?
N Oh, er, no thanks. I'm not very hungry.
S The lasagne is delicious, Dad.
M Yes, it is.
F Thank you.
***
S I'll do the washing-up, Mum.
F No, I'll do it.
N Er, where's the bathroom?
***
N Did you watch the match this evening, John? Chelsea and Arsenal. It was fantastic!
F No, I didn't watch it. I don't like football at all. In fact, I hate it.
N Oh.
M So what are you going to do when you finish university, Nigel?
N Er, I don't know.
F What are you studying at university?
N Sociology.
F Why did you choose sociology?
N Because I thought it was easy.
M Is it interesting?
N It's OK. Er... What was Suzy like as a little girl, Marion? Do you have any photos of her?
M Photos of Suzy? Yes, we have thousands of photos. She was a lovely little girl, wasn't she, John?
F Yes, she was. A beautiful little girl.
N Can I see some?
S Oh no, please.
M John, can you bring the photo albums? ... Look and this is one when she was three years old.
F And this is when we went to Disneyland. That's Suzy with Mickey and Minnie Mouse.
N Ah! She was *so* sweet.
F Would you like another beer, Nigel?
N Yes, please, John.

f Tell Sts to listen again and this time to answer the two questions. Give Sts a few minutes to see what they can remember, then play the audio again if necessary.

Get Sts to compare with a partner, and then check answers.

1 He arrives late; he calls them by their first names he gives his opinion too strongly about meat eaters; he doesn't say anything positive about the food; he doesn't offer to help with the washing-up; he doesn't find out before meeting him if the father likes football; he wasn't very good at answering questions about himself; his answers are very short, so the conversation dies.
2 He asks to see photos of Suzy as a child and he says she looked 'sweet'.

Extra support

- If there's time, you could get Sts to listen again with the script on *p.122*, so they can see exactly what they understood / didn't understand. Translate / explain any new words or phrases.

g Do this as an open-class activity.

2 GRAMMAR uses of the infinitive with *to*

a Tell Sts to focus on sentences a–d from the article and rules 1–4. They must match a sentence with a rule.

Get Sts to compare with a partner, and then check answers.

a 2 b 3 c 4 d 1

b Tell Sts to look back at gaps 2–8 in the article and to decide which rule 1–4 they follow.

Get Sts to compare with a partner, and then check answers.

2 to make (Rule 3)
3 not to be (Rule 2)
6 to answer (Rule 2), to know (Rule 1)
7 to do (Rule 1)
8 not to talk (Rule 1)

c **3 24**))) Tell Sts to go to **Grammar Bank 7A** on *p.138*. Focus on the example sentences and play the audio for Sts to listen and repeat. Encourage them to copy the rhythm. Then go through the rules with the class.

Additional grammar notes

- The infinitive has two forms in English:
  1 ***work*** is the form which is given in a dictionary. Sts have seen this used in present simple questions and negatives, e.g. *Do you work?*, *I didn't work*, and after the modal verb *can*.
  2 ***to work*** Sts should already be familiar with the infinitive with *to* used after some verbs such as *want* and *would like*, e.g. *I want to come with you*.

! The infinitive of purpose is only used to express a [+] reason. To express a [−] reason we use *in order not to* or *so as not to*, e.g. *We took a taxi so as not to be late* NOT ~~*We took a taxi not to be late*~~. At this level it is better not to point this out unless it comes up.

Focus on exercises **7A** on *p.139*. Sts do the exercises individually or in pairs.

Check answers, getting Sts to read the full sentences.

a 1 E 2 D 3 F 4 A 5 C

b 1 to meet 2 to do 3 to go 4 not to make 5 to learn 6 not to drive 7 to look for

Extra idea

- Put Sts into small groups. Get them to try to think of at least two answers to each of the questions below, using *to* + infinitive. Why do people...?
  – go to parties – go on holidays – go to a gym
  – get married – learn English

Tell Sts to go back to the main lesson **7A**.

Extra support

- If you think Sts need more practice, you may want to give them the Grammar photocopiable activity at this point.

3 VOCABULARY verbs + infinitive

a Here Sts focus on the verbs before the infinitives. Tell Sts not to look at the article and to complete the gaps in 1–4.

Check answers.

1 need 2 want 3 Offer 4 try

b Tell Sts to go to **Vocabulary Bank *Verb forms*** on *p.158*. Focus on part **1 Verbs + infinitive**.

Focus on **a** and get Sts to complete the ***to* + verb** column with the verbs from the list.

3 25 Now do **b**. Play the audio for Sts to check their answers. Give further practice of any words your Sts find difficult to pronounce.

> **3 25**
> **Verbs + infinitive**
> 1 We've decided **to go** to France for our holiday.
> 2 Don't forget **to turn off** all the lights.
> 3 We hope **to see** you again soon.
> 4 I'm learning **to drive**. My test's next month.
> 5 I need **to go** to the supermarket. We don't have any milk.
> 6 He offered **to help** me with my CV.
> 7 They're planning **to get married** soon.
> 8 He pretended **to be** ill, but he wasn't really.
> 9 He's promised **to pay** me back when he gets a job.
> 10 Remember **to bring** your dictionaries to class tomorrow.
> 11 It was very cloudy and it started **to rain**.
> 12 I'm trying **to find** a job, but it's very hard.
> 13 I want **to catch** the six o'clock train.
> 14 I'd like **to buy** a new car next month.

Now do **c** and tell Sts, in pairs, to cover the ***to* + verb** column. They must try to remember and say the full sentence.

Tell Sts to go back to the main lesson **7A**.

Extra support

- If you think Sts need more practice, you may want to give them the Vocabulary photocopiable activity at this point.

4 PRONUNCIATION & SPEAKING

weak form of *to*, linking

> **Pronunciation notes**
>
> **Weak form of *to***
>
> - The word *to* is usually unstressed in a sentence (unless it comes at the end of a question, e.g. *Who are you talking to?*) and is pronounced as a weak form /tə/, e.g. *I never speak to* /tə/ *Jane*.
> - It's important for Sts to be aware of the way two consonant sounds are linked (see information box in the Student's Book) as this will help them to understand spoken language when this linking occurs. It will also help them to speak in a more natural way.

a **3 26** Tell Sts to listen to the two sentences and especially to how the word *to* is pronounced.

Play the audio once for Sts just to listen and elicit that *to* isn't stressed and is pronounced /tə/.

> **3 26**
> See sentences in Student's Book on *p.53*

b **3 27** Focus on the **Linking words with the same consonant sound** box and go through it with Sts.

Now tell them they are going to hear six sentences and they must write them down. Play the audio, pausing after each sentence to give Sts time to write. Play again if necessary.

Get Sts to compare with a partner, and then check answers.

> **3 27**
> 1 He promised to help me.
> 2 Don't forget to turn off the lights.
> 3 It's difficult to say.
> 4 I don't know what to do.
> 5 Do you want to come with me?
> 6 It's important not to be late.

In pairs, Sts practise saying the sentences.

c This speaking activity reinforces the pronunciation practised in **b**. Quickly go through the questions and make sure Sts understand them.

Put Sts in pairs, **A** and **B**. **A** asks the first six questions to **B**, who answers giving as much information as possible. Then **B** asks the next six questions to **A**.

Get feedback from the class.

Extra support

- Get Sts to choose questions to ask you first. Encourage them to ask follow-up questions for more information. You could write a few question words, e.g. *Why? When?*, etc. on the board to remind them.

d Put Sts in pairs, **A** and **B**. Tell Sts to go to **Communication *How to...***, **A** on *p.103*, **B** on *p.107*.

Go through the instructions with them carefully, and make sure Sts know what they have to do.

A and **B** read their ***How to...*** texts. Give them time to try to memorize the information and deal with any vocabulary problems. They both close their books.

A then tells **B** the five tips. Encourage **B** to note down the main point of each tip. Then **A** and **B** decide which they think is the most important tip.

B now tells **A** the five tips in his / her text (and **A** notes down the main points) and they again decide which is the most important one.

When they have finished, get feedback from some pairs about which tip they thought was the most important.

Tell Sts to go back to the main lesson **7A**.

5 WRITING

In pairs, Sts now write their ***How to...*** article. First, they must choose one of the two titles and then they must write at least four tips.

When they have finished, make sure they check their work for mistakes.

Then they could swap articles with another pair.

G uses of the gerund (verb + *-ing*)
V verbs + gerund: *like, can't stand*, etc.
P the letter *i*

7B Being happy

Lesson plan

A magazine article in which different journalists from the same magazine talk about their idea of happiness provides the context for Sts to learn three common uses of the verb + -ing form (often called the gerund).

The lesson begins with grammar and the magazine article presents examples of the gerund. The vocabulary focus is on common verbs which are followed by the gerund. In Pronunciation Sts look at the two pronunciations of the letter *i* and learn some spelling and pronunciation rules. The speaking and listening activity focusses on singing and Sts listen to an interview with the director of a singing school and a woman who did a singing course there. In Writing Sts write their own sentences about their idea of happiness.

STUDY LINK
- Workbook 7B
- iTutor
- www.oup.com/elt/englishfile

Extra photocopiable activities

- **Grammar** Infinitive with *to* or verb + *-ing p.181*
- **Communicative** Find someone who... *p.228* (instructions *p.203*)
- **Vocabulary** Verb forms, infinitive or gerund *p.257* (instructions *p.246*)
- **Song** *Don't Stop Me Now p.274* (instructions *p.265*)
- **www.oup.com/elt/teacher/englishfile**

Optional lead-in (books closed)

- Write the following words on the board HAPPY, SAD, DARK, WEAK. Ask Sts what part of speech they are, and elicit that they are adjectives. Then tell Sts that by adding four letters to the end of these adjectives, you make them into nouns, and see if anyone comes up with *-ness*. Write the nouns on the board (*happiness, sadness*, etc.), and model and drill pronunciation.
- You could also teach a few more *-ness* nouns from other adjectives Sts know, e.g. *kindness, laziness, tidiness*, etc.

1 GRAMMAR uses of the gerund

a Books open. Put Sts in pairs and get them to discuss the questions. You could answer the questions yourself first.

Get some feedback from the class.

b Focus on the article and photos. Tell Sts to read the text once and then write the letter of the photos in paragraphs 1–6.

You may want to pre-teach some vocabulary, e.g. *leftovers, scales, a suitcase, baggage reclaim, a bargain*, etc. or you may prefer to deal with these in context after Sts have read the text.

Check answers.

1 E	3 C	5 F
2 D	4 B	6 A

c Sts read the article again and tick the people that they agree with and cross any they don't agree with.

Get Sts to compare their choices with a partner, and then get feedback from the whole class to find out which one(s) are the most popular / unpopular.

d Tell Sts to focus on the highlighted phrases in paragraph 1 and to try and find the three examples for 1–3.

Check answers.

1 using leftovers
2 making something
3 making soup

Extra challenge

- Try to elicit from Sts these spelling rules:
  1 Add *-ing* to the infinitive form, e.g. *work – working*.
  2 With monosyllabic verbs (ending in one vowel and one consonant) you double the final consonant and add *-ing*, e.g. *sit – sitting*, etc.
  3 With verbs which end in *e*, cut the *e* and add *-ing* (except *be*), e.g. *make – making*, etc.

e 3 28))) Tell Sts to go to **Grammar Bank 7B** on *p.138*. Focus on the example sentences and play the audio for Sts to listen and repeat. Encourage them to copy the rhythm. Then go through the rules with the class.

Additional grammar notes

- It is very likely that in your Sts' L1 an infinitive form will be used in places where English uses an *-ing* form.

! In British English it is much more common to use a gerund after *like, love*, and *hate* especially when you are speaking about general likes and dislikes. However, an infinitive can often be used without any real difference in meaning.

Spelling rules

- You may want to point out that verbs which are stressed on the last syllable also double the final consonant, e.g. *begin – beginning, prefer – preferring*.

! *travel – travelling* is an exception: it is stressed on the first syllable, but doubles the final consonant.

Gerund or infinitive?

- Sts are asked to discriminate between the gerund and infinitive in the second exercise in the Grammar Bank. Before doing it you could get Sts to quickly look again at the rules for both (see **Grammar Banks 5A** and **5B** *p.134*).

! Remind Sts that *like* is usually followed by the gerund, e.g. *I like travelling*, but *would like* is followed by the infinitive, e.g. *I would like to travel around the world.*

Focus on the exercises for **7B** on *p.139*. Sts do the exercises individually or in pairs.

Check answers, getting Sts to read the full sentences.

a	1	swimming	5	texting
	2	practising	6	being
	3	remembering	7	Travelling
	4	Teaching	8	studying
b	1	Doing	5	to drive
	2	not to have	6	raining
	3	to park	7	cooking, doing
	4	reading	8	getting up

Tell Sts to go back to the main lesson **7B**.

Extra support

- If you think Sts need more practice, you may want to give them the Grammar photocopiable activity at this point.

f Tell Sts they are going to write a paragraph similar to the ones in **1b**. Write HAPPINESS IS... on the board and tell Sts they should write between 10 and 25 words about their idea of happiness.

g When Sts have finished writing, put them in small groups of four. Tell Sts to exchange their pieces of writing in their groups and read the paragraphs written by their groupmates. When they have finished reading all of them, they should give their opinion.

Get some feedback from various groups.

2 VOCABULARY & SPEAKING verbs + gerund

a Here Sts learn some other common verbs which take the gerund form. Tell Sts to go to **Vocabulary Bank *Verb forms*** on *p.158* and look at part **2 Verbs + gerund (verb + *-ing*)**.

Focus on **a** and get Sts to complete the **gerund** column with the verbs from the list.

3 29 Now do **b**. Play the audio for Sts to check answers. Give further practice of any words your Sts find difficult to pronounce.

3 29

Verbs + gerund

1 I enjoy **reading** in bed.
2 Have you finished **tidying** your room?
3 I want to go on **working** until I'm 60.
4 I hate **being** late when I'm meeting someone.
5 I like **having** breakfast in a café.
6 I love **waking up** on a sunny morning.
7 I don't mind **doing** the ironing. It's quite relaxing.
8 She spends hours **talking** on the phone.
9 It started **raining** at 5.30 in the morning.
10 Please stop **making** such a noise. I can't think.
11 I don't feel like **cooking** today. Let's go out for lunch.

Remind Sts that *I don't mind (doing something)* = although I don't enjoy it, it isn't a problem for me. Point out the asterisk by *start* and tell Sts that it can be used with a gerund or infinitive with no difference in meaning, e.g. *It started raining* or *It started to rain*.

Now do **c** and tell Sts, in pairs, to cover the **gerund** column. They must try and remember the full sentences.

Tell Sts to go back to the main lesson **7B**.

Extra support

- If you think Sts need more practice, you may want to give them the Vocabulary photocopiable activity at this point.

b Here Sts get some oral practice of the new vocabulary. Focus on the task. Highlight that Sts only have to choose five things they want to talk about from the ten possibilities. Give them a minute to choose their five things.

! Highlight that *dream of* is used for daydreaming, i.e. something we would love to do; *dream about* is used for dreaming while actually asleep, e.g. *I dreamt about you last night.*

Extra support

- Sts could write down their answers to help prepare them for the speaking.

c Demonstrate the activity by choosing a few things from the list and talking about them yourself. Encourage the class to ask you for more information, e.g. *Why (not)?*

In pairs, **A** tells **B** his / her five things and **B** asks for more information.

When you think the **A**s have finished, get them to swap roles.

Monitor and help while Sts are talking. Correct Sts if they use an infinitive instead of an *-ing* form.

Get some feedback from the class.

Extra idea

- Get fast finishers to choose more topics to talk about.

3 PRONUNCIATION the letter *i*

Pronunciation notes

- There are several clear spelling / pronunciation rules for words with the letter *i*, but there are a few common exceptions like *live* (v), which trip Sts up sometimes. By this time Sts will instinctively pronounce most of these words correctly.

a Focus on the activity and elicit the two sounds and words.

Give Sts two minutes to put the words in the right column.

Get Sts to compare with a partner.

b 3 30 Play the audio for Sts to listen and check.

Check answers.

> 3 30
> fish /ɪ/ give, miss, skin, slim, thin, which, win, with
> bike /aɪ/ find, high, hire, kind, like, mind, night, right, time

Play the audio again for Sts to listen and repeat. Give more practice if these sounds are a problem for your Sts.

Then give Sts some time, in pairs, to work out the rules and elicit them.

> *i* + one consonant + *e* is usually pronounced /aɪ/.
> The exception is *give*.
> *ind* and *igh* are usually pronounced /aɪ/.
> *i* between consonants is usually pronounced /ɪ/, e.g. *miss*.

You could point out that while the verb *live* is pronounced /lɪv/, the adjective *live* as in *live music* is pronounced /laɪv/. This difference between the verb and adjective sometimes confuses Sts.

c 3 31 Here Sts do the same as in **a**, but with two-syllable words.

Give Sts time to decide if the letter i is pronounced /ɪ/ or /əɪ/.

Now play the audio for Sts to listen and check.

Check answers.

> 3 31
> fish /ɪ/ engine, practise, promise, service
> bike /aɪ/ arrive, decide, invite, online, revise, surprise

Play the audio again for Sts to listen and repeat.

d Get Sts to do this in pairs or do it as a class activity.

Check the answer.

> When the *i* is pronounced /ɪ/, the stress in the verb is on the first syllable. When the *i* is pronounced /aɪ/, the stress is on the second syllable.

Extra support

- Before Sts answer the question, elicit which words in **c** are verbs.

4 SPEAKING & LISTENING

a Focus on the photos and ask Sts what all the photos have in common (They all show people singing and looking happy).

In pairs, get Sts to ask and answer the questions. Make sure they understand the words *karaoke* and *choir*. Model and drill their pronunciation, /kæri'əʊki/ and /'kwaɪə/.

Get some feedback from the class.

b Focus on the task and make sure Sts understand statements 1–7.

In pairs, Sts tell each other if they think the statements are true or false.

Get some feedback from the class, but do not yet tell them if they are right or not.

c 3 32 Tell Sts they are going to listen to an interview with Martin, a director of a singing school, and Gemma, a student who did a course there. Explain that they will hear them talking about the things in 1–7.

Play the audio once the whole way through. Sts listen and check their answers to **b**. Play the audio again if necessary.

Check answers and ask if any pairs had predicted correctly.

Extra support

- Read through the script and decide if you need to pre-teach any new lexis before Sts listen.

> 1 T 2 T 3 F 4 F 5 F 6 T 7 F

> 3 32
> (script in Student's Book on *p.122*)
> **I = interviewer, M = Martin, G = Gemma**
> **I** Good morning and welcome. In today's programme we're going to talk about singing. In the studio we have Martin, the director of a singing school in London, and Gemma, a student at Martin's school. Good morning to both of you.
> **M and G** Good morning.
> **I** First, Martin, can you tell us, why is it a good idea for people to learn to sing?
> **M** First, because singing makes you feel good. And secondly, because singing is very good for your health.
> **I** Really? In what way?
> **M** Well, when you learn to sing, you need to learn to breathe correctly. That's very important. And you also learn to stand and sit correctly. As a result, people who sing are often fitter and healthier than people who don't.
> **I** Are your courses only for professional singers?
> **M** No, not at all. They're for everybody. You don't need to have any experience of singing. And you don't need to be able to read music.
> **I** So how do your students learn to sing?
> **M** They learn by listening and repeating. Singing well is really 95% listening.
> **I** OK. Gemma. Tell us about the course. How long did it last?
> **G** Only one day. From ten in the morning to six in the evening.
> **I** Could you already sing well before you started?
> **G** No, not well. I have always liked singing. But I can't read music and I never thought I sang very well.
> **I** So what happened on the course?
> **G** Well, first we did a lot of listening and breathing exercises, and we learnt some other interesting techniques.
> **I** What sort of things?
> **G** Well, for example we learnt that it is easier to sing high notes if you sing with a surprised look on your face!
> **I** Oh really? Could you show us?
> **G** Well, I'll try.
> **I** For those of you at home, I can promise you that Gemma looked very surprised. Were you happy with your progress?
> **G** Absolutely. At the end of the day we were singing in almost perfect harmony. It was amazing. In just one day we really were much better.
> **I** Could you two give us a little demonstration?
> **M and G** Oh, OK...

d Go through the six multiple-choice questions.

Then play the audio again for Sts to listen and choose the right answer. Play any parts of the audio again if necessary.

Check answers.

> 1 a 2 b 3 a 4 c 5 b 6 b

Extra support

- If there's time, you could get Sts to listen again with the script on *p.122*, so they can see exactly what they understood / didn't understand. Translate / explain any new words or phrases.

e Finish by asking Sts if they would like to learn to sing (better) and which tips from the audio they could use.

5 3 33 SONG *Don't Stop Me Now* ♫

This song was originally made famous by the British rock band Queen in 1978. For copyright reasons this is a cover version. If you want to do this song in class, use the photocopiable activity on *p.274*.

3 33

Don't Stop Me Now

Tonight I'm gonna have myself a real good time
I feel alive
And the world is turning inside out, yeah!
I'm floating around in ecstasy, so
(Don't stop me now)
(Don't stop me) 'cause I'm having a good time, having a good time
I'm a shooting star leaping through the sky like a tiger
Defying the laws of gravity
I'm a racing car passing by like Lady Godiva
I'm gonna go, go, go, there's no stopping me
I'm burning through the sky, yeah!
Two hundred degrees, that's why they call me Mister Fahrenheit
I'm travelling at the speed of light, I wanna make a
Supersonic man out of you

Chorus
(Don't stop me now) I'm having such a good time, I'm having a ball
If you wanna have a good time, just give me a call
'Cause I'm having a good time
Yes I'm having a good time, I don't want to stop at all

I'm a rocket ship on my way to Mars on a collision course
I am a satellite, I'm out of control
I am a machine, ready to reload
Like an atom bomb, about to explode
I'm burning through the sky, yeah!
Two hundred degrees, that's why they call me Mister Fahrenheit
I'm trav'ling at the speed of light, I wanna make a
Supersonic woman of you

(Don't stop me, don't stop me, don't stop me)
Hey hey hey!
(Don't stop me, don't stop me, Ooh ooh ooh)
I like it (Don't stop me, don't stop me)
Have a good time, good time
(Don't stop me, don't stop me)
Ooh ooh, alright

Oh, burning through the sky, yeah!
Two hundred degrees, that's why they call me Mister Fahrenheit
Trav'ling at the speed of light, I wanna make a
Supersonic man out of you

Chorus

G *have to, don't have to, must, mustn't*
V modifiers: *a bit, really*, etc.
P *must, mustn't*

7C Learn a language in a month!

Lesson plan

The title and main context of this lesson were inspired by an article in the British press where an experiment was done to see how well someone could learn a foreign language in just a month. When the month was up, the person travelled to the country itself and carried out a series of tasks to see how much he or she had learnt. The lesson begins with a grammatical focus on modal verbs expressing obligation: *have to / don't have to* and *must*, and there is a pronunciation focus on *must* and *mustn't*. Then Sts read an article about an experiment to see how much Spanish a British student, Max, can learn in a month and then they listen to hear how Max got on in Spain when his course finished. Then there is a vocabulary focus on modifiers like *quite, really*, and *incredibly* before Sts talk about their experiences as learners of English. In Writing Sts write a formal email to a language school asking for information.

STUDY LINK
- Workbook 7C
- iTutor
- iChecker
- www.oup.com/elt/englishfile

Extra photocopiable activities

- **Grammar** *have to, don't have to, must, mustn't p.182*
- **Communicative** In the UK *p.229* (instructions *p.203*)
- **www.oup.com/elt/teacher/englishfile**

Optional lead-in (books closed)

- Ask Sts what rules there are in the class, and elicit their ideas onto the board, writing them up in imperatives, e.g. *Do homework every day. Don't miss classes. Turn off your mobile phone. Don't speak in* (Sts' L1), etc.
- Then ask Sts which two they think are the most important.

1 GRAMMAR *have to, don't have to, must, mustn't*

a Books open. Focus on the notices and rules 1–4, and get Sts to match them.

Check answers.

1 C	2 B	3 D	4 A

b Focus on the highlighted expressions in **a** and questions 1 and 2. Give Sts a few moments to answer the questions and then check answers. Make sure Sts understand the words *obligation / obligatory, permitted*, and *against the rules*.

1 You have to / You must
2 a You mustn't
b You don't have to

Extra challenge

- Get Sts in pairs to cover rules 1–4 and just look at the notices. Encourage them to test each other by pointing to a notice and asking *What does this mean?* Their partner responds *It means you….*

Extra idea

- If there are any other notices (relating to rules / obligations) in your school, remind Sts of them and elicit what they mean, e.g. No smoking – *You mustn't smoke*, etc.

c 3 34))) 3 35))) Tell Sts to go to **Grammar Bank 7C** on *p.138*. Focus on the example sentences and play the audio for Sts to listen and repeat. Encourage them to copy the rhythm. Then go through the rules with the class.

Additional grammar notes

have to* and *must

- At Pre-intermediate level *have to* and *must* can be treated as synonyms as a way of expressing obligation. We tend to use *have to* more often than *must* when there is an external obligation, i.e. a law or a rule, e.g. *You have to wear a seat belt in a car in the UK.*
- Watch out for the typical mistake of using *to* with *must*: e.g. *I must to go to the bank.*
- Highlight the impersonal use of *You* when we talk about rules and laws, e.g. *You have to drive on the left.*

don't have to* and *mustn't

- The typical mistake here is when Sts use *don't have to* instead of *mustn't*, e.g. *You don't have to smoke in class.* (*You mustn't smoke…*)

Focus on the exercises for **7C** on *p.139*. Sts do the exercises individually or in pairs.

Check answers, getting Sts to read the full sentences.

a	1 has to		5 have to
	2 have to		6 doesn't have to
	3 Does ... have to		7 have to / must
	4 have to		8 Do ... have to
b	1 mustn't		5 mustn't
	2 have to		6 must
	3 don't have to		7 have to
	4 ✓		8 ✓

Tell Sts to go back to the main lesson **7C**.

Extra support

- If you think Sts need more practice, you may want to give them the Grammar photocopiable activity at this point.

d In pairs, get Sts to complete the four sentences about their school.

e Put two pairs together and get them to read their sentences to each other. They should then choose the most important rule.

Get some feedback from various groups.

2 PRONUNCIATION *must, mustn't*

Pronunciation notes

- *must* is usually pronounced strongly /mʌst/ especially when we want to emphasize that something is important, e.g. *You MUST HELP me.* But it can also be pronounced weakly /məst/, e.g. *I must REMEMBER to DO it.*
- The first *t* in *mustn't* is silent. Sometimes it can be difficult for Sts to hear the difference between the positive and negative form.

a 3 36 Focus on the activity and tell Sts that they are going to hear the sentences and that they need to identify the silent letter in *mustn't*.

Play the recording once and elicit that it is the first letter *t* (*mustn't*) which is not pronounced.

3 36
See sentences in Student's Book on *p.56*

Now play the audio again, pausing after each sentence for Sts to repeat.

b 3 37 Tell Sts they are either going to hear five sentences with either *must* or *mustn't* and they must write them down.

Play the audio, pausing after each sentence to give Sts time to write. Play again if necessary.

Get Sts to compare with a partner, and then check answers.

3 37
1 I mustn't forget her birthday.
2 She must help you.
3 We must call him at work.
4 You mustn't tell her husband.
5 He mustn't be late.

3 READING & LISTENING

a Focus on the questions and elicit some opinions from the class. Try to get a short discussion going if Sts seem to be interested in the topic.

b Focus on the photo and tell Sts that they are going to read about a British journalist who tried to learn Spanish on an intensive course. Make sure Sts understand what *an intensive course* means.

Focus on the instructions and go through questions 1–6 making sure Sts understand them.

Give Sts a few minutes to read the article once.

Then get them to cover the article and answer the questions.

Get Sts to compare with a partner, and then check answers.

1 They have a reputation for being bad at languages.
2 They wanted Max to learn a new language in a month.
3 Because he would like to visit Spain and Latin America.
4 In London for one month.
5 Easy: Vocabulary: Some words are similar to English words.
Difficult: Grammar: the verbs change for each person; pronunciation
6 1 Order a drink and a sandwich (ask how much it is and understand the price)
2 Ask for directions in the street
3 Get a taxi to a famous place
4 Leave a message on a phone
Rules: You mustn't use a dictionary or phrase book, speak no English, and you mustn't use your hands, mime, or write anything.

Deal with any new vocabulary.

c 3 38 Focus on tests 1–4 in the article and ask Sts the two questions. Get some feedback from the class.

Then play the audio of Max doing the tests in Madrid. Sts just listen to hear which test was the easiest and which was the most difficult.

Check answers.

Extra support

- Read through the script and decide if you need to pre-teach any new lexis before Sts listen.

The easiest test was getting a drink and a sandwich in a bar.
The most difficult was getting a taxi to a famous place.

3 38
(script in Student's Book on *p.122*)
J = journalist, P = Paula, W = waiter, Pb = passer-by, T = taxi driver, L = Lola

J I arrived at Madrid airport where I met Paula. *Hola Soy Max.*
P *Encantada. Soy Paula.*
J Paula took me to my hotel and that evening we went to the centre of Madrid and it was time for my first test. I had to order a sandwich and a drink in a bar, then ask for the bill. I sat down at the bar and I tried to order a beer and a ham sandwich. *Por favor, una cerveza y un bocadillo de jamón.*
W *En seguida.*
J Fantastic! The waiter understood me first time. My pronunciation wasn't perfect, but I got my beer and my sandwich. I really enjoyed it. But then the more difficult bit. Asking for the bill... *¿Cuánto es?*
W *Seis noventa.*
J *¿Cómo?*
W *Seis noventa.*
J Six ninety. I understood! Paula gave me eight points for the test. I was very happy with that. Next we went out into the street. Test number two was asking for directions and (very important!) understanding them. We were in a narrow street and I had to stop someone and ask them for the nearest chemist, Una farmacia. I stopped a woman. At first I didn't understand anything she said!
Pb *Siga todo recto y tome la segunda por la derecha. Hay una farmacia en esa calle.*
J I asked the woman to speak more slowly.
Pb *Todo recto y tome la segunda calle por la derecha DERECHA.*
J I got it this time, I think. The second street on the right. I followed the directions and guess what. There was a chemist there! Seven points from Paula. Test number three. I wasn't looking forward to this one. I had to get a taxi to a famous place in Madrid. Paula wrote down the name of the place on a piece of paper. It was the name of the football stadium where Real Madrid play. We stopped a taxi. *El Bernabéu, por favor.*
T *¿Qué? ¿Adónde?*
J He didn't understand me. I tried again, but he still didn't understand. I was desperate, so I said, *'Real Madrid, Stadium, football'.*
T *¡Ah! El Santiago Bernabéu.*

J Finally! Paula only gave me five because I ended up using English. Still, at least I made the taxi driver understand where I wanted to go. And so to the final test. I had to leave a message in Spanish on somebody's voicemail. I had to give my name, spell it, and ask the person to call me back. Paula gave me the number – it was one of her friends called Lola – and I dialled. I was feeling a bit nervous at this point, because speaking on the phone in a foreign language is never easy.
L *Deje su mensaje después de la señal.*
J *Er. Buenas noches. Soy Max. Max. M-A-X. Er... Por favor... llámame esta noche... Oh yes... a las 8.30 er, Gracias.* Well, my grammar wasn't right, but I left the message. Half an hour later, at half past eight Lola phoned me. Success! Paula gave me eight points. That was the end of my four tests. Paula was pleased with me. My final score was seven. I was quite happy with that. So, how much can you learn in a month? Well, of course you can't learn Spanish in a month, but you can learn enough to survive if you are on holiday or on a trip. Now I want to go back to England and try and learn some more. *¡Adiós!*

d Focus on the task and quickly go through sentences 1–7 before playing the audio.

Play the audio again, pausing to give Sts time to mark them T or F. Play all or part of the audio again if necessary.

Check answers.

1 F (The waiter understood him first time.)
2 F (It was six euros ninety.)
3 F (It was the second street on the right.)
4 F (He didn't understand.)
5 T
6 F (His final mark was seven.)
7 F (You can't learn Spanish in a month, but you can learn enough to survive.)

Extra support

- If there's time, you could get Sts to listen again with the script on *p.122*, so they can see exactly what they understood / didn't understand. Translate / explain any new words or phrases.

4 VOCABULARY modifiers

a In this activity Sts revise / learn some useful modifiers. Focus on the two examples and elicit the meaning of the bold words (very = a lot; a bit = a little).

Focus on the chart. Make sure Sts understand that they have to complete it with the words in the list in order of difficulty. Elicit the first one (*incredibly*) from the whole class.

Check answers.

Spanish is	incredibly really very quite a bit not very	difficult.

Go through the ***a bit*** information box with the class.

You could also highlight that:

– *incredibly* /ɪn'kredəbli/ has the stress on the second syllable.

– *really* is a little stronger than *very*. Compare *She's very well* and *She's really well.*

– *quite* means an intermediate amount – neither a lot nor a little.

b Give Sts time to complete the sentences so that they are true for them and then get them to compare their answers with a partner.

Get some feedback from the class.

5 SPEAKING

a Focus on the questions and the example. In pairs or small groups, Sts discuss how well they would do in the tests.

Get some feedback from the class.

b Here Sts do a short speaking activity based on their experience in using English. Quickly run through the questions before Sts start.

Put Sts in pairs and get them to ask and answer the questions. Either **A** can ask **B** all the questions and then they swap roles or they can take turns to ask and answer. Encourage them to use *What about you?* after they have answered.

Get some feedback from the class about their experiences.

6 WRITING a formal email

Tell Sts to go to **Writing *A formal email*** on *p.115*.

a Tell Sts to read the email and tick the questions that Antonio asks the school.

Check answers.

Sts should tick:
How much do the courses cost?
When do the courses start and finish?
Where can I stay?

b Now tell Sts to look at the highlighted expressions. They are all for a formal email / letter. Sts need to write the equivalent expressions for an informal email / letter.

Check answers.

1 Dear X / Hi / Hello
2 I'm writing
3 I'd like
4 Look forward to hearing from you. / Can't wait to hear from you.
5 Lots of love / Love

c Get Sts to read the two advertisements for courses. They must choose one and write a formal email asking two or three questions.

d You may like to get Sts to do the writing in class or you could set it as homework. Get them to write the email, making sure they write two paragraphs according to the model.

e Sts should check their emails for mistakes, and then swap them with another student to read.

Vocabulary	feeling ill: a headache, a cough, etc.
Function	describing symptoms; buying medicine; talking about possessions
Language	*I have a cold; I'm allergic to...; I've got...*

PRACTICAL ENGLISH

Episode 4 At the pharmacy

Lesson plan

In this lesson Sts get practice with describing symptoms and buying medicine. Early in the morning, Rob and Jenny go running in Central Park, and Jenny invites Rob for dinner. However, Rob isn't feeling too well, and in the afternoon he goes to a pharmacy. Later, in the evening, he has dinner at Jenny's apartment.

STUDY LINK

- **Workbook** At the pharmacy
- **iTutor**
- **www.oup.com/elt/englishfile**

Test and Assessment CD-ROM

- **Quick Test 7**
- **File 7 Test**

www.oup.com/elt/teacher/englishfile

Optional lead-in (books closed)

- Before starting Episode 4, elicit what Sts can remember about Episode 3, e.g. ask them *What does Rob buy? Why? What happens when he buys them? What does Rob agree to do with Jenny?, etc.*
- Alternatively, you could play the last scene of Episode 3.

1 RUNNING IN CENTRAL PARK

a **3 39** Books open. Focus on the photos and elicit what Sts think is happening. Do not tell them if they are right or not yet.

Now focus on the question and play the audio once the whole way through for Sts to check their ideas.

Check answers.

Jenny is. Rob says he is, but he is very tired.

3 39

(script in Student's Book on *p.122*)

J = **Jenny**, **R** = **Rob**

J Are you OK?
R Me? Never better.
J It's beautiful here, isn't it? I think this is my favourite place in New York.
R Yeah, it's great.
J So how's it all going? Are you happy you came?
R To Central Park? At seven fifteen in the morning?
J To New York, Rob.
R Yeah. Of course I'm happy. It's fantastic.
J Really? You aren't just saying that.
R No, I mean it.
J You need to get in shape, Rob.
R I know. I am a bit tired of eating out all the time. It isn't good for my figure.
J It's the restaurants you go to! Why don't you come over to my place after work? I could make you something a little healthier.
R I'd really like that. Thanks.
J So, how do you feel now? Are you ready to go again?
R Oh yes! I'm ready for anything.
J Are you sure you're OK?
R Absolutely.
J OK. We'll only go around two more times.
R Two? Excellent!

b Focus on questions 1–6 and give Sts time to read them.

Play the audio again the whole way through.

Get Sts to compare with a partner, and play again if necessary.

Check answers.

1 Never better.
2 It is beautiful and her favourite place in New York.
3 Yes.
4 He is tired of eating out.
5 She invites him to have dinner at her place.
6 Twice. / Two more times.

Extra support

- If there's time, you could get Sts to listen again with the script on *p.123*, so they can see exactly what they understood / didn't understand. Translate / explain any new words or phrases.

2 VOCABULARY feeling ill

a Focus on the title and elicit / teach the meaning of *ill*.

Now focus on the question *What's the matter?* and make sure Sts understand it.

Tell Sts to match the phrases and pictures.

Get them to compare with a partner.

b **3 40** Play the audio for Sts to listen and check.

3 40

What's the matter?

2 I have a headache.	5 I have a temperature.
4 I have a cough.	6 I have a bad stomach.
1 I have flu.	3 I have a cold.

Model and drill the sentences. You might want to contrast *I have a cold* (= I am ill) and *I am cold* (= I am feeling cold, but not ill).

Play it again, pausing after each phrase for Sts to repeat. Give further practice of words your Sts find difficult to pronounce.

Tell Sts to cover the phrases and practise saying them with a partner.

Extra challenge

- Get Sts to give some advice.

3 GOING TO A PHARMACY

a 3 41 Focus on the title and the **British and American English** box under the dialogue on *p.59*.

Now focus on the instructions and sentences 1–4.

Play the audio once the whole way through. Play again if necessary.

Get Sts to compare with a partner, and then check answers.

1 flu 2 ibuprofen 3 four hours 4 $6.99

3 41 3 42
P = **pharmacist**, **R** = **Rob**
P Good morning. Can I help you?
R I'm not feeling very well. (*repeat*) I think I have flu. (*repeat*)
P What are your symptoms?
R I have a headache and a cough. (*repeat*)
P Do you have a **temperature**?
R No, I don't think so. (*repeat*)
P Are you allergic to any drugs?
R I'm allergic to penicillin. (*repeat*)
P No **problem**. This is ibuprofen. It'll make you feel **better**.
R How many do I have to take? (*repeat*)
P **Two** every four hours.
R Sorry? How often? (*repeat*)
P **Two** every four hours. If you don't feel better in **48** hours, you should see a doctor.
R OK, thanks. How much is that? (*repeat*)
P That's $6.99, please.
R Thank you. (*repeat*)
P You're **welcome**.

You might want to tell Sts that ibuprofen is like aspirin, it reduces pain. You could also elicit / teach that penicillin is an antibiotic.

b Now focus on the dialogue in the chart. Elicit who says the **You Hear** phrases (the pharmacist) and who says the **You Say** phrases (the customer, here Rob). These phrases will be useful for Sts if they need to go to a pharmacy / chemist.

Give Sts a minute to read through the dialogue and think what the missing words might be. Then play the audio again, and get Sts to complete the gaps. Play again if necessary.

Get Sts to compare with a partner, and then check answers.

See words in **bold** in script 3.41

Go through the dialogue line by line with Sts, helping them with any words or expressions they don't understand. Elicit / explain the meaning of *symptoms*. You might also want to highlight the phrase *to be allergic to sth*. Model and drill *allergic* /ə'lɜːdʒɪk/. Ask a few Sts *Are you allergic to anything?*

c 3 42 Now focus on the **You Say** phrases and tell Sts they're going to hear the dialogue again. They should repeat the **You Say** phrases when they hear the beep. Encourage them to copy the rhythm and intonation.

Play the audio, pausing if necessary for Sts to repeat the phrases.

d Put Sts in pairs, **A** and **B**. **A** is Rob and **B** is the pharmacist. Get Sts to read the dialogue aloud, and then swap roles.

e In pairs, Sts do another roleplay. Go through the instructions with them. **A** (book closed) should choose another illness from **2**. **B** (book open) starts with *Can I help you?*

Monitor and help.

Extra support

- Demonstrate the activity by getting a good student to play the pharmacist and you pretend to feel ill.

f When they have finished, they should swap roles.

You could get a few pairs to perform in front of the class.

4 DINNER AT JENNY'S APARTMENT

a 3 43 Focus on the picture and ask Sts some questions, e.g. *Where are Rob and Jenny? What's happening?*, etc.

Focus on sentences 1–5 and go through them with Sts.

Then play the audio once the whole way through for them to mark the sentences T (true) or F (false). Make it clear that they don't need to correct the false sentences yet. Play again if necessary.

Get Sts to compare with a partner, and then check answers.

1 F 2 T 3 T 4 F 5 F

3 43
(script in Student's Book on *p.123*)
R = **Rob**, **J** = **Jenny**
R That was a lovely meal. Thanks, Jenny.
J That's OK.
R It's been great being in New York. You know, your offer to work here came at a very good time for me.
J Really?
R Yeah, I was looking for something new. Something different. You see, I broke up with my girlfriend a few months before I met you.
J Oh... right...
R What about you?
J What about me?
R You know... relationships?
J Oh, I've been too busy recently to think about relationships. Getting this job at the magazine was a really big thing for me. I guess that's taken up all my time and energy.
R But that isn't very good for you. Only thinking about work, I mean.
J Why didn't you tell me you weren't feeling well this morning? We didn't have to go for a run.
R I wanted to go. It was nice.
J Well, I'm glad you're feeling better. Would you like another coffee?
R No, thanks. I think I should get back to the hotel now, I've got a really busy day tomorrow. Do you have a telephone number for a taxi?
J Yeah... but it's much easier to get a cab on the street.
R Oh, OK, then.
J I'll see you in the morning, if you're feeling OK.
R Oh, I'm sure I'll be fine! Thanks again for a great evening.
J Any time.
R Goodnight.
J Night, Rob.

b Play the audio again, so Sts can listen again and correct the false sentences.

Get Sts to compare with a partner, and then check answers.

1 Rob broke up with his girlfriend **a few months** before he met Jenny.
4 Rob wants to go back to his hotel **because he wants to go to bed early as he has a busy day the next day.**
5 Jenny **doesn't call** a taxi.

Extra support

- If there's time, you could get Sts to listen again with the script on *p.123*, so they can see exactly what they understood / didn't understand. Translate / explain any new words or phrases.

c 3 44 Focus on the ***have got*** box and go through it with the class.

Play the audio once the whole way through for Sts just to listen.

3 44
I've got a busy day tomorrow.
Have you got any children?
Yes, I have. I've got a girl and boy.
No, I haven't. I haven't got children.

Now play it again, pausing after each phrase, and get Sts to repeat.

In *English File* Sts have been taught to use *Do you have..?, I don't have..., I have...* to talk about possession as we believe it is the easiest form for Sts to acquire and the most international. However, it is important that they are aware of, and can recognize, the *have got* form of *have* which is especially common in spoken English among UK native speakers of English (although the *have / do you have* form is also common). We normally contract *have got*, e.g. *I've got a headache*. Point out that you cannot use *have got* when you are using *have* with another meaning, e.g. *have dinner, have a shower*. If you want to go into the grammar of *have got* in more detail with your Sts, tell them to go to *p.165*. Go through the rules (audio 3.45), and get them to do the exercises in pairs. The answer key is at the end of this lesson.

d Put Sts in pairs. Focus on the instructions and the example.

Monitor and help, making sure Sts use *have got* correctly.

Get some feedback from various pairs.

Extra idea

- Tell Sts to add two more possessions to ask their partner about.

e Focus on the **Social English phrases**. In pairs, get Sts to think about what the missing words could be.

Extra challenge

- In pairs, get Sts to complete the phrases before they listen.

f 3 46 Play the audio for Sts to listen and complete the phrases.

Check answers.

3 46

Rob	That was a lovely **meal**.
Rob	That isn't very **good** for you.
Jenny	I'm **sure** I'll be fine.
Rob	I think I **should** get back to the hotel now.
Rob	I'm **glad** you're feeling better.
Rob	Thanks again for a **great** evening.
Jenny	**Any** time.

If you know your Sts' L1, you could get them to translate the phrases. If not, get Sts to have a look at the phrases again in context in the script on *p.123*.

g Now play the audio again, pausing after each phrase for Sts to listen and repeat.

Finally, focus on the **Can you...?** questions and ask Sts if they feel confident they can now do these things. If they feel that they need more practice, tell them to watch the episode again and practise the language on their *iTutor*.

Answer key for the *have got* appendix

a
1 She hasn't got any brothers.
2 Have you got a big flat?
3 We haven't got a lot of work today.
4 Has your sister got a boyfriend?
5 Roger and Val have got a beautiful garden.
6 I have got a really good teacher.
7 My brother hasn't got a job at the moment.
8 They've got the same colour eyes.
9 Have we got a meeting today?
10 He hasn't got many friends at work.

b
1 haven't got
2 Has ... got
3 've got
4 haven't got
5 has got
6 haven't got
7 Have ... got
8 's got
9 Have ... got
10 haven't got

G *should*
V *get: get angry, get lost*, etc.
P /ʊ/ and /uː/, sentence stress

8A I don't know what to do!

Lesson plan

In this lesson Sts learn to use *should* / *shouldn't* for giving advice. The lesson begins with Sts reading three emails which were sent to a newspaper 'problem page' by men seeking advice. This leads into the grammar presentation, which is followed by a pronunciation focus on the /ʊ/ and /uː/ sounds, and on sentence stress. Then there is a listening and speaking activity where Sts hear a radio phone-in programme and discuss the advice that is given to two callers. Vocabulary focusses on different meanings of *get*, which are recycled in a questionnaire. Finally, in Writing Sts write a response to a person who is asking for advice.

STUDY LINK

- **Workbook** 8A
- **iTutor**
- **www.oup.com/elt/englishfile**

Extra photocopiable activities

- **Grammar** *should p.183*
- **Communicative** I need some advice *p.230* (instructions *p.203*)
- **Vocabulary** *get p.258* (instructions *p.246*)
- **Song** *Why Do I Feel So Sad? p.275* (instructions *p.265*)
- **www.oup.com/elt/teacher/englishfile**

Optional lead-in (books closed)

- Write on the board I NEED SOME ADVICE. Ask Sts what they think *advice* means, and elicit also that it is a noun, and that the verb is *advise*. Point out that the verb is /ədˈvaɪz/ and the noun is /ədˈvaɪs/. Tell Sts that *advice* is uncountable in English – it can't be used in the plural, e.g. *My sister usually gives me good advice* NOT ~~good advices~~.

1 READING

a Books open. Focus on the two questions and give Sts a couple of minutes to discuss them in pairs or small groups. If you did the **Optional lead-in**, only focus on the second question.

Get feedback from the class. Elicit also the idea of contacting a radio programme or a magazine / internet problem page. Find out from the class what they think of these more impersonal options and ask if Sts think this is better than asking a family member or friend.

b Focus on the title and elicit that in the UK men have the reputation of being bad at talking about their feelings. Ask if this is true in your Sts' country.

Now focus on the instructions and get Sts to read problems A–C and then match two pieces of advice to each problem.

Get Sts to compare with a partner, and then check answers.

Problem A 4 and 6
Problem B 2 and 5
Problem C 1 and 3

Extra support

- Before Sts read the problems and advice, you might want to pre-teach some vocabulary, e.g. *an impulse, have second thoughts, attend, an argument*, etc.

c Focus on the instructions. Tell Sts to read the problems and advice again and get them, in pairs, to guess the meaning of the highlighted verb phrases in the text. Tell them to read the whole sentence as the context will help them guess.

Check answers, either explaining in English, translating into Sts' L1, or getting Sts to check in their dictionaries.

Deal with any other new vocabulary.

d In pairs, Sts discuss which piece of advice they agree with most for each of the three problems. Then they should think of more suggestions for each problem.

Get feedback. First elicit which piece of advice is better for each problem, and then ask if Sts have any other suggestions. You could also tell them what you think.

2 GRAMMAR *should*

a Get Sts to underline the seven examples of *should* / *shouldn't* in the problems and advice in **1**, and to answer the two questions.

Check answers.

1 What should I do? (in B)
2 Should I go... or should I suggest separate holidays? (in C)
3 You should tell your girlfriend... (in 3)
4 I think you should go for it. (in 4)
5 You should be there. (in 5)
6 You shouldn't do anything in a hurry. (in 6)

1 *should* is used to give advice; *you should* = I think it's a good idea. It is not an obligation, and is not as strong as *you have to* or *you must*.
2 To make a negative add *not* (*should not* = *shouldn't*) and to make a question use an infinitive without *to*, e.g. *Should I go?*

b 3 47))) Tell Sts to go to **Grammar Bank 8A** on *p.140*. Focus on the example sentences and play the audio for Sts to listen and repeat. Encourage them to copy the rhythm. Then go through the rules with the class.

Additional grammar notes

- *Should* does not usually cause problems as it has a clearly defined use and the form is simple. Remind Sts to use the infinitive without *to* after *should*.
- You may want to point out to Sts the alternative form *ought to*, but *should* is more common, especially in spoken English.
- The main problem with *should* is the pronunciation, i.e. the silent *l* (see Pronunciation notes in **3**).

Focus on the exercises for **8A** on *p.141*. Sts do them individually or in pairs.

Check answers, getting Sts to read the full sentences.

a	1	shouldn't	5	should
	2	should	6	should
	3	should	7	should
	4	shouldn't	8	shouldn't
b	1	should wear	5	shouldn't drive
	2	should study	6	should go
	3	shouldn't walk	7	should spend
	4	should relax	8	shouldn't have

Tell Sts to go back to the main lesson **8A**.

Extra support

- If you think Sts need more practice, you may want to give them the Grammar photocopiable activity at this point.

3 PRONUNCIATION /ʊ/ and /uː/, sentence stress

Pronunciation notes

- *Should* (like *would* and *could*) is often mispronounced partly because of the silent *l*, but also because *ou* is not normally pronounced /ʊ/.
- The focus on /ʊ/ and /uː/ will give Sts further practice of this sound and contrast it with the long /uː/. It is worth pointing out to Sts that one of the main problems with these two sounds is words with *oo*, which can be pronounced either way. There is no rule, so Sts need to learn each word as it comes up.

a  Focus on the instructions and question.

Play the audio once for Sts just to listen to the sounds and words, and answer the question.

Check the answer.

The /uː/ sound is a longer sound.

3 48

See words in Student's Book on *p.61*

Play the audio again, pausing after each word and sound for Sts to repeat.

b **3 49** Tell Sts to decide if the words in the list are sound 1 (ʊ) or sound 2 (uː).

Play the audio for Sts to listen and check.

Check answers.

3 49

sound 1: /ʊ/ book, could, foot, look
sound 2: /uː/ flew, food, school

Now ask Sts *Which consonant is not pronounced in* should, would, *and* could? and elicit the answer.

It is the *l*.

Now play the audio again for Sts to listen and repeat.

STUDY LINK Sts can practise these sounds on the *iTutor* and on the *English File* Pre-intermediate website.

c **3 50** Now tell Sts they are going to listen to six sentences with *could*, *should*, and *would* (in any form, positive, negative or interrogative) and they must write them down.

Extra support

- Highlight that *should*, *could*, and *would* in the affirmative form are unstressed, but the negative forms *shouldn't* | *couldn't* | *wouldn't* are always stressed.

Play the audio, pausing after each sentence to give Sts time to write.

Check answers.

3 50

1 What should I do?
2 You should read a good book.
3 You could send her an email.
4 I wouldn't like to be in your situation.
5 Could you help me with this?
6 You shouldn't worry about it.

d Play the audio again, pausing after each sentence for Sts to listen and repeat.

Then repeat the activity eliciting responses from individual Sts.

e Put Sts in pairs, **A** and **B**. Tell Sts to go to **Communication *What should I do?***, **A** on *p.103*, **B** on *p.108*.

Go through the instructions with them carefully and make sure Sts know what they have to do.

A starts by telling **B** about his / her problem. **B** listens and offers advice. **A** responds to **B**'s advice by accepting it or rejecting it. Then they swap roles.

Monitor and help while Sts do the activity. Don't interrupt and correct, but make notes of any common errors and go through these on the board afterwards.

Get some feedback from the class.

Extra support

- Before you do the activity, you might want to pre-teach some vocabulary, e.g. *allergic*, *bark*, *cough*, etc.

Tell Sts to go back to the main lesson **8A**.

8A

4 LISTENING & SPEAKING

a 3 51 Focus on the task and tell Sts they are going to listen to someone with a problem phoning a radio programme. They must listen and write down the caller's problem. Tell Sts to copy the chart on a piece of paper, so that they have more space to write.

Play the audio once the whole way through. Then play it again if necessary.

Extra support

- Read through the scripts and decide if you need to pre-teach any new lexis before Sts listen.

3 51

(script in Student's Book on *p.123*)

P = presenter, K = Kevin

P Welcome to this morning's edition of *What's the Problem?* Today we're talking about friends, so if you have a problem with one of your friends, and you'd like our psychologist Catherine to give you some advice, just phone us on 800 700 550. Our first caller today is Kevin from Birmingham. Hello, Kevin.

K Hi.

P What's the problem?

K Yes. My problem is with my best friend Alan. Well, the thing is, he's always flirting with my girlfriend.

P Your best friend flirts with your girlfriend?

K Yes, when the three of us are together he always says things to my girlfriend like, 'Wow! You look fantastic today' or 'I love your dress, Suzanna', things like that. And when we're at a party he often asks her to dance.

P Do you think he's in love with your girlfriend?

K I don't know... but I'm getting really stressed about it. What can I do?

b Get Sts to compare their answers and discuss what advice they would give the man.

Check what the man's problem is, making sure Sts understand the word *flirt*.

His best friend flirts with his girlfriend.

Elicit some advice from the class for this man's problem.

Extra support

- First, check as a class what the man's problem is. Then put Sts in pairs and get them to discuss what advice they would give the man. Finally, get some feedback.

c 3 52 Now tell Sts they are going to listen to the expert's advice. They must make notes, so they can then compare it to their advice. Play the audio once the whole way through. Then play it again if necessary.

Check the answer first, and then find out what Sts think of the advice.

The expert's advice is for Kevin to talk to his girlfriend first to see how she feels. If she doesn't like the way Alan behaves, then Kevin should talk to Alan and tell him to stop.

3 52

(script in Student's Book on *p.123*)

P = presenter, C = Catherine, K = Kevin

P Well, let's see if our expert can help. Catherine?

C Hello, Kevin. Have you talked to your girlfriend about this?

K No, I haven't. I don't want Suzanna to think I'm jealous.

C Well, first I think you should talk to her, ask her how she feels, and what she thinks of Alan's behaviour. Perhaps she thinks it's fine, and they are just good friends. That it's just his personality. If that's what she thinks, then I think you should accept it and relax.

K What should I do if she also finds it... er difficult, er uncomfortable?

C Then I think you should talk to Alan. Tell him that he's a good friend, but that you and Suzanna have problems with the way he behaves. I'm sure he'll stop doing it. He's probably never thought it was a problem.

K Thanks very much for that. I'll talk to Suzanna tonight.

d 3 53 3 54 Now tell Sts they are going to hear another caller. They must listen to find out what the woman's problem is. Play the audio once the whole way through. Then play it again if necessary.

Get Sts to compare their answers and discuss what advice they would give the woman.

Check what the woman's problem is.

Her husband's ex-wife rings him once a week for a chat and always asks him for help if she has a problem.

Now elicit some advice from the class.

3 53

(script in Student's Book on *p.123*)

P = presenter, M = Miranda

P And our next caller is Miranda from Brighton. Hi, Miranda.

M Hi.

P And what's your problem?

M My problem is with my husband's ex-wife. They divorced five years ago, before I met him. But she still phones him at least once a week to chat, and if she has a problem in her flat or with her car, she always calls him and asks him to come and help her.

P Does your husband have children with his ex-wife?

M No, they don't have any children. That's why I think she should stay out of our lives.

P Catherine, over to you. What do you think Miranda should do?

Now tell Sts they are going to listen to the expert's advice. They must make notes, so they can then compare it to their advice. Play audio 3.54 once the whole way through. Then play it again if necessary.

Check the answer first, and then find out what Sts think of the advice.

The expert's advice is for Miranda to meet her friend Bill every time her husband meets his ex-wife.

3 54

(script in Student's Book on *p.123*)

C = Catherine, M = Miranda, P = presenter

C Hi, Miranda. Well, the first thing is have you spoken to your husband about this?

M Yes, I have. He thinks I'm being difficult. He feels sorry for his ex – she's on her own, she doesn't have a partner.

C OK. Miranda, do you have any male friends, men who are just good friends?

M Yes, I have a friend called Bill. We've been friends since I was a teenager.

C That's perfect. My advice is this: when your husband's ex-wife phones and asks him to go and see her, phone Bill and arrange to meet and have a drink, or go to the cinema. Every time your husband meets his ex or has a long phone call, then you meet Bill or have a long phone call. He'll soon see what's happening, and he'll stop seeing his ex.

M I think that's a great idea. Thank you, Catherine.

P And the next caller is...

Extra support

- If there's time, you could get Sts to listen again with the scripts on *p.123*, so they can see exactly what they understood / didn't understand. Translate / explain any new words or phrases.

5 VOCABULARY *get*

a Focus on the instructions, the three sentences, and the verbs in the list. Get Sts to match them and then compare with a partner.

Check answers.

1 b 2 a 3 c

b Tell Sts to go to **Vocabulary Bank** ***get*** on *p.159*. Focus on the ***get*** box and go through it with the class.

Get Sts to do **a** individually or in pairs. Many of these words / phrases may already be familiar to them.

 Now do **b**. Play the audio for Sts to check answers. Play it again, pausing after each phrase for Sts to repeat. Give further practice of words and phrases your Sts find difficult to pronounce.

3 55

get
5 get angry
3 get divorced
6 get fit
4 get lost
2 get married
1 get nervous
7 get better
9 get colder
8 get worse
11 get a job
12 get a newspaper
10 get a ticket
15 get on a bus / get off a bus
13 get on well with
14 get up
16 get home
18 get to school
17 get to work
19 get an email
21 get a present
20 get a text message

Finally, do **c** and get Sts to cover the words and look at the pictures. They can test themselves or a partner.

Tell Sts to go back to the main lesson **8A**.

Extra support

- If you think Sts need more practice, you may want to give them the Vocabulary photocopiable activity at this point.

c Focus on the questionnaire and go through the questions. Get Sts to ask you one or two of the questions. Sts then ask and answer in pairs.

Monitor and help, making sure they are using *get* correctly.

Get feedback from a few pairs.

6 WRITING

a Focus on the instructions and problems. Tell Sts to read both problems and to choose one to respond to with some advice.

Go through the **Language for giving advice** box with the class and then tell them:

- to use either *you should / shouldn't* to give advice and explain why.
- to use the messages from **1** as a model.
- not to put the number of the problem. They should end with their names.
- to write their note on a separate piece of paper (not in their notebooks).

Sts should write about 50 words. Monitor and help with spelling, etc.

Extra idea

- Fast finishers could write another response for the other problem.

b Now put Sts into groups of four (or take in the notes and redistribute them). Each student then reads his / her note to the group and they decide which problem it is answering, and if they think it's good advice or not. They should take notes, so they can give feedback later.

Get feedback by going through the two problems and asking Sts what advice was given, and which advice they think is best.

Tell Sts to go back to the main lesson **8A**.

7  SONG *Why Do I Feel So Sad?* ♫

This song was originally made famous by American singer Alicia Keys in 2001. For copyright reasons this is a cover version. If you want to do this song in class, use the photocopiable activity on *p.275*.

3 56

Why Do I Feel So Sad?
Friends we've been for so long, now true colours are showing
Makes me wanna cry, oh yes it does, 'Cause I had to say goodbye

Chorus
By now I should know, that in time things must change, so it shouldn't
Be so bad, so why do I feel so sad?

How can I adjust, to the way that things are going, it's
Killing me slowly, Oh I just want it to be how it used to be

'Cause I wish that I could stay, but in time things must change
So it shouldn't be so bad, so why do I feel so sad

You cannot hide the way you feel inside I realize
Your actions speak much louder than words, so tell me why, oh

Chorus

By now, by now I should know, that in time things must grow
And I had to leave you behind, so why
Do I feel so sad, if it couldn't be that bad
Tell me why

Chorus

G *if* + present, *will* + infinitive (first conditional)
V confusing verbs: *carry, wear, win, earn*, etc.
P linking

8B If something can go wrong, ...

Lesson plan

This lesson presents the first conditional through the humorous context of 'Murphy's Law', which states that if something bad can happen, it will happen. The lesson begins with a reading text about the origins of Murphy's Law and Sts try to match two halves of some common examples. This leads into the grammar presentation of the first conditional which is followed by a pronunciation focus on linking using conditional sentences. The vocabulary and speaking focus is on verbs which are often confused, like *know / meet* and *borrow / lend*, which are practised in a questionnaire. Finally, there is a listening activity which picks up on the theme of things going wrong. Sts listen to the true story of a Swedish couple who, when travelling, experienced seven natural disasters, including an earthquake.

STUDY LINK
- **Workbook** 8B
- **iTutor**
- **www.oup.com/elt/englishfile**

Extra photocopiable activities

- **Grammar** *if* + present, *will* + infinitive (first conditional) *p.184*
- **Communicative** On the Trans-Siberian Railway *p.231* (instructions *p.204*)
- **Vocabulary** Confusing verbs *p.259* (instructions *p.247*)
- **www.oup.com/elt/teacher/englishfile**

Optional lead-in (books closed)

- Write MURPHY'S LAW on the board and elicit from the class anything they know about it. Try to elicit a concrete example of one of Murphy's Laws. If the class don't seem to have much idea, you could ask them *What always happens if you drop a piece of bread or toast on the floor? Which way does it fall?* (with the side with the butter on the floor). You could use mime to help make this clear.

1 READING

a Books open. Sts will see the first conditional presented in this reading text about Murphy's Law. Focus on the question. Sts will probably try to express that the queue they were in before will move faster. Then, if you didn't do the **Optional lead-in**, tell Sts that this is an example of what we call Murphy's Law and ask if they have heard of this law before.

b Focus on the text and tell Sts to read the two paragraphs (up to where the examples start). Give Sts a few minutes to read and answer the questions.

Check answers.

Murphy was an American aerospace engineer.
His law is 'if something can go wrong, it will go wrong.'

c Give Sts time to read the examples of Murphy's Law (1–8) and to match them to the correct endings A–H.

Extra challenge

- You could get Sts to cover the endings (A–H) and to try to guess how sentences 1–8 could finish. Accept any logical ending, without worrying about correct grammar at this point. Then get Sts to uncover A–H and match them to sentences 1–8.

Check answers. Explain / translate *spill* (= accidentally let a liquid fall).

1 A 2 G 3 E 4 H 5 D 6 C 7 F 8 B

d In pairs, small groups, or as a whole class, Sts answer the question. You could tell Sts if these things happen to you.

2 GRAMMAR *if* + present, *will* + infinitive

a In pairs, Sts cover A–H in **1c** and try to remember the Laws using the first half of the sentences in the article as prompts.

b Now tell Sts to focus on the full sentences and to decide which structures are used in both parts.

Check answers and explain that sentences with *if* are often called conditional sentences, and that this structure (a sentence with *if* + present, + future) is often called *the first conditional*.

The verb after *if* is in the present simple and the other verb is in the future (*will / won't* + infinitive).

c **4 2**))) Tell Sts to go to **Grammar Bank 8B** on *p.140*. Focus on the example sentences and play the audio for Sts to listen and repeat. Encourage them to copy the rhythm. Then go through the rules with the class.

Additional grammar notes

- Since first conditional sentences refer to future possibilities, some Sts may try to use the future after *if*. Typical mistake: *If he'll phone, I'll tell him.*
- The present simple is also used rather than *will* after *when*, e.g. *I'll tell him when he arrives.* You may want to point this out in this lesson.

Focus on the exercises for **8B** on *p.141*. Sts do them individually or in pairs.

Check answers, getting Sts to read the full sentences.

a 1 D 2 G 3 E 4 F 5 A 6 B

b 1 tell, won't tell
2 don't write, won't remember
3 Will ... call, get
4 'll help, ask
5 'll phone, hear
6 'll miss, move
7 listen, 'll understand
8 won't be, are
9 'll drive, give

Tell Sts to go back to the main lesson **8B**.

Extra support

- If you think Sts need more practice, you may want to give them the Grammar photocopiable activity at this point.

d Focus on the prompts for Sts to make new 'Murphy's Laws'. Highlight that there is not one right answer. Remind Sts of the original Law: if something can go wrong, it will go wrong.

While Sts complete their laws in pairs, monitor and help with vocabulary and spelling.

e Put Sts in small groups or get them to stand up and mill, and get them to read their 'laws' to each other.

Get feedback and write the 'laws' on the board. Accept all logical endings.

Possible endings
1 they won't have your size.
2 the bus will come.
3 you will be more confused after the call than before. / you will wait for hours listening to music.
4 you will need to make an urgent call. / a lot of people will call you.
5 you will find the 'lost' glove.

3 PRONUNCIATION linking

a 4 3))) Here Sts practise deciphering connected speech. Focus on the **Sound linking** box and go through it with the class.

Tell Sts to look at the five sentences and to pay particular attention to how some words are linked. Play the audio once for Sts just to listen.

4 3)))
See sentences in Student's Book on *p.63*

Then play the audio again, pausing after each sentence for Sts to repeat and copy the rhythm.

b 4 4))) Tell Sts they are going to hear five sentences said at normal speed. The first time tell them just to listen, not to write. Then play the audio again, pausing after each sentence to give Sts time to write.

Check answers, eliciting the sentences onto the board.

4 4)))
1 If you don't eat something soon, you'll be hungry later.
2 I'm sure she'll come if you ask her.
3 You'll earn more money if you work at weekends.
4 If the film's in French, we won't understand a word.
5 If I cook lunch, will you cook dinner?

Play the audio again pausing for Sts to repeat the sentences and copy the rhythm.

Then repeat the activity eliciting responses from individual Sts.

4 VOCABULARY & SPEAKING

confusing verbs

a Focus on the question and elicit answers from the class.

know = have met and seen sb before
meet = get to know sb for the first time
wear = have on your body, e.g. clothes, glasses
carry = have sth in your hand, e.g. a bag, an umbrella

b Tell Sts to go to **Vocabulary Bank *Confusing verbs*** on *p.160* and get Sts to do **a** individually or in pairs. Many of these words / phrases may already be familiar to them.

4 5))) Now do **b**. Play the audio for Sts to check answers. Give further practice of any words your Sts find difficult to pronounce.

4 5)))
Confusing verbs
2 wear jewellery, carry a bag
8 win a medal, earn a salary
5 know somebody well, meet somebody for the first time
1 hope that something good will happen, wait for a bus
3 watch TV, look at a photo
11 look happy, look like your mother
4 miss the bus, lose a match
9 bring your dictionary, take an umbrella
6 look for your glasses, find your glasses
10 say sorry, tell a joke
7 lend money to somebody, borrow money from somebody

– *win / earn*:
you win a sports match, something in a competition, lottery, etc.
you earn money when you work

– *hope / wait*:
hope = what you want to happen, e.g. I hope that it's sunny tomorrow.
wait = sit / stand and do nothing until something happens, e.g. wait for the doctor

– *watch / look at*:
you watch something where there is movement, e.g. we watched a cricket match in the park, we watched the children playing.
you look at something static, e.g. a photo, somebody's passport

– *look / look like*:
we use *look* + adjective, e.g. you look tired.
we use *look like* + a noun, e.g. you look like Brad Pitt.

– *miss / lose*:
you miss a class, a bus a plane (e.g. if you are late / ill)
you lose a sports match or lose an object, e.g. your keys

– *bring / take*:
this depends on where the speaker is. The teacher (at school) says: Don't forget to bring your book to class tomorrow. The student (at home) says: I must remember to take my book today.

– *look for* / *find*:
look for is the action of trying to locate something you have lost or need, e.g. I'm looking for a new job.
find is used when you have located it, e.g. I have found a new job.

– *say* / *tell*:
say is used like this:
Jack said, 'hello.'
Jack said hello **to** me yesterday.

Susan told a lie.
Susan told me a lie.

– *lend* / *borrow*:
I lent my brother some money.
My brother borrowed some money from me.

! Some of these verbs are often confused because in your Sts' L1, one verb may be used for both meanings. For this reason it's better for Sts to learn these verbs in a phrase, e.g. *know someone well*, *meet someone for the first time*, etc. rather than just learning a translation of the verb in isolation.

Go through the ***hope* and *expect*** and ***look* and *look like*** box with the class.

Finally, get Sts to do **c** in pairs. **A** says a verb and **B** a continuation, and then they swap roles.

Tell Sts to go back to the main lesson **8B**.

Extra support

- If you think Sts need more practice, you may want to give them the Vocabulary photocopiable activity at this point.

c Get Sts to read questions 1–6 and to circle the right verb in each one.

Get Sts to compare with a partner, and then check answers.

1 look like
2 missed
3 take
4 earn
5 meet
6 tell

Now put Sts in pairs and get them to ask and answer the questions.

Get some feedback from the class.

5 LISTENING

a In pairs, get Sts to think of three things that could go wrong when on holiday. Elicit some ideas from various pairs, e.g. the hotel could be awful, the weather could be bad, you could lose your credit cards, etc. Make sure that you include the weather, even if Sts haven't come up with it.

b Now focus on words 1–7 and definitions A–G. Tell Sts to match the words to their definitions.

Check answers. Model and drill any words which are difficult for your Sts.

2 G 3 D 4 B 5 A 6 F 7 C

c **4 6**))) Focus on the photo and heading.

Now tell Sts to listen to a travel programme about the Swedish couple's trip. Sts must draw the route on the map.

Play the audio once the whole way through. Play the audio again if necessary and then check answers.

Extra support

- Read through the script and decide if you need to pre-teach any new lexis before Sts listen.

Stockholm → Munich (south Germany) → Thailand → Bali (Indonesia) → Perth (western Australia) → Cairns → Brisbane → Auckland (New Zealand)→ Tokyo (Japan) → China → Stockholm

4 6)))

(script in Student's Book on *p.123*)
And to finish our programme today – the incredible story of a Swedish couple who went on holiday and survived no fewer than seven natural disasters!
Stefan and Erika Svanström started their four-month trip last December. They were travelling with their young baby daughter. First, they flew from Stockholm to Munich. But when they arrived in Munich they couldn't get their connecting flight to Thailand because there was a terrible blizzard in South Germany – the worst snowstorm for 100 years! They had to wait at the airport for 24 hours. Mrs Svanström said, 'We just thought things will get better.' When they finally got to Thailand, they had a relaxing few weeks. But that was the last time they could really relax. From Thailand they flew to the island of Bali in Indonesia, a popular holiday destination. When they arrived in Bali they were expecting blue skies and sun, but what they got were terrible monsoon rains – the worst monsoons for many years. Mrs Svanström said, 'Now we were thinking, what will happen next?' They decided not to stay in Bali, but to go to Australia. They flew to Perth in Western Australia, but hours after they arrived Perth suffered terrible forest fires, and the streets were full of smoke. They travelled north to Cairns, and arrived just in time for Cyclone Yasi – one of the worst cyclones ever to hit the city. They had to leave their hotel and spend 24 hours in a shopping centre with 2,500 other people.
Could things get any worse? Yes, they could. The Svanström family left Cairns and travelled south to Brisbane to visit friends, but the city was suffering from the worst floods in its history. So they left Brisbane and booked to fly to Christchurch in New Zealand. But just before their plane left Brisbane some friends phoned them to say that Christchurch had been hit by an earthquake and a large part of the city was destroyed. Their plane landed in another city, Auckland. They travelled around New Zealand for a while, and then they flew to Japan. On March the 11th they were having lunch in a restaurant in Tokyo when suddenly everything began to shake. It was an earthquake – 9 on the Richter scale and one of the worst that ever hit Japan. And after the earthquake came a devastating tsunami. Fortunately, Mr and Mrs Svanström and their child were not hurt. They travelled from Japan to China for the last part of their holiday. Luckily, they didn't have any more natural disasters, and they arrived safely home in Stockholm on the 29th of March.
Mr Svanström said, 'We have learnt that in life you should always expect the worst but hope for the best. Also you need to be prepared for anything.'

Now play the audio again and get Sts to write down which disaster happened in each place.

Check answers.

Munich (south Germany): a blizzard
Bali (Indonesia): monsoon
Perth (western Australia): forest fires
Cairns: cyclone
Brisbane: floods
Tokyo (Japan): earthquake and tsunami

d Give Sts time to look at questions 1–7 and then play the audio again.

Get Sts to compare with a partner, and then check answers.

1 24 hours
2 Sunny weather
3 Perth
4 In a shopping centre
5 Because Christchurch had been hit by an earthquake.
6 They were having lunch.
7 They went to China. Nothing happened.

Extra support

- If there's time, you could get Sts to listen again with the script on *p.123*, so they can see exactly what they understood / didn't understand. Translate / explain any new words or phrases.

e Do this as an open-class activity. You could also tell Sts what you think.

Extra challenge

- Ask Sts if they have experienced any of the natural disasters mentioned. If so, where were they and what did they do?

G possessive pronouns
V adverbs of manner: *dreamily, completely*, etc.
P sentence rhythm

8C You must be mine

Lesson plan

The context of this lesson is short story by the famous American writer O. Henry (1862–1910), which has a characteristic 'twist' at the end.

Sts read and listen to the first part of the story and then practise reading aloud with good sentence rhythm in Pronunciation. Then they hear the rest of the story in Listening. Make sure that you allow time to do the reading, pronunciation, and listening in the same class. Examples taken from the story lead into the grammar focus on possessive pronouns. Finally, there is a vocabulary focus on using adverbs. This lesson provides a good opportunity to remind Sts of the value of reading 'Graded Readers' (sometimes called Easy Readers) in English. Reading 'Graded Readers' helps to consolidate what Sts already know and to build their vocabulary. Some 'Graded Readers' also have an accompanying audio CD, which can be used to help to improve Sts' listening comprehension and pronunciation. You could recommend the Oxford Bookworm series level 2, which has a selection of other O. Henry stories in a book called *New Yorkers*.

STUDY LINK
- **Workbook** 8C
- **iTutor**
- **iChecker**
- **www.oup.com/elt/englishfile**

Extra photocopiable activities
- **Grammar** Possessives pronouns *p.185*
- **Communicative** Reading questionnaire *p.232* (instructions *p.204*)
- **www.oup.com/elt/teacher/englishfile**

Optional lead-in (books closed)

- Write this question on the board and get Sts to ask each other in pairs.
  WHICH OF THESE THINGS DO YOU READ IN ENGLISH?
  – school or university textbooks
  – websites
  – video or computer game instructions
  – song lyrics
  – Graded Readers
  – anything else

  Remind Sts that Graded Readers are books which are written in simple language using grammar and vocabulary according to level.
- Get feedback from the class and use this opportunity to stress the importance of reading in English outside class. If you haven't already done so, draw Sts' attention to Graded Readers, particularly if your school has a library. If not, you could consider starting a class library by getting Sts to buy one book each and then swapping the books among all the Sts in the class. You could also have a wall chart recording the books Sts have read and a brief comment or score.

1 READING

a Books open. Focus on the task and tell Sts, to look at the picture and the three questions. Elicit answers from the class.

1 The woman has red curly hair and blue eyes, and is wearing a dark green skirt and a white top. The man has dark hair and a big moustache. He is wearing a shirt and tie, and a coat and hat.
2 Outside the woman's flat / house.
3 In the 19th century.

b 4 7 Tell Sts they are going to read and listen to an extract from *Girl* by O. Henry. You might want to tell them that his real name was William Sydney Porter (1862–1910) and that he was a famous American author.

Play the audio once the whole way through while Sts follow **Part 1** of the story.

See Part 1 in Student's Book on *p.64*

Then give Sts time to read **Part 1** again without the audio. In pairs, Sts answer questions 1–5.

Check answers to 1–4 and elicit ideas for 5.

1 He gave Hartley Vivienne's address. He offered to follow her.
2 He left the detective's office and went to find where Vivienne lived.
3 She looked about 21, her hair was red gold, and her eyes blue.
4 Because she hadn't answered his letter.
5 Sts' own answers

c In pairs, Sts look at the words and phrases from the story and try to guess their meaning.

Check answers, either explaining in English, translating into Sts' L1, or getting Sts to check in their dictionaries.

Deal with any other new vocabulary.

d 4 8 Before telling Sts to read and listen to **Part 2**, go through the **Glossary** on *p.65* with them.

Then play the audio once the whole way through while Sts read **Part 2** of the story.

See Part 2 in Student's Book on *p.65*

Then give Sts time to read **Part 2** again without the audio. In pairs, Sts answer questions 1–6.

Check answers to 1–4 and elicit ideas for 5 and 6.

! At this stage of the story Sts will probably assume that Hartley is in love with Vivienne and wants her to come and live with him. They will also probably imagine that Héloise is his wife. Don't confirm or reject these assumptions.

1 She doesn't think she would enjoy living in the suburbs.
2 He told her she could come to the city whenever she wants.
3 At the Montgomerys'.
4 Because she has someone else.
5 and 6 Sts' own answers

e Focus on the **Adverbs of manner** bbox and go through it with the class.

In pairs, Sts look at the highlighted adverbs in the story and try to guess their meaning.

Check answers, either explaining in English, translating into Sts' L1, or getting Sts to check in their dictionaries.

Deal with any other new vocabulary.

2 PRONUNCIATION sentence rhythm

Pronunciation notes

- Reading aloud in class is an activity which divides teachers. Some feel that it can give Sts valuable pronunciation practice while others find it painful. We believe that in small doses it can be helpful to improve Sts' awareness of word and sentence rhythm. However, we believe that reading aloud needs to be focussed, with short pieces of text which all Sts can work on (with teacher correction). This can be much more effective than just getting Sts to read a text aloud around the class with each person reading a different sentence.

a  Focus on the task and on the last five lines of the story on *p.65*. Get Sts to read the two questions and then play the audio.

Check answers.

a punctuation b the adverbs, i.e. *masterfully, calmly*

4 9

'Vivienne,' said Hartley, masterfully. 'You must be mine.'
Vivienne looked him in the eye.
'Do you think for one moment,' she said calmly, 'that I could come to your home while Héloise is there?'

Play the extract again and ask Sts to focus on the rhythm of the sentences, and how the speaker pauses.

Now give Sts a few moments to read the text aloud (quietly) to themselves. Tell them to try to get the right rhythm, to pause momentarily when there is a comma and to read the two lines with adverbs (*masterfully* and *calmly*) in the appropriate way.

Then choose a couple of Sts to read the text aloud to the class with good rhythm, correcting them as necessary.

b Focus on the **Reading aloud** box and go through it with the class. Then tell Sts to go to **Communication *Reading dialogue*** on *p.104*.

Go through the instructions with them carefully and model and drill the four names. Put Sts in pairs. Then focus on the adverbs in brackets and make sure Sts know what they mean. Remind Sts that they need to read the paragraph that follows the adverb in that way, e.g. *anxiously*, *slowly*, etc.

Give them time to act out the dialogue and swap roles. Remind Sts to stress words which should be stressed and to pause momentarily when there is a comma.

When they have finished, get some pairs to perform in front of the class.

Tell Sts to go back to the main lesson **8C**.

3 LISTENING

a  Tell Sts they are going to listen to **Part 3** of the story and they must answer questions 1–3.

Play the audio once the whole way through. Then play it again if necessary.

Get Sts to compare with a partner, and then check answers to 1 and 2. Elicit ideas for 3, but don't tell Sts if they are right yet.

Extra support

- Read through the scripts and decide if you need to pre-teach any new lexis before Sts listen, e.g. *drunk*, *scream*, *whisper*.

1 That she will go.
2 To be Hartley's.
3 Sts' own answer

4 10

(script in Student's Book on *p.123*)

Part 3

'Héloise will go,' said Hartley angrily. 'I haven't had one day without problems since I met her. You are right, Vivienne. Héloise must go before I can take you home. But she will go. I have decided...'
'Then,' said Vivienne, 'my answer is yes. I will be yours.' She looked into his eyes and Hartley could hardly believe his luck.
'Promise me,' he said.
'I promise,' repeated Vivienne, softly.
At the door he turned and looked at her happily, 'I will come for you tomorrow,' he said.
'Tomorrow,' she repeated with a smile.
An hour and forty minutes later Hartley stepped off the train when it stopped in the suburbs, and walked to his house.
As he walked towards the door a woman ran to him. She had black hair and was wearing a long white dress. They kissed, and walked into the house.

b **4 11** Now tell Sts they are going to listen to **Part 4** of the story and they must answer questions 1–3.

Play the audio once the whole way through. Then play it again if necessary.

Get Sts to compare with a partner, and then check answers.

1 Hartley's wife.
2 The Montgomerys' cook.
3 Hartley's cook.

4 11

(script in Student's Book on *p.124*)

Part 4

'My mother is here,' the woman said. 'But she's leaving in half an hour. She came to have dinner, but there's nothing to eat.'
'I have something to tell you,' said Hartley. He whispered something in her ear.
His wife screamed. Her mother came running into the hall.
The woman screamed again, but it was a happy scream – the sound of a woman whose husband loved her.

> 'Oh, mother!' she cried, 'What do you think? Vivienne is coming to be our cook! She is the cook that was with the Montgomerys. She's going to be ours! And now, dear,' she told her husband, 'you must go to the kitchen and tell Héloise to leave. She has been drunk again all day.'

Extra support

- If there's time, you could get Sts to listen again with the scripts on *pp.123–124*, so they can see exactly what they understood / didn't understand. Translate / explain any new words or phrases.

c Do this as a whole class activity. You could tell Sts your reaction the first time you read the story.

4 GRAMMAR possessive pronouns

a Tell Sts to look at sentences 1–4, which are from the story, and to complete the gaps.

Check answers.

1 my	2 your	3 mine	4 yours

b 4 12 Tell Sts to go to **Grammar Bank 8C** on *p.140*. Focus on the example sentences and play the audio for Sts to listen and repeat. Focus particularly on the pronunciation of *ours* /'aʊəz/ and *theirs* /ðeəz/, and encourage them to copy the rhythm. Then go through the rules with the class.

Additional grammar notes

- Sts will probably need reminding of how possessive adjectives (*my, your, his*, etc.) are used and in particular how they agree with the subject of a sentence, not the object (e.g. ***Jack** helps **his** sister a lot*. NOT ~~*Jack helps **her sister** a lot*~~.) and how they never change (e.g. *your books* NOT ~~*yours books*~~).
- When Sts learn possessive pronouns, e.g. *These are yours / hers / ours*, they may then tend to start adding an *s* to possessive adjectives.
- This is also a good moment to remind Sts about how object pronouns are used (e.g. *He loves me*).

Focus on the exercises for **8C** on *p.141*. Sts do them individually or in pairs.

Check answers, getting Sts to read the full sentences.

a	1 my	4 her	7 theirs
	2 yours	5 mine	8 your
	3 ours	6 their	9 hers
b	1 Hers	5 theirs	
	2 him	6 us	
	3 their	7 our	
	4 ours	8 its	

Tell Sts to go back to the main lesson **8C**.

Extra support

- If you think Sts need more practice, you may want to give them the Grammar photocopiable activity at this point.

c 4 13 Focus on the instructions and the example. Tell Sts they are going to listen to seven sentences and each time they must change the object for a possessive pronoun. Play the audio, pausing after each sentence for Sts to make the transformation.

4 13

1 It's my book. (*pause*) It's mine.
2 It's her scarf. (*pause*) It's hers.
3 They're our coats. (*pause*) They're ours.
4 It's his bike. (*pause*) It's his.
5 It's your phone. (*pause*) It's yours.
6 It's their house. (*pause*) It's theirs.
7 They're your sweets. (*pause*) They're yours.

Then repeat the activity eliciting responses from individual Sts.

5 WRITING using adverbs

a Focus on the instructions and get Sts to make adverbs from the adjectives in the list.

Get Sts to compare with a partner, and then check answers.

angrily	lazily	quietly	sadly	seriously	slowly

Extra support

- Elicit from Sts these basic rules for formation of adverbs:

Adjective	Adverb	
quiet sadly	quiet**ly** sad**ly**	Add *-ly*
possi**ble** comforta**ble**	possi**bly** comforta**bly**	Change *-ble* to *-bly*
lazy angry	laz**ily** angr**ily**	~~y~~ Add *-ily*
good fast hard	**well** **fast** **hard**	Irregular

b 4 14 Get Sts to read sentences 1–6 and to think what the missing adverb from **a** might be.

Now play the audio the whole way through. Then play it again, pausing after each sentence for Sts to write an adverb to describe how the person is speaking.

Get Sts to compare with a partner, and then check answers.

1 sadly	3 slowly	5 lazily
2 angrily	4 quietly	6 seriously

4 14

1 'I'm sorry, but I don't love you.'
2 'Give me back all my letters.'
3 'I think... I have an idea.'
4 'Don't make a noise. Everyone is asleep.'
5 'I don't feel like doing anything.'
6 'This is a very important matter.'

c Focus on the task, and remind Sts that at the end of the story Hartley tells his wife to tell the cook (Héloise) to leave. Give Sts, e.g. five minutes, to write their short scene. Tell them that they should also include at least two adverbs in their dialogues after *said*.

Get Sts to perform their dialogues in front of the class. You could get them to vote for the best ones.

7 & 8 Revise and Check

For instructions on how to use these pages see *p.38*.

STUDY LINK
- iTutor

Test and Assessment CD-ROM
- Quick Test 8
- File 8 Test

GRAMMAR

1 a	6 a	11 a
2 c	7 a	12 b
3 b	8 c	13 b
4 c	9 c	14 c
5 b	10 b	15 c

VOCABULARY

a 1 meet, 2 tell, 3 miss, 4 hope, 5 wears

b 1 forget, 2 learn, 3 try, 4 promise, 5 enjoy, 6 mind, 7 hate, 8 finish

c 1 Very, 2 incredibly, 3 bit, 4 rather, 5 quite

d 1 lost, 2 home / back, 3 better, 4 tickets, 5 on, 6 divorced, 7 from

PRONUNCIATION

a 1 give, 2 child, 3 choose, 4 sandwich, 5 wear

b 1 pretend, 2 important, 3 remember, 4 salary, 5 quietly

CAN YOU UNDERSTAND THIS TEXT?

a Because they are lazy.
b Students should tick: 2, 4, 6, 7

CAN YOU UNDERSTAND THESE PEOPLE?

4 15

1 c 2 c 3 a 4 c 5 a

1
I = interviewer, S = Stacey
I What's your idea of happiness?
S Happiness is having just enough money to live by and have enough, and having people that love you, having a family.

2
I = interviewer, H = Heba
I What foreign languages do you speak?
H I speak Arabic and French, a little bit of French.
I How well do you speak them?
H I'm very fluent in Arabic, and not as fluent in French.

3
I = interviewer, R = Ruth
I If you have a problem, who do you ask for advice, friends or family? Why?
R It depends what sort of problem it is. Quite often I would ask my mum for advice, but if it's a problem maybe about relationships or something, I would probably ask my friends.

4
I = interviewer, B = Ben
I What advice would you give someone who can't sleep at night?
B I would say that they should probably cut down on caffeine, or perhaps they're suffering from stress at work, so they should try and reduce their stress.

5
I = interviewer, N = Nick
I Do you think the Americans are bad at language learning? Why?
N Americans, I think they're not as good at learning languages as people in Europe. Sometimes I think Americans aren't as interested in learning other languages as foreigners are.

G *if* + past, *would* + infinitive (second conditional)
V animals: lion, tiger, goat, etc.
P word stress

9A What would you do?

Lesson plan

A survival quiz where Sts have to choose what they would do in a variety of situations involving animals and insects is the context for Sts to learn about the second conditional for hypothetical and imaginary situations. The lesson begins with reading where Sts read and answer the questions in the quiz and then find out if they have chosen the best option. Questions from the quiz are used to lead into Grammar where the second conditional is analysed and practised. In Vocabulary Sts learn the names of common animals, and pronunciation focusses on how to pronounce the words for animals in English which may be similar in Sts' own language. Finally, both the grammar and vocabulary are recycled and practised in Speaking.

STUDY LINK

- **Workbook** 9A
- **iTutor**
- **www.oup.com/elt/englishfile**

Extra photocopiable activities

- **Grammar** *if* + past, *would* + infinitive (second conditional) *p.186*
- **Communicative** I think you'd... *p.233* (instructions *p.204*)
- **Vocabulary** Animal quiz *p.260* (instructions *p.247*)
- **www.oup.com/elt/teacher/englishfile**

Optional lead-in (books closed)

- Give Sts, in pairs, three minutes to brainstorm words they know for animals. Elicit answers, getting Sts to spell the words and write them on the board. Elicit the correct pronunciation.
- You could also write the animals in columns depending on whether they are wild animals, farm animals, insects, etc.

1 READING & SPEAKING

a Books open. Focus on the photos and list of animals, and elicit the pronunciation of each one.

Now focus on the instructions and the quiz. Tell Sts, in pairs, to just complete each gap in the questions with one of the animals in the list.

Check answers.

1 dog	3 snake	5 jellyfish
2 bee	4 bull	6 shark

Extra support

- Before Sts do the quiz, check it for words and phrases which your Sts might not know and be ready to help with these.

b Focus on the highlighted verbs and verb phrases. Get Sts, in pairs, to guess their meaning. Tell them to read the whole sentence as the context will help them guess.

Check answers, either explaining in English, translating into Sts' L1, or getting Sts to check in their dictionaries.

Go through the three alternatives for each quiz question and deal with any other new vocabulary.

c Give Sts a few minutes to read the questions again and choose their answers.

Get Sts to compare their choices with a partner. Encourage them to try to say why they have chosen each option.

d Put Sts into groups of three. Tell them to go to **Communication *Would you know what to do?*,** **A** on *p.104*, **B** on *p.108*, and **C** on *p.110*. Explain that all the **A**s are going to read the answers to **In the city**, the **B**s to **In the country**, and the **C**s to **In the water**.

! If the number of Sts you have does not divide into groups of three, have one or two pairs, where they read and tell each other the answers to **A** and **B**, and then simply read the answers to **C**.

Go through the instructions with them carefully. Monitor and help with vocabulary while they are reading.

When Sts have read their answers, put them back into their groups, so they can tell each other what the right answers are and why the others are wrong.

When they have finished, they could see who in their group got the most answers correct.

Tell Sts to go back to the main lesson **9A**.

e Do the questions as a whole-class activity. If you have been in any of the situations, tell the class about it.

2 GRAMMAR *if* + past, *would* + infinitive

a Focus on the task. Get Sts to look at questions 1–6 in the quiz in pairs, or go through them with the whole class.

Check answers.

They are all about an imagined future.
The tense of the verb after *if* is the past simple.

b **4 16**)) Tell Sts to go to **Grammar Bank 9A** on *p.142*. Focus on the example sentences and play the audio for Sts to listen and repeat. Encourage them to copy the rhythm. Then go through the rules with the class.

Additional grammar notes

- Sts may find it strange to be using past tenses in the *if* half of these conditional sentences and it needs emphasizing that they do not refer to the past, but rather to a hypothetical situation.
- Sts have seen and used *would* / *wouldn't* + infinitive before with the verb *like*, so should not have problems with the form of *would*.

- Highlight that we often use the expression *If I were you, I'd…* to give advice.

Focus on the exercises for **9A** on *p.143*. Sts do them individually or in pairs.

Check answers, getting Sts to read the full sentences.

a 1 E 2 D 3 C 4 F 5 G 6 B

b
1 would buy, had
2 tried, would like
3 would learn, worked
4 rented, could
5 would see, lived
6 wouldn't go, were
7 would take, didn't have
8 wouldn't cycle, had
9 Would … leave, got
10 wouldn't be, had to

Tell Sts to go back to the main lesson **9A**.

Extra support

- If you think Sts need more practice, you may want to give them the Grammar photocopiable activity at this point.

c Tell Sts to complete the five sentences, so they are true for themselves.

Get Sts to compare their sentences with a partner, and then get some feedback from the class. Make sure they are not pronouncing the silent *l* in *would* / *wouldn't*.

3 VOCABULARY animals

a Tell Sts to go to **Vocabulary Bank *Animals*** on *p.161* and get Sts to do **a** individually or in pairs.

4 17 Now do **b**. Play the audio for Sts to check answers. Play it again, pausing after each one for Sts to repeat. Give further practice of words your Sts find difficult to pronounce.

4 17

Animals

20 bee	25 pig	22 jellyfish
14 butterfly	7 sheep	30 kangaroo
27 fly	2 bat	9 lion
8 mosquito	19 bear	18 monkey
29 spider	28 bird	24 mouse
1 bull	12 camel	6 rabbit
21 chicken	13 crocodile	26 shark
16 cow	15 dolphin	17 snake
10 goat	4 elephant	11 tiger
23 horse	3 giraffe	5 whale

Ask Sts why the words are in three groups and elicit / explain that the first group are all insects or arachnids, the second group are farm animals, and the third group are wild animals. Model and drill the pronunciation of *insects* /ˈinsekts/ and *wild* /waɪld/.

Finally, do **c** and get Sts to cover the words and look at the pictures. They can test themselves or a partner.

Tell Sts to go back to the main lesson **9A**.

Extra support

- If you think Sts need more practice, you may want to give them the Vocabulary photocopiable activity at this point.

b **4 18** This listening consists only of sound effects and its aim is to recycle the animal vocabulary in a fun and amusing way. Play the audio pausing after each sound for Sts to say or write the name of the animal.

Check answers.

4 18

(Sound effects)

1 chicken	6 dolphin
2 horse	7 lion
3 monkey	8 bull
4 snake	9 sheep
5 elephant	10 mosquito

Extra idea

- You could make this a team game where you divide the class into two or more teams and play the audio twice for them to decide which animals they are and write them down. The team with the most right answers wins.

4 PRONUNCIATION word stress

a Focus on the **Stress in words that are similar in other languages** box and go through it with the class.

Tell Sts to look at the animal words in the list and to underline the stress.

b **4 19** Play the audio for Sts to listen and check.

Check answers.

4 19

camel	giraffe
crocodile	kangaroo
dolphin	lion
elephant	mosquito

If you are teaching a monolingual class, ask them if the stress is in the same place in their L1.

c Quickly go through questions 1–8 making sure Sts understand them.

Put Sts in pairs and get them to ask and answer the questions.

Get some feedback from the class by asking individual Sts for some of their answers.

5 SPEAKING

Go through the questions and make sure Sts understand them all.

Then focus on the **Talking about imaginary situations** box and go through it with the class. Get some Sts to choose a question to ask you. Answer, giving as much detail as you think Sts will understand and trying to use some of the phrases in the box.

Put Sts into groups of three, and tell them to take turns to choose a question they want to ask their partners. They should also answer that question themselves. Encourage Sts to ask for more information (*Why?*, etc.).

Monitor and help Sts, correcting any misuse of tenses in the second conditional.

Get some feedback from the class, asking if anyone found their partners' answers surprising / amusing, etc.

G present perfect + *for* and *since*
V phobias and words related to fear: *afraid, frightened*, etc.
P sentence stress

9B I've been afraid of it for years

Lesson plan

In this lesson Sts study the present perfect with *for* and *since* to talk about unfinished actions or states. The context is phobias and the lesson begins with Vocabulary where Sts learn the words for some common phobias and words related to fear. In Listening and Speaking Sts hear three people talking about phobias they suffer from (all real answers) and they then talk about people they know with phobias. In Grammar, examples of the present perfect are taken from the listening activity and analysed before Sts go to the Grammar Bank. In Pronunciation Sts work on sentence stress in present perfect sentences to prepare them for the speaking activity, a survey in which Sts find out how long their classmates have done certain things. The lesson finishes with reading where Sts read about a possible new cure for phobias.

STUDY LINK
- Workbook 9B
- iTutor
- www.oup.com/elt/englishfile

Extra photocopiable activities

- **Grammar** Present perfect + *for* and *since p.187*
- **Communicative** Famous phobias *p.234* (instructions *p.205*)
- **www.oup.com/elt/teacher/englishfile**

Optional lead-in (books closed)

- Play *Hangman* with the word PHOBIA. Elicit the pronunciation (reminding Sts that *ph* is always pronounced /f/).
- Then ask Sts *How do you feel if you have a phobia of something?* and elicit *afraid* (or *frightened* | *scared*).

1 VOCABULARY phobias and words related to fear

a Books open. Get Sts to focus on the picture and see how many things they can see that people have a phobia of. If you didn't do the **Optional lead-in**, make sure Sts know what *phobia* means (i.e. a strong, abnormal, sometimes irrational fear of something).

Sts might say: spiders, flying, snakes, small spaces, the number 13, bats, public speaking, clowns, high places, and injections

Then elicit any other things Sts can think of that people sometimes have phobias of and write them on the board.

b Focus on the names of five phobias and explanations A–E, and give Sts time to try to match them. Sts probably won't know some of the phobia words, but should be able to match most of them.

Get Sts to compare with a partner, and then check answers.

1 D   2 B   3 E   4 C   5 A

c Focus on the task and give Sts time to find the words in the text.

Get Sts to compare with a partner, and then check answers.

1 fear (in E)
2 terrified (in A)
3 frightened (in B) and scared (in D)

2 LISTENING & SPEAKING

a 4 20)) Focus on the instructions and tell Sts to copy the chart on a piece of paper, so that they have more space to write. Now tell Sts that the first time they listen they only need to answer the question *What is he | she afraid of?* for the three speakers.

Play the audio once the whole way through.

Check answers.

Extra support

- Read through the scripts and decide if you need to pre-teach any new lexis before Sts listen.

Speaker 1	She is afraid of bats.
Speaker 2	He has claustrophobia.
Speaker 3	She is afraid of clowns.

4 20))
(script in Student's Book on *p.124*)
I = interviewer, W = woman, M = man
1
I Do you have any phobias?
W1 Yes, I'm terrified of bats.
I Really? How long have you had the phobia?
W1 I've had it for about 40 years! Since I was 12 years old. At my school we had a swimming pool, and the changing rooms were in an old building near the pool. On the first day at school our teacher told us that there were bats in there and that we shouldn't move around too much as they might start flying around and get into our hair. She also said we mustn't turn the lights on because this would wake up the bats. We had to change as quickly and quietly as possible.
I Did a bat every fly into your hair?
W1 No, nothing ever happened, but I was terrified just at the thought of it.
I Does it affect your life at all?
W1 Yes, I often feel very nervous or start to panic if I'm outside when it's beginning to get dark, which is when bats appear. If I'm sitting in my garden in the evening, I always have a tennis racquet, so if a bat flies near me, I can protect myself. And I can't watch a TV documentary about bats, or even look at them in photos.

2
I Do you have any phobias?
M Yes, I get very bad claustrophobia.
I How long have you had the phobia?
M It just started one morning about ten years ago. I was going to work on the train and it was very crowded. I started thinking that if there were an accident I'd never get out. I had a panic attack and I sort of felt my heart beating very quickly. I had to get off the train.
I How does your phobia affect your life?
M Well, I can't travel on crowded trains. I never ever travel on the underground because my worst nightmare would be if the train stopped in the tunnel. I also try to avoid lifts. What else? Oh yes, if I'm flying, I must have an aisle seat. I can't sit by the window.
3
I Do you have any phobias?
W2 Yes, I have a quite unusual phobia. I'm scared of clowns.
I Clowns, really? How long have you had it?
W2 I've had it for a long time. Since I was a child.
I How did it start?
W2 Well, I remember I went on a school trip to the circus when I was six or seven years old and there were clowns. I thought they were sort of stupid, but I wasn't really afraid of them. Then I went to a birthday party and there were clowns and they were showing us how to paint our faces, and I found I didn't like being near them. At first I just didn't like them, but over the years my feelings have changed to fear.
I Does your phobia affect your life at all?
W2 Not really because, luckily, I don't see clowns very often!

b Now play the audio again and get Sts to answer questions 2 and 3 for each speaker.

Get Sts to compare with a partner and play the audio again if necessary.

Check answers.

Question 2	**Speaker 1**	It started when she was 12.
	Speaker 2	It started about ten years ago.
	Speaker 3	It started when she was six or seven.
Question 3	**Speaker 1**	She is nervous if she is outside when it gets dark. She can't look at pictures of bats.
	Speaker 2	He can't go on crowded trains. He never uses the underground and he needs an aisle seat on a plane.
	Speaker 3	It doesn't.

Finally, ask the class *Which person is most affected by their phobia?* and elicit some answers.

Extra support

- If there's time, you could get Sts to listen again with the script on *p.124*, so they can see exactly what they understood / didn't understand. Translate / explain any new words or phrases.

c Put Sts in pairs and get them to answer the three questions.

Get some feedback from the class. You could also tell them what you think.

3 GRAMMAR present perfect + *for* and *since*

a Tell Sts to focus on the extract from the first interview and to answer the four questions.

Get Sts to compare with a partner, and then check answers.

1 When she was 12.
2 Yes.
3 The present perfect.
4 *for, since*

b **4 21** Tell Sts to go to **Grammar Bank 9B** on *p.142*. Focus on the example sentences and play the audio for Sts to listen and repeat. Encourage them to copy the rhythm. Then go through the rules with the class.

Additional grammar notes

- The present perfect with *for* and *since* can be tricky for Sts as they may use a different structure in their language to express this concept, e.g. the present tense. Typical mistake: *I live here since three years / since three years ago.*
- The important thing to highlight is that the present perfect with *for* and *since* is used to say how long a situation has continued from the past until now, i.e. we use it for situations which are still true, e.g. *I've been in this class for two years* (= I started two years ago and I am still in this class now).
- In the following lesson the present perfect for unfinished actions / periods of time will be contrasted with the past simple for finished actions / periods.

Focus on the exercises for **9B** on *p.143*. Sts do the exercises individually or in pairs.

Check answers, getting Sts to read the full sentences.

a
1 How long have you been frightened of clowns?
2 How long has your sister had her car?
3 How long have you lived here?
4 How long has your dad been a teacher?
5 How long have you known your boyfriend?
6 How long has Britain been in the EU?
7 How long have you had your cat?
8 How long has he worked for the same company?

b
1 I've been frightened of clowns since I was a child.
2 She's had her car for three years.
3 I've lived here for a long time.
4 He's been a teacher since 1990.
5 I've known my boyfriend since May.
6 It's been in the EU since 1973.
7 We've had our cat for about two years.
8 He's worked for the same company since 2008.

Tell Sts to go back to the main lesson **9B**.

Extra support

- If you think Sts need more practice, you may want to give them the Grammar photocopiable activity at this point.

c **4 22** Focus on the instructions and the example. Tell Sts to listen to the word(s) and then make a phrase using *for* or *since*.

Play the audio and elicit the phrases.

1 1984 (*pause*) since 1984
2 five months (*pause*) for five months
3 three weeks (*pause*) for three weeks
4 last week (*pause*) since last week
5 yesterday morning (*pause*) since yesterday morning
6 20 minutes (*pause*) for 20 minutes
7 I was a child (*pause*) since I was a child
8 2010 (*pause*) since 2010

Then repeat the activity eliciting responses from individual Sts.

4 PRONUNCIATION sentence stress

a 4 23 Here Sts practise sentence rhythm in the present perfect to prepare for the speaking activity in **5**.

Play the audio once the whole way through. Then play it again pausing after each section for Sts to repeat, building up to the whole sentence / question. Encourage them to copy the rhythm.

> **4 23**
> See sentences in Student's Book on *p.71*

Now get them to practise the phrases in pairs.

b 4 24 Now tell Sts they are going to hear five sentences / questions and they must write them down.

Play the audio, pausing after each line to give Sts time to write. Play the audio again if necessary.

Check answers.

> **4 24**
> 1 How long have you worked here?
> 2 They've been married for 20 years.
> 3 She hasn't travelled by plane since 2005.
> 4 How long has he lived in Italy?
> 5 We've known them for a long time.

In pairs, get Sts to practise saying the sentences.

5 SPEAKING

a Focus on the chart and instructions. Elicit the answer to the two questions from the class.

> The two verb forms are the present simple and the present perfect.
> The missing words are *Do you / Are you* and *have you.*

Elicit the past participles of the four verbs (*had, lived, known, been*).

Extra support

- Check Sts can make the questions correctly by getting them to ask you some of the questions first. Give short, natural answers with *for* and *since*, and some more information if you can as a model for how Sts should answer.

b Tell Sts they are going to move around the class asking other Sts the questions. If someone says *Yes, I do / am* to the first question (the present simple question), then they must ask the follow-up question (the present perfect question). They should try to find someone different for each question. Encourage Sts to ask for and give as much information as they can so that the survey becomes more of a conversation rather than just question and answer.

When Sts have finished, get some feedback.

6 READING

a Do this as a open-class activity.

b Focus on the title of the text and make sure Sts understand the word *pill*. Now tell Sts to read the text and mark sentences 1–6 T (true) or F (false).

Get Sts to compare with a partner, and then check answers.

> 1 F (Different phobias affect at least a quarter of the population.)
> 2 F (They discovered that a drug for tuberculosis can help.)
> 3 T
> 4 F (It does not work for everybody.)
> 5 T
> 6 T

Extra support

- Before Sts read the text, check it for words and phrases which your Sts might not know and be ready to help with these while they are answering the questions or afterwards. You may even want to pre-teach some words / phrases to lighten the load.

c Get Sts, in pairs, to guess the meaning of the highlighted words and phrases in the text. Tell them to read the whole sentence as the context will help them guess.

Check answers, either explaining in English, translating into Sts' L1, or getting Sts to check in their dictionaries.

Deal with any other new vocabulary.

d In pairs or small groups, Sts discuss the two questions.

Get some feedback from the class.

G present perfect or past simple? (2)
V biographies
P word stress, /ɔː/

9C Born to sing

Lesson plan

The main focus of this lesson is how to describe your or somebody else's life. The lesson begins with Sts learning the vocabulary for verb phrases often used in biographies. There is then a pronunciation focus on the word stress in these phrases, and on the /ɔː/ sound. This lexis is recycled in reading where Sts read about the lives of the famous reggae singer Bob Marley and his son Ziggy Marley. The contrast between the verb forms used for the father (who is dead) and his son, who is still alive, is used to show Sts a fundamental difference between how the past simple and the present perfect are used in English. In Listening Sts hear about another famous son from the music world: Enrique Iglesias (son of the Spanish singer Julio). The lesson finishes with a speaking activity where Sts talk about the life of an older person who they know well. This leads into writing where Sts are asked to write a short biography about either the person they have just talked about or another member of their family.

STUDY LINK
- **Workbook** 9C
- **iTutor**
- **iChecker**
- **www.oup.com/elt/englishfile**

Extra photocopiable activities

- **Grammar** Present perfect or past simple? *p.188*
- **Communicative** Like mother, like daughter *p.235* (instructions *p.205*)
- **Song** *You're My #1 p.276* (instructions *p.265*)
- **www.oup.com/elt/teacher/englishfile**

Optional lead-in (books closed)

- Ask Sts in pairs to brainstorm famous people whose parents are / were also famous, e.g. Angelina Jolie and Jon Voight, Melanie Griffiths and Tippi Hedren, etc.
- Elicit answers, getting Sts to tell you what the people do, and write their names on the board.

1 VOCABULARY & PRONUNCIATION

biographies, word stress, /ɔː/

Pronunciation notes

- The most common spellings of the /ɔː/ sound are *or* (when it is stressed), *al*, and *aw*.
- However, words beginning *wor-* are pronounced /ɜː/, e.g. *work*, *world*, *worse*, etc., which is confusing for Sts who often pronounce these words with the /ɔː/ sound. Learning the rule here should help them to avoid this common pronunciation error.

a **4 25** Books open. Focus on the list of phrases. Elicit / teach the meaning of *events* (things which happen to you). Go through the list, making sure Sts understand them all.

Give Sts time to mark the stress on the highlighted words.

Play the audio for Sts to listen and check their answers.

Then play the audio again for Sts to repeat.

4 25
marry somebody
get married
go to primary school
have children
go to secondary school
go to university
separate
get divorced
retire

b Tell Sts to number the expressions in **a** in a logical order. Elicit that the first expression is *be born*.

Put Sts into pairs and get them to compare their order with a partner. Do they agree?

Finally, elicit from the class the usual order of the expressions.

A possible order

1	be born	8	get married
2	go to primary school	9	have children
3	go to secondary school	10	separate
4	leave school	11	get divorced
5	go to university	12	retire
6	get a job	13	die
7	fall in love		

Extra idea

- You could get Sts to mark the expressions: E = everybody does it, S = some people do it, M = most people do it.

c **4 26** Focus on the sound picture and elicit the word and sound.

Then play the audio for Sts to listen.

4 26
See words in Student's Book on *p.72*

Now play the audio again and get Sts to listen and repeat.

d Focus on the words in the list and tell Sts that some of them have the /ɔː/ sound. Sts should say the words and circle the ones with the /ɔː/ sound. Remind them that it is easier if they say the words aloud to themselves.

Get Sts to compare with a partner.

e 4 27 Play the audio for Sts to listen and check.

Check answers.

more	ball
small	form
walk	bought
talk	four

4 27
See words in Student's Book on *p.72*

Now ask Sts *What rule can you see for words with wor + consonant?* and elicit the answer.

They are pronounced /ɜː/.

Now play the audio again for Sts to listen and repeat.

STUDY LINK Sts can practise these sounds on the *iTutor* and on the *English File* Pre-intermediate website.

2 READING

a Tell Sts they are going to read a text about Bob and Ziggy Marley. Ask the class if they have heard of them. Elicit the kind of music they play (reggae) and ask Sts if they have heard their music and if they like it. Sts are more likely to know Bob Marley, who is world-famous, than his son, who is still building his music career.

When Sts have read the introduction, ask them what the title *Like father like son* means (= the son is doing the same as his father did, i.e. making a career in music).

b Focus on the task and tell Sts, in pairs, to read each paragraph and decide if it refers to Bob Marley (BM) or Ziggy Marley (ZM).

Check answers.

BM 2, 6, 7, 9, 10 **ZM** 1, 3, 4, 5, 8

c Still in pairs, **A** re-reads about Bob Marley and **B** about Ziggy Marley.

Now books closed, **A** tells **B** everything he / she can remember about Bob.

3 GRAMMAR present perfect or past simple? (2)

a Give Sts a minute or so to answer question 1.

Check answers and elicit a few examples.

All the verbs are in the past tense because he is dead (*he was born, he made, he died*, etc.).

Now focus on question 2 and give Sts a minute or so to answer it.

Check answers and elicit a few examples. Highlight that if you are talking about the life of a person who is dead, you only use the past simple. If you are talking about the life of someone who is still alive, you will probably use the present, the past, and the present perfect.

Past simple *he was born, he was 13, he formed a band...and played*
This tense is used for finished events in his life, e.g. his childhood and early life.
Present simple *they have three children*
This tense is sued for a situation which is true now in the present.
Present perfect *he has been a musician, he has lived, he has won*
This structure is used for actions or states which started in the past and are still true in the present, i.e. he started being a musician when he was 13 and is still a musician now.

b 4 28 Tell Sts to go to **Grammar Bank 9C** on *p.142*. Focus on the example sentences and play the audio for Sts to listen and repeat. Encourage them to copy the rhythm. Then go through the rules with the class.

Additional grammar notes

- The contrast between the past simple and the present perfect was first focussed on in **4B** (See **Grammar Bank 4B** *p.132*).
- Highlight that the present perfect is used in the examples about Ziggy Marley because his career as a musician hasn't finished. He is still a musician and will probably make more albums.
- The past tense is used for Bob Marley because the sentences refer to a finished period of time. Bob Marley won't win a Grammy Award now because he is dead, so 'didn't win' is used. If he was still alive and making albums, then 'hasn't won' would be used.

Focus on the exercises for **9C** on *p.143*. Sts do the exercises individually or in pairs. Check answers.

a 1 He left
2 I lived
3 She's lived
4 My sister had
5 I've worked
6 The city has changed
7 They were
8 met, was

b 1 has he lived, moved
2 did Picasso die, did he live, left
3 have they been, 've been, met, was

Tell Sts to go back to the main lesson **9C**.

Extra support

- If you think Sts need more practice, you may want to give them the Grammar photocopiable activity at this point.

4 LISTENING

a Tell Sts to look at the photos of another famous father and son. Ask *What's their surname?* and elicit *Iglesias*. Then ask the class who they think is more famous.

b Explain the task and focus on 1–7. In pairs, Sts quickly try to guess what connection there might be between the information in 1–7 and Enrique Iglesias.

Listen to their ideas, but do <u>not</u> tell them if they are right or not.

c 4 29 Play the audio once and tell Sts not to write anything, just to listen, to see whether they guessed the connections correctly.

Then play the audio again, and get Sts to make notes. Pause the audio as necessary to give Sts time to make their notes.

Get Sts to compare with a partner and play the audio again if necessary.

Now elicit answers. Don't expect Sts to have all the information given.

Extra support

- Read through the scripts and decide if you need to pre-teach any new lexis before Sts listen.

1 He was born in Madrid in 1975.
2 He moved to Miami to live with his father.
3 Enrique Martinez is the name he used to get a record contract, when he sent his first songs to a record company.
4 'Enrique Iglesias' is the name of his first album, which he made in 1995.
5 His fourth album 'Escape' was his biggest commercial success in 2001.
6 Anna Kournikova became his girlfriend some years ago, and possibly still is.
7 100 million is the number of albums he has sold.

4 29

(script in Student's Book on *p.124*)

Good evening and welcome to *Top Sounds*, our weekly music programme, and tonight the focus is on the Latin music star Enrique Iglesias. As I'm sure you all know, Enrique Iglesias is the son of the Spanish singer Julio Iglesias, who is one of the most successful singing artists of all time.

Enrique was born in Madrid, Spain in 1975. His mother is Isabel Preysler, a journalist and TV host from the Philippines. When he was three years old his parents got divorced and later he moved to Miami to live with his father. He started studying Business at Miami University, but he left after a year because he wanted to become a musician. He didn't want his father to know about his music career and he didn't want to use his famous surname to be successful. So when he sent some of his songs to several record companies he used the name Enrique Martinez and he eventually got a contract with a Mexican record company.

He made his first album called 'Enrique Iglesias' in 1995, which won him a Grammy. He then made two more albums and he had many hits in the Latin music charts. At first Enrique sang mainly in Spanish, but later he began to sing more and more in English, too.

His fourth album, 'Escape' in 2001, was his biggest commercial success and included the singles *Escape* and *Hero* (sung in English), which became hits all over the world and made Enrique an international star. Since then he has made five other albums and has also had a few acting parts in films and TV programmes.

Also in 2001, he began dating the Russian tennis player, Anna Kournikova, but they kept their relationship very private. Today, Enrique Iglesias is recognized as one of the most popular artists in Latin America. He has sold 100 million albums, which makes him one of the best-selling artists of all time.

Extra support

- If there's time, you could get Sts to listen again with the script on *p.124*, so they can see exactly what they understood / didn't understand. Translate / explain any new words or phrases.

d Sts can answer the questions in pairs, small groups, or as a whole class. If they do the activity in pairs or small groups, get some feedback.

5 SPEAKING & WRITING

a In this activity Sts put into practice the contrast between the past simple and the present perfect through talking about an older person – a friend or member of their family.

Focus on the activity and give Sts five minutes to think about who they are going to talk about and to prepare their answers to the questions. Stress that it should be an older person, not a younger one.

Focus on the question prompts and quickly elicit the questions. You could demonstrate the activity by getting the class to ask you about one of your grandparents, elderly relatives, or a friend.

Extra support

- Get Sts to write the questions in their notebooks before they ask them. When they ask the questions, get them to ask the questions from the prompts and not just read them.

b Sit Sts in pairs, ideally face-to-face. Set a time limit for **A** to interview **B**. Encourage **B** to give as much information as possible and **A** to ask extra questions where possible.

Then Sts swap roles.

Find out if they found any similarities between their two people.

c Tell Sts to go to **Writing *A biography*** on *p.116* and to do **a**. Tell them not to worry about the gaps in the biography.

When they have finished, elicit three things about Norah Jones that they have remembered.

Now tell Sts to do **b** by putting the verbs in brackets in the past simple or present perfect.

Check answers.

2 separated	5 met	8 has made
3 has been	6 have worked	9 has won
4 went	7 moved	10 broke up

Now focus on the **Writing a biography** box and go through it with the class.

For **c**, you may like to get Sts to do the writing in class or you could set it as homework. Get them to write a biography of someone who is still alive, so someone they know or a famous person. Make sure they write three paragraphs by following the model.

In **d**, Sts should check their biography for mistakes, and if they did the writing in class, they could then swap the biography with other Sts to read. You could do the question *Which of your classmates' biographies is the most interesting?* as an open class. If they do it for homework, tell them to attach a photo of the person.

Tell Sts to go back to the main lesson **9C**.

6  **SONG** *You're My #1* ♫

This song was originally made famous by Spanish singer Enrique Iglesias in 1999. For copyright reasons this is a cover version. If you want to do this song in class, use the photocopiable activity on *p.276*.

4 30

You're My #1

I've kissed the moon a million times
Danced with angels in the sky
I've seen snowfall in the summertime
Felt the healing of the powers above
I've seen the world from the highest mountain
Tasted love from the purest fountain
I've seen lips that spark desire
Felt the butterflies a hundred times

I've even seen miracles
I've felt the pain disappear
But still haven't seen anything
That amazes me quite like you do

Chorus
You bring me up when I'm feeling down
You touch me deep you touch me right
You do the things I've never done
You make me wicked you make me wild
'Cause baby, you're my number one

I've sailed in a perfect dream
I've seen the sun make love to the sea
I've kissed the moon a million times
Danced with angels in the sky

I've even seen miracles
I've seen the tears disappear
But still haven't seen anything
That amazes me quite like you do

Chorus x2

Vocabulary directions: *traffic lights, take the..., etc.*
Function asking for and understanding directions in the street and for public transport; apologizing
Language *How do I get to...?, How many stops is that?, I'm terribly sorry*, etc.

PRACTICAL ENGLISH

Episode 5 Getting around

Lesson plan

In this lesson Sts learn how to give and understand simple directions both for in the street and for public transport.

In the storyline, Rob is with Holly in Brooklyn. Jenny rings to confirm their dinner date in Manhattan. She gives Rob directions on the subway to the restaurant. However, Rob arrives late. When he gets there Jenny is leaving the restaurant, after having waited an hour, and they have an argument.

STUDY LINK
- **Workbook** Getting around
- **iTutor**
- **www.oup.com/elt/englishfile**

Test and Assessment CD-ROM
- **Quick Test 9**
- **File 9 Test**
- **www.oup.com/elt/teacher/englishfile**

Optional lead-in (books closed)

- Elicit from the class what happened in the previous episode. Ask some questions, e.g. *What did Rob and Jenny do in the morning? Why did Rob go to the pharmacy? What did he buy? Where did Rob go in the evening?*
- Alternatively, you could play the last scene of Episode 4.

1 HOLLY AND ROB IN BROOKLYN

a 4 31 Books open. Focus on the photos and elicit what Sts think is happening. Do not tell them if they are right or not yet.

Focus on sentences 1–6 and give Sts time to read them. Then play the audio once the whole way through for them to mark the sentences T (true) or F (false). Make it clear that they don't need to correct the false sentences yet. Play again if necessary.

Get Sts to compare with a partner, and then check answers.

1 T	3 F	5 F
2 T	4 T	6 F

4 31
(script in Student's Book on *p.124*)
H = **Holly**, **R** = **Rob**, **J** = **Jenny**
H That was a good day's work, Rob. You did a great interview.
R You took some great photos, too. They're really nice.
H Thanks. Hey, let's have another coffee.
R I don't know. I have to get to Manhattan.
H You don't have to go right now.
R I'm not sure. I don't want to be late.
H Why do you have to go to Manhattan?
R I've got a... erm...
H A date? You have a date?
R Mm hm.
H Is it with anybody I know?
R No, it isn't. Anyway, excuse me a minute. I need to go to 'the restroom'.
H That's very American. I'll order more coffees.
R OK.
J (on the phone) Rob?
H Is that you, Jennifer?
J Oh, hi Holly. Erm... is Rob there?
H Yeah, one second. Rob! Not anybody I know, huh?
R Hi, Jenny.
J Rob? Are you still in Brooklyn?
R Yeah.
J You know the reservation at the restaurant's for eight, right?
R Don't worry. I'll be there! Oh, how do I get to Greenwich Village on the subway?

b Play the audio again, so Sts can listen again and correct the false sentences.

Get Sts to compare with a partner, and then check answers.

3 He has **a date** in Manhattan.
5 **Jenny** phones Rob.
6 The restaurant is booked for **8** o'clock.

Elicit from Sts that the restaurant is in Greenwich Village, a well-known area of Manhattan, and that Greenwich is pronounced /grenɪtʃ/.

Now focus on the **British and American English** box and go through it with the class.

Extra support

- If there's time, you could get Sts to listen again with the script on *p.124*, so they can see exactly what they understood / didn't understand. Translate / explain any new words or phrases.

2 VOCABULARY directions

a Tell Sts to look at the pictures and then complete phrases 1–5.

Get Sts to compare with a partner.

b 4 32 Play the audio for Sts to listen and check.

4 32
1 Turn **left**.
2 Go **straight** on.
3 Take the **next** turning on the right.
4 Turn right at the **traffic** lights.
5 Go round the **roundabout** and take the third exit.

Now play the audio for Sts to listen and repeat the phrases.

3 ASKING HOW TO GET THERE

a 4 **33**))) Focus on the map of the New York subway and ask Sts *Is Rob in Manhattan or Brooklyn now?* (Brooklyn) *Is the restaurant in Brooklyn?* (No, it isn't. It's in Greenwich Village, Manhattan.)

Make sure Sts can see where Rob is on the map.

Tell Sts that they are going to hear Rob asking Jenny for directions and they need to listen to the directions and try to mark the route on the map. Play the audio at least twice.

Get Sts to compare with a partner, and then check that they have marked the right route.

! The map in the Student's Book has been adapted and is simplified rather than strictly accurate.

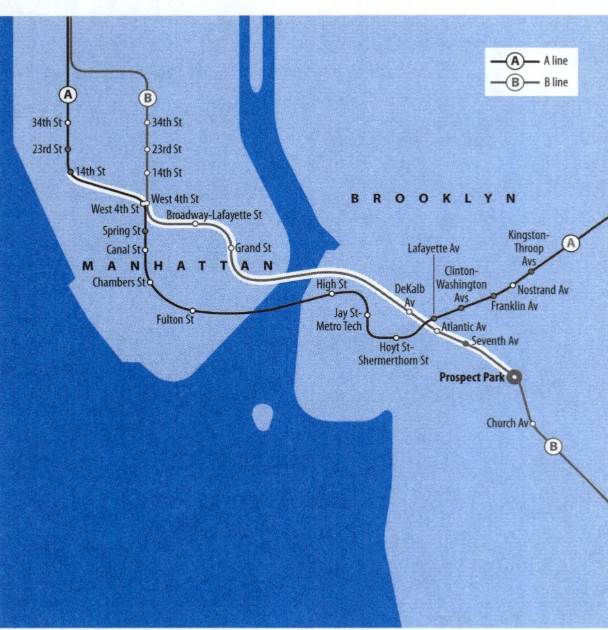

4 **33**)))
R = **Rob**, **J** = **Jenny**
R How do I get to Greenwich Village on the subway? (*repeat*)
J Go to the subway station at Prospect Park. **Take** the B train to West 4th Street.
R How many stops is that? (*repeat*)
J Six or seven.
R OK. And then? (*repeat*)
J From West 4th Street take the A train, and get **off** at 14th Street.
R Could you say that again? (*repeat*)
J OK. From Prospect Park take the B train to West 4th Street, and then take the A train to 14th Street. That's only one **stop**.
R Where's the restaurant? (*repeat*)
J Come out of the subway on Eighth Avenue, go **straight** on for about 50 yards, and take the **first** left. That's Greenwich Avenue. The restaurant's on the **right**. It's called 'The Tea Set'.
R OK, thanks. See you later. (*repeat*)
J And don't get **lost**!

b Now focus on the dialogue in the chart. Elicit that the **You Say** phrases is what Rob says and the **You Hear** phrases are said by Jenny, who is giving Rob directions. These phrases will be useful for Sts if they need to ask for directions.

Give Sts a minute to read through the dialogue and think what the missing words might be. Then play the audio again, and get Sts to complete the gaps. Play again if necessary.

Get Sts to compare with a partner, and then check answers.

See words in **bold** in script 4.33

Go through the dialogue line by line with Sts, helping them with any words or expressions they don't understand.

c 4 **34**))) Now focus on the **You Say** phrases and tell Sts they're going to hear the dialogue again. They should repeat the **You Say** phrases when they hear the beep. Encourage them to copy the rhythm and intonation.

Play the audio, pausing if necessary for Sts to repeat the phrases.

d Put Sts in pairs, **A** and **B**. **A** is Rob and **B** is Jenny. Get Sts to read the dialogue aloud, and then swap roles.

e In pairs, Sts roleplay asking for and giving simple directions using the subway map. Go through the instructions with them. **A** starts with *Go to the subway station at Lincoln Center...*

Monitor and help with any issues relating to directions.

Extra support

- Demonstrate the activity by giving the class directions to somewhere on the map and then ask them where they are.

f When they have finished, they should swap roles.

You could get a few pairs to perform in front of the class.

4 ROB IS LATE...AGAIN

a 4 **35**))) Focus on the pictures and ask Sts some questions, e.g. *What's happening?*, *How do they look?*, etc.

Get Sts to focus on the question or get them to close their books and write it on the board.

Play the audio once the whole way through and then check the answer.

No, it isn't.

4 **35**)))
(script in Student's Book on *p.124*)
R = **Rob**, **J** = **Jenny**
R Jenny! I'm here.
J Hi.
R I'm so sorry. There was a problem on the underground.
J We call it the subway here.
R Right. Anyway, the train stopped for about 20 minutes. I tried to call, but there was no signal.
J I've been here since seven forty-five.
R I know. I ran from the underground... subway station... I'm so sorry.
J You're always late. It's funny, isn't it?
R I said I'm sorry. Look, why don't we go back inside the restaurant?
J I waited for an hour for you. I don't want to stay here any more.

R Maybe we could... we could go for a walk. We could find another restaurant.
J I don't feel like a walk. It's been a long day.
R OK.
J But the night is still young. Maybe you have time to meet up with Holly again.
R Holly?
J I'm sorry. I didn't mean to say that.
R I don't care about Holly.
J Forget it, Rob. Now if you don't mind, I'd like to go home.
R Listen to me, Jenny. Holly is just a colleague.
J I said forget it. It's OK.
R No, it isn't OK. Look. I know I'm always late. And I know the underground is the subway. But that's not the point! I'm not interested in Holly. I came to New York because of you. The only person I'm interested in is you!

b Now give Sts time to read questions 1–5.

Play the audio again the whole way through. Play the audio again if necessary.

Get Sts to compare with a partner, and then check answers.

1 He says there was a problem on the underground.
2 An hour.
3 Go back in the restaurant, go for a walk, or go to a different restaurant.
4 He could meet up with Holly.
5 Jenny.

Extra support

- If there's time, you could get Sts to listen again with the script on *p.124*, so they can see exactly what they understood / didn't understand. Translate / explain any new words or phrases.

c Focus on the **Social English phrases**. In pairs, get Sts to think about what the missing words could be.

Extra challenge

- In pairs, get Sts to complete the phrases before they listen.

d **4 36** Play the audio for Sts to listen and complete the phrases.

Check answers.

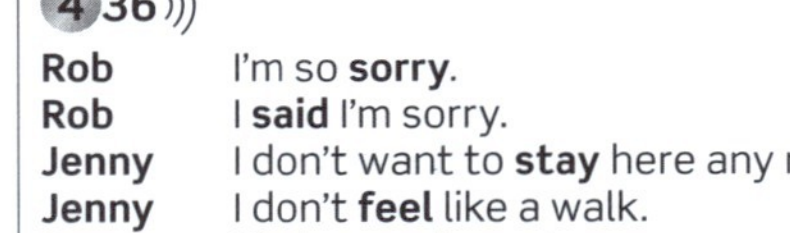

4 36

Rob	I'm so **sorry**.
Rob	I **said** I'm sorry.
Jenny	I don't want to **stay** here any more.
Jenny	I don't **feel** like a walk.
Jenny	It's been a **long** day.
Jenny	I didn't **mean** to say that.

If you know your Sts' L1, you could get them to translate the phrases. If not, get Sts to have a look at the phrases again in context in the script on *p.124*.

e Now play the audio again, pausing after each phrase for Sts to listen and repeat.

Finally, focus on the **Can you...?** questions and ask Sts if they feel confident they can now do these things. If they feel that they need more practice, tell them to watch the episode again and practise the language on their *iTutor*.

G passive
V verbs: *invent, discover,* etc.
P /ʃ/, *-ed*, sentence stress

10A The mothers of invention

Lesson plan

We often assume that most inventors are men. This lesson challenges this assumption and shows that women were responsible for several significant inventions of the last century. The lesson begins with Listening where Sts hear a radio programme about five everyday items invented by women. These inventions provide the context for the introduction of the present and past forms of the passive in Grammar. In Reading and Vocabulary the focus is on verbs which are frequently used in the passive, e.g. *designed, discovered, based (on)*, which leads into reading where Sts read some interesting and amusing facts about how some other famous things came to be invented. This is followed by a pronunciation focus on the /ʃ/ sound, the pronunciation of *-ed* in past participles, and sentence stress in passive sentences. The lesson ends with Speaking, where Sts ask each other quiz questions. The title of the lesson echoes the famous saying of the Greek philosopher, Plato, 'Necessity is the mother of invention.'

STUDY LINK

- **Workbook** 10A
- **iTutor**
- **www.oup.com/elt/englishfile**

Extra photocopiable activities

- **Grammar** Passive *p.189*
- **Communicative** General knowledge quiz *p.236* (instructions *p.205*)
- **www.oup.com/elt/teacher/englishfile**

Optional lead-in (books closed)

- Write the following phrase on the board:
  THE MOST USEFUL INVENTION OF THE LAST CENTURY WAS...
- Give Sts, in pairs, two or three minutes to complete the sentence by deciding what they think was the most useful invention of the 20th century.
- Get feedback and write Sts ideas on the board. Then get Sts to vote, with a show of hands, for the most useful invention.

1 LISTENING

a Books open. Focus on the photos. Make sure Sts understand what all the words mean, e.g. *disposable* = you throw it away after you have used it once, *bullet-proof* = bullets from a gun can't go through it, etc., and model and drill pronunciation.

Give Sts, in pairs, a couple of minutes to guess which five things were invented by women. Do not check answers yet.

b 4 37 Focus on the task and play the audio for Sts to check their answers to **a**.

Check answers. Get feedback to find out if Sts had guessed correctly.

Extra support

- Read through the script and decide if you need to pre-teach any new lexis before Sts listen.

The five inventions are:
the dishwasher, windscreen wipers, disposable nappies, Tipp-Ex, and the bullet-proof vest.

(script in Student's Book on *pp.124–125*)
P = presenter, S = Sally

P Good afternoon, and welcome to another edition of *Science Today*. In today's programme we are going to hear about women inventors. When we think of famous inventors we usually think of men, people like Alexander Graham Bell, Guglielmo Marconi, Thomas Edison. But, as Sally will tell us, many of the things which make our lives easier today were invented by women.

S That's absolutely right. Let's take the dishwasher for example. This was invented by a woman called Josephine Cochrane in 1886. She was a rich American who gave a lot of dinner parties. But she was annoyed that her servants used to break plates and glasses when they were washing up after a party. So, Josephine decided to try and invent a machine which could wash a lot of plates and glasses safely. Apparently she said, 'If nobody else is going to invent a dishwasher, then I will!' She designed the machine, and then she found a company to make it. At first only hotels and restaurants bought Josephine's new machine, but today the dishwasher is used by millions of people all over the world.
The car was invented by a man, but it was a woman, Mary Anderson, who in 1903 solved one of the biggest problems of driving. Until her invention it was impossible for drivers to see where they were going when it was raining or snowing. They had to open their window. The name of Mary's invention? Windscreen wipers.
An invention that definitely improved the lives of millions of people was disposable nappies. They were invented by a woman called Marion Donovan. Her father and uncle were inventors, and when she had young children she sat down and invented a nappy that you could use and then throw away. Anybody who has a small baby will know what a big difference disposable nappies make to our lives. But although she invented it in 1950, it wasn't until 1961 that an American company bought Marion's idea. Today millions of disposable nappies are used every day and Marion's invention has been made more eco-friendly. Now you can buy biodegradable nappies!
And now to our next inventor. In 1956, Bette Nesmith Graham was working as a secretary. Like all secretaries at that time she used to get very frustrated and angry when she made typing mistakes. In those days if you made a mistake, you had to get a new sheet of paper and start again from the beginning. Then she had a brilliant idea, which was to use a white liquid to paint over mistakes. Her invention is called Tipp-Ex today. Mrs Graham was a divorced mother and her invention made her a very rich woman. Her son, Mike Nesmith became a famous pop star – he was a member of the American group, The Monkees.
And finally... policemen, soldiers, and politicians all over the world are protected by something which was invented by a woman. In 1966 Stephanie Kwolek invented Kevlar, a special material which was very light, but incredibly strong, much stronger than metal. This material is used to make bullet-proof vests. Stephanie's invention has probably saved thousands of lives.

P Thanks very much, Sally. So... if you thought that everything was invented by men, think again.

Now play the audio again for Sts to complete 1–5 with the names of the inventions.

Check answers.

1 dishwasher	4 Tipp-Ex
2 Windscreen wipers	5 bullet-proof vest
3 Disposable nappies	

c Focus on the questions. Play the audio again for Sts to listen for more detail. Pause the audio after each invention to give Sts time to write their answers.

Get Sts to compare what they understood with a partner, then play the audio again if necessary.

Check answers.

1 Her servants used to break plates and glasses when they were doing the washing-up.
2 It was impossible for drivers to see where they were going.
3 More than 55 million.
4 She was a secretary.
5 It was very light, but incredibly strong (stronger than metal).

Extra challenge

- Ask a few more questions to check comprehension, e.g. *Who was Josephine Cochrane?* (A rich American woman) *Was the car invented by a woman?* (No) *Why has the invention of disposable nappies helped many women?* (Because they used to spend many hours a day washing nappies.), etc.

Extra support

- If there's time, you could get Sts to listen again with the script on *pp.124–125*, so they can see exactly what they understood / didn't understand. Translate / explain any new words or phrases.

d Focus on the question and get feedback from the whole class.

2 GRAMMAR passive

a Focus on the task and the example. Give Sts time to make four more true sentences.

Check answers.

2 Disposable nappies were invented by Marion Donovan.
3 More than 55 million nappies are used every day.
4 Mrs Graham's invention is called Tipp-Ex today.
5 Policemen all over the world are protected by the bullet-proof vest.

b Focus on the two sentences, a and b, and read the three questions aloud to the class. Elicit answers from the whole class, getting a majority opinion on each one and confirming if it is right or wrong.

1 Yes   2 b   3 a

c 4 38))) Tell Sts to go to **Grammar Bank 10A** on *p.144*. Focus on the example sentences and play the audio for Sts to listen and repeat. Make sure they pronounce the *-ed* endings in the participles correctly and encourage them to copy the rhythm. Then go through the rules with the class.

Additional grammar notes

- This lesson provides an introduction to the passive and Sts are taught present and past forms only.
- The formation of the passive is not difficult for Sts as it is composed of known items: the verb *be* and a past participle.
- The passive is often used in English where other languages use an impersonal subject.

Extra challenge

- You may want to point out to Sts that all other forms of the passive are made simply by changing the form of *be*, e.g. *will be made, has been made*, etc.

Focus on the exercises for **10A** on *p.145*. Sts do the exercises individually or in pairs.

Check answers, getting Sts to read the full sentences.

a 1 were invented
2 are educated
3 was discovered
4 was woken
5 is played
6 were recorded
7 are made
8 are sung
9 aren't usually seen
10 wasn't built

b 1 The iPod and the iPhone were designed by Jonathan Ive.
2 Olive oil is produced by most Mediterranean countries.
3 Uranus was discovered by Herschel in 1781.
4 The *Men in Black* films were directed by Barry Sonnenfeld.
5 *Mr and Mrs Clark and Percy* was painted by David Hockney in 1970–1971.
6 *Blue Suede Shoes* wasn't written by Elvis Presley.
7 The Harry Potter books were written by JK Rowling.
8 Daihatsu cars are made in Japan.

Tell Sts to go back to the main lesson **10A**.

Extra support

- If you think Sts need more practice, you may want to give them the Grammar photocopiable activity at this point.

3 READING & VOCABULARY verbs: *invent, discover*, etc.

a This exercise teaches / revises verbs which are often used in the passive and which Sts will later use in **Speaking**.

Get Sts to match the verbs in the list with the definitions and check answers.

1 discover	3 design
2 base	4 invent

b Focus on the text and the verbs in the list. Give Sts a few minutes to complete the text using the past participle of the correct verb from the list.

Get Sts to compare with a partner, and then check answers.

1 designed	5 shown	9 discovered
2 given	6 played	10 based
3 invented	7 called	
4 opened	8 used	

c Focus on the task and make sure Sts understand that one of the pieces of information in the text is not true. Give Sts a minute or so to re-read the text and decide, in pairs, which piece of information is not true.

Get feedback, asking Sts to explain their guess. Tell them that the invented piece of information is the fact that golf is so called because its letters stand for **G**entlemen **O**nly **L**adies **F**orbidden. This is not true, although the game was originally played by men. The word *golf* is thought to come from the Dutch word *kolf* meaning stick.

Extra idea

- Ask Sts to choose five words or phrases from the text that they want to learn and to write them with their translation in their notebooks or vocabulary books. Get some feedback on which words Sts have chosen.

Extra challenge

- Get Sts to read the text again and to try to remember the information. Then tell Sts to cover the text. Write on the board:
  Nike
  Tinned food
  Monopoly
  Golf
  Botox
  House M.D.
- Sts, in pairs, try to remember as much as they can from the text for each thing. Then get feedback from the whole class to see how much they can collectively remember.

4 PRONUNCIATION /ʃ/, *-ed*, sentence stress

Pronunciation notes

/ʃ/

- The /ʃ/ sound can be a problem for Sts who do not have it in their language. Here Sts are shown the typical letter combinations which produce this sound, *sh*, *ti* + consonant, and *cia* + consonant, and the less typical *ch*. Words where *ch* is pronounced /ʃ/ generally come from the French, e.g. *chef*, *chic*, etc.

-ed

- The pronunciation rules for the past participles in passive sentences are of course the same for regular past simple *-ed* ending verbs.
- *-ed* can be pronounced in three different ways:
  1 *-ed* is pronounced /t/ after verbs ending in these unvoiced* sounds: /k/, /p/, /f/, /s/, /ʃ/, and /tʃ/, e.g. *looked, hoped, laughed, passed, washed, watched.*
  2 After voiced* endings *-ed* is pronounced /d/, e.g. *arrived, changed, showed.*
  3 After verbs ending in /t/ or /d/ the pronunciation of *-ed* is /ɪd/, e.g. *hated, decided.*
- The difference between 1 and 2 is very small and only occasionally causes communication problems. The most important thing is for Sts to be clear about rule 3, i.e. when they should pronounce *-ed* /ɪd/.

***Voiced and unvoiced consonants**

- Voiced consonant sounds are made in the throat by vibrating the vocal chords, e.g. /b/, /l/, /v/, etc. Unvoiced consonant sounds are made in the mouth without vibration in the vocal chords, e.g. /k/, /p/, /t/, /s/, etc.
- You can demonstrate this to Sts by getting them to hold their hands against their throats. For voiced sounds they should feel a vibration in their throat, but not for unvoiced sounds.

a 4 39 Focus on the sound picture and elicit the word and sound.

Now play the audio for Sts to listen.

See words in Student's Book on *p.77*

Now play the audio again and get Sts to listen and repeat.

b Focus on the first question and elicit the answer regarding the four different spellings.

sh, ti, ci, and *ch*

Now tell Sts to go to the **Sound Bank** on *p.167* to check which spelling they think is not typical.

Check the answer.

ch is not typical.

STUDY LINK Sts can practise these sounds on the *iTutor* and on the *English File* Pre-intermediate website.

c This activity revises the pronunciation of *-ed* endings. Focus on the chart and remind Sts that the *-ed* ending can be pronounced in these three different ways.

Give Sts, in pairs, a couple of minutes to try and put the verbs in the list in the right column. They will find the /t/ and /d/ ones the most difficult to distinguish between.

d 4 40 Play the audio for Sts to check their answers.

tie /t/	based, produced
dog /d/	called, designed, discovered, used
/ɪd/	created, directed, invented, painted

Then play the audio again for Sts to underline the stressed syllable in each multi-syllable verb.

Check answers.

See underlining in script 4.40

Finally, play the audio again for Sts to listen and repeat.

e  Now tell Sts they are going to listen to six sentences and they must write them down.

Play the audio, pausing after each sentence to give Sts time to write. Play the audio again if necessary.

Check answers.

4 41

1 The washing machine was invented in the USA.
2 These photos were taken with an iPhone.
3 This wine is produced near here.
4 Who was the film directed by?
5 Who were those pictures painted by?
6 The cash machine wasn't invented until 1967.

Then repeat the activity getting individual Sts to say the sentences.

Extra challenge

- Play the audio again and get Sts to underline the stressed words. Elicit the answers onto the board (See underlining in script 4.41).

5 SPEAKING

Put Sts into pairs, **A** and **B**, and tell them to go to **Communication *Passives quiz***, **A** on *p.105*, **B** on *p.109*. Give Sts time to complete their sentences and choose the correct answers.

Get Sts to sit face-to-face if possible. **A** reads his / her sentences to **B**, who listens and says if **A**'s sentences are right or wrong, and corrects the wrong answers.

Sts then swap roles.

Monitor and help as Sts do the task, making sure they are forming the passive and pronouncing the past participle correctly.

End the activity when the majority of pairs have finished.

Extra support

- Put two **A**s together and two **B**s; let them complete their sentences with the correct passive form and answer option (a, b, or c). Then, put one **A** with one **B** and get them to read each other their sentences.

G *used to*
V school subjects: *history, geography*, etc.
P *used to / didn't use to*

10B Could do better

Lesson plan

In this lesson Sts learn to use *used to* to talk about repeated past actions, and the main context is school experiences. The lesson begins with a vocabulary focus on school subjects. Then Sts read some extracts from some famous people's school reports, which are used to present the grammar of *used to / didn't use to*. This is followed by a pronunciation focus on how to pronounce the new language. In Listening Sts listen to six people talking about their memories of school, which leads into Speaking where Sts talk about their own experiences at primary or secondary school.

STUDY LINK
- **Workbook** 10B
- **iTutor**
- **www.oup.com/elt/englishfile**

Extra photocopiable activities

- **Grammar** *used to p.190*
- **Communicative** My past *p.237* (instructions *p.206*)
- **Song** *ABC p.277* (instructions *p.266*)
- **www.oup.com/elt/teacher/englishfile**

Optional lead-in (books closed)

- Write on the board:
  WHAT PRIMARY / SECONDARY SCHOOL DID YOU GO TO?
  DID YOU LIKE THEM? WHY (NOT)?
- Model and drill the pronunciation of *primary* and *secondary*.
- Answer the question yourself and tell Sts a bit about your school experience. Then get them to ask and answer in pairs, and get some feedback.

1 VOCABULARY school subjects

a Books open. Focus on the instructions and report. Elicit what a report is, and model and drill the pronunciation
...ɔːt/. Also model and drill the pronunciation of
...ˈsʌbdʒɪkts/. Give Sts time to complete the
...ching the school subjects and pictures.

...ith a partner.

...s to listen and check. Point
...*ture* /ˈlɪtrətʃə/ each
...l (the *o* in *history*

...ogy)

Then play the audio again for Sts to repeat.

Tell Sts, individually or in pairs, to cover the words in **a**, look at the pictures and try to remember the words.

c Focus on the task and do the question as an open-class. Model and drill the pronunciation of *behaviour*.

d Focus on the ***good at*** box and go through it with the class.

Now focus on the task and the speech bubble. Demonstrate the activity by talking about the subjects yourself.

Put Sts in pairs and give them a few minutes to talk to each other.

Get some feedback from the class.

2 GRAMMAR *used to*

a Put Sts in pairs or small groups and get them to discuss the questions. Make sure they understand the word *term* (= one of the three periods that the school or college year is divided into). To start Sts off, you could tell them about yourself.

Get some feedback from the class.

b Focus on the book cover and tell Sts it's a book with extracts from famous British people's school reports, either from primary or secondary school. You could tell them that the title 'Could do better' was a typical comment that teachers often made in reports. Now tell Sts that they are going to read some of the extracts, and should decide if the comments are positive or negative.

Check answers.

They are all negative.

c Now tell Sts to read the reports again and then match the initials to sentences 1–5.

Get Sts to compare with a partner, and then check answers.

1 WC	3 KF	5 PD
2 JL	4 HF	

Now read the reports aloud to the class, eliciting / explaining the meaning of new words and phrases.

d Now give Sts a minute to look back at the sentences in **c** and to answer the two questions.

1 b 2 b

e **4 43**)) Tell Sts to go to **Grammar Bank 10B** on *p.144*. Focus on the example sentences and play the audio for Sts to listen and repeat. Encourage them to copy the rhythm. Then go through the rules with the class.

Additional grammar notes

- *Used to* only exists in the past, and is used for past habits or states. Sts may not have an equivalent form in their language. If they do have an equivalent verb, it may also exist in the present (for present habits), which means Sts may try to say *I use to* for present habits rather than using the present simple and an adverb of frequency (*I usually …*). Typical mistake: *I use to go to the gym every Friday.*

! Sts might confuse *used to* + infinitive with the past of the verb *use*, e.g. *I used my dictionary when I did my English homework.*

Focus on the exercises for **10B** on *p.145*. Sts do the exercises individually or in pairs.

Check answers, getting Sts to read the full sentences.

a
1 He used to have long hair.
2 He didn't use to wear glasses.
3 He didn't use to have a beard.
4 He used to play football.
5 He didn't use to wear a tie.

b
1 My sister used to hate maths, but she loves it now.
2 Where did you use to work?
3 I didn't use to like vegetables when I was a child.
4 What did you use to do in the summer holidays when you were young?
5 The British didn't use to drink a lot of coffee.
6 This building used to be a cinema.
7 Did your brother use to teach here?
8 I didn't use to be a Manchester United fan.
9 Did Jeff use to have a motorbike?
10 Telegrams used to be a way of sending important messages.

Tell Sts to go back to the main lesson **10B**.

Extra support

- If you think Sts need more practice, you may want to give them the Grammar photocopiable activity at this point.

3 PRONUNCIATION *used to / didn't use to*

Pronunciation notes

- As mentioned earlier, Sts might confuse *used to* + infinitive with the past of the verb *use*. As well as having a completely different meaning the two verbs are pronounced differently (*used to* is pronounced /ˈjuːstə/ and *used* (past of *use*) is /juːzd/. The final /t/ in *used* and the /t/ in *to* are run together and make one /t/ sound.

a 4 44 Focus on the **Pronouncing *used to*** box and go through it with the class. Model and drill the pronunciation of *used to* /ˈjuːstə/.

Now focus on the task. Play the audio once for Sts just to listen.

Then play it again for them to underline the stressed words.

Check answers.

4 44
1 He used to hate school.
2 I used to be good at French.
3 They didn't use to behave well.
4 She didn't use to wear glasses.
5 Did you use to walk to school?

Extra challenge

- You could ask Sts to guess and underline the stressed words before they listen to the audio. Elicit again the kind of words that are usually stressed / unstressed (see **Pronunciation notes** in **2B**).

Play the audio again, pausing after each sentence for Sts to listen and repeat.

Then repeat the activity eliciting responses from individual Sts.

b 4 45 Focus on the task and tell Sts they are going to hear six more sentences with a form of *used to* in them. They must write them down.

Play the audio, pausing after each sentence to give Sts time to write. Play again if necessary.

Elicit the sentences onto the board.

1 Where did you use to live?
2 I didn't use to like exams.
3 I used to have long hair.
4 Did you use to work hard?
5 I used to be very shy.
6 I didn't use to do any sport.

4 LISTENING

a 4 46 Focus on the task and make sure Sts know what they have to do. Tell them that all the speakers are talking about their memories of secondary school. Play the audio once the whole way through and get Sts to decide how each person felt about school. Play again if necessary.

Check answers.

Extra support

- Read through the script and decide if you need to pre-teach any new lexis before Sts listen.

1 ✗	3 ✓	5 ✓✗
2 ✓✗	4 ✗	6 ✓

4 46
(script in Student's Book on *p.125*)
I = interviewer, M = man, W = woman

1
I Did you like school?
M1 No, definitely not.
I Why?
M1 I didn't like most of the lessons – I was always bored
I hated exams. And the worst thing of all was PE. W
went to school we used to play rugby. Ugh – it wa

2
I Did you like school?
W1 I loved primary school, but I didn't really like
school.
I Why not?
W1 Well, the school was very big and it was
impersonal. It took me a very long time
there. And I'm not really very academ
We used to get loads of homework,

3
I Did you like school?
W2 Er yes, I did.
I Why?
W2 I was very curious about everything when I was little so I liked school because I learned about new things. And of course I used to see my friends every day. The other thing I loved was the library – my school had a fantastic library – I even used to stay on there after class just to read. Oh dear, I sound very goody-goody – but it's true!

4
I Did you like school?
M2 Not especially.
I Why?
M2 It was a boys' school and I got a bit fed up with just being with boys all the time.

5
I Did you like school?
W3 It was all right – some bits were better than others, of course. The lessons I liked depended very much on the teacher – so for example, physics and English were great, but chemistry and history were terrible. I generally liked sport, except in the winter. I made some good friends at school, and I'm still in touch with a few of them 30 years later, so I suppose that's positive!

6
I Did you like school?
M3 Actually, I used to really love school. Lessons were fine, and I always did well without having to work too hard. But the real reason I loved school was because I had a very good social life. I had lots of friends and we used to play football in the playground at lunchtime. I was one of the gang, I felt that I belonged there. I've never really felt like that since then.

b Tell Sts that they are now going to hear the people again and they must answer the questions. Give Sts some time to read the questions before playing the audio.

Play the audio again and then check answers.

Speaker 4 didn't like being at a same-sex school.
Speaker 6 didn't use to study a lot, but got good marks.
Speaker 5 had a very good physics teacher.
Speaker 1 hated doing sport.
Speaker 2 liked one school, but not another.
Speaker 3 used to read a lot at school.

Extra challenge

- Elicit as many details as possible about each speaker.

c In pairs or small groups, Sts answer the question.

Get some feedback from the class.

Extra support

If there's time, you could get Sts to listen again with ...ript on *p.125*, so they can see exactly what they ...d / didn't understand. Translate / explain ...or phrases.

...ages of your Sts, ...imary or ...utes to ...ed to do

...out a few of

b Put Sts into groups of three **A**, **B**, and **C** (or pairs if this is not feasible). Tell **A** to talk about the first thing in the list in **a** and to tell **B** and **C** about how they used to be. **B** and **C** ask for more information when they can, and then talk about themselves. Then **B** talks to **A** and **C** about the second thing in the list, etc., and they carry on taking turns to start each topic.

Get quick feedback from the groups and find out if Sts had anything in common.

6 4 47 SONG *ABC*

This song was originally made famous by The Jackson 5 in 1970. For copyright reasons this is a cover version. If you want to do this song in class, use the photocopiable activity on *p.277*.

4 47

ABC

You went to school to learn, girl
Things you never, never knew before
Like I before E except after C
And why two plus two makes four, now now now,
I'm gonna teach you (Teach you, teach you)
All about love, dear (All about love)
Sit yourself down, take a seat
All you gotta do is repeat after me.

Chorus
A B C, Easy as
One, two, three, Or simple as
Do re mi, A B C,
One, two, three, baby, you and me girl!
A B C, Easy as
One, two, three, Or simple as
Do re mi, A B C,
One, two, three, baby, you and me girl!

Come on, let me love you just a little bit!
Come on, let me love you just a little bit!
I'm a going to teach how to sing it out!
Come on, come on, come on, let me show you what it's all about!

Reading, writing, arithmetic are the
Branches of the learning tree
But listen without the roots of love every day, girl
Your education ain't complete
T, T, T, Teacher's gonna show you (Show you, show you)
How to get an A! (How to get an A, girl!)
Spell 'me' (me) 'you' (you), (Add the two!)
Listen to me baby, that's all you gotta do!

Chorus

G *might*
V word building: noun formation, e.g. *decide – decision*
P diphthongs

10C Mr Indecisive

Lesson plan

This lesson presents the modal verb *might* used to express possibility through the context of a person who is very indecisive. The lesson begins with grammar and a dialogue between Adrian ('Mr Indecisive') and his friend, Tina. In the Grammar Bank Sts see that *may* is an alternative to *might* although this is not practised in the lesson. In Pronunciation Sts work on some common diphthongs. Then in Speaking they interview each other to find out whether they are indecisive and this leads into reading an article which asks whether there is too much choice in today's world. Finally, in Vocabulary Sts get some practice in word building (formation of nouns).

STUDY LINK
- **Workbook** 10A
- **iTutor**
- **iChecker**
- **www.oup.com/elt/englishfile**

Extra photocopiable activities

- **Grammar** *might* (possibility) *p.191*
- **Communicative** Match it! *p.238* (instructions *p.206*)
- **www.oup.com/elt/teacher/englishfile**

Optional lead-in (books closed)

- Write DECIDE on the board. Ask Sts what it means and which part of speech it is (verb, noun, etc.) and elicit that it's a verb. Ask where the stress is and mark it on the board (de<u>ci</u>de). Then ask *What's the noun from 'decide'?* and elicit that it's *de<u>ci</u>sion*. Teach / elicit the phrase *make a decision*. Then elicit / teach the adjective *de<u>ci</u>sive* and its meaning (it describes a person who can make decisions quickly) and then teach / elicit the opposite *inde<u>ci</u>sive*.

1 GRAMMAR *might*

a Books open. Focus on the photo, and elicit that the man is indecisive, i.e. he finds it difficult to make decisions. Elicit the meaning of what the woman is thinking (*make up your mind* = make a decision). If you didn't do the **Optional lead-in**, write INDE<u>CI</u>SIVE on the board and underline the stressed syllable.

Then focus on the questions. Get some answers from the class. If you know someone who is indecisive, you could tell the class about them.

b 4 48 Tell the class they are going to listen to the two people in the photo having a conversation. Get them to close their books or cover the dialogue in **c** and listen for what Adrian decides to do in the end.

Get Sts to compare their answers with a partner. Play again if necessary.

Check answers.

Adrian decides to go to the party. He decides to drive and to pick Tina up at 9.00.

4 48
T = Tina, A = Adrian
T Hi, Adrian.
A Oh, hi Tina.
T It's Alice's party tonight. You are going, aren't you?
A I don't know. I'm not sure. <u>I might **go**</u>, but <u>I might not</u>. I can't decide.
T Oh, come on. It'll be good. Lots of Alice's friends are going to be there. <u>You might **meet someone**</u>.
A Yes, that's true… OK. I'll go then.
T Great. Shall we get a taxi there?
A No, I'll take my car… No, wait. <u>It might **be difficult** to park</u>. Let's get a taxi.
T Fine. What time shall I get the taxi for? 9.30?
A Yes… No… Listen. I'll take my car. I'll pick you up at 9.00.
T Are you sure about that?
A Yes, I'm sure… I think.

c Tell Sts to listen again and complete the gaps. Play the audio, pausing if necessary for Sts to write.

Check answers.

See **bold** words in script 4.48

d 4 49 Tell Sts that Adrian now phones Tina. They must listen and find out what happens.

Check answers.

Tina is waiting for Adrian, who is half an hour late. He has changed his mind again.

4 49
T Adrian! Where are you? It's nearly half past nine.
A Sorry, Tina. Listen. I've changed my mind. I'm not going to go to the party.
T I don't believe it. You are the most indecisive person I've ever met.
A Well, I suppose I could go…
T Aghh!!

e Focus on the instructions. Elicit that the first example is *I might go*, and get Sts to underline the rest.

Check answers.

See underlining in script 4.48

We use *might* (+ infinitive) to talk about a possibility.

f 4 50 Tell Sts to go to **Grammar Bank 10C** on *p.144*. Focus on the examples and play the audio for Sts to listen and repeat. Encourage them to copy the rhythm. Then go through the rules with the class.

Additional grammar notes
- *Might* and *may* are synonyms, but *might* is probably more frequent in spoken English, which is why the presentation focusses on this form. However, *may* is also commonly used, especially in writing, so it is important that this is pointed out to Sts.

- At this level *might* is taught more for recognition than production as it is an example of 'late assimilation' language. In conversation Sts are more likely to try to express the same idea in another way, e.g. by using *maybe, possibly,* or *It's possible.*

Focus on the exercises for **10C** on *p.145*. Sts do them individually or in pairs.

Check answers, getting Sts to read the full sentences.

a 1 H 2 G 3 A 4 C 5 B 6 I 7 F 8 E

b
1 might be ill.
2 might be in a meeting.
3 might not like it.
4 might not have time.
5 might have fish and chips.
6 might be cold.

Tell Sts to go back to the main lesson **10C**.

Extra support

- If you think Sts need more practice, you may want to give them the Grammar photocopiable activity at this point.

g Focus on the task and the example in the speech bubbles. You could demonstrate the activity by answering a couple of the questions yourself.

Make sure Sts understand that they must give two possibilities each time and return the question with *What about you?* Put Sts in pairs and get them to ask and answer the five questions.

Get some feedback from the class.

2 PRONUNCIATION diphthongs

Pronunciation notes

- A diphthong is a combination of two vowel sounds which run together to produce a new sound. For example, the diphthong /eə/ is a combination of /e/ and /ə/. There are eight diphthongs in English, which are all practised here.

a 4 51 Look at the eight picture words and sounds, and tell Sts to listen to how they are pronounced. Play the audio once for Sts to just listen.

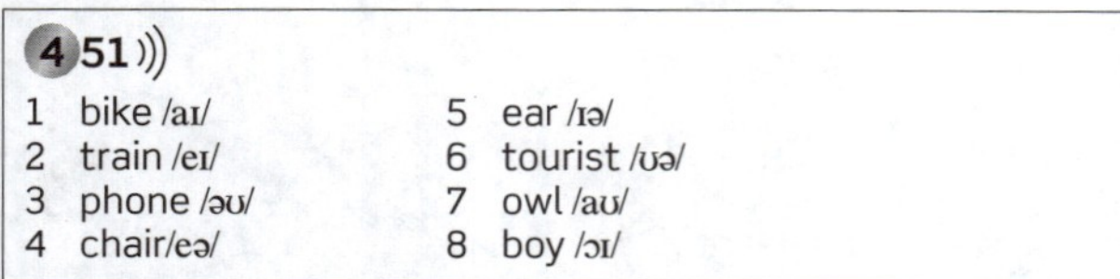

4 51

1 bike /aɪ/	5 ear /ɪə/
2 train /eɪ/	6 tourist /ʊə/
3 phone /əʊ/	7 owl /aʊ/
4 chair/eə/	8 boy /ɔɪ/

Now play the audio again for Sts to listen and repeat each sound. Play again if necessary, concentrating especially on any sounds your Sts find more difficult to make.

b Tell Sts to look at all the words in each category and to find the odd word out, i.e. the one that doesn't have the same diphthong sound. Remind Sts that this kind of exercise is easier if they say the words aloud to themselves.

Get Sts to compare their answers.

c 4 52 Now play the audio for Sts to listen and check.

Check answers.

1 since	5 where
2 key	6 bus
3 trousers	7 borrow
4 near	8 town

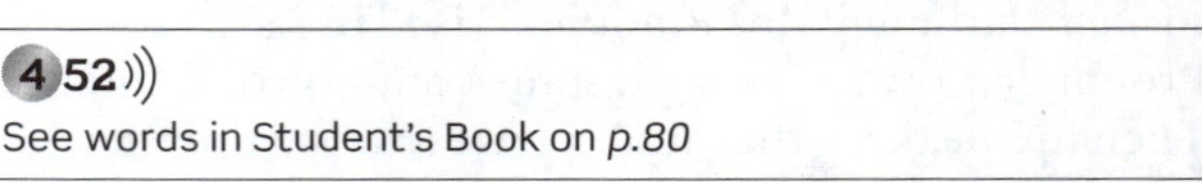

4 52

See words in Student's Book on *p.80*

Then play the audio, pausing after each line for Sts to listen and repeat.

3 SPEAKING & READING

a Focus on the **Are you indecisive?** questionnaire and put Sts in pairs. Remind Sts of the phrase *change your mind* (= make a decision and then change it). Tell them they are going to interview each other to find out who the more indecisive of the two of them is.

Give Sts time to interview each other. Monitor and encourage them to ask for / give more information, and to illustrate their answers with examples.

Get feedback from various pairs, and find out (with a show of hands) if the majority of the class is indecisive or decisive.

Extra idea

- You could get Sts to interview you first. Give as many examples as you can.

b Tell Sts they are going to read an article about choice and the first sentence from each paragraph is missing. They must read the article and complete the gaps with sentences A–E.

Get Sts to compare with a partner, and then check answers.

1 C 2 A 3 D 4 E 5 B

Deal with any new vocabulary.

c Finally, get Sts, in pairs or small groups, to discuss the question.

Get feedback and find out, with a show of hands, which area Sts think offers too much choice.

Extra challenge

- Ask the class *Can you remember a time when you had too much choice?* and elicit answers, e.g. in a mobile phone shop or when buying a pair of shoes. Ask Sts how they finally made their choice.

4 VOCABULARY word building: noun formation

a Focus on the **Noun formation** box and go through it with the class.

Now focus on the chart, point out the two sections, and make sure Sts know all the verbs. In the first section, highlight the *-ion* ending and the spelling changes. Then elicit the next noun (*information*) and get Sts to continue in pairs.

b 4 53 Play the audio Sts to listen and check.

Check answers.

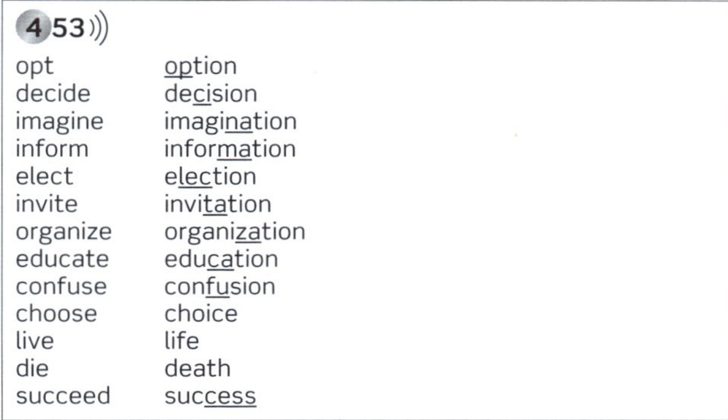
4 53

opt	option
decide	decision
imagine	imagination
inform	information
elect	election
invite	invitation
organize	organization
educate	education
confuse	confusion
choose	choice
live	life
die	death
succeed	success

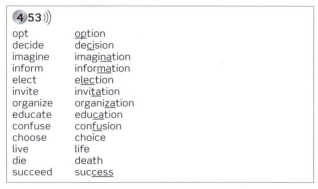

Now play the audio again, pausing after each word for Sts to underline the stress.

Check answers and elicit that *-tion* and *-sion* are pronounced /ʃn/ or /ʒn/ (*imagination* and *decision*), and that the stress is always on the syllable before this ending.

Finally, play it one more time for Sts to listen and repeat.

Extra idea

- Get Sts to write four questions using the nouns from **a**, e.g. *Do you have a good imagination?* Sts then ask and answer in pairs.

9 & 10 Revise and Check

For instructions on how to use these pages see *p.38*.

STUDY LINK
- **iTutor**

Test and Assessment CD-ROM
- **Quick Test 10**
- **File 10 Test**

GRAMMAR

1 b 6 a 11 b
2 c 7 c 12 b
3 a 8 a 13 c
4 c 9 b 14 a
5 c 10 c 15 c

VOCABULARY

a 1 election 5 death
2 decision 6 success
3 choice 7 imagination
4 organization

b 1 goat (the others can fly)
2 lion (the others are farm animals)
3 spider (the others are sea animals)
4 fear (the others are adjectives)
5 marks (the others are school subjects)

c 1 retire 4 based
2 fell 5 designed
3 discovered

d 1 kangaroo (also koala) 5 terrified
2 bee 6 separate
3 crocodile 7 science
4 bull 8 report

PRONUNCIATION

a 1 bear 4 nervous
2 cow 5 subject
3 children

b 1 gi<u>raffe</u> 4 re<u>tire</u>
2 <u>el</u>ephant 5 de<u>sign</u>
3 <u>se</u>condary

CAN YOU UNDERSTAND THIS TEXT?

a They pushed the swimmers together and swam around them.

b 1 F 3 T 5 F 7 F 9 T
2 T 4 F 6 T 8 F

CAN YOU UNDERSTAND THESE PEOPLE?

4 54

1 c 2 c 3 b 4 b 5 a

4 54

1
I = interviewer, D = David
I Do you have a phobia?
D Yes, I don't like being in confined spaces, like a cave.
I How long have you had it?
D Since I was a child.
I How does it affect your life?
D I try not to go into caves, or very small spaces.

2
I = interviewer, Jo = Joanna
I What animal would you most like to see in the wild, for example on a safari? Why?
Jo Well, I've already been on safari, so I've seen quite a few of them, but we didn't see any leopards when I went on safari, so I'd really like to see a leopard in the wild.

3
I = interviewer, P = Polly
I Did you like school?
P Yeah, I loved school.
I Why?
P Because you learnt lots of new things, there was lots of sport to do, and all your friends were at school.
I What were your best and worst subjects?
P Maybe languages, I liked French, but also science, maths, and worst subject? I don't know I liked them all.

4
I = interviewer, SJ = Sarah Jane
I What do you do?
SJ I'm a teacher.
I How long have you been a teacher?
SJ Six years.

5
I = interviewer, J = Justin
I What's your favourite building in New York?
J Probably the Empire State Building.
I Why do you like it?
J I like the décor, I like the design of it, and it's because it's centralized, it's just the perfect location for that kind of a skyscraper.
I What do you know about it?
J I know it was put together in the late 20s, and it opened in 1931, I think.

G expressing movement: *go over*, etc.
V sports: *team player*, etc.; expressing movement: *into, through*, etc.
P sports

11A Bad losers

Lesson plan

In this lesson Sts learn how we express movement in English using a verb and an adverb or preposition, e.g. *walk under the bridge*, *go out of the door*, and the context is sport. At the start of the lesson in Pronunciation and Speaking Sts practise pronouncing the names of sports in English before doing a questionnaire about which sports they like and don't like, etc. In Vocabulary they focus on words which describe movement (*up, down, along, through*, etc.) and in Grammar they learn how to combine these words with a verb to express movement. In Reading and Speaking Sts read a newspaper article about some famous bad losers in sporting history and talk about their own experiences of good and bad losers. Finally, in Writing Sts read a model essay about football on TV, and then write an essay of their own.

STUDY LINK

- **Workbook** 11A
- **iTutor**
- **www.oup.com/elt/englishfile**

Extra photocopiable activities

- **Grammar** Expressing movement *p.192*
- **Communicative** The race *p.239* (instructions *p.206*)
- **Vocabulary** Expressing movement *p.261* (instructions *p.247*)
- **Song** *The Final Countdown p.278* (instructions *p.266*)
- **www.oup.com/elt/teacher/englishfile**

Optional lead-in (books closed)

- Write SPORTS on the board and give Sts, in pairs, two minutes to think of English words for sports. Tell them that they must try to write down at least ten. Tell them to keep their lists as they will be using them later.

1 PRONUNCIATION & SPEAKING sports

Pronunciation notes

- Some words for sports in other languages are similar to the English word or even the same. However, the pronunciation is usually different. This means that there may often be interference from Sts' L1 when they use the English word for a particular sport.

a Books open. Focus on the photos and ask Sts to name all the sports. Write their answers on the board.

1 tennis	3 skiing	5 cycling	7 rugby
2 high jump	4 basketball	6 handball	

b 4 55 Focus on the list of sports. Put Sts in pairs and get them to say together how they think they are pronounced, and to underline the stressed syllable.

Play the audio once for Sts to check their answers, pausing before each word and eliciting the pronunciation from an individual student (or the whole class), and then letting them hear the pronunciation on the audio.

Play the audio again for Sts to underline the stressed syllable in each one and then check answers.

> 4 55
> athletics, baseball, basketball, boxing, cycling, football, golf, handball, hockey, motor racing, rugby, skiing, tennis, volleyball, windsurfing

Now, play the audio again getting Sts to listen and repeat.

Finally elicit any other sports Sts know, e.g. karate, judo, table tennis, etc. If you did the **Optional lead in**, now ask Sts if they have any sports in their lists which have not been named so far. Elicit their spelling and pronunciation, and write them on the board.

c Focus on the **Verbs with sports** box and go through it with the class.

Extra idea

- Draw three columns on the board and write PLAY, GO, and DO at the top of each one. Get Sts to put the sports in **a** and **b** in the right column, or if you did the **Optional lead-in**, add other sports Sts came up with to the columns.

Some examples:

PLAY	GO	DO
handball	sailing	gymnastics
hockey	riding	karate
badminton	climbing	athletics
ping-pong	motor racing	boxing

Now focus on the sports questionnaire and go through the questions, making sure Sts understand them. Demonstrate the activity by answering some of the questions yourself.

Put Sts in pairs and get them to ask and answer the questions. Encourage them to ask for and give more information so that this becomes a conversation rather than just questions and answers.

Get some feedback from the class.

2 VOCABULARY sports, expressing movement

a Focus on the task and tell Sts to put the words in the list in the correct column.

Get Sts to compare with a partner, and then check answers, making sure Sts know what all the words mean. Model and drill pronunciation.

athletics	**football**	**golf**	**tennis**
lap	corner	bunker	match point
track	penalty	hole	serve

Elicit any other words Sts know related to those four sports.

b 4 56 Focus on the task and make sure Sts know what a sports commentary is. Tell Sts to listen and name the four sports.

Play the audio once the whole way through. Then play it again if necessary, pausing after each commentary to elicit the sport.

1 golf	2 football	3 athletics	4 tennis

4 56

1 Oh, that's a really long one! Oh, dear! boy! The ball has gone into the lake. And that might be the end of his hopes of winning the US Open this year.
2 It's a penalty! Yes, the referee has given a penalty in the last minute of the game! This is England's big chance. The goalkeeper is waiting on his line. Here we go! Oh no, he's missed it! The ball has gone over the bar! I don't believe it. England have missed a penalty in the last minute.
3 And there's the bell for the last lap! Now they have to run round the track one more time in this 10,000 metres final, and the African runners are in first, second and third positions, but the Brazilian is coming up fast in the outside lane. This is going to be a fantastic finish!
4 And it's match point for the second time. A very hard serve, but it goes into the net... Second serve. The serve is good, and that's a very hard return, but the ball has gone out! And so we have a new Wimbledon ladies' champion.

c Tell Sts they are going to listen to the commentaries again and to complete sentences 1–4 with one word. You might want to tell Sts that there is one sentence for each of the four sports.

Play the audio again, pausing after each sport for Sts to write the missing word.

Check answers. For number 3 Sts may say *around*. Tell them that the commentator said *round*, but that *around* is a synonym and would also be correct in this context.

1 into	2 over	3 round	4 out

Now tell Sts to look at drawings a–d and to match each one with a sentence.

Check answers.

1 b	2 c	3 a	4 d

d Tell Sts to go to **Vocabulary Bank *Expressing movement*** on *p.162* and get them to do **a** individually or in pairs.

4 57 Now do **b**. Play the audio for Sts to check answers. Play it again, pausing after each phrase for Sts to repeat. Give further practice of words and phrases your Sts find difficult to pronounce.

4 57

Expressing movement

6 under the bridge	3 over the bridge
11 along the street	12 up the steps
10 round the lake	7 past the church
8 through the tunnel	9 towards the lake
4 into the shop	1 down the steps
2 across the road	5 out of the shop

Focus on the ***in(to)* and *out (of)*** box and go through it with the class.

Focus on **c**. Get Sts to cover the words in **a** and look at the pictures. From memory they take turns to tell their partner where the dog went.

Finally, focus on the ***away, off,* and *back*** box and go through it with the class.

Tell Sts to go back to the main lesson **11A**.

Extra support

- If you think Sts need more practice, you may want to give them the Vocabulary photocopiable activity at this point.

3 GRAMMAR expressing movement

a Focus on the activity and check that Sts understand the verbs in the list. Then get Sts to complete the sentences.

Check answers.

1 throw	2 kick	3 hit	4 run

b In pairs, Sts try to think of three possible verbs to complete the gap in the sentence. Point out to Sts that the verbs must be in the past simple.

Check answers.

Possible answers
ran, drove, cycled, jogged

c 4 58 Tell Sts to go to **Grammar Bank 11A** on *p.146*. Focus on the example sentences and play the audio for Sts to listen and repeat. Encourage them to copy the rhythm. Then go through the rules with the class.

Additional grammar notes

- In English, movement is expressed by adding a preposition or adverb of movement to a verb, e.g. *walk **up** the steps, climb **over** the wall*. In your Sts' L1 this may be expressed in a different way, e.g. by just using a single verb.

Focus on the exercises for **11A** on *p.147*. Sts do the exercises individually or in pairs.

Check answers, getting Sts to read the full sentences.

a	1 to, into	3 along	5 towards	7 round
	2 past	4 over	6 over, into	8 across
b	1 over	3 down	5 out	7 up
	2 in	4 into	6 out of	

Tell Sts to go back to the main lesson **11A**.

Extra challenge

- With a class which is very keen on sport, you could get Sts to practise more sports rules. Put Sts in groups of four: **A, B, C, D. A** thinks of a sport he / she knows well. The others have to guess it by asking a maximum of ten *yes* / *no* questions, e.g. *Is it a team sport? Do you play it inside? Do you have to throw the ball?*, etc. When they have guessed, **B** thinks of a sport, etc.

Extra support

- If you think Sts need more practice, you may want to give them the Grammar photocopiable activity at this point.

d Focus on the instructions and the example. Before Sts start, you could pre-teach some words they might need, e.g. *jump, bar, basket, goal, line*, etc.

Put Sts in pairs and get them to say what they can see in the pictures, using the right verb and preposition.

Get some feedback from the class.

2 He's jumping over the bar.
3 He's skiing down the mountain.
4 He is throwing the ball into the basket.
5 He's cycling around the track.
6 He is throwing the ball into the goal.
7 One player is pulling the other player down. The other player is running towards the (touch)line.

4 READING & SPEAKING

a Put Sts in pairs or small groups and get them to answer the questions. Model and drill the pronunciation of *loser*.

Get some feedback from the class. You could also tell the class about you and your family / friends.

b Focus on the text and the five questions, making sure Sts understand them. Tell Sts to read the text and find the names. They should not worry about the gaps.

Get Sts to compare with a partner, and then check answers.

1 John McEnroe	4 Nelson Piquet
2 John Howard	5 Luciano Gaucci
3 Jon Drummond	

Extra support

- Read the introduction with the class and elicit the meaning of the vocabulary, e.g. *dignity*, *blame sb*, *defeat*, *refuse*, and *opponent*.

c Set Sts a time limit to read the text again and complete the gaps with the prepositions.

Get Sts to compare with a partner, and then check answers.

1 out	3 down	5 out of
2 in	4 past	6 out of

d Tell Sts to look at the highlighted words in the text related to sport and, in pairs, to try to guess their meaning.

Check answers, either explaining in English, translating into Sts' L1, or getting Sts to check in their dictionaries. If Sts are using dictionaries, remind them that the words are related to sport, so they need to find the relevant definitions.

Extra challenge

- You could get Sts to underline other words in the text related to sport. Check answers.

your opponent, athletics, runner, the track, was serving, his serve, Grand Prix, footballer, World Cup, semi-final, the match, the president of the club, the player's contract, the medals ceremony, the medals, the English players

Deal with any other vocabulary problems, and write any useful new vocabulary on the board for Sts to copy into their notebooks.

e Put Sts in pairs. Sts take turns to ask a partner the questions. The first two relate to the article.

Monitor and help while Sts are doing the activity.

Finally, get feedback from the class about their opinions on the three questions.

5 WRITING an opinion essay

a In pairs, Sts discuss the question.

Get some feedback from the class.

b Tell Sts to go to **Writing *An opinion essay*** on *p.117*.

Focus on the instructions in **a** and get Sts to read the article. Tell them not to worry about the gaps, but help them with any vocabulary problems. When they have finished, elicit whether Sts agree or not with the writer's arguments. You could even have a vote with a show of hands.

Now do **b** and get Sts to read the article again and complete the gaps with the words and phrases in the list.

Check answers.

2 Firstly	4 Thirdly	6 To conclude
3 for example	5 Finally	7 Instead

Finally, focus on the essay title in **c**. Put Sts in pairs and get them to decide if they agree with the title or not, and what their reasons are. You might want to change *reality shows* in the essay title to *channels*, *American series*, or whatever you think is more appropriate depending on what TV is like in your Sts' country.

Go through the layout of the article in **d** with the class, pointing out the three different sections. You may like to get Sts to do the writing in class or you could set it as homework.

Focus on **e** and make sure Sts check their articles for mistakes. Then get Sts to read each other's articles and find out how many agree with each other.

Extra support

- Ask Sts if they agree with the title *There are too many reality shows on TV* and put them in pairs or small groups with someone who has the same opinion. Together, they can think of their reasons why before starting to write.

Tell Sts to go back to the main lesson **11A**.

6 4 59 SONG *The Final Countdown* ♫

This song was originally made famous by the Swedish band Europe in 1986. For copyright reasons this is a cover version. If you want to do this song in class, use the photocopiable activity on *p.278*.

4 59

The Final Countdown

We're leaving together, but still it's farewell
And maybe we'll come back to earth, who can tell
I guess there is no one to blame
We're leaving ground (leaving ground)
Will things ever be the same again?

Chorus
It's the final countdown
The final countdown

We're heading for Venus, Venus, and still we stand tall
Cause maybe they've seen us and welcome us all
With so many light years to go and things to be found (to be found)
I'm sure that we all miss her so

Chorus

G word order of phrasal verbs
V phrasal verbs: *look up, look after, find out*, etc.
P linking

11B Are you a morning person?

Lesson plan

This lesson provides a gentle introduction to phrasal verbs and how they work. Phrasal verbs are an important feature of English, and are very frequently used by native speakers. At this level Sts only need to know the most common ones like *wake up, turn on / off, look for*, etc.

The context is waking up in the morning and whether we are 'a morning person' or not. The lesson begins with Speaking and Reading where Sts talk about waking up in the morning and how they feel. Then they read an interview with a BBC journalist, who works on an early morning music programme, in which she talks about her early morning routine. In Vocabulary the focus is on common phrasal verbs and in Grammar the word order of phrasal verbs is analysed. In Pronunciation Sts have more practice of linking and the lesson finishes with speaking where phrasal verbs are recycled and practised in a questionnaire.

STUDY LINK
- Workbook 11B
- iTutor
- www.oup.com/elt/englishfile

Extra photocopiable activities

- **Grammar** Word order of phrasal verbs *p.193*
- **Communicative** Phrasal verb dialogues *p.240* (instructions *p.206*)
- **Vocabulary** Phrasal verbs *p.262* (instructions *p.247*)
- **www.oup.com/elt/teacher/englishfile**

Optional lead-in (books closed)

- Draw a clock on the board and quickly revise telling the time. Then say a few digital times to Sts (e.g. 8.15, 11.40, etc.) and elicit the other way of saying them (a quarter past eight, twenty to twelve).
- Then tell Sts to continue in pairs. **A** says a digital time and **B** has to say it the other way. Then **B** says a digital time, etc. Stop the activity when you think Sts have had enough practice.

1 SPEAKING & READING

a Books open. Read the questions with the class, making sure Sts remember the meaning of all the verbs, e.g. the difference between *wake up* (= stop sleeping) and *get up* (= leave your bed).

Now put Sts in pairs and get them to interview their partner.

Get some feedback from the class. You could also tell the class about yourself.

b Focus on the title of the article and explain that an early bird is a person who gets up, arrives, etc. very early. You could also write the idiom on the board 'the early bird catches the worm'. Elicit / explain that it means it is a good thing to get up early, and ask Sts if they have an equivalent idiom in their language.

Focus on the instructions, the introduction, and establish who Sara Mohr-Pietsch is. Get Sts to read the interview and match the questions and answers. The first one has been done for them.

Get Sts to compare with a partner, and then check answers.

2 C 3 D 4 B 5 A 6 E 7 H 8 F 9 I

c Tell Sts to cover Sara's answers and to look at questions A–I. They should now tell their partner what they can remember about her answers.

Extra idea

- Put Sts in pairs, **A** and **B**. **B** (book open) reads questions A–E to **A** (book closed) who answers them, whilst **B** checks if **A** is right. They then swap roles and **B** answers questions F–I.

d In pairs, Sts discuss the two questions. You could demonstrate the activity by answering the two questions yourself.

Get some feedback from the class.

2 VOCABULARY phrasal verbs

a Focus on the instructions and give Sts a few minutes to work out what the highlighted phrases mean in the three sentences.

You could remind Sts of the meaning of *turn off* by for example turning off the light. Elicit / teach that here *picks me up* = comes to her house to take her to work. Remind Sts of the other meaning of *pick up*, e.g. *pick up the paper*. Elicit / teach the meaning of *give it up* = stop doing.

b Focus on the **Phrasal verbs** box and go through it with the class.

! Technically a phrasal verb is a verb + particle. The particle can be a preposition or an adverb. However, at this level it is probably easier to call them 'prepositions', which many of them are, rather than confusing Sts with a new term.

Now elicit answers for questions 1–3.

1 look for   2 try on   3 get on with

c Tell Sts to go to **Vocabulary Bank** ***Phrasal verbs*** on *p.163* and get them to do **a** individually or in pairs.

5 2))) Now do **b** and play the audio for Sts to listen and check their answers. Give further practice of any words your Sts find difficult to pronounce.

5 2))

Phrasal verbs

9 The match will be over at about 5.30.
4 I need to give up smoking.
1 Don't throw away that letter!
10 Turn down the music! It's very loud.
5 Turn up the TV! I can't hear.
7 He looked up the words in a dictionary.
2 Could you fill in this form?
12 I want to find out about hotels in Madrid.
8 It's bedtime – go and put on your pyjamas.
11 Could you take off your boots, please?
3 My sister's looking after Jimmy for me today.
6 I'm really looking forward to the holidays.

Focus on the box explaining the three types of phrasal verbs and go through it with the class, making sure Sts understand the difference between them.

Now focus on **c**. Give Sts a few minutes to test themselves or each other. Encourage them to say the whole sentence, as learning phrasal verbs in context makes it easier to remember their meaning.

Now tell Sts to focus on **d**. Elicit the meaning of these phrasal verbs from Sts.

Tell Sts to go back to the main lesson **11B**.

Extra idea

- Write the following phrasal verbs that Sts already know on the board: PUT ON / TAKE OFF, TURN DOWN, LOOK AFTER, THROW AWAY, WANT TO GIVE UP, LOOK FORWARD TO.
- Put Sts in pairs and get them to think of two things for each phrasal verb.
- Get some feedback from the class.

Extra support

- If you think Sts need more practice, you may want to give them the Vocabulary photocopiable activity at this point.

3 GRAMMAR word order of phrasal verbs

a Here Sts focus on the grammar of phrasal verbs. Focus on the picture and instructions.

Get Sts to compare which words they have underlined and check answers.

the alarm clock in the first two sentences, *it* in the third

b Focus on the instructions and check Sts know the difference between a noun and a pronoun. Get Sts to read and complete the rules.

Check answers.

1 noun 2 pronoun

c 5 3)) Tell Sts to go to **Grammar Bank 11B** on *p.146*. Focus on the example sentences and play the audio for Sts to listen and repeat. Encourage them to copy the rhythm. Then go through the rules with the class, and remind Sts that the green phrasal verbs in the **Vocabulary Bank** are type 1, the red are type 2, and the blue are type 3.

Additional grammar notes

- Sts will probably ask *How do we know if a phrasal verb which takes an object is type 2 or type 3?* There is no easy rule. Tell them:
  1 To always put new phrasal verbs into an example sentence, and if they are type 2, to write the object in the middle, e.g. *turn (the radio) down.*
  2 In a dictionary, a type 2 phrasal verb will always be given with *sth / sb* between the verb and the particle, e.g. *turn sth down.*

Now focus on the exercises for **11B** on *p.147*. Sts do them individually or in pairs.

Check answers, getting Sts to read the full sentences.

a
1 look after my sister
2 go out this evening
3 ✓
4 looking for a new job
5 ✓
6 try them on
7 ✓
8 get on with her
9 take it back
10 get up in the morning

b
1 them up
2 it on
3 up
4 them in
5 it back
6 on
7 down

Tell Sts to go back to the main lesson **11B**.

Extra support

- If you think Sts need more practice, you may want to give them the Grammar photocopiable activity at this point.

4 PRONUNCIATION linking

a 5 4)) Here Sts practise deciphering connected speech and all the examples involve phrasal verbs. Write on the board as an example GET UP and remind Sts that when a word ends with a consonant sound and the next word begins with a vowel sound, they are linked together and sound like one word, especially when people speak quickly. Draw a linking mark on the sentence between the final *t* in *get* and the *u* in *up*.

Play the audio once for Sts to hear the six sentences. Tell them just to listen, not to write.

Then play the audio again, pausing after each sentence to give Sts time to write.

Check answers, eliciting the sentences onto the board.

5 4))

1 There's a wet towel on the floor. Please **pick it up**.
2 I can't concentrate with that music on. Please **turn it off**.
3 If you don't know what the word means, **look it up**.
4 Why have you taken your coat off? **Put it on**!
5 This book was very expensive. Please **look after it**.
6 Why are you wearing your coat in here? **Take it off**!

b Play the audio again, pausing for Sts to repeat the sentences and copy the rhythm.

Put Sts in pairs and get them to practise saying the sentences.

5 SPEAKING

a Go through the questionnaire with Sts, making sure they understand all the vocabulary.

Then give Sts some time to think of their answers.

b Put Sts in pairs, **A** and **B**. **A** (book open) asks **B** (book closed) the first four questions. **B** must answer all the questions, giving as much information as possible, and add *What about you?* for **A** to answer them too.

Then **B** (book open) asks **A** (book closed) the next four questions and **A** must answer, giving as much information as possible, and add *What about you?* for **B** to answer them too.

Get some feedback from various pairs.

G *so, neither* + auxiliaries
V similarities
P /ð/ and /θ/, sentence stress

11C What a coincidence!

Lesson plan

The topic of this lesson is coincidences. The structure *So am I, Neither am I* is presented through the true case of identical twins who were separated at birth, but reunited 40 years later. The pronunciation focus is on the two possible pronunciations of *th*, /ð/ as in *neither* and /θ/ as in *both*, and sentence stress in phrases like *So am I, Neither do I*, and Sts then have a speaking activity where they try to find things they have in common. At this level Sts will find it hard to manipulate this structure with much fluency, so here just practise using the present forms *So am / do I, Neither am / do I*.

The vocabulary focus is on different words / phrases used to express similarity, and the lesson ends with a listening about another more modern real-life coincidence, where a man and a woman find out via the internet that they have exactly the same name (Kelly Hildebrandt), and subsequently meet and marry.

STUDY LINK
- **Workbook** 11C
- **iTutor**
- **iChecker**
- **www.oup.com/elt/englishfile**

Extra photocopiable activities

- **Grammar** *so, neither* + auxiliaries *p.194*
- **Communicative** Are we the same? *p.241* (instructions *p.207*)
- **www.oup.com/elt/teacher/englishfile**

Optional lead-in (books closed)

- Ask the class if anybody has a twin brother or sister, eliciting or teaching the meaning of *twin*. If not, find out if anyone in the class knows two people who are twins. If any student has a twin brother or sister or knows twins, ask them if they are *identical twins* and teach / elicit the meaning. Then ask if the identical twins are similar or different in personality and interests.

1 GRAMMAR *so, neither* + auxiliaries

a Books open. Focus on the lesson title and elicit / teach the meaning. Then focus on the photo, and ask *What do the two men look like?*, e.g. *The man on the left has dark hair*, etc.

Ask Sts if the two men look similar and elicit that they are twins.

b Focus on the instructions. Give Sts time to read the text and answer the questions.

Get Sts to compare with a partner, and then check answers.

1 They are American identical twins.
2 Because they were adopted by two different families when they were babies.
3 He decided to find and contact his brother.
4 It took him six weeks.

Deal with any other new vocabulary.

c 5.5 Either tell Sts to cover the dialogue or get them to close their books. Tell them to listen to the dialogue and to find three things the brothers have in common. Tell Sts that there are more than three things that they have in common.

Before playing the audio you might want to tell Sts that *neither* can be pronounced /ˈnaɪðə/ or /ˈniːðə/, and that in this audio they will hear the American version /ˈniːðə/.

Play the audio once the whole way through. Play again if necessary.

Elicit answers from the class onto the board. You may need to teach the word *both* here.

Sts should mention three of these:
Both men have been married twice, they both have a son called James Allen, neither went to college, they were both terrible students, they both have a dog called Toy, they don't do any exercise, they own the same car (a Chevrolet), and they both drink Miller Lite beer.

5.5
A Hi! I'm Jim.
B So **am** I. Great to meet you. Sit down. Are you married, Jim?
A Yes... well, I've been married twice.
B Yeah? So **have** I. Do you have any children?
A I have one son.
B So **do** I. What's his name?
A James Allen.
B That's amazing! My son's name is James Allen too!
A Did you go to college, Jim?
B No, I didn't.
A Neither **did** I. I was a terrible student.
B So **was** I. Hey, this is my dog Toy.
A I don't believe it! My dog's called Toy too!
B He wants to go outside. My wife usually takes him. I don't do any exercise at all.
A Don't worry. Neither **do** I. I drive everywhere.
B What car do you have?
B A Chevrolet.
A So **do** I!
A and B Let's have a beer, Jim.
A What beer do you drink?
B Miller lite.
A So **do** I!

Extra challenge

- Tell Sts to try and hear as many things as possible that the men have in common.

d Now tell Sts to listen again and to complete the gaps in the dialogue. Play the audio once and then play it again if necessary.

Get Sts to compare with a partner, and then check answers.

1 am	3 do	5 was	7 do
2 have	4 did	6 do	8 do

e Do this as an open-class question.

f Put Sts in pairs and focus on the instructions. Give Sts time to answer the questions.

Check answers.

1 [+] *So* (*am*, *have*, etc.) *I*.
[–] *Neither* (*did*, *do*, etc.) *I*.
2 It changes to follow the tense or form used by the first speaker.

g 5 6 Tell Sts to go to **Grammar Bank 11C** on *p.146*. Focus on the example sentences and play the audio for Sts to listen and repeat. Encourage them to copy the rhythm. Then go through the rules with the class.

Additional grammar notes

- The main problem Sts may have is thinking that *So* (*do*) *I* is used to agree with a statement and *Neither* (*do*) *I* to disagree. It is important to stress that both are used to say that two people have the same opinion or do the same thing, but we use *So*, etc. when it is a [+] thing and *Neither*, etc. when it is a [–] thing.
- Sts will probably already know the expression *Me too*, which is a 'short cut' way to express *So do I*, etc. You may want to teach Sts the negative version, *Me neither*.

Focus on the exercises for **11C** on *p.147*. Sts do them individually or in pairs.

Check answers, getting Sts to read the full sentences.

a	1	am	6	can
	2	did	7	would
	3	was	8	did
	4	do	9	would
	5	have	10	can
b	1	So do I.	5	Neither do I.
	2	Neither am I.	6	So can I.
	3	So did I.	7	So do I.
	4	Neither have I.	8	So am I.

Tell Sts to go back to the main lesson **11C**.

Extra support

- If you think Sts need more practice, you may want to give them the Grammmar photocopiable activity at this point.

2 PRONUNCIATION /ð/ and /θ/, sentence stress

Pronunciation notes

/ð/ and /θ/

- Sts should be aware by now of the small difference between these two sounds, as they occur in so many common words. Here they get some extra practice to help them to hear the difference and produce the two sounds.

Sentence stress

- The important thing for Sts to remember here is that the auxiliary verb is not stressed, but *So* / *Neither* and the subject pronoun are.
- You may also want to highlight that with *Neither am I* the three words are all run together.

a 5 7 Focus on the two sound pictures *mother* /ð/ and *thumb* /θ/, and play the audio once for Sts just to listen to the sounds and words. Encourage Sts to try to approximate the *th* sound as far as possible and to hear the difference between the voiced sound /ð/ and the unvoiced sound /θ/ although they may find this quite difficult.

5 7
See words in Student's Book on *p.89*

Then play the audio again, pausing for Sts to repeat the words and sounds.

b 5 8 Focus on the words and get Sts to add them to the right rows in **a**.

Play the audio for Sts to listen and check.

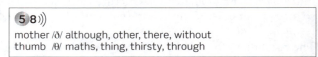

5 8
mother /ð/ although, other, there, without
thumb /θ/ maths, thing, thirsty, through

Then play it again, pausing after each one and get Sts to repeat.

STUDY LINK Sts can practise these sounds on the *iTutor* and on the *English File* Pre-intermediate website.

c 5 9 Play the audio once for Sts just to listen.

Then play it again, pausing for Sts to repeat each line.

Then tell them to underline the stressed words. Play the audio again for them to check.

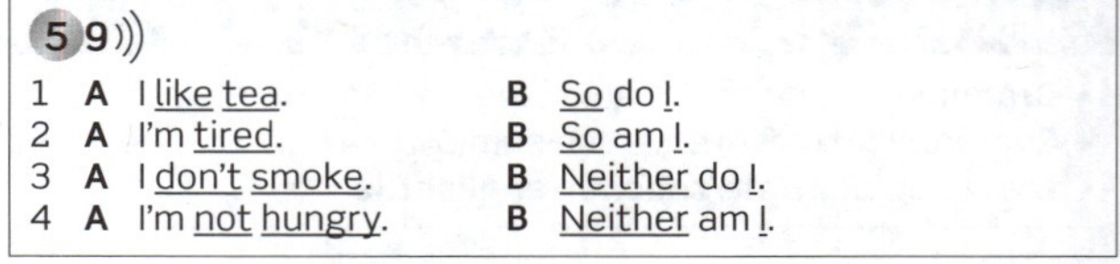
5 9
1 A I like tea. B So do I.
2 A I'm tired. B So am I.
3 A I don't smoke. B Neither do I.
4 A I'm not hungry. B Neither am I.

In pairs, get Sts to practise the dialogues.

d 5 10 Focus on the instructions and the example. Explain that Sts are going to hear a sentence on the audio, and they have to use *So* ______ *I* or *Neither* ______ *I* to say that they are the same. You might want to stress that Sts mustn't think about themselves, but simply answer so that they agree with the speaker.

Play the audio, pausing after the first sentence, to elicit *So do I* from the whole class. Continue, pausing the audio after each sentence to elicit a response.

5 10
1 I catch the bus to work. (*pause*) So do I.
2 I like chocolate. (*pause*) So do I.
3 I'm happy. (*pause*) So am I.
4 I'm not angry. (*pause*) Neither am I.
5 I don't like football. (*pause*) Neither do I.
6 I'm going out tonight. (*pause*) So am I.
7 I have a big family. (*pause*) So do I.
8 I'm not English. (*pause*) Neither am I.
9 I live in a flat. (*pause*) So do I.

Then repeat the activity eliciting responses from individual Sts.

Extra support

- Write *So* ______ *I* and *Neither* ______ *I* on the board for Sts to focus on.

3 SPEAKING

a Focus on the instructions. Make sure Sts understand all the categories in brackets, and give them a few minutes to complete the sentences.

b Go through the instructions and focus on the speech bubbles. Demonstrate by going to different Sts and saying *I love* (whatever kind of music you like) to individual Sts until somebody says *So do I*. If they don't like it, encourage them to say a whole sentence, e.g. *I don't like it. / I hate it.*

Tell Sts to stand up and start saying their sentences from **a** to each other to find someone who is the same. Stop the activity when one student has a name for all his / her sentences.

Get some feedback from the class.

4 VOCABULARY similarities

a Here Sts learn some different ways of expressing similarities. Focus on the text about the two Jims. Get Sts to read it once without worrying about the gaps. Then ask them to tell you some more of the similarities between the two Jims.

Now get Sts to read it again and complete the gaps with words from the list.

Get Sts to compare with a partner, and then check answers.

1 like	3 similar	5 identical	7 neither
2 both	4 as	6 so	

Highlight that the *So... Neither...* structure can be used with all persons, e.g. *I live in London and so do my parents / they*, etc. Highlight the difference between *similar* and *the same*.

Extra challenge

- You may also want to teach the rules for the position of *both*, i.e. before the main verb but after *be*.

b Say the first two sentences about yourself. Encourage Sts to ask for more information.

Then give Sts a few moments to complete the sentences with a family word.

! For 4, 5, and 6 they need to add other words too. They can use the same family member more than once.

Sts discuss their answers with a partner.

Get feedback by eliciting different sentences from several pairs.

5 LISTENING

a 5 11 Focus on the photo. Then, before playing the audio, check Sts know the meaning of *coincidence* (if you didn't focus on the lesson title) and drill the pronunciation.

Extra idea

- You could ask Sts to predict what they think the coincidence might be.

Now play the audio for Sts to listen and answer the question.

Get Sts to compare with a partner, and then check answers.

Extra support

- Read through the script and decide if you need to pre-teach any new lexis before Sts listen.

They have the same name and surname.

5 11

(script in Student's Book on *p.125*)
And our last story on today's *New Hour* is about an incredible coincidence. Have you ever put your name into Google or Facebook to see what come up?
One evening last April, an American woman Kelly Hildebrandt did just that. She was feeling bored, so she put her name into Facebook. She has quite an unusual name, so she was amazed to discover that there was another person on Facebook with exactly the same name and surname as her – but with one big difference. The other Kelly Hildebrandt was a *man*, and he lived in Texas. Kelly sent him a message and they began to email each other. Later they started to phone each other every day, and finally they met in person. They discovered that they had more in common than just their name – they both love the beach, and they both really enjoy cooking. Soon they realized that they were in love. At first they were worried that they might be related, but they found out that there was no family connection at all, and in October Kelly asked Kelly to marry him. The two Kellys call each other 'Kelly girl' and 'Kelly boy', and they say that having the same name often causes confusion. Once when Kelly boy booked travel tickets for them, the travel agent almost cancelled one ticket because he thought that booking two tickets with the same name was a mistake. But there is one thing that the two Kellys are very clear about – if they have children, they definitely won't call them Kelly!

b Give Sts time to read questions 1–8 before playing the audio again. Then play again if necessary.

Get Sts to compare with a partner, and then check answers.

1 Because she was bored.
2 That a man had exactly the same name and surname as her.
3 She sent him a message.
4 They both love the beach and cooking.
5 Because they thought they might be related.
6 They call each other 'Kelly boy' and 'Kelly girl'.
7 A travel agent nearly cancelled a ticket.
8 They are not going to call their children Kelly.

Extra support

- If there's time, you could get Sts to listen again with the script on *p.125*, so they can see exactly what they understood / didn't understand. Translate / explain any new words or phrases.

c Do this as an open-class activity.

Function	phone somebody and say who you are / who you want to talk to; leave a message for somebody; respond to news
Language	*That's great news; I'll explain later*, etc.

PRACTICAL ENGLISH

Episode 6 Time to go home

Lesson plan

In this final Practical English lesson Sts learn some vocabulary related to phoning, leaving messages, and responding to news.

Rob and Jenny are depressed that his stay in New York is coming to an end. Rob goes off to do his last interview. Meanwhile Barbara is trying to get hold of him. Rob gets her message, and tries to phone her back, but has problems getting through. In the final scene Rob and Jenny meet in Central Park. They both have news for each other. Jenny tells hers first – she has sent Barbara an email to say she is resigning as she wants to move to London. However, Rob's news is that Barbara has offered him a permanent job in New York, which he has accepted. Jenny desperately phones Barbara and tells her not to open the email, and all ends well. They have a future in New York.

The story is continued in New York in *English File* Intermediate.

STUDY LINK

- **Workbook** Time to go home
- **iTutor**
- **www.oup.com/elt/englishfile**

Test and Assessment CD-ROM

- **Quick Test 11**
- **File 11 Test**
- **www.oup.com/elt/teacher/englishfile**

Optional lead-in (books closed)

- Elicit what happened in the last episode by asking some questions, e.g. *How did Rob get to his date with Jenny? Did they have a good meal at the restaurant?*, etc.
- Alternatively, you could play the last scene of Episode 5.

1 ROB AND JENNY TALK ABOUT THE FUTURE

a 5 12))) Books open. Focus on the photo and elicit what Sts think Jenny and Rob are talking about.

Focus on sentences 1–6 and go through them with Sts. Then play the audio once the whole way through for them to mark the sentences T (true) or F (false). Make it clear that they don't need to correct the false sentences yet. Play again if necessary.

Get Sts to compare with a partner, and then check answers.

1 F	3 T	5 T
2 F	4 F	6 F

5 12)))

(script in Student's Book on *p.125*)

J = **Jenny**, **R** = **Rob**, **B** = **Barbara**

J I can't believe it. Your month here is nearly over. It's gone so fast.
R I know. I've had a great time, Jenny.
J Me too. It's been really special. But...
R But what?
J It won't be the same when you're in London and I'm here.
R But we'll still be in touch. You can visit me in London and I can come back here to see you.
J It still won't be the same.
R No. No, it won't.
J Maybe... I could come back to London with you?
R You can't do that Jenny. You've just got this job.
J That's true.
R Well, we still have some time together. We're going out for dinner tonight!
J Yes, and I'm going to take you somewhere really nice.
R Look at the time. I have to go now; it's my last interview in New York. I don't want to be late.
J OK. See you later then.
R Bye.

***

B Jenny, is Rob here?
J Oh, you just missed him, Barbara.
B I really need to talk to him. I'll try him on his cell phone... (on the phone) Hello, Rob? It's Barbara. Can you give me a call? There's something I'd like to talk about.

Now focus on the **British and American English** box and go through it with the class.

b Play the audio again, so Sts can listen again and correct the false sentences.

Get Sts to compare with a partner, and then check answers.

1 Rob is going home **soon**.
2 He says Jenny can visit London and he can come back to New York.
4 He **doesn't think** it's a good idea.
6 Barbara wants to talk to **Rob**.

Ask Sts what they think Barbara wants to talk about, and elicit ideas, but don't tell them the answer yet.

Extra support

- If there's time, you could get Sts to listen again with the script on *p.125*, so they can see exactly what they understood / didn't understand. Translate / explain any new words or phrases.

2 ON THE PHONE

a 5 13))) Focus on the three photos and elicit what Sts think is happening.

Focus on the instructions and the two questions. Alternatively, you could get Sts to close their books and write the questions on the board.

Play the audio once the whole way through.

Get Sts to compare with a partner, and play the audio again if necessary.

Check answers.

1 He wants to speak to Barbara.
2 He has to call three times.

5 13))) 5 14)))

M = man, R = Rob, Re = receptionist, B = Barbara

M Hello. Broadway Grill.
R Oh, sorry. I have the wrong number. (*repeat*)

***

Re *NewYork24seven*. **How** can I help you?
R Hello. Can I speak to Barbara Keaton, please? (*repeat*)
Re Just a second. I'll put you **through**... Hello.
R Hi, is that Barbara? (*repeat*)
Re No, I'm sorry. She's not at her **desk** right now.
R Can I leave a message, please? (*repeat*)
Re Sure.
R Can you tell her Rob Walker called? (*repeat*) I'll call back later. (*repeat*)
Re I'll give her the **message**. You could try her cell phone.
R Yes, I'll do that. Thank you. (*repeat*)

***

B I'm sorry, I can't take your **call** at the moment. Please **leave** a message after the beep.
R Hello, Barbara. This is Rob returning your call. (*repeat*)

***

Re *NewYork24seven*. How can I help you?
R Hello. It's Rob again. (*repeat*) Can I speak to Barbara, please? (*repeat*)
Re Just a second... I'm sorry, the line's **busy**. Do you want to hold?
R OK, I'll hold. (*repeat*)
B Hello.
R Hi, Barbara. It's me, Rob. (*repeat*)
B Rob, hi! I tried to call you earlier.
R What did you want to talk about? (*repeat*)

b Now focus on the dialogue in the chart. Ask Sts *Who says the **You Hear** sentences in each conversation?* and elicit that first it is a man working in a restaurant, then the receptionist at *NewYork24seven*, and finally Barbara.

Then ask *Who says the **You Say** sentences?* and elicit that it is Rob. Tell Sts that if they want to make a call, they will need the You Say phrases.

Give Sts a minute to read through the dialogue and think what the missing words might be. Then play the audio again, and get Sts to complete the gaps. Play again if necessary.

Get Sts to compare with a partner, and then check answers.

See words in **bold** in script 5.13

Go through the dialogue line by line with Sts, helping them with any words or expressions they don't understand.

c **5 14)))** Now focus on the **You Say** phrases. Tell Sts they're going to hear the dialogue again. They should repeat the **You Say** phrases when they hear the beep.

Play the audio, pausing if necessary for Sts to repeat the phrases. Encourage them to copy the rhythm and intonation.

d Put Sts in pairs, **A** and **B**. Tell **A** to read the part of the man, the receptionist, and Barbara, and **B** to read Rob. In pairs, Sts read the dialogue aloud. Then **A** and **B** swap roles.

e Sts now roleplay the same conversations, but this time the person taking the part of Rob closes his / her book and does it from memory.

f Sts swap roles when they have finished.

You could get some pairs to perform in front of the class.

3 IN CENTRAL PARK AGAIN

a **5 15)))** Focus on the pictures and ask Sts what's happening.

Get Sts to focus on the question or get them to close their books and write it on the board.

Play the audio once the whole way through and then check the answer.

It is a happy ending.

5 15)))

(script in Student's Book on *p.125*)

R = Rob, J = Jenny

R Jenny!
J Rob! I have something to tell you.
R I have something to tell you too. You go first.
J Well, I thought again about moving to London...
R But you don't need to move to London.
J What?
R Barbara called me earlier.
J What about?
R She offered me a job. Here, in New York!
J What?! Oh, that's great news.
R You don't seem very pleased.
J I am, I mean, it's great! It's just that...
R What?
J I sent Barbara an email this morning.
R And?
J I told her I was quitting, and moving to London.
R Don't worry. Maybe she hasn't read your email yet.
J I'll call her.
B Hello, Barbara Keaton.
J Barbara? It's Jenny.
B Oh, hi Jenny.
J Um, have you read your emails recently? There's one from me.
B Oh yes. I can see it. I haven't opened it yet.
J Don't open it! Delete it! Please just delete it. I'll explain later.
B OK. It's gone. Is everything all right, Jenny?
J Yes, thanks. Never better.

b Focus on the questions and give Sts time to read them.

Play the audio once the whole way through.

Get Sts to compare with a partner, and then play again if necessary.

Check answers.

1 They both have news.
2 Barbara offered Rob a job in New York.
3 She sent Barbara an email. She quit her job.
4 Jenny asks Barbara to delete her email.

Extra support

- If there's time, you could get Sts to listen again with the script on *p.125*, so they can see exactly what they understood / didn't understand. Translate / explain any new words or phrases.

c Focus on the **Social English phrases**. In pairs, get Sts to think about what the missing words could be.

Extra challenge

- In pairs, get Sts to complete the phrases before they listen.

d 5 16))) Play the audio for Sts to listen and complete the phrases.

Check answers.

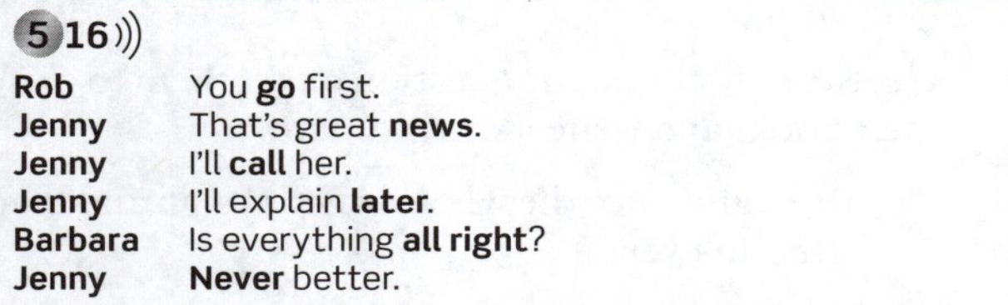

5 16)))

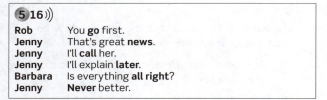

Rob	You **go** first.
Jenny	That's great **news**.
Jenny	I'll **call** her.
Jenny	I'll explain **later**.
Barbara	Is everything **all right**?
Jenny	**Never** better.

If you know your Sts' L1, you could get them to translate the phrases. If not, get Sts to have a look at the phrases again in context in the script on *p.125*.

e Now play the audio again, pausing after each phrase for Sts to listen and repeat.

Finally, focus on the **Can you...?** questions and ask Sts if they feel confident they can now do these things. If they feel that they need more practice, tell them to watch the episode again and practise the language on their *iTutor*.

G past perfect
V verbs phrases: *get into the swimming pool*, etc.
P contractions: *had / hadn't*

12A Strange but true!

Lesson plan

In this lesson the past perfect is presented through the context of strange but true stories from around the world. The lesson begins with reading and speaking, where Sts read some stories and choose the best option to fill gapped sentences. In Grammar, sentences from one of the stories are analysed to present the past perfect. Pronunciation focusses on how to pronounce the contracted forms of *had*. The lesson finishes with listening, where Sts listen to another strange but true story.

STUDY LINK
- **Workbook** 12A
- **iTutor**
- **www.oup.com/elt/englishfile**

Extra photocopiable activities

- **Grammar** Past perfect *p.195*
- **Communicative** Match the sentences *p.242* (instructions *p.207*)
- **www.oup.com/elt/teacher/englishfile**

Optional lead-in (books closed)

- Revise irregular past participles, by saying a verb from the *Irregular Verbs* list on *p.164* and eliciting the past simple and past participle.
- Then ask Sts *When do you use past participles?* and elicit in the present perfect (with *have*) and the passive (with *be*). Now tell Sts they're going to learn another form where the past participle of the verb is used.

1 READING & SPEAKING

a Books open. Focus on the title of the lesson and emphasize that the stories that Sts are going to read really are true. Now focus on the four pictures that go with each story and ask Sts what they can see.

Now tell Sts to read the stories and to complete each gap with a sentence.

Get Sts to compare with a partner, and then check answers. If Sts ask what the structure *had* + past participle is, you can explain that this is the past perfect, which they are going to study later, but ideally they should be able to deduce the meaning from the context.

Australia	2	**Italy**	5
England	4	**Sweden**	7

Now go through the four stories and deal with any vocabulary problems. You could also ask comprehension questions to check Sts' understanding, e.g. *Why were the swimmers surprised? How did the shark get into the swimming pool?*, etc.

b Focus on the instructions. Tell Sts that all the verb phrases are from the stories, but they should try and match them without looking back at the stories.

Get Sts to compare with a partner, and then check answers.

2 F 3 E 4 J 5 A 6 C 7 B 8 I 9 D 10 G

Ask Sts which story they think is the strangest.

2 GRAMMAR past perfect

a Focus on the sentences and get Sts to answer the questions in pairs, or answer them as a whole class.

Check answers.

1 B happened first
2 *had* + the past participle (= the past perfect)

b Give Sts time to do the exercise in pairs or individually.

Check that Sts have underlined the right examples.

England: had gone, had left, had run away, had gone, had got, had travelled
Italy: had decided
Sweden: had got confused, had put, had sat down

Elicit that all these actions happened before the main part of the story.

c **5 17**)) Tell Sts to go to **Grammar Bank 12A** on *p.148*. Focus on the example sentences and play the audio for Sts to listen and repeat. Encourage them to copy the rhythm. Then go through the rules with the class.

Additional grammar notes

- The form and use of the past perfect is not normally problematic for most Sts, but the concept may be difficult if Sts do not have the same grammatical structure in their L1.
- The past perfect is very common after verbs like *realized, remembered, saw*, etc., e.g. *I suddenly realized that I had forgotten my sister's birthday.*

Focus on the exercises for **12A** on *p.149*. Sts do them individually or in pairs.

Check answers, getting Sts to read the full sentences.

a 1 G 2 D 3 A 4 F 5 E 6 B

b 1 didn't recognize, had changed
2 phoned, had left
3 turned on, had already finished
4 didn't lend, hadn't watched
5 had closed, arrived
6 got, had broken
7 had stopped, left

Tell Sts to go back to the main lesson **12A**.

Extra support

- If you think Sts need more practice, you may want to give them the Grammar photocopiable activity at this point.

d Give Sts time to complete the five sentences with their own ideas.

e Put Sts in pairs and get them to compare their sentences with a partner.

Get some Sts to read their sentences to the class.

Possible completions
1 I'd left my passport at home.
2 all our plants had died.
3 I'd already seen it.
4 hadn't studied.
5 where we had parked.

f Focus on the instructions and put Sts in pairs.

Then give Sts time to re-read the stories. Encourage them to use their own words when they re-tell.

Make sure they swap roles.

Extra support

- You could write some words or phrases on the board as prompts to help Sts re-tell the stories, e.g. Australia: Sydney, swimmers, swimming pool, assistants, shark, wave, etc.

3 PRONUNCIATION contractions: *had / hadn't*

Pronunciation notes

- Native speakers tend to contract *had* in the past perfect to *'d* when they speak. It is important that Sts are made aware of this as it will help them to understand past perfect sentences in spoken English. Here Sts practise understanding and producing contractions, but at this level teachers should not worry at all if Sts use the full form.
- Remind Sts that the *'d* contraction can also be *would*, e.g. *I'd like to be rich.*

a 5 18 Focus on the **Contractions: past perfect** box and go through it with the class.

Now tell Sts they are going to hear six sentences in the past perfect and they must write them down.

Play the audio, pausing after each sentence to give Sts time to write. Play again if necessary.

Get Sts to compare with a partner, and then check answers.

5 18
1 I didn't know that she'd lost her job.
2 I remembered that I'd seen the film before.
3 He failed his exam because he hadn't studied.
4 I'd left my phone at home, so I couldn't call you.
5 When he arrived we hadn't finished our dinner.
6 When we came out of the cinema, it'd stopped raining.

Elicit that *had* is not stressed in [+] sentences. In pairs, get Sts to practise saying the sentences. Monitor and help with rhythm and pronunciation.

! Point out to Sts that *it'd* has an extra /ə/ sound between the /t/ and the /d/ sounds, i.e. /ɪtəd/

b Put Sts in pairs, **A** and **B**, and get them to sit face-to-face if possible. Tell them to go to **Communication *What had happened?***, **A** on *p.104*, **B** on *p.109*.

Go through the instructions and make sure Sts understand what they have to do.

Give Sts time to think of verbs that could go into the sentences.

Extra support

- Demonstrate the activity by writing this sentence on a piece of paper:
  WHEN I GOT TO CLASS I SUDDENLY REMEMBERED THAT I HADN'T DONE MY HOMEWORK.
- Then write on the board:
  WHEN I GOT TO CLASS I SUDDENLY REMEMBERED THAT I __________ MY HOMEWORK. [−]
- Tell Sts that you have written the complete sentence on a piece of paper, and that you want them to guess the missing words. Tell them what's missing is a past perfect verb, and that the [−] sign means that it is a verb in the negative. Get the class to guess the missing verb. If they suggest something which is grammatically correct, but not what you have on your piece of paper, e.g. *hadn't brought*, say *Try again.* Carry on until somebody says *hadn't done.*

Monitor while Sts are doing the activity, and encourage them to say the sentences with the right rhythm.

Extra challenge

- Fast finishers could try to invent a sentence of their own with the verb missed out to read to the class for them to guess the missing verb.

Tell Sts to go back to the main lesson **12A**.

4 LISTENING

a 5 19 Tell Sts they are going to listen to another news story and they must put the events in the order in which they happened. Give Sts time to read the sentences quickly.

Play the audio once the whole way through. Play again if necessary.

Get Sts to compare with a partner, and then check answers.

Extra support

- Read through the script and decide if you need to pre-teach any new lexis before Sts listen, e.g. *attack, jump, snore.*

1 Katie came home from work.
2 Joey attacked her.
3 Joey sat on her plate.
4 Joey went to sleep.
5 Katie met her neighbour.

5 19

(script in Student's Book on *p.125*)
And finally on *News Today*, here's a funny story to cheer you up on a Monday morning.
On Saturday night Katie Parfitt, a nurse from Manchester, came home from work. As soon as she opened the door, she realized that her cat, Joey, was behaving rather strangely. Instead of being pleased to see her, he started attacking her, and then, when she sat down to have something to eat, Joey jumped onto the table and sat on her plate. Then he jumped down onto the floor and immediately went to sleep. He slept all night, snoring very loudly. Katie couldn't understand what the matter was with Joey – he had never behaved like this before. However, when she met her neighbour the next morning, the mystery was solved.

b Put Sts in pairs and get them to tell each other what they think had happened.

Elicit some ideas, but do not tell Sts if they are right.

c **5 20** Now tell Sts they are going to hear the rest of the news story. They need to listen to see if they had guessed correctly. Play the audio once the whole way through and get Sts to tell each other what they understood, and then play the audio again.

Finally, elicit what had happened (Joey had drunk some beer that was on the floor of a pub and had got drunk).

5 20

(script in Student's Book on *p.125*)
My neighbour told me that he was having a drink in our local pub, on Saturday. Suddenly he saw my cat Joey walk in through the door – it was open because it was a hot day. And then one of the people spilled his glass of beer on the floor and Joey starting drinking it – he was probably thirsty. So of course when Joey got home he was completely drunk! I took him to vet the next day, but luckily he's fine now.

Extra support

- If there's time, you could get Sts to listen again with the scripts on *p.125*, so they can see exactly what they understood / didn't understand. Translate / explain any new words or phrases.

G reported speech
V *say* or *tell*?
P double consonants

12B Gossip is good for you

Lesson plan

This lesson provides a clear and simple introduction to reported (or indirect) speech. Sts simply learn to deal with reported statements – reported questions are taught in *English File* Intermediate. The context for the presentation is the topic of gossiping. The lesson begins with Speaking and Listening where Sts talk about gossiping and then listen to a conversation between two elderly women, who are gossiping about a conversation they overheard between a young couple, who live next door. The grammar section presents reported speech by contrasting what Emma actually said and how one of the old women reported it to her friend. Vocabulary focusses on the different ways *say* and *tell* are used, and in speaking Sts practise reporting what other Sts have said. In Pronunciation there is a focus on how double consonants are pronounced. Sts then read an article about some research that has been done into why people gossip, and the lesson finishes with the song *I Heard It Through the Grapevine*.

STUDY LINK
- **Workbook** 12B
- **iTutor**
- **www.oup.com/elt/englishfile**

Extra photocopiable activities

- **Grammar** Reported speech *p.196*
- **Communicative** Really? How amazing! *p.243* (instructions *p.207*)
- **Song** *I Heard It Through the Grapevine p.279* (instructions *p.267*)
- **www.oup.com/elt/teacher/englishfile**

Optional lead-in (books closed)

- Write these three sentences on the board:
  'YOU'LL NEVER GUESS WHAT JAMES TOLD ME THE OTHER DAY!'
  'HAVE YOU HEARD ABOUT WHAT HAPPENED TO SUSAN YESTERDAY?'
  'I SAW THE BOSS IN THE CINEMA THE OTHER DAY. YOU'LL NEVER BELIEVE WHO SHE WAS WITH.'
- Now ask the class what the three sentences are examples of and try to elicit that it is somebody talking to a friend about another person, and elicit / teach the verb *gossip*.

1 SPEAKING & LISTENING

a Focus on the dictionary definition of *gossip*. Model and drill the pronunciation.

Put Sts in pairs and get them to discuss the questions.

Get some feedback from the class.

b **5 21** Tell Sts they are going to listen to a conversation between two women and they must answer the question *What has happened to Jack and Emma?*

Now play the audio once the whole way through. Play again if necessary.

Get Sts to compare with a partner, and then check the answer.

Jack and Emma have broken up.

Extra support

- Read through the script and decide if you need to pre-teach any new lexis before Sts listen.

5 21
(script in Student's Book on *p.125*)
I = Iris, R = Rosemary
I Hello, Rosemary. How are you this morning?
R Hello, Iris. I'm fine thanks, but you'll never guess what's happened. Jack and Emma have broken up!
I No! Jack and Emma from number 36? That can't be true. I saw them last week and they looked really happy.
R No, it's definitely true. I heard them shouting. They were having a terrible argument.
I No! When?
R Last night. After he came home from work.
I What did they say?
R Well, I wasn't really listening...
I Of course not.
R But I couldn't help hearing. She was talking so loudly and of course the walls are very thin...
I So what did they say?
R Well, she said she that was going to stay with her mum! She told him that she wouldn't come back.
I Ooh, how awful. What about the children?
R She said she'd taken them to her sister. I suppose she'll take them with her in the end. And anyway, then five minutes later I saw her leaving the house with a suitcase!
I No! Why do you think she's leaving him? Is he seeing another woman?
R I don't know. Ooh, here's my bus.
I I must go and tell Mrs Jones at number 14. She always thought there was something... something strange about him.

Now tell Sts they will hear the conversation again and they must answer questions 1–5. Give them a few minutes to read all the options.

Now play the audio the whole way through. Play again if necessary.

Get Sts to compare with a partner, and then check answers.

1 a 2 c 3 c 4 b 5 c

c **5 22** Now tell Sts they are going to listen to what Jack and Emma actually said when Rosemary overheard them. They must listen for any differences between what Rosemary told Iris and what Jack and Emma really said.

Play the audio once the whole way through. Play again if necessary.

Get Sts to compare with a partner, and then check answers.

No, she wasn't. She either misunderstood a lot of what she heard, or only heard part of the conversation. In fact, Emma isn't leaving Jack, she is going to look after her mother, who has had an accident.

5 22)))
(script in Student's Book on *p.125*)
J = Jack, E = Emma
J Hi, Emma. I'm back. Where are you?
E I'm upstairs in the bedroom. I'm packing.
J Why? Where are you going?
E I'm going to stay with my mum.
J What's happened to her?
E She's had an accident. She fell over in the street yesterday and she's broken her leg.
J How awful! Poor thing. Shall I go and make you a cup of tea?
E That's be lovely. Thanks, darling.
J How long do you think you'll have to stay?
E I won't come back until the weekend, I don't think. I'll have to make sure she's OK. I've taken the children to my sister's for the night and she'll take them to school tomorrow morning. Can you pick them up after school?
J Of course I can, darling. Now don't worry about anything. We'll be absolutely fine. Drink your tea and I'll go and get your suitcase.
E Thanks, darling. The taxi'll be here in five minutes.

Extra challenge

- Ask Sts some comprehension questions, e.g. *Why was Emma packing?* (To go and stay at her mother's) *Why was she going to her mother's?* (Because she'd broken her leg), etc.

Extra support

- If there's time, you could get Sts to listen again with the scripts on *p.125*, so they can see exactly what they understood / didn't understand. Translate / explain any new words or phrases.

2 GRAMMAR reported speech

a Focus on the instructions and the extracts. Give Sts time, in pairs, to underline the words that are different.

Check answers.

She said that <u>she</u> <u>was</u> going to stay with <u>her</u> mum.
She told him that <u>she</u> <u>wouldn't</u> come back.
She said <u>she'd</u> taken them to <u>her</u> sister.

b 5 23))) Tell Sts to go to **Grammar Bank 12B** on *p.148*. Focus on the example sentences and play the audio for Sts to listen and repeat. Encourage them to copy the rhythm. Then go through the rules with the class.

Additional grammar notes

- This is an introduction to reported (or indirect) speech. The reporting of sentences with *say* and *tell* is covered here, but not reported questions, e.g. *He asked me if I lived near here.*
- You may want to point out to Sts that when people report a past tense statement they sometimes do not make the change to the past perfect, e.g.

  Direct speech: 'I saw Jack at the party.'

  Reported speech: Jane told me she saw / had seen Jack at the party.
- Sts tend to confuse the verbs *say* and *tell*, and may try to use *say* with a person. Typical mistake: ~~*He said me that he was tired.*~~

Focus on the exercises for **12B** on *p.149*. Sts do the exercises individually or in pairs.

Check answers, getting Sts to read the full sentences.

a 1 was hungry
2 didn't like sad films
3 would call the doctor
4 had bought a new phone
5 lived in the city centre
6 couldn't do it
7 had seen *Eclipse* at the cinema

b 1 'I'm studying German.'
2 'My car has broken down.'
3 'I'll send you an email.'
4 'We're in a hurry.'
5 'I haven't finished my essay yet.'
6 'I won't arrive on time.'
7 'I've just arrived.'

Tell Sts to go back to the main lesson **12B**.

Extra support

- If you think Sts need more practice, you may want to give them the Grammar photocopiable activity at this point.

c 5 24))) Focus on the instructions and examples. Tell Sts that they must begin the sentences with *He said that* or *She said that* depending on whether they hear a male voice or a female voice. Do the first two as a class.

Play the audio, pausing after the direct speech sentence for the class to make the transformation into reported speech.

5 24)))
1 I'm in a hurry. (*pause*) She said that she was in a hurry.
2 I'll write. (*pause*) He said that he would write.
3 I didn't see it. (*pause*) She said that she hadn't seen it.
4 I'm hungry. (*pause*) He said that he was hungry.
5 I'll be late. (*pause*) She said that she would be late.
6 I've finished. (*pause*) He said that he had finished.
7 I'm coming. (*pause*) She said that she was coming.
8 I'll do it again. (*pause*) He said that he would do it again.
9 I had a great time. (*pause*) She said that she had had a great time.
10 I'm tired. (*pause*) He said that he was tired.

Then repeat the activity eliciting responses from individual Sts.

3 VOCABULARY *say* or *tell*?

Focus on the task and give Sts time to complete the sentences.

Get them to compare with a partner, and then check answers.

Extra support

- If Sts are having problems with *say* / *tell*, get them to look back at the note in **Grammar Bank 12B** on *p.148*.

1 said	3 said	5 said	7 say
2 told	4 told	6 tell	8 tell, say

4 SPEAKING

a Focus on the task and the four topics. Give Sts a minute or so to think about what they want to say. Point out that the information can be true, but they could also invent it if they want. Highlight that it must be interesting information, for example not just *My grandmother was born in 1940.*

Put Sts into pairs and give them time to talk to each other. Remind Sts that the person listening must take some notes.

Make sure Sts swap roles.

Extra idea

- To help Sts to get the idea of the activity, begin by whispering a piece of real or invented gossip to one student. Then get the class to ask the student *What did he / she say?* Now encourage the student to report what you said using reported speech.

b Get Sts to change partners and explain that they must now tell their new partner what their first partner told them. To do this they must change the information into reported speech.

Give Sts time to report their conversations to their new partners and to decide if they think their previous partners were telling the truth.

Then Sts should go back to their original partners and find out if they were telling the truth or not.

Get feedback by asking individual Sts to report one exchange.

5 PRONUNCIATION double consonants

Pronunciation notes

- Here Sts learn two clear rules about how vowel sounds are normally short sounds before a double consonant, and how double consonants themselves (e.g. *ss*, *rr*, etc.) are pronounced exactly the same as a single consonant.

a Tell Sts to look at the five vowel sound pictures and to match each one with a group of words a–e.

b 5 25 Play the audio for Sts to listen and check.

See **bold** in script 5.25

5 25

1d	cat /æ/	happy, married, nappies, rabbit, baggage
2b	up /ʌ/	hurry, rubbish, runner, summer, butterfly
3c	fish /ɪ/	written, miss, bitten, different, middle
4e	egg /e/	letter, better, message, umbrella, tennis
5a	clock /ɒ/	gossip, offer, sorry, bottle, robber

Play the audio again for Sts to listen and repeat.

c Focus on the **Double consonants** box and go through it with the class.

Tell Sts, in pairs, to try to pronounce the words in the list. Then they should look them up and find out how to pronounce them and what they mean.

Check answers.

kettle /ˈketl/	pottery /ˈpɒtəri/	supper /ˈsʌpə/
nanny /ˈnæni/	slippers /ˈslɪpəz/	

Still in pairs Sts practise saying the words.

6 READING

a Focus on the title and ask Sts why / how they think gossip might be good for us.

Now tell Sts to read the article and mark 1–5 T (true) or F (false). Remind them to correct the F ones.

Get Sts to compare with a partner, and then check answers.

1 T
2 T
3 T
4 F (People enjoy sharing bad news about people they dislike.)
5 F (Men gossip with their wives or girlfriends.)

b Now focus on the highlighted verbs and verb phrases and get Sts in pairs to try to guess their meaning from the context.

Check answers, either explaining in English, translating into Sts' L1, or getting Sts to check in their dictionaries.

Deal with any other new vocabulary.

c Do this as an open-class activity. After Sts have given their opinions, tell them what you think.

7 5 26 SONG *I Heard It Through the Grapevine* ♫

This song was originally made famous by American singer Marvin Gaye in 1968. For copyright reasons this is a cover version. If you want to do this song in class, use the photocopiable activity on *p.279*.

5 26

I Heard It Through the Grapevine

Ooh, I bet you're wondering how I knew
'bout your plans to make me blue
With some other guy that you knew before.
Between the two of us guys you know I love you more.
It took me by surprise I must say,
When I found out yesterday. Don't you know that...

Chorus
I heard it through the grapevine
Not much longer would you be mine. Oh
I heard it through the grapevine, Oh
I'm just about to lose my mind.
Honey, honey yeah.
(Heard it through the grapevine, not much longer would you be my baby, ooh)

I know that a man ain't supposed to cry,
But these tears I can't hold inside.
Losin' you would end my life you see,
'Cause you mean that much to me.
You could have told me yourself
That you love someone else. Instead...

Chorus

People say believe half of what you see,
Son, and none of what you hear.
But I can't help being confused
If it's true please tell me dear?
Do you plan to let me go
For the other guy you loved before? Don't you know...

Chorus

12C The *English File* quiz

Lesson plan

In this final lesson Sts learn to use questions without auxiliaries (*Who painted this picture?*, etc.) and contrast them with questions with auxiliaries (*When did he paint it?*). The grammar is presented through a quiz, which tests Sts' memory on information that has come up in the book. If your Sts have only used the second half of *English File* Pre-intermediate (i.e. Multipack B), they should just do the second half of the quiz, i.e. questions 8–15. Then in writing and speaking Sts write their own quiz to practise making questions with or without auxiliaries.

STUDY LINK

- **Workbook** 12C
- **iTutor**
- **iChecker**
- **www.oup.com/elt/englishfile**

Extra photocopiable activities

- **Grammar** Questions with and without auxiliaries *p.197*
- **Communicative** Hollywood quiz *p.244* (instructions *p.208*)
- **www.oup.com/elt/teacher/englishfile**

Optional lead-in (books closed)

- Write these three jumbled questions on the board and give Sts, in pairs, a couple of minutes to write them with the words in the right order.
  1 YOU IN COFFEE MUCH SUGAR HOW DO TAKE?
  2 DOES 'TO GOSSIP' MEAN WHAT?
  3 SCHOOL GO WHAT YOU TO DID?
- Check answers and ask Sts to tell you what is the normal word order in questions with the present simple and past simple to elicit **Q**uestion word **A**uxiliary **S**ubject **I**nfinitive. Remind Sts that prepositions usually come at the end of a question (e.g. *What school did you go* ***to****? Who did you play tennis* ***with****?*)

1 How much sugar do you take in coffee?
2 What does 'to gossip' mean?
3 What school did you go to?

- Then ask a different student each question.

1 GRAMMAR questions without auxiliaries

a Books open. Focus on the instructions and tell Sts that the questions in the quiz are based on lessons (Files 1–11) in the Student's Book.

Put Sts in pairs and set a time limit for them to answer as many questions as possible from memory. Tell Sts to use the illustrations to help them. (See **Lesson plan** above if you are using Multipack B.)

b When the time limit is up, ask Sts how many questions they could answer from memory.

Now tell them that they must find the answers to the questions they couldn't answer by looking back at lessons in Files 1–11.

Check answers.

Extra challenge

- You could do **1a** as a competition and when the time limit is up, find out which pair(s) got the most answers right.

1 The British artist David Hockney
2 She took part in an anti-government demonstration in 1968 and her rich grandfather disinherited her.
3 Osaka Airport in Japan
4 A younger man who has a relationship with an older woman
5 Sarah Ferguson's
6 Vitamin D
7 Hugh Laurie
8 Murphy's Law
9 Seven
10 The American writer O. Henry
11 Bob Marley
12 A woman (Josephine Cochrane)
13 Winston Churchill
14 The American tennis player, John McEnroe
15 Kelly Hildebrandt

c Now tell Sts to only focus on questions 1 and 2 in the quiz and to answer the questions.

Get Sts to compare with a partner, and then check answers.

1 Question 1 doesn't have an auxiliary verb in it, but question 2 does have one (*did*).
2 *Who* is the subject.
3 Caroline de Bendern is the subject.
4 3, 7, 10, 11, 12, 13, and 14.

Highlight that when the question word (usually *who* or *which*) is the subject of the sentence, QUASI (**Q**uestion word, **A**uxiliary verb, **S**ubject, **I**nfinitive) does not apply, because the question word and the subject are the same.

d 5 27))) Tell Sts to go to **Grammar Bank 12C** on *p.148*. Focus on the example sentences and play the audio for Sts to listen and repeat. Encourage them to copy the rhythm. Then go through the rules with the class.

Additional grammar notes

- Sts will already have met questions without auxiliaries, e.g. *Who knows the answer?*, etc., but until now this type of question has not been focussed on.

- Highlight that:
  - the vast majority of questions in the past and present follow the **QUASI** rule.
  - the only question words which can be the subject of a question, and may not need an auxiliary verb, are:
    Who?, e.g. *Who wrote the song?*
    Which?, e.g. *Which singer sang My Way?*
    What?, e.g. *What happened?*
    How many / much?, e.g. *How many students came?*
  - Questions beginning with *When?*, *Why?*, *Where?*, *How long?*, etc. always need an auxiliary.

Focus on the exercises for **12C** on *p.149*. Sts do the exercises individually or in pairs.

Check answers, getting Sts to read the full sentences.

a 1 happened
 2 does this word mean
 3 came
 4 goes
 5 won
 6 did the teacher say
 7 made

b 1 When did Barack Obama become president of the USA? (In 2008)
 2 Which US state starts with the letter 'H'? (Hawaii)
 3 Which books were written by J.R R. Tolkien? (*The Lord of the Rings*, *The Hobbit*, etc.)
 4 Who won the football World Cup in 2010? (Spain)
 5 Which sport uses the lightest ball? (ping-pong / table tennis)
 6 Where did the 2008 Olympics take place? (Beijing, China)
 7 Which company did Steve Jobs start? (Apple Inc.)

Tell Sts to go back to the main lesson **12C**.

Extra support

- If you think Sts need more practice, you may want to give them the Grammar photocopiable activity at this point.

2 WRITING & SPEAKING

a Put Sts into pairs, **A** and **B**, and get them to sit face-to-face if possible. Tell them to go to **Communication *General knowledge quiz***, **A** on *p.105*, **B** on *p.110*.

Focus on the instructions and make sure Sts are clear what they have to do. Remind Sts that the correct answer is the one in bold. Highlight that all the questions in the quiz are questions without auxiliaries.

Give Sts time to complete their questions. Monitor and make sure Sts are forming the questions correctly.

Extra support

- You could elicit some or all of the questions first, making sure that Sts can pronounce the past tense forms correctly.

Now tell **A**s to ask their questions first. Highlight that they should give the three alternatives each time.

Then Sts swap roles.

Get feedback to see who got the most right answers.

Tell Sts to go back to the main lesson **12C**.

b Focus on the instructions and categories. In pairs, Sts write their own quiz. Set a time limit for Sts to write their questions and remind them that they must know the answers to their questions.

Monitor and help where necessary.

c Put two pairs together and get them to ask each other their questions.

Get some feedback from the class on how well they did in the quizzes.

Extra idea

- Get each pair to ask their questions to the whole class. They score a point for each question to which nobody knew the answer.

11 & 12 Revise and Check

For instructions on how to use these pages see *p.38*.

STUDY LINK
- iTutor

Test and Assessment CD-ROM
- Quick Test 12
- File 12 Test
- Progress Test Files 7–12
- End-of-course Test

GRAMMAR

1 c
2 a
3 c
4 b
5 a
6 c
7 b
8 b
9 a
10 c
11 a
12 c
13 a
14 c
15 c

VOCABULARY

a 1 through
2 into
3 along
4 towards
5 past
6 off
7 up
8 down
9 back
10 out

b 1 identical
2 as
3 similar
4 neither
5 both

c 1 go
2 put
3 tell
4 look
5 leave
6 turn
7 have
8 get
9 give
10 do

PRONUNCIATION

a 1 put
2 find
3 through
4 neither
5 message

b 1 athletics
2 towards
3 forward
4 similar
5 different

CAN YOU UNDERSTAND THIS TEXT?

a They both had a life-saving heart operation in the same hospital, on the same day performed by the same heart surgeon.

b 8 Their daughter was born.
1 They both had a heart operation in the same hospital.
5 Alistair had another heart operation.
7 They got married.
4 They discovered that they had been in the same hospital twenty years earlier.
3 They discovered they had the same heart problem.
2 They met at a swimming pool.
6 Alistair asked Alison to marry him.

CAN YOU UNDERSTAND THESE PEOPLE?

5 28

1 b 2 a 3 c 4 a 5 c

5 28

1
I = interviewer, N = Nick
I Do you know any twins?
N Yes, I have a really good friend who has an identical twin brother.
I Are they very similar?
N They look exactly the same, but their personalities couldn't be more different.

2
I = interviewer, R = Ruth
I Are you a good or bad loser?
R I'm a good loser, I think.
I Why?
R Well, I think the best person wins, and if I'm not the best person, then that's OK.

3
I = interviewer, H = Hew
I Do you do any sport or exercise?
H Yes.
I What do you do?
H Play football, squash, cricket, tennis, a bit of hockey every now again and again, and I cycle.
I Do you enjoy it?
H Yeah, otherwise I wouldn't do it.

4
I = interviewer, A = Andy
I Are you a morning or evening person?
A Normally a morning person.
I Why?
A Because I have much more energy in the morning. I used to be an evening person, but not so much now.

5
I = interviewer, Al = Alison
I Who do you think gossip more, men or women?
Al I think men think women gossip more, but in fact men like to gossip too.
I Why?
Al I think everybody likes to gossip sometimes because they're interested in what other people are doing, and they enjoy gossiping.

Photocopiable activities

Contents

Photocopiable material

- There is a **Grammar activity** for each main (A, B, and C) lesson of the Students' Book.
- There is a **Communicative activity** for each main (A, B, and C) lesson of the Students' Book.
- There is a **Vocabulary activity** for each main (A, B, and C) lesson of the Students' Book.
- There is a **Songs activity** for each main (A, B, and C) lesson of the Students' Book. The recording of the song can be found in the main lesson on the Class CD.

Using extra activities in mixed ability classes

Some teachers have classes with a very wide range of levels, and where some Sts finish SB activities much more quickly than others. You could give these fast-finishers a photocopiable activity (Grammar, Vocabulary, or Communicative) while you help the slower students. Alternatively some teachers might want to give faster Sts extra oral practice with a communicative activity while slower students consolidate their knowledge with an extra grammar activity.

Tips for using Grammar activities

The Grammar activities are designed to give students extra practice in the main grammar point from each lesson. How you use these activities depends on the needs of your students and the time you have available. They can be used in the lesson if you think all of your class would benefit from the extra practice or you could set them as homework for some or all of your students.

- All of the activities start with a writing stage. If you use the activities in class, get Sts to work individually or in pairs. Allow Sts to compare before checking the answers.
- The activities have an Activation section that gets Sts to cover the sentences and to test their memories. If you are using the activities in class, Sts can work in pairs and test their partner. If you set them for homework, encourage Sts to use this stage to test themselves.
- If Sts are having trouble with any of the activities, make sure they refer to the relevant Grammar Bank in the Student's Book.
- Make sure that Sts keep their copies of the activities and that they review any difficult areas regularly. Encourage them to go back to activities and cover and test themselves. This will help with their revision.

Grammar Activity Answers

1A word order in questions

2 How are you today?
3 Where are you from?
4 What year were you born?
5 Where do you live?
6 Do you live in a house or a flat?
7 Do you have any pets?
8 Can you speak any other languages?
9 Why are you studying English?
10 What TV programmes do you watch?
11 How often do you use a computer?
12 What kind of magazines do you read?
13 What did you have for breakfast?
14 Did you do any sport yesterday?
15 Where were you at ten o'clock last night?

1B present simple

2 does his sister look like? **3** do you know **4** doesn't make **5** don't eat **6** finishes **7** don't get on **8** Do they go **9** Does Lucy prefer **10** Do your sisters have **11** do you relax **12** stops **13** doesn't study **14** do you live **15** has **16** does **17** start **18** don't use **19** wear **20** Does your girlfriend have

1C present simple or present continuous

1 **2** want **3** don't understand **4** play **5** love **6** 'm selling **7** want

2 **8** Do you need **9** 'm just looking **10** Are...looking **11** 'm thinking **12** have **13** wear

3 **14** 're reading **15** don't believe **16** hate **17** need **18** is studying **19** 's walking **20** isn't walking **21** 's flying

2A past simple: regular and irregular verbs

1 **2** did...stay **3** stayed **4** booked **5** arrived **6** didn't like **7** left **8** rented **9** were **10** started **11** didn't finish **12** loved

2 **13** took **14** was **15** did...happen **16** went **17** wasn't **18** Did...see **19** came **20** wasn't **21** did...have **22** knew

3 **23** Did...have **24** was **25** stayed **26** thought **27** didn't go **28** did...do **29** Did...go **30** spent **31** argued **32** bought **33** didn't buy

2B past continuous

a **2** rang; was driving **3** arrived; was making **4** were playing; started **5** were having; took **6** heard; were travelling

b **2** looked **3** didn't see **4** were holding **5** weren't waiting **6** didn't know **7** was **8** decided **9** went **10** looked **11** were waiting **12** caught **13** stopped **14** got **15** walked **16** gave **17** was talking **18** ran **19** was carrying **20** read **21** was waiting **22** thought **23** were **24** said

2C time sequencers and connectors

a **2** d; because **3** e; although **4** a; so **5** i; but **6** h; because **7** j; so **8** f; but **9** b; although **10** c; but

b **2** when **3** although **4** because **5** but **6** One evening **7** so **8** Although **9** suddenly **10** So **11** two minutes later **12** so **13** because **14** Next day **15** but

3A *be going to* (plans and predictions)

a **2** 's going to rain **3** 's going to buy a new car **4** 're going to play football **5** 's going to watch TV **6** isn't going to swim **7** 're going to see a film **8** 're going to go to (Berlin)

b **2** 'm going to get **3** Are...going to do **4** 'm not going to do **5** are...going to go **6** 're going to get **7** 's going to work **8** Is...going to have

3B present continuous (future arrangements)

3 Who's he taking to the hospital on Tuesday? He's taking his Mum.
4 When is he working? He's working on Monday morning and Wednesday afternoon.
5 Is he having dinner with Frank on Monday? Yes, he is.
6 What's he doing on Sunday morning? He's meeting Ellie at the station.
7 What's he doing on Friday night? He's going to Frank's party.
8 When is he going to the dentist? He's going on Friday morning.
9 What's he doing on Saturday morning? He's shopping for Ellie's present.
10 When is he playing tennis? He's playing tennis on Tuesday afternoon.
11 Who's he seeing on Saturday afternoon? He's seeing George.
12 When is he helping his Dad? He's helping his Dad on Thursday afternoon.
13 Is he going to the theatre on Wednesday? Yes, he is.
14 Is he meeting George at the museum? No, he isn't.
15 What's he doing on Sunday evening? He's driving to Wales with Ellie.

3C defining relative clauses

2 who cuts **3** where...borrow **4** where...sleep **5** which...drink **6** which...listen **7** who designs **8** where...have **9** where...look at **10** which...wear **11** where...buy **12** which...cut **13** which...put on **14** who flies **15** who visits

4A present perfect + *yet, just, already*

a
2 Has he cleaned the floor yet? Yes, he has.
3 Has he done the ironing yet? No, he hasn't.
4 Has he taken out the rubbish yet? No, he hasn't.
5 Has he done the shopping yet? Yes, he has.

6 Has he done the washing yet? Yes, he has.
7 Has he cleaned the window yet? No, he hasn't.
8 Has he tidied his desk yet? No, he hasn't.
9 Has he laid the table yet? Yes, he has.
10 Has he made his bed yet? No, he hasn't.

b 2 He's just been on holiday. 3 They've just arrived. 4 She's just washed her hair. 5 He's just bought a ring. 6 We've just had lunch.

4B present perfect or past simple?

a
2 I've never flown in a helicopter.
3 Has she ever been late for work?
4 He hasn't bought any expensive clothes.
5 She's met a lot of famous people.
6 We've never seen a Spike Lee film.
7 She's won a lot of prizes for her novels.
8 Have you ever lost a credit card?
9 I've never worked in a shop or a restaurant.
10 Have you ever sold something on eBay?
11 He's fallen off his bike five times.
12 I haven't read any of *The Lord of the Rings* books.

b 2 have 3 went 4 Did...buy 5 bought 6 did...pay 7 've worn 8 Have...ever heard 9 haven't 10 saw 11 Was 12 liked

4C *something, anything, nothing*, etc.

2 anywhere; somewhere 3 anything; nowhere 4 nobody 5 something 6 anywhere 7 Somebody; anybody 8 anything; nothing; anything 9 somewhere 10 Somebody; anything; anybody

5A comparative adjectives and adverbs, *as...as*

a
2 Spain is hotter than France.
3 The sandwiches are more expensive than the drinks.
4 David speaks Italian better than Kim.
5 Sydney is farther / further from London than Delhi.
6 He's taller than his brother.
7 Claire works harder than Sally.
8 The traffic at 8.30 is worse than the traffic at 9.30.
9 Harry writes more quickly than Paul.
10 Life in the city is more stressful than life in the country.

b
2 France isn't as hot as Spain.
3 The drinks aren't as expensive as the sandwiches.
4 Kim doesn't speak Italian as well as David.
5 Delhi isn't as far from London as Sydney is.
6 His brother isn't as tall as him.
7 Sally doesn't work as hard as Claire.
8 The traffic at 9.30 isn't as bad as the traffic at 8.30.
9 Paul doesn't write as quickly as Harry.
10 Life in the country isn't as stressful as life in the city.

5B superlatives (+ *ever* + present perfect)

a 2 the cheapest 3 the most boring 4 the meanest 5 the most impatient 6 the quietest 7 the emptiest 8 the laziest

b
2 What's the most difficult language you've ever learnt?
3 What's the best restaurant you've ever been to?
4 What's the most expensive gadget you've ever bought?
5 What's the coldest place you've ever visited?
6 What's the longest journey you've ever made?
7 What's the most delicious food you've ever eaten?
8 What's the most beautiful place you've ever been to?
9 What's the most boring film you've ever seen?
10 Where's the furthest / farthest you've ever been on holiday?

5C quantifiers, *too, not enough*

2 a lot of 3 too 4 enough money 5 How much 6 too 7 a little 8 too much 9 much 10 patient enough 11 Too much 12 How many 13 too much 14 enough time 15 too many 16 a few 17 well enough 18 very little 19 a little 20 too many

6A *will / won't* (predictions)

a 2 h; won't understand 3 g; won't be 4 i; won't have 5 a; won't get 6 e; 'll feel 7 k; 'll lose 8 l; 'll get 9 d; 'll last 10 b; 'll be 11 c; 'll pass 12 j; 'll love

b b P c O d O e O f P g P h P i O j O k P l O

6B *will / won't* (promises, offers, decisions)

2 Shall...close 3 won't tell 4 'll call 5 Shall...take 6 won't happen 7 'll have 8 'll be 9 'll help 10 'll think 11 'll make 12 'll ask

6C review of verb forms: present, past, and future

2 don't answer; 'll call 3 isn't playing 4 haven't made 5 'm going to sell 6 did...get; got 7 'll help 8 was driving 9 don't drink 10 Have...spoken 11 were...doing 12 does...work 13 won't hurt 14 'm not working 15 've...seen 16 are...wearing / are...going to wear 17 'll meet 18 are...doing; Do...want 19 did...dream 20 did...take; was walking

7A uses of the infinitive with *to*

2 to pass 3 not to tell 4 to build 5 to use 6 to print 7 to turn off 8 to go 9 to be 10 to swim 11 not to worry 12 to learn 13 to lock 14 to see 15 to get 16 to cry 17 to make 18 to say 19 to ask 20 not to know

7B infinitive or verb + *-ing*?

3 to come 4 not talking 5 to see 6 to earn 7 relaxing; not doing 8 to give 9 to learn 10 winning 11 not to hit 12 drinking; talking 13 to go 14 stopping 15 going 16 to be 17 to go 18 Eating 19 not to understand 20 remembering

7C *have to, don't have to, must, mustn't*

2 don't have to pay 3 must wear 4 mustn't touch 5 don't have to pay 6 mustn't take 7 have to be 8 mustn't play 9 mustn't put 10 don't have to come 11 must drive 12 must wear

8A *should*

2 should ask 3 should tell 4 should get 5 shouldn't sit 6 should get up 7 shouldn't think; should say 8 shouldn't go 9 should learn 10 should go

8B *if* + present, *will* + infinitive (first conditional)

1 **2** 'll get **3** get **4** 'll catch **5** catch **6** won't do **7** don't do **8** won't get

2 **9** lend **10** 'll buy **11** have **12** 'll start **13** have **14** 'll lend **15** lend **16** 'll be able to buy

3 **17** can't **18** won't go **19** don't go **20** won't meet **21** never meet **22** won't get **23** don't get **24** won't have

4 **25** talk **26** 'll miss **27** miss **28** 'll be **29** 'm **30** 'll be **31** is **32** 'll lose

8C possessive pronouns

a **2** her **3** your; my **4** theirs **5** yours; mine **6** our

b **1** his; him **2** Our; we **3** She; her; her **4** theirs; them; they **5** Its; its **6** mine; yours; my; my; you; her; she

9A *if* + past, *would* + infinitive (second conditional)

a **2** 'd feel; did **3** 'd be; didn't live **4** wouldn't swim; were **5** 'd ask; could speak **6** Would she buy; had **7** weren't; 'd go **8** wouldn't be; weren't / wasn't

b **3** studied **4** 'll lend **5** weren't / wasn't **6** don't see **7** won't say **8** don't hurry up **9** wouldn't go **10** would…do

9B present perfect + *for* and *since*

2 have…had; 've had; for **3** have…been married; 've been married since **4** have…known; 've known; for **5** have…lived; 've lived; since **6** have…had; 've had; since **7** have…been; 've been; since

9C present perfect or past simple?

1 've loved; wasn't; started
2 Has…finished; finished; hasn't decided
3 've lived; lived; did…leave; retired
4 saw; told; Have…lived; 've never been; 's visited
5 Have…heard; 've separated; thought
6 's been; fell; got; were

10A passive

2 was designed **3** are checked **4** were built **5** are shown **6** was discovered **7** weren't used **8** were worn **9** was invented **10** is played **11** was painted **12** is…pronounced

10B *used to*

2 She used to play **3** She didn't use to ride **4** She used to wear **5** She didn't use to have **6** She used to be **7** She didn't use to wear **8** She didn't use to play **9** He used to watch **10** He didn't use to do **11** He didn't use to wear **12** He used to have **13** He used to be **14** He used to wear **15** He didn't use to eat **16** He used to have

10C *might*

2 might be **3** might like **4** might not go **5** might meet **6** might fall **7** might not have **8** might phone **9** might go **10** might not say **11** might be

11A expressing movement

2 out of / through **3** under **4** (a)round **5** towards **6** along **7** through **8** up **9** into **10** across **11** down **12** down

11B word order of phrasal verbs

a **2** putting on **3** writing down **4** picking up **5** going away **6** throwing away **7** looking for **8** getting up **9** taking off **10** getting on

b **2** turn it up **3** looking after them **4** call her back **5** Turn off your mobiles / turn your mobiles off **6** pick them up **7** look for them **8** pay me back

11C *so, neither* + auxiliaries

3 Neither can I **4** Neither am I **5** So have I **6** Neither did I **7** So was I **8** Neither have I **9** So am I **10** So do I **11** Neither do I **12** So did I **13** So was I **14** Neither have I **15** So do I **16** Neither will I **17** So am I **18** So would I **19** So will I **20** So have I

12A past perfect

2 was; hadn't taken **3** didn't work; hadn't turned it on **4** couldn't take; had forgotten **5** 'd never flown; were **6** arrived; hadn't brought **7** 'd just had; wasn't **8** had to; 'd lost **9** ran; hadn't paid **10** arrived, had gone out **11** could; 'd learnt **12** was; 'd been

12B reported speech

a **2** he didn't like the music **3** he'd done his homework **4** it would be expensive **5** she wasn't going to the party **6** he'd lost the match **7** he loved her **8** she'd found his keys

b **2** 'It won't hurt.' **3** 'It's my mother's car.' **4** 'I've finished my homework.' **5** 'I can't swim.' **6** 'I will always love you.' **7** 'We want to check out.' **8** 'I don't speak English.'

12C questions with and without auxiliaries

2 Martin Scorsese
3 Who painted *The Scream*? Edvard Munch
4 Where do manga comics come from? Japan
5 Who invented the World Wide Web? Tim Berners-Lee
6 Which country has a blue and yellow flag? Sweden.
7 When did the Second World War end? 1945
8 Which country won the 2010 World Cup? Spain
9 Which superhero film did Christoper Nolan direct in 2008? *The Dark Knight*
10 How many countries belong to the United Nations? 193
11 Who did Tom Cruise marry in 2006? Katie Holmes
12 Where do people speak Yorùbá? West Africa

1A GRAMMAR word order in questions

a Put the words in the right order to make questions.

1 name / your / 's / what
What's your name ? Luca.

2 how / you / are / today
____________________ ? Fine, thank you.

3 from / you / where / are
____________________ ? Italy.

4 year / what / you / born / were
____________________ ? 1983.

5 live / you / where / do
____________________ ? Rome.

6 in / a / flat / you / do / live / or / a / house
____________________ ? In a house.

7 have / do / pets / you / any
____________________ ? Yes, I do – a dog and a goldfish.

8 any / can / other / languages / you / speak
____________________ ? Yes, French and Russian.

9 English / why / are / studying / you
____________________ ? Because I need it for my job.

10 TV / you / do / what / watch / programmes
____________________ ? Music programmes on MTV and the news on CNN.

11 use / how / computer / you / often / do / a
____________________ ? Every day – I use it at work.

12 read / of / do / what / kind / magazines / you
____________________ ? I read car magazines.

13 breakfast / have / did / what / you / for
____________________ ? Coffee and bread with jam.

14 do / did / you / any / yesterday / sport
____________________ ? Yes, I went swimming.

15 last / you / were / where / night / ten o'clock / at
____________________ ? I was at my friend's house.

b **Test your memory.** Cover the questions. Look at the answers. Can you remember the questions?

activation

c Work with a partner. Ask and answer the questions in **a**.

1B GRAMMAR present simple

a Complete the sentences with the present simple of the verbs in brackets.

1 Why *do you want* to have straight hair? (you / want)
2 What ________________? (his sister / look like)
3 How many really clever people ________________? (you / know)
4 **A** Is that book funny?
B Not very. It ________________ me laugh. (not make)
5 I ________________ fish. (not eat)
6 Jon ________________ work at six o'clock. (finish)
7 My mother and I ________________ very well. (not get on)
8 ________________ to the gym every day? (they / go)
9 ________________ fish or meat? (Lucy / prefer)
10 ________________ blonde hair? (your sisters / have)
11 How ________________ after work? (you / relax)
12 **A** Is he talkative?
B Yes, he never ________________ talking! (stop)
13 He ________________ in the evening. (not study)
14 Excuse me, ________________ here? (you / live)
15 Yuri ________________ a beard and a moustache. (have)
16 Clara ________________ yoga every day. (do)
17 We usually ________________ work at eight o'clock. (start)
18 My parents ________________ Facebook or Twitter. (not use)
19 I sometimes ________________ jeans. (wear)
20 ________________ a car? (your girlfriend / have)

activation

b Write three sentences about what you do at the weekend, and three about what a person in your family does. Use adverbs or expressions of frequency.

1C GRAMMAR present simple or present continuous?

a Complete the sentences with the present simple or present continuous of the verbs in brackets.

1 **A** Why [1]*are* you *taking* (take) a photo of your guitar?

B I [2]______________ (want) to sell it on eBay.

A Why? I [3]______________ (not understand). You [4]______________ (play) your guitar every day! You [5]______________ (love) it!

B I [6]______________ (sell) my old one because I [7]______________ (want) to buy a new one.

A Oh, OK.

2 **A** Hi. [8]______________ (need) any help?

B No, thanks. I [9]______________ (just look).

A [10]______________ you ______________ (look) for anything in particular?

B Yes, I [11]______________ (think) of getting a jacket.

A This is one of our bestsellers. It's real leather. I [12]______________ (have) it and I [13]______________ (wear) it all the time.

B Yes, it's lovely. Where can I try it on?

3 **A** You [14]______________ (read) a book about modern art! I [15]______________ (not believe) it! You [16]______________ (hate) modern art!

B I know. But now I [17]______________ (need) to learn about it.

A Why?

B Because my girlfriend [18]______________ (study) it at college this year and she loves it.

A What's that picture on the left? Can I see it?

B It's a woman, and I think she [19]______________ (walk) in a garden...I don't really know.

A Let me see... No, she [20]______________ (not walk). She [21]______________ (fly).

B Oh, yes!

activation

b Practise the dialogues in **a** with a partner.

2A GRAMMAR past simple: regular and irregular verbs

a Complete the dialogues with the past simple of the verbs in brackets.

1 **A** Is this your first time in the UK, Anna?

B No, I [1]*had* a holiday in Scotland last year.

A Really? I love Scotland! Where [2]__________ you __________ (stay)?

B We [3]__________ (stay) in Edinburgh. We [4]__________ (book) a hotel online, but unfortunately when we [5]__________ (arrive) we [6]__________ (not like) it. So we [7]__________ (leave) that hotel and [8]__________ (rent) an apartment. It was great! What about you? When [9]__________ (be) you in Scotland?

A Oh, a long time ago. I [10]__________ (start) a university course there. I [11]__________ (not finish) the course, but I [12]__________ (love) Scotland!

2 **A** What's the problem, sir?

B Somebody [13]__________ (take) my clothes and bag when I [14]__________ (be) in the sea!

A When [15]__________ this __________ (happen)?

B I [16]__________ (go) for a swim at 11 o'clock. I [17]__________ (not be) in the water for very long – about 15 minutes.

A [18]__________ you __________ (see) the person take your things?

B No. When I [19]__________ (come) out of the water, my bag [20]__________ (not be) there.

A What [21]__________ you __________ (have) in your bag? Anything valuable?

B Yes! My mobile phone, credit cards... Oh, I [22]__________ (know) it was a bad idea to leave my bag on the beach...

3 **A** Ruth! You're back! [23]__________ you __________ (have) a good time?

B No. It [24]__________ (be) awful.

A Why? What happened?

B We [25]__________ (stay) in a really basic apartment, and Tom [26]__________ (think) the city was dangerous at night, so we [27]__________ (not go) out much in the evening.

A What [28]__________ you __________ (do) during the day? [29]__________ you __________ (go) sightseeing?

B Yes, we visited all the famous places. But we [30]__________ (spend) a lot of money on food and we [31]__________ (argue) a lot about it. Tom [32]__________ (buy) very expensive souvenirs for all his family! I [33]__________ (not buy) anything.

activation

b Cover the dialogues and look at the pictures. Try to remember what happened to Anna, the man on the beach, and Ruth and Tom.

2B GRAMMAR past continuous

a Look at the pictures and write the sentences. Use the past simple and past continuous.

1 She *saw* the spider when she *was buying* some fruit. (see, buy)

2 His mobile __________ when he __________. (ring, drive)

3 Neil __________ late when his boss __________ a speech. (arrive, make)

4 They __________ football when it __________ to rain. (play, start)

5 We __________ a party when I __________ this photo. (have, take)

6 We __________ the result when we __________ in France. (hear, travel)

b Complete the story with the past simple or past continuous of the verbs in brackets.

When Alex Jones [1]*arrived* (arrive) at JFK International Airport, she [2]__________ (look) around, but she [3]__________ (not see) anybody there to meet her. A lot of people [4]__________ (hold) cards with names on them, but they [5]__________ (not wait) for her. She [6]__________ (not know) what to do, but it [7]__________ (be) a beautiful, sunny day, so she [8]__________ (decide) to go to the hotel on her own. She [9]__________ (go) outside and [10]__________ (look) for a taxi. A lot of people [11]__________ (wait), so she [12]__________ (catch) the airport bus into New York. The bus [13] __________ (stop) in Manhattan, quite near the hotel, and she [14]__________ (get) off. She [15]__________ (walk) into the hotel and [16]__________ (give) her name, Alexandra Jones. She [17]__________ (talk) to the receptionist when suddenly a man [18]__________ (run) up to her. He [19]__________ (carry) a card which [20]__________ (read) 'Mr Jones'.
'Ms Jones? I'm terribly sorry! I [21]__________ (wait) for you at the airport, but I [22]__________ (think) you [23]__________ (be) a man!'
'That's OK,' [24]__________ (say) Alex. 'It happens to me all the time!'

activation

c Cover sentences 1–6 in **a**. Look at the pictures and remember the sentences.

2C GRAMMAR time sequencers and connectors

a Match the sentence halves and (circle) the correct word: *so*, *but*, *because*, or *although*.

1 The weather was awful, [g]
2 I didn't give him my phone number [ ]
3 She didn't like the song [ ]
4 It was her birthday, [ ]
5 He's an intelligent student, [ ]
6 I ran to the shop [ ]
7 They didn't want to dance, [ ]
8 We didn't go anywhere special, [ ]
9 It was a sad story [ ]
10 We drove along the street very slowly, [ ]

a **so / but** I invited her to dinner.
b **because / although** it had a happy ending.
c **but / so** we couldn't find the house.
d **because / although** I didn't want him to call me.
e **because / although** it was by one of her favourite bands.
f **so / but** we had a wonderful evening.
g **but / (so)** we didn't go out.
h **although / because** I was in a hurry.
i **because / but** he's very lazy.
j **so / because** they left the club early.

activation

b Complete the story with the time sequencers and connectors in the list.

although (x2) because (x3) but (x2) next day one evening so (x3) suddenly two minutes later when

Don't always listen to the sat nav...

Oscar Peters never wanted a sat nav [1] *because* he didn't like technology. And [2] __________ his brother gave him one as a birthday present, it directed him into a difficult situation.

'My brother Jez loves gadgets and technology. Last year he gave me a sat nav for my birthday, [3] __________ he knew I didn't really want one. Jez uses his sat nav all the time [4] __________ he likes listening to instructions, [5] __________ I prefer using a map.

[6] __________, a friend of a friend phoned. She needed my help, [7] __________ I agreed to drive to her house. [8] __________ I had a map in the car, I decided to use the sat nav to find her village. It was dark, and I wanted to get there as quickly as possible.

Everything was going fine. I was nearly there, but then [9] __________ I saw there was a small river on the left. I could see that there was a road which went through the water to the other side of the river. The sat nav said 'Turn left!'

[10] __________ I followed the instruction and turned left into the water. The sat nav said 'Go straight on!', but [11] __________ my car was completely stuck in the mud.

I had my mobile with me, [12] __________ I phoned my friend and she came to the river to help. I felt terrible [13] __________ she got very cold and wet in the water.

[14] __________, a tractor pulled my car out of the river, [15] __________ it was completely ruined by the water. I can't believe I made such a stupid – and expensive – mistake!'

3A GRAMMAR *be going to* (plans and predictions)

a What's going to happen? Write a sentence with *be* + *going to* for pictures 1–8 and a verb from the list.

buy go ~~miss~~ play rain see not swim watch

1 *He's going to miss the bus.*
2 It ____________________.
3 He ____________________.
4 They ____________________.
5 She ____________________.
6 He ____________________.
7 They ____________________.
8 They ____________________ Berlin.

b Complete the dialogues with the correct form of *be* + *going to* and a verb from the list.

do have get (x2) go ~~miss~~ not do work

1 **A** We [1]*'re going to miss* the plane!
B No, we're not... Wait a minute.
A What are you doing?
B I [2]____________________ a trolley. I can't carry all these bags.

2 **A** [3]____________ you ____________________ your homework this evening?
B No, I'm not. I'm really tired. In fact, I [4]____________________ anything – just sleep!

3 **A** So, do you like it here in Oxford?
B Yes, we love it! But we're only here for a short time. We're going to visit lots of different places.
A Where [5]____________ you ____________ next?
B Liverpool. We [6]____________________ the train there.

4 **A** How's your daughter?
B She's fine, thanks.
A Does she have any plans for the summer?
B Yes. She [7]____________________ in a bookshop for six weeks.
A [8]____________ she ____________________ a holiday?
B No, I don't think she is.

activation

c Cover sentences 1–8 in **a**. Look at the pictures and remember the sentences. Then practise the dialogues in **b** with a partner.

3B GRAMMAR present continuous (future arrangements)

a Look at Luke's diary. Write the questions and the answers. Use the present continuous.

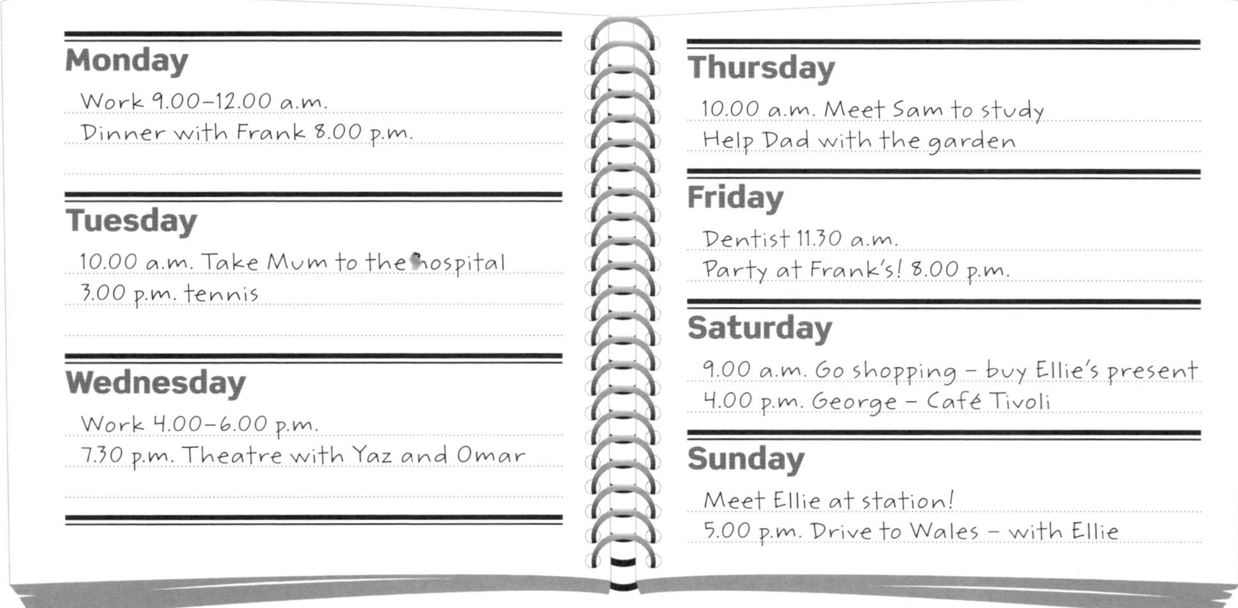

1 / meet Sam on Monday?
'Is he meeting Sam on Monday?' 'No, he isn't.'

2 When / go to the station?
'When is he going to the station?' 'He's going to the station on Sunday.'

3 Who / take to the hospital on Tuesday?

4 When / work?

5 / have dinner with Frank on Monday?

6 What / do on Sunday morning?

7 What / do on Friday night?

8 When / go to the dentist?

9 What / do on Saturday morning?

10 When / play tennis?

11 Who / see Saturday afternoon?

12 When / help his Dad?

13 / go to the theatre on Wednesday?

14 / meet George at the museum?

15 What / do on Sunday afternoon?

activation

b Write down one arrangement that you have each day next week. Tell a partner. Use the present continuous.

3C GRAMMAR defining relative clauses

a Complete the definitions with *who*, *which*, or *where* and the correct form of a verb in the list.

borrow ~~build~~ buy cut (x2) design drink fly have listen
look at put on sleep visit wear

1 A **builder** is a person <u>*who builds*</u> houses.
2 A **hairdresser** is somebody ________ ________ your hair.
3 A **library** is a place ________ you can read or ________ books.
4 A **campsite** is a place ________ people ________ in tents.
5 **Mugs** are things ________ you ________ from.
6 An **iPod** is something ________ you ________ to music with.
7 An **architect** is someone ________ ________ buildings.
8 An **internet café** is a place ________ you can send emails and ________ a coffee.
9 An **art gallery** is a place ________ you ________ paintings.
10 **Trainers** are shoes ________ people ________ for sport.
11 A **bookshop** is a place ________ you ________ books.
12 **Scissors** are things ________ you use to ________ paper with.
13 **Lipstick** is something ________ you ________ your lips.
14 A **pilot** is a person ________ ________ planes.
15 A **tourist** is a person ________ ________ another country.

activation

b **Test your memory.** Cover the definitions. Look at the pictures. Can you remember the definitions?

4A GRAMMAR present perfect + *yet, just, already*

a Write questions and answers for the picture. Use present perfect + *yet* / *already*.

1 do / the washing-up
Has he done the washing-up yet?
No, he hasn't.

2 clean / the floor
______________________________?
______________________________.

3 do / the ironing
______________________________?
______________________________.

4 take out / the rubbish
______________________________?
______________________________.

5 do / the shopping
______________________________?
______________________________.

6 do / the washing
______________________________?
______________________________.

7 clean / the window
______________________________?
______________________________.

8 tidy / his desk
______________________________?
______________________________.

9 lay / the table
______________________________?
______________________________.

10 make / his bed
______________________________?
______________________________.

b Write sentences for the pictures. Use *just* + present perfect.

1 She / make / breakfast
She's just made breakfast.

2 He / be on holiday
______________________________.

3 They / arrive
______________________________.

4 She / wash her hair
______________________________.

5 He / buy a ring
______________________________.

6 **A** Would you like a cake?
B No, thanks. We / have lunch
______________________________.

activation

c Write sentences that are true for you. Say two things you've already done today, two things you haven't done yet, and two things you've just done.

4B GRAMMAR present perfect or past simple?

a Write sentences in the present perfect.

1 you / ever **eat** / octopus
Have you ever eaten octopus ____________?

2 I / never **fly** / in a helicopter
____________.

3 she / ever **be** / late for work
____________?

4 he / not **buy** / any expensive clothes
____________.

5 she / **meet** / a lot of famous people
____________.

6 we / never **see** / a Spike Lee film
____________.

7 she / **win** / a lot of prizes for her novels
____________.

8 you / ever **lose** / a credit card
____________?

9 I / never **work** / in a shop or a restaurant
____________.

10 you / ever **sell** / something on eBay
____________?

11 he / **fall off** / his bike five times
____________!

12 I / not **read** / any of *The Lord of the Rings* books
____________.

b Complete the dialogues with the correct form of the verb: present perfect or past simple.

A [1]*Have* you *ever been* (ever / go) to an auction?

B Yes, I [2]____________. I [3]____________ (go) to one about two years ago.

A [4]____________ you ____________ (buy) anything?

B Yes, I [5]____________ (buy) a necklace.

A How much [6]____________ you ____________ (pay) for it?

B A fortune! But I [7]____________ (wear) it a lot. I love it.

A [8]____________ you ____________ (ever / hear) the group *Muse*?

B No, I [9]____________. What kind of music do they play?

A Rock music. I [10]____________ (see) them in concert last month.

B [11]____________ (be) it a good concert?

A Yes, I really [12]____________ (like) it.

activation

c Practise the dialogues in **b** with a partner. Then ask each other questions beginning *Have you ever been to...*(place)*?* and *Have you ever heard the group...* (a song or a musician)*?* and have short conversations.

4C GRAMMAR *something, anything, nothing, etc.*

a Complete the dialogues with the words from the list. Write your answers in the column on the right.

anybody (x2) anything (x4) anywhere (x2) nobody ~~nobody~~ nothing nowhere
somebody (x2) ~~somebody~~ something somewhere (x2)

1 **A** Why are you looking out of the window?
B I think there's ▬ in the house opposite. *somebody*
A But ▬ has lived there for years! *nobody*
B I know, that's why I'm looking.

2 **A** Are you going ▬ this summer? ______
B We haven't decided yet. But my wife wants to go ▬ nice and hot. ______

3 **A** I'm so bored. There isn't ▬ to do in this town! ______
B That's not true. There are lots of things to do.
A But there's ▬ for young people to go. ______

4 **A** I phoned your office at 2.00 today, but ▬ answered. ______
B Sorry. We were all at lunch.

5 **A** I'm hungry. I need ▬ to eat. ______
B Well, there's food in the fridge.

6 **A** Where did you go last night?
B I didn't go ▬. I was too tired. I stayed in. ______

7 **A** ▬ told me that their new album is very good. ______
B Really? I don't know ▬ who likes it. ______

8 **A** Did you buy ▬ this afternoon? ______
B No, ▬. I didn't see ▬ that I liked. ______ ______

9 **A** Where are the keys?
B They're ▬ in the kitchen. ______

10 **A** ▬ told Eva about the party. Was it you? ______
B Me? No, I haven't said ▬ to ▬. ______ ______

activation

b Work with a partner. Cover the column on the right. Read the dialogues aloud with the missing words.

5A GRAMMAR comparative adjectives and adverbs, *as...as*

a Write sentences about the pictures using comparative adjectives and adverbs.

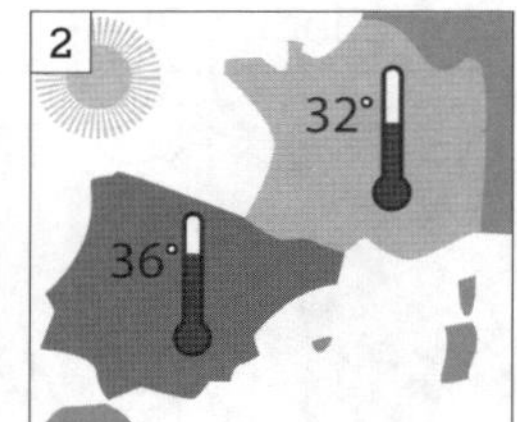

1 He's / happy / his wife
He's happier than his wife.

2 Spain is / hot / France
____________________.

3 The sandwiches are / expensive / the drinks
____________________.

4 David speaks Italian / good / Kim
____________________.

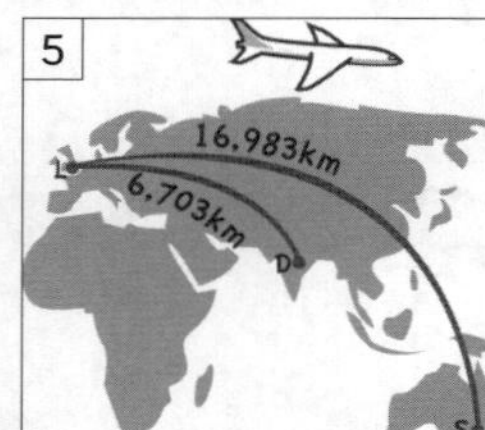

5 Sydney is / far from London / Delhi
____________________.

6 He's / tall / brother
____________________.

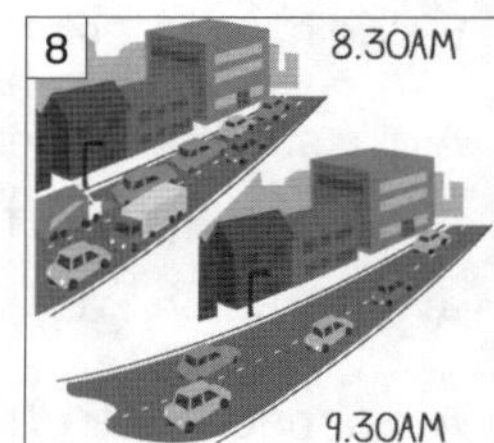

7 Claire works / hard / Sally
____________________.

8 The traffic at 8.30 is / bad / the traffic at 9.30
____________________.

9 Harry writes / quickly / Paul
____________________.

10 Life in the city is / stressful / life in the country
____________________.

b Rewrite the sentences from **a** using *not as…as*.

1 His wife *isn't as happy as him.*
2 France ____________________.
3 The drinks ____________________.
4 Kim ____________________.
5 Delhi ____________________.
6 His brother ____________________.
7 Sally ____________________.
8 The traffic at 9.30 ____________________.
9 Paul ____________________.
10 Life in the country ____________________.

activation

c Cover the sentences and look at the pictures. For each picture, say a sentence a) with a comparative adjective or adverb and b) with *not as…as*.

5B GRAMMAR superlatives (+ *ever* + present perfect)

a Write the opposite superlatives.

1 the most unfriendly *the friendliest*
2 the most expensive ________
3 the most exciting ________
4 the most generous ________
5 the most patient ________
6 the loudest ________
7 the most crowded ________
8 the most hard-working ________

b Write the questions with the superlative form of the adjective and *ever* + present perfect.

1 Who / generous / person you / meet
Who's the most generous person you've ever met?
2 What / difficult / language you / learn
________?
3 What / good / restaurant you / be to
________?
4 What / expensive / gadget you / buy
________?
5 What / cold / place you / visit
________?
6 What / long / journey you / make
________?
7 What / delicious / food you / eat
________?
8 What / beautiful / place you / be / to
________?
9 What / boring / film you / see
________?
10 Where / far / you / be on holiday
________?

activation

c Work with a partner. Ask and answer the questions in **b**.

5C GRAMMAR quantifiers, *too*, *not enough*

a Choose the correct word or phrase for each sentence. ~~Cross out~~ the wrong form.

1 The fish was delicious, but I found ~~**a little**~~ / **a few** bones.
2 A good diet can prevent **lot of** / **a lot of** illnesses.
3 'How was the job interview?' 'It was OK. I wasn't **too** / **enough** nervous.'
4 I think I have **enough money** / **money enough** to pay for this.
5 **How much** / **many** milk do you drink?
6 You should be friendly, but not **too** / **too much** friendly.
7 Could I have **a little** / **a few** milk, please?
8 She spends **too many** / **much** money on shoes.
9 You don't do **many** / **much** exercise.
10 I can't teach children. I'm not **patient enough** / **enough patient**.
11 **Too much** / **many** chocolate isn't good for you.
12 **How many** / **much** hours do you study each day?
13 Don't spend **too much** / **many** time at the computer.
14 I couldn't finish the work because I didn't have **time enough** / **enough time**.
15 I have **too many** / **much** clothes. I can never decide what to wear.
16 We're buying **a little** / **a few** things for our new flat.
17 Are you **enough well** / **well enough** to go to work today?
18 I'm going to have **very little** / **very few** free time this weekend.
19 He does **a few** / **a little** housework every day.
20 We buy **too many** / **much** vegetables. We never eat them all!

activation

b Complete the sentences so that they are true for you. Compare your answers with a partner. Tell your partner more information.

I don't eat enough…
I spend too much money on…
I watch too many…
I drink too much…
I don't do enough…
People in my country are too…

6A GRAMMAR *will / won't* (predictions)

a Read sentences 1–12 and match them to predictions a–l. Complete the predictions with *will / won't*. Use the verbs in brackets.

1 'I don't believe it. I've broken Sam's laptop.' [*f*]
2 'Marc's going to see a film in English tonight.' [ ]
3 'There's a new drinks machine in the office.' [ ]
4 'The teacher isn't going to be here tomorrow.' [ ]
5 'My brother's going to sell his car.' [ ]
6 'I've started going swimming every day.' [ ]
7 'Esther's going to buy another mobile phone.' [ ]
8 'My daughter has a degree in IT.' [ ]
9 'My new coat was really expensive!' [ ]
10 'The meeting starts at 2.30.' [ ]
11 'I'm taking my driving test tomorrow.' [ ]
12 'We're going to Brazil next month.' [ ]

a 'He ______________ much money for it. It's very old.' (not get)
b 'Yes, and I'm sure it ______________ really boring!' (be)
c 'Don't worry. You ______________ easily.' (pass)
d 'Yes, but it ______________ a long time.' (last)
e 'That's good. You ______________ much healthier.' (feel)
~~f~~ 'Oh no. He*'ll be* really angry.' (be)
g 'The coffee ______________ very good.' (not be)
h 'He ______________ anything!' (not understand)
i 'Great! So we ______________ the exam!' (not have)
j 'Lucky you! You ______________ the people and the scenery.' (love)
k 'She ______________ it, just like the other two.' (lose)
l 'She ______________ a good job, I'm sure.' (get)

b Read the conversations again. Are the predictions in **a** optimistic or pessimistic? Write O or P.

a [*P*] b [ ] c [ ] d [ ] e [ ] f [ ]
g [ ] h [ ] i [ ] j [ ] k [ ] l [ ]

activation

c Work with a partner. **A** read sentences 1–12. **B** read the predictions. Use positive or negative intonation. Then swap roles.

6B GRAMMAR *will / won't* (promises, offers, decisions)

a Complete the dialogues with *will* / *won't* or *shall* and the correct verb from the list.

ask be call close have help make ~~not forget~~
not happen not tell take think

1 **A** Please can you post this letter for me today? It's very important.
B Don't worry, I *won't forget*.

2 **A** I'm cold.
B ________ I ________ the window?

3 **A** It's a secret. You're the only person who knows.
B It's OK. I ________________ anyone.

4 **A** Oh, hello Nina. I can't talk now. I'm at work.
B No problem. I ________________ you back this evening.

5 **A** I bought this toy for my son's birthday, but it doesn't work.
B I'm going into town soon. ________ I ________ it back for you?

6 **A** You're 15 minutes late!
B I'm very sorry. It ________________ again.

7 **A** So, a mineral water and an egg sandwich. Anything else?
B Yes, I ________________ a packet of crisps, please.

8 **A** Please don't go!
B Don't worry. I ________________ back soon.

9 **A** I'm going to paint my flat at the weekend.
B I ________________ you if you like.

10 **A** What are your plans for the summer?
B I'm going to travel around Italy. Why don't you come with me?
A Maybe! I ________________ about it.

11 **A** I've had a terrible day today.
B Sit down, and I ________________ you a cup of tea.

12 **A** I'm nervous about the test tomorrow.
B OK. Give me the book. I ________________ you some of the questions.

activation

b Practise the dialogues in **a** with a partner.

6C GRAMMAR review of verb forms: present, past, and future

Complete the dialogues with the correct form of the verbs in brackets: present simple, present continuous, past simple, past continuous, present perfect, *going to* + infinitive, *will* / *won't* + infinitive.

1 **A** *Does* your sister sometimes *get* (get) angry with you?
B Only if I take her clothes without asking.

2 **A** They __________ (not answer) the phone after six o'clock. The office is closed.
B OK, I __________ (call) them tomorrow.

3 **A** Our goalkeeper __________ (not play) very well at the moment.
B That's strange. He's usually so good.

4 **A** Sorry, I __________ (not make) anything for dinner yet.
B That's OK. I'm not very hungry.

5 **A** Have you decided what to do with your car?
B Yes. I __________ (sell) it next month.

6 **A** How __________ they __________ (get) home last night?
B They __________ (get) a taxi.

7 **A** Oh, dear. I'm not very good at this.
B Don't worry. I __________ (help) you.

8 **A** Do you know about the election results?
B Yes, I heard about them on the news when I __________ (drive) home.

9 **A** Coffee isn't very good for you, you know.
B Well, I __________ (not drink) very much – just one cup a day.

10 **A** __________ you ever __________ (speak) to your mother about the problem?
B Yes, I have. But it was a long time ago.

11 **A** What __________ you __________ (do) when I phoned?
B I was having a shower.

12 **A** Where __________ Jack __________ (work)?
B He works in London.

13 **A** I'm a bit nervous about the injection, Doctor.
B Don't worry. It __________ (not hurt).

14 **A** Hi, can you talk now?
B Yes, I __________ (not work) at the moment.

15 **A** I __________ just __________ (see) the new *James Bond* film.
B Did you like it?
A Yes, I did. But not as much as the last one.

16 **A** What __________ you __________ (wear) to the party tonight?
B Probably black jeans and a white top.

17 **A** My plane is arriving at one o'clock in the afternoon.
B OK, we __________ (meet) you at the airport.

18 **A** What __________ you __________ (do) tomorrow afternoon?
B Nothing. Why?
A __________ you __________ (want) to see a film?

19 **A** What __________ you __________ (dream) about last night?
B I can't remember!

20 **A** Where __________ you __________ (take) this photo?
B When I __________ (walk) in the Himalayas.

[ ] **20**

16–20 Excellent. You can use the past, present, and future very well.

11–15 Quite good, but check the rules in the Grammar Bank (Student's Book *p.136*) and look at the exercise again.

1–10 This is difficult for you. Read the rules in the Grammar Bank (Student's Book *p.136*). Then ask your teacher for another photocopy and do the exercise again at home.

7A GRAMMAR uses of the infinitive with *to*

a Complete each sentence with *to* + a verb from the list. Write your answers in the **infinitives with *to*** column.

ask be build cry get go learn lock make not know not tell
pass print say see ~~start~~ swim turn off use not worry

		infinitives with *to*
1	Are you ready ______ work now?	*to start*
2	It's not difficult ______ the first year exam.	
3	Promise ______ anyone about this. It's a secret.	
4	They're planning ______ a supermarket there.	
5	Can you show me how ______ the new coffee machine?	
6	You need ______ your boarding pass before you go to the airport.	
7	Don't forget ______ the computer when you leave.	
8	Does he know where ______ when he arrives?	
9	She shouldn't pretend ______ happy if she isn't.	
10	Is it safe ______ in this river?	
11	Try ______ about your exam. You'll pass easily.	
12	What's the best way ______ a new language?	
13	Did you remember ______ the door?	
14	It was really nice ______ you again.	
15	I can't think what ______ her for her birthday.	
16	He tried to tell her that he was leaving her, but she started ______.	
17	It's really important ______ a good impression on your first day in a new job.	
18	He phoned her ______ that he was sorry.	
19	I don't know who ______ for advice.	
20	Don't worry. It's quite normal ______ all the answers.	

activation

b Cover the **infinitives with *to*** column. Read the sentences aloud with the missing infinitives.

7B GRAMMAR infinitive with *to* or verb + *-ing*?

Complete the sentences with the verbs in brackets with *to* + infinitive or a verb + *-ing*.

1 I can't promise *to be* (be) on time.

2 *Swimming* (swim) is better exercise than running.

3 Would you like __________ (come) to my party?

4 Do you mind __________ (not talk) so loudly?

5 It was very interesting __________ (see) my old school again.

6 He works at weekends __________ (earn) more money.

7 On Sundays she likes __________ and __________ (relax, not do) anything.

8 We were unhappy with the service, so the restaurant offered __________ (give) us a free dinner.

9 Is it difficult __________ (learn) Japanese?

10 He's very competitive. He thinks __________ (win) is the most important thing.

11 She tried __________ (not hit) the man, but she was driving too fast.

12 They spent all night __________ coffee and __________ (drink, talk).

13 Do you need __________ (go) to the bathroom?

14 They drove without __________ (stop) for 6 hours.

15 We're thinking of __________ (go) to Mexico for our holidays next year.

16 I'm very happy __________ (be) here again.

17 I decided __________ (go) camping because I didn't have much money.

18 __________ (eat) cakes and junk food will make you fat.

19 He pretended __________ (not understand) the police officer.

20 Are you good at __________ (remember) people's names?

[ ] **20**

16–20 Excellent. You can use the infinitive and verb + *-ing* very well.

11–15 Quite good, but check the rules in the Grammar Bank (Student's Book *p.138*) and look at the exercise again.

1–10 This is difficult for you. Read the rules in the Grammar Bank (Student's Book *p.138*). Then ask your teacher for another photocopy and do the exercise again at home.

7C GRAMMAR *have to, don't have to, must, mustn't*

a Complete the sentences with *have to* / *don't have to* / *must* / *mustn't* + a verb from the list.

be come drive pay (x2) play put take touch ~~turn off~~ wear (x2)

1 You *must turn off* your phone.

2 Children ______________________.

3 You ______________________ a jacket.

4 You ______________________ the door.

5 You ______________________ anything now.

6 You ______________________ photos.

7 You ______________________ over 18 to see this film.

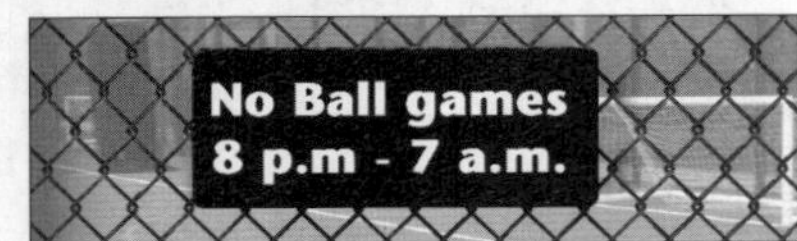

8 You ______________________ football here at night.

9 You ______________________ your feet on the seats.

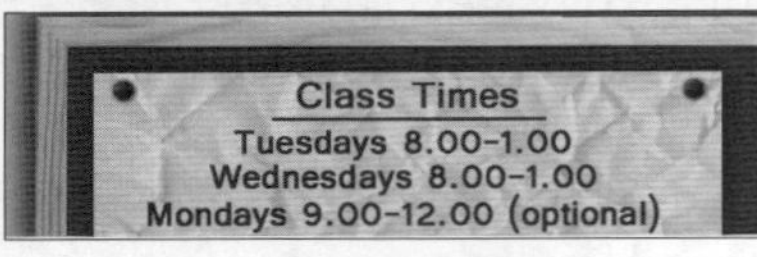

10 You ______________________ to class on Mondays.

11 You ______________________ in one direction.

12 You ______________________ sports shoes here.

activation

b **Test your memory.** Cover the sentences. Look at the signs and remember the sentences.

8A GRAMMAR *should*

a Look at pictures 1–10. Use *should* / *shouldn't* + a verb from the list to complete dialogues 1–10.

ask go (x2) get get up learn say sit tell think ~~use~~

1 **A** What are you doing?
B I'm trying to open this packet.
A You *shouldn't use* a knife! You'll cut yourself!

2 **A** I can't do this exercise. It's too difficult.
B You ______________ the teacher for some help.

3 **A** I'm really annoyed with Paula.
B Why?
A Because she's always on the computer. She never talks to me!
B You ______________ her how you feel. Maybe she doesn't know.

4 **A** Angela's leaving work at the end of the month. She's going to have a baby.
B We ______________ her a present.

5 **A** You ______________ so near the television.
B Why not?
A It's not good for your eyes.

6 **A** I miss the bus for college nearly every day.
B You ______________ earlier.

7 **A** Good luck for the match!
B Thanks, but I'm sure I'm going to lose.
A You ______________ like that! Be positive!
B What do mean?
A You ______________ to yourself, 'I'm going to win! I'm going to win!'

8 **A** Come on. Get up. It's 9.30.
B But I'm tired.
A You ______________ to bed so late.

9 **A** Can you make me an omelette, please?
B Make it yourself!
A I don't know how to.
B You ______________ how to cook then!

10 **A** I'd love to travel round the world.
B Do you have enough money for the trip?
A Well, yes.
B Then I think you ______________!

activation

b **Test your memory.** Cover the dialogues. Look at the pictures and remember the advice.

8B GRAMMAR *if* + present, *will* + infinitive (first conditional)

a Complete the stories with the correct form of the verbs in brackets.

1

If you [1]*don't take* an umbrella, you [2]__________ wet. (not take, get)

If you [3]__________ wet, you [4]__________ a cold. (get, catch)

If you [5]__________ a cold, you [6]__________ well in your exam tomorrow. (catch, not do)

If you [7]__________ well in your exam, you [8]__________ a place at university. (not do, not get)

2

If you [9]__________ me £3,000, I [10]__________ a good computer. (lend, buy)

If I [11]__________ a good computer, I [12]__________ my own business. (have, start)

If I [13]__________ my own business, I [14]__________ you some money. (have, lend)

If I [15]__________ you some money, you [16]__________ a new car. (lend, can buy)

3

If I [17]__________ borrow your dress, I [18]__________ to the party. (not can, not go)

If I [19]__________ to the party, I [20]__________ anyone. (not go, not meet)

If I [21]__________ anyone, I [22]__________ married. (never meet, not get)

If I [23]__________ married, you [24]__________ any grandchildren. (not get, not have)

4

If I [25]__________ to you now, I [26]__________ the bus. (talk, miss)

If I [27]__________ the train, I [28]__________ late for work. (miss, be)

If I [29]__________ late for work, my boss [30]__________ angry with me. (be, be)

If my boss [31]__________ angry with me, I [32]__________ my job. (be, lose)

activation

b Cover the stories and look at the pictures. Try to remember the stories.

1 If you don't take an umbrella, …

2 If you lend me £3,000, …

3 If I can't borrow your dress, …

4 If I talk to you now, …

8C GRAMMAR possessive pronouns

a Circle the correct word in the dialogues.

1 **A** Is that Bill's camera?
B No, it's **our** / **ours**. Why?

2 **A** She says she's 25.
B 25! That's not **her** / **hers** real age.

3 **A** Can you move **your** / **yours** car, please?
B Sorry? That's not **my** / **mine** car.

4 **A** Andy and Gina's cat is so sweet! When did they get it?
B I don't think it's **their** / **theirs**, actually. It's the neighbours'.

5 **A** I love this motorbike! Is it **your** / **yours**?
B No, it's not **my** / **mine**, unfortunately.

6 **A** Have you seen this photo in the newspaper?
B Wait a minute! Thy're **our** / **ours** children!

b Complete the sentences with the correct subject or object pronouns (*I*, *me*, *you*, etc.) and possessive adjectives or pronouns (*my*, *mine*, *etc.*).

1 If Andrew doesn't leave soon, *he*'ll miss __________ train. I think you should tell __________ to hurry.

2 My sister and I work in the same office. __________ hours are the same, so __________ often have lunch together.

3 Do you know where Sally is? __________ isn't at __________ desk, and one of the secretaries is looking for __________.

4 My parents live near me in London. My flat is very small but __________ is enormous. I often tell __________ that __________ don't need all that space.

5 Look at that dog. __________ looks really ill and __________ leg is hurt.

6 **A** Is that your phone ringing?
B No, __________ has a different ringtone. Isn't it __________?
A No, __________ phone's in __________ bag.
B It's probably Anne's then. Could __________ call __________? I think __________'s in the bathroom.

activation

c Write four sentences that are true for you using *I*, *me*, *my*, and *mine*.

9A GRAMMAR *if* + past, *would* + infinitive (second conditional)

a Write second conditional sentences for the pictures.

1 Which *would you choose* if you *could* only have one? (you choose, can)

2 You __________ better if you __________ more exercise. (feel, do)

3 They __________ happier if they __________ in that cage. (be, not live)

4 I __________ there if I __________ you. (not swim, be)

5 I __________ somebody if I __________ French. (ask, can speak)

6 __________ it if she __________ the money? (she buy, have)

7 If she __________ ill, she __________ to work. (not be, go)

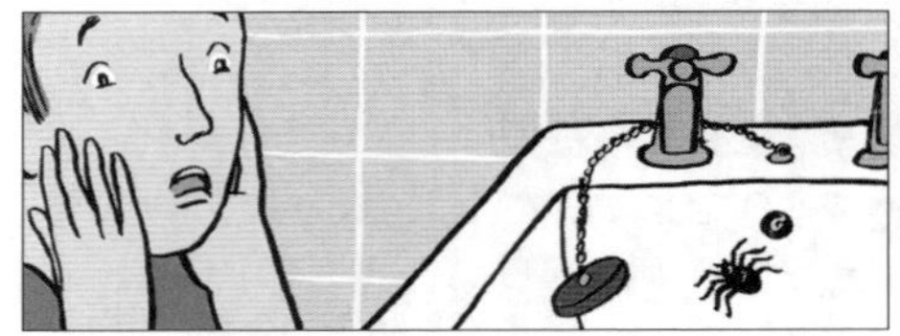

8 He __________ scared if it __________ so big. (not be, not be)

b First or second conditional? Complete the sentences with the correct form of the verb.

1 What will we do tomorrow if it *rains* (rain)?
2 If I had a lot of money, I *'d buy* (buy) a horse.
3 She'd pass her exams if she __________ (study) harder.
4 I'm sure she __________ (lend) you the money if you ask her nicely.
5 I'd like your dog more if he __________ (not be) so noisy!
6 If I __________ (not see) you this evening, I'll see you on Friday.
7 I __________ (not say) anything to James if you don't want me to.
8 If you __________ (not hurry up), we'll miss the train.
9 If I were you, I __________ (not go) to the UK in the winter.
10 What __________ you __________ (do) if you found a snake in your bed?

activation

c Cover the sentences in **a** and look at the pictures. Remember the second conditionals.

9B GRAMMAR present perfect + *for* and *since*

a Complete the sentences with the present perfect of the verb given + *for* or *since* if necessary.

four years

work

1 **A** How long *has* your daughter *worked* in New York?

B She*'s worked* there *for* four years.

have

2 **A** How long ______ you ______ your cat?

B I ______ it ______ a few weeks now.

a few weeks

1981

be married

3 **A** How long ______ you ______?

B I ______ ______ 1981.

know

4 **A** How long ______ they ______ each other?

B They ______ each other ______ 50 years.

50 years

2006

live

5 **A** How long ______ you ______ here?

B We ______ here ______ 2006.

have

6 **A** How long ______ you ______ this phobia?

B I ______ it ______ about 2010.

A Ah...

about 2010

I was 17

be

7 **A** How long ______ you ______ in this team?

B I ______ in it ______ I was 17.

b **Test your memory.** Cover the sentences. Look at the pictures. Can you remember the sentences?

activation

c Write four sentences about yourself, two with the present perfect + *for*, and two with the present perfect + *since*.

9C GRAMMAR present perfect or past simple?

a Complete the dialogues with the present perfect or the past simple.

1 **A** How long *have* you *played* (play) the violin?
B Since I *was* (be) four. I __________ (love) music all my life.
A Was it a difficult instrument to learn?
B Yes. I __________ (not be) very good when I __________ (start).

2 **A** __________ your brother __________ (finish) university?
B Yes, he __________ (finish) three weeks ago.
A What's he going to do now?
B He __________ (not decide) yet.

3 **A** Where do your parents live?
B They __________ (live) in Brighton since last year. But before that they __________ (live) in Birmingham.
A Why __________ they __________ (leave) Birmingham?
B Because my dad __________ (retire).

4 **A** I __________ (see) Oliver yesterday. He __________ (tell) me about your plans to move to Australia.
B Yes, I'm very excited... and a bit nervous too.
A __________ you ever __________ (live) abroad before?
B No, never. I __________ (never be) very interested in foreign travel.
A How about your wife?
B Oh, Lily loves travelling! She __________ (visit) lots of different countries.

5 **A** __________ you __________ (hear) about Andy and Francesca?
B No. What?
A They __________ (separate).
B Really? That's a shame. I __________ (think) they were very happy together.

6 **A** Is your brother married?
B Yes, he __________ (be) married for ages. About ten years. He __________ (fall) in love with Sarah when they were both at secondary school. They __________ (get) married when they __________ (be) only 18.

b Practise the dialogues in **a** with a partner.

activation

c Write a four-line dialogue beginning with *Have you ever...?*

10A GRAMMAR passive

a Look at the pictures. Complete the sentences with present or past passive.

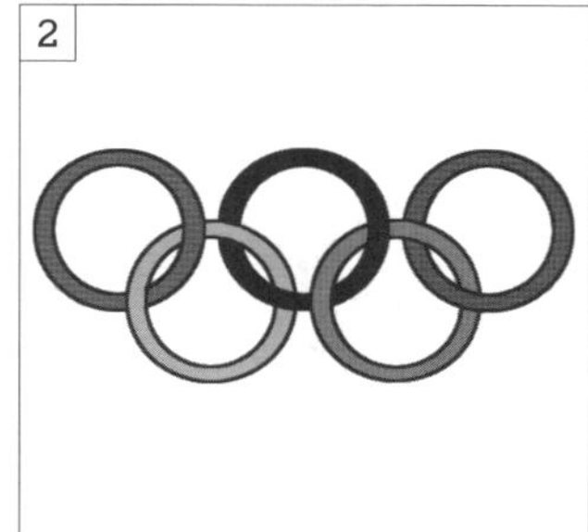

1 'Romeo Must Die' *is based* on 'Romeo and Juliet'. (base)

2 The symbol of the Olympic Games ______________________ in 1912. (design)

3 All bags ______________________ very carefully at airports these days. (check)

4 The Pyramids ______________________ nearly 5,000 years ago. (build)

5 About 350 films ______________________ at the Berlin Film Festival every year. (show)

6 P4 is a very small new moon which ______________________ in 2011. (discover)

7 Seat belts ______________________ in planes until the 1930s. (not use)

8 These suits ______________________ by Elvis Presley. (wear)

9 The first smartphone ______________________ in 1992 by IBM. (invent)

10 *Pétanque* ______________________ a lot all over France. (play)

11 This ______________________ by Picasso. (paint)

12 How ______________________ this name ______________________? (pronounce)

b Cover the sentences. Look at the pictures. Can you remember the sentences?

activation

c 1 Write two past passive sentences about inventions or discoveries made by someone from your country.

2 Write two present passive sentences about things that are produced, grown, or made somewhere in your country.

10B GRAMMAR *used to*

a Look at how Alice and Johnny have changed. For each person, write eight sentences using *used to* / *didn't use to* about what they were like in the past.

1 She used to wear dresses.
2 ____________ the violin.
3 ____________ a motorbike.
4 ____________ glasses.
5 ____________ a tattoo on her arm.
6 ____________ very calm and quiet.
7 ____________ jeans and t-shirts.
8 ____________ the guitar.

9 ____________ TV all day.
10 ____________ any sport or exercise.
11 ____________ a suit and tie.
12 ____________ a beard and a moustache.
13 ____________ a bit overweight.
14 ____________ jeans.
15 ____________ healthy food.
16 ____________ long hair.

activation

b Look at the pictures. Make sentences with *used to* and *didn't use to* about Alice and Johnny.

c Write two sentences with *used to* and two sentences with *didn't use to* about yourself.

10C GRAMMAR *might*

a Complete the dialogues with *might* or *might not* + a verb from the list.

be (x2) ~~buy~~ fall go (x2) have like meet phone say

1 **A** I think I <u>*might buy*</u> this T-shirt.
B Don't be silly. It's much too small for you.

2 **A** Are you going to go to the party?
B I'm not sure. My ex-husband ______________ there and I really don't want to see him.

3 **A** What's this? It looks very strange.
B It's a special dish from my country. Try it, you ______________ it.

4 **A** I ______________ to class tomorrow. I think I'll have to work late.
B OK. I'll text you and tell you what there is for homework.

5 **A** Are you going to be in this evening?
B I'm not sure. I ______________ some friends for a drink.

6 **A** Look, Mummy, I can ride a bicycle without using my hands!
B Oh, be careful! You ______________!

7 **A** Where are you going for your holiday?
B I don't know. I'm really busy at work, so I ______________ a holiday this year.

8 **A** Are you going to send Adam an email?
B No, I think I ______________ him. It's quicker.

9 **A** How are you going to get there?
B I ______________ by train... but maybe it's better to drive... I don't know...
A Come on – you need to make a decision!

10 **A** Are you going to tell Anna about seeing Mike in the pub?
B I don't know. I ______________ anything.

11 **A** I ______________ late tomorrow. I'm seeing the doctor at 8.30.
B OK. Thanks for telling me.

b Practise the dialogues in **a** with a partner.

activation

c Write two things you might do next weekend, and two things you might not have time to do tomorrow.

11A GRAMMAR expressing movement

a Complete the sentences with a preposition of movement.

1 A police helicopter flew *over* the houses.
2 The rock star threw a TV ____________ the window.
3 A bird flew ____________ the bridge.
4 They danced ____________ the fire.
5 The sheriff walked ____________ the saloon.
6 The cat ran ____________ the wall.
7 The road goes ____________ the village.
8 The boy is climbing ____________ the tree.
9 He jumped ____________ the swimming pool.
10 The dog swam ____________ the river.
11 The policemen fell ____________ the stairs.
12 The skiers are skiing ____________ the mountain.

activation

b **Test your memory.** Cover the sentences. Look at the pictures and remember the sentences.

11B GRAMMAR word order of phrasal verbs

a What are the people doing? Complete each sentence with a phrasal verb. Use one word from each list.

get (x2) go look pick put take throw ~~turn~~ write

away (x2) down for off ~~on~~ on (x2) up (x2)

1 She's *turning on* the TV.
2 He's ____________ his shoes.
3 They're ____________ the questions.
4 He's ____________ her books.
5 She's ____________ for the weekend.
6 He's ____________ his newspaper.
7 She's ____________ her phone.
8 He's ____________ early.
9 She's ____________ her coat.
10 They're ____________ well.

b Circle the right answer. Tick (✓) if both are correct.

1 Can I **try on this jacket / try this jacket on**, please? ✓
2 I can't hear the music. Can you **turn it up / turn up it**?
3 They're my sister's children. I'm **looking after them / looking them after**.
4 Jane called when you were out. Can you **call her back / call back her**?
5 **Turn off your mobiles / Turn your mobiles off** before the exam begins.
6 Your clothes are all over the floor. Please **pick up them / pick them up**.
7 I can't find my car keys. Can you help me **look for them / look them for**?
8 If I lend you the money, when will you **pay me back / pay back me**?

activation

c Cover the sentences in **a**. Look at the pictures and say what's happening.

11C GRAMMAR *so, neither* + auxiliaries

a Complete the dialogues with *So* + auxiliary + *I* or *Neither* + auxiliary + *I*.

1 **A** I don't like that new building much.
B *Neither do I*. It looks like a spaceship.

2 **A** I passed the exam!
B *So did I*! I got 92%.

3 **A** I can't swim, I'm afraid.
B ______________. Perhaps we should have lessons.

4 **A** I'm not very hungry.
B ______________. I'll just have a sandwich.

5 **A** I've finished university.
B ______________. I'm looking for a job now!

6 **A** I didn't like the film.
B ______________. It was too slow.

7 **A** I was born in 1989.
B Really? ______________.

8 **A** I don't have any brothers or sisters.
B ______________. But I have lots of cousins.

9 **A** I'm going to stay at home this evening.
B ______________. I'm quite tired.

10 **A** I have to go to work on Saturday.
B ______________. I hate working at the weekends.

11 **A** I don't get on with Lydia very well.
B ______________. We don't really have much in common.

12 **A** I got married in 2005.
B ______________. But I got divorced a year later!

13 **A** I was working in London last year.
B ______________. What a coincidence!

14 **A** I haven't been to South America.
B ______________, but I'd love to go.

15 **A** I want to go to the beach today.
B ______________. It's a beautiful day.

16 **A** I won't go to that restaurant again.
B ______________. The food was awful.

17 **A** I'm going to stop using *Facebook*.
B ______________. I spend too much time on it.

18 **A** I'd like to go to New Zealand.
B ______________. They say it's beautiful.

19 **A** I'll do my homework on the bus.
B ______________. It's very easy.

20 **A** I have a twin sister.
B ______________. That's amazing!

b Practise the dialogues in **a** with a partner.

activation

c Write a two-line dialogue with *So* + auxiliary + *I*, and another with *Neither* + auxiliary + *I*.

12A GRAMMAR past perfect

a Look at the pictures and complete the sentences. Use the past simple and past perfect.

1. When they *got* (get) to the station the train *had already left* (already leave).
2. She ______________ (be) very cold because she ______________ (not take) her coat.
3. The printer ______________ (not work) because he ______________ (not turn it on).
4. I ______________ (not can) take a photo of the crocodile because I ______________ (forget) to charge the battery.
5. They ______________ (never fly) before and they ______________ (be) very nervous.
6. When he ______________ (arrive) at the pool he realized he ______________ (not bring) his swimsuit.
7. She ______________ (just have) dinner, so she ______________ (not be) hungry.
8. She ______________ (have to) pay again because she ______________ (lose) her ticket.
9. The waitress ______________ (run) after him because he ______________ (not pay) the bill.
10. The fire engine ______________ (arrive) after the fire ______________ (go out).
11. They ______________ (can) speak French because they ______________ (learn) it at school.
12. She ______________ (be) tired because she ______________ (be) in the queue all night.

activation

b Cover the sentences. Look at the pictures and remember the sentences.

c Continue these sentences with the past perfect.

I didn't recognize him because…

My father was really angry because…

When I got to school today I realized that…

12B GRAMMAR reported speech

a Change the direct speech to reported speech.

1 She said that *she couldn't see anything.*
2 He told her that ________________.
3 He told his father that ________________.
4 The man said that ________________.
5 She said that ________________.
6 He told his wife that ________________.
7 He told her that ________________.
8 She said that ________________.

b Change the reported speech to direct speech.

1 She said that she wasn't very hungry.
'I'm not very hungry.'

2 The nurse told the man that it wouldn't hurt.
____

3 He told the police that it was his mother's car.
____

4 She said that she had finished her homework.
____

5 He told the instructor that he couldn't swim.
____

6 He told her that he would always love her.
____

7 They said that they wanted to check out.
____

8 He told the woman that he didn't speak English.
____

12C GRAMMAR questions with and without auxiliaries

a Make questions using the present simple or past simple. Then circle the correct answer.

1 Where / polar bears / live
Where do polar bears live? — the North Pole (circled) / the South Pole

2 Who / direct / the film *Hugo* in 2011
Who directed the film Hugo in 2011? — Woody Allen / Martin Scorsese

3 Who / paint / *The Scream*
______________________________? — Gustav Klimt / Edvard Munch

4 Where / manga comics / come from
______________________________? — Japan / China

5 Who / invent / the World Wide Web
______________________________? — Bill Gates / Tim Berners-Lee

6 Which country / have / a blue and yellow flag?
______________________________? — Greece / Sweden

7 When / the Second World War / end
______________________________? — 1945 / 1955

8 Which country / win / the 2010 World Cup
______________________________? — Italy / Spain

9 Which superhero film / Christopher Nolan in 2008 / direct
______________________________? — *Elektra* / *The Dark Knight*

10 How many countries / belong to / the United Nations
______________________________? — 127 / 193

11 Who / Tom Cruise in 2006 / marry
______________________________? — Katie Holmes / Penélope Cruz

12 Where / people / speak / Yorùbá
______________________________? — West Africa / East Africa

activation

b **Test your memory**. Cover the questions. Look at the answers. Can you remember the questions?

Communicative Activity Instructions

Tips for using Communicative activities

- We have suggested the ideal number of copies for each activity. However, you can often manage with fewer, e.g. one copy per pair instead of one per student.
- When Sts are working in pairs, if possible get them to sit face to face. This will encourage them to really talk to each other and also means they can't see each other's sheet.
- If your class doesn't divide into pairs or groups, get two Sts to share one role, or get one student to monitor, help, and correct.

Extra idea

- If some Sts finish early, they can swap roles and do the activity again, or you could get them to write some of the sentences from the activity.

1A Student profile

A pairwork activity

Sts interview each other and complete a form for their partner. The forms revise question forms and provide the teacher with useful information about Sts. Copy one sheet per person.

Language

What's your name? What do you do? Where were you born? etc.

- Give each student one sheet. Focus on the questions. Give Sts, in pairs, a few minutes to decide what each question should be.
- Check answers. Model and drill the questions for Sts to copy the rhythm.

1 What's your first name?
2 What's your surname?
3 Where are you from?
4 Where do you live? / What's your address?
5 What's your email address?
6 What do you do?
7 Where were you born?
8 What languages do you speak?
9 What do you like doing in your free time?
10 Which social networks do you use? / Which social networks are you a member of?

- Demonstrate the activity by getting Sts to ask you the first two questions. Encourage them to ask you to spell your name and surname. Put Sts in pairs to interview each other and thell them to write the information in the forms. Make sure they cover the questions and ask them from memory.
- You could collect in the forms for your own reference.

1B Ask me a question

A pairwork / group work activity

Sts practise using the present simple tense. Copy and cut up one set of cards per group of three Sts (or per pair).

Language

What does your mother look like? How many brothers and sisters do you have? What do you usually have for breakfast? etc.

- Put Sts in groups of three (or pairs). Give each group a set of cut-up cards. Demonstrate the activity by writing on the board *Where / your mother work? What time / you get up?* and eliciting that Sts need to add *do* or *does*. Ask a student the question and then ask follow-up questions to get as much information as possible.
- In their groups, **A** takes a card and asks the other two Sts the question. Then **B** and **C** do the same.
- Encourage Sts to ask for and give as much information as possible.
- Monitor and help where necessary, particularly with question formation.
- When Sts have finished, get feedback from the class on some of their answers.

1C At an art gallery

A pairwork information gap activity

Sts describe their pictures to each other to find ten differences between them. Copy one sheet per pair and cut into **A** and **B**.

Language

prepositions of place, parts of the body
On the left there's a painting of a woman. She's smiling.
In my picture she isn't smiling. She's looking sad.

- Pre-teach / revise any words you think the Sts don't know or may have forgotten, e.g. *statue, attendant, sculpture, audioguide*. Also pre-teach expressions they will needs, e.g. *on the left*.
- Put Sts into pairs A and B and give out the sheets. Sit A and B so they can't see each other's sheet. Focus on the instructions and explain that they both have a picture of the same art gallery but there are ten differences between the two pictures.
- Sts describe their pictures to each other and find and circle the differences. Demonstrate being both A and B, e.g.:
  A *In my picture there's a painting of a chair.*
  B *In my picture, there's a chair and a cat is sitting on the chair.*

- Sts continue in pairs to find nine more differences. Check the differences orally in class, writing up any difficult sentences for Sts to copy.

1 In **A** there's a painting of a woman looking sad. In **B** the woman is smiling.
2 In **A** a man and a woman with a child are looking at a picture. In **B** the child is sitting on the floor crying.
3 In **A** there's a painting of a chair. In **B** a cat is sitting on the chair.
4 In **A** a man and a woman are sitting down talking. In **B** they are looking at a guidebook.
5 In **A** a student is listening to an audioguide. In **B** the students doesn't have an audioguide.
6 In **A** a man is sitting on a seat reading a paper. In **B** a man is sitting on a seat sending a text.
7 In **A** the girl in jeans has short hair. In **B** the girl in jeans has long hair.
8 In **A** a man is holding a camera. In **B** the man is taking a photograph.
9 In **A** there's a statue with no right arm. In **B** there's a statue with no left arm.
10 In **A** a woman is touching a sculpture. In **B** the woman is looking at the sculpture.

2A Bingo!

A grammar and pronunciation game

Sts revise irregular past tense forms. Copy and cut up one sheet per 20 Sts. If you have more than 20 students, get some Sts to share a card.

Language
Irregular past tenses

- Put Sts in pairs and give each pair a card. Give them time to remember the past tense of each verb.
- Tell Sts they are going to play 'past tense bingo'. Explain that you will say the past tense of different verbs. If they have the infinitive of the verb on their card, they cross through it. When they have crossed through all nine verbs, they shout *Bingo!*
- Go to the *Irregular verb list* (SB *p.155*) and start saying the past tense verbs in random order. Use a pencil to tick the verbs you have read out.
- When a student shouts *Bingo!*, get him / her to read out the nine verbs, saying the infinitive and the past tense. Check they are all verbs that you have ticked. If the verbs are correct, the student is the winner. If they have made a mistake, the game continues.

Extra idea

- Play the game with new cards, or get Sts to play in groups when one student reads out the past tenses.

2B Fake or real?

A pairwork story-telling activity

Sts read and retell information to their partner. Copy one sheet per pair. Cut each sheet into three parts: the two photos, and then **A** / **B** sheets.

Language
Past simple and past continuous
The shark began to attack the man.
He was driving his car around the lake.

- Put Sts in pairs and get them to sit face to face if possible. Give each pair the first part of the sheet (the photos).
- Focus on the photos. Ask Sts what they can see and what they think is happening in the photos. Elicit / teach *shark*, *ladder*, *lake*, *monster*.
- Tell Sts they are going to read the stories behind the photos. Explain that their partner has a different story and later they will have to tell their partner about what they have read.
- Now tell Sts to read the text and highlight important information to help them remember the story, e.g. What was happening when the photo was taken, names, dates, places, etc. Sts should read their text at least twice. Give them plenty of time to do this.
- Sts **A** and **B** take turns to talk about their photo and, from memory, to tell their partner as much about the story as possible. Monitor and help.
- Ask Sts to decide together if they think their photos were fake or real, and why. Get feedback from the class.
- Now tell Sts to read the text to see if their photo is fake or real. Then tell them to tell their partner the information, using their own words.
- When they have finished the activity, ask the class if they know of any other famous photos which are fakes.

2C Sentence race

A group activity

Sts race to complete sentences. Copy one sheet per four or five Sts.

Language
Connectors: *so, because, but, although*

- Put Sts into pairs and give them a sheet face down.
- Tell Sts they have to finish the sentences as quickly as they can in a logical and correct way.
- Say "Go!" and tell Sts to turn over their sheet and start writing. Set a time limit. Monitor while Sts are writing to make sure their sentences make sense.
- When the time limit is up (or when one pair has finished) stop the activity and check answers. The pair with the most correct sentences is the winner.

Extra idea

- Cut the sheet into strips. Put Sts into teams and give each team a strip. When they have written the sentence they have to come up to you and show it to you. If it is correct, give them another strip. The first group to write 20 correct sentences is the winner.

3A Find a partner

A class mingle

Sts choose a holiday from a variety of options then try to find somebody who's made exactly the same choice. Copy one sheet per student.

> **Language**
> *going to*
> *Where are you going to go?*
> *Are you going to go in May or June?*
> holiday facilities
> travel verbs

- Give out the sheets. Give Sts time to read the adverts and deal with any vocabulary problems that come up.
- Focus on **a**. Sts read the four questions and individually make their choices.
- Focus on **b**. Demonstrate the activity. Choose a holiday and options. Ask Sts *Where are you going to go?* until you find someone who has chosen the same destination as you. Then ask *When are you going to go?* etc., to try to find someone who has chosen the same options.
- Sts do the same, first with the student next to them, then by standing up and moving around the class. Make sure that Sts use *going to, by, on* + date.
- If Sts quickly find somebody with exactly the same holiday details, tell them to find as many other people as they can.
- Get some feedback. Ask *Who found a partner? Which was the most popular holiday?*

3B Come fly with me!

A pairwork information gap activity

Sts complete questions and ask each other for some missing information. Copy one sheet per pair and cut into **A** and **B**.

> **Language**
> present continuous for future
> *Who are you flying with? How much are you taking?*
> travel vocabulary

- Put Sts in pairs and give out the sheets. Sit **A** and **B** so that they can't see each other's sheets. Explain that they have one completed boarding card and another boarding card with missing information.
- Give Sts time to read both boarding cards and deal with any vocabulary problems that come up.
- Focus on the questions in **a**. Tell **A** and **B** to look at the boarding card with the missing information. They have to complete questions 1–6 individually using the present continuous to find out the missing information from their partner. Set a time limit, e.g. 8–10 minutes. Monitor and check that Sts are writing the correct questions.

1 Who are you flying with?
2 When are you leaving?
3 Where are you flying from?
4 Where are you flying to?
5 What time are you leaving?
6 What time are you arriving?

- Quickly check all the questions before starting the activity. Elicit the questions and write them on the board if necessary.
- Focus on **b**. Student **A** asks **B** his / her questions and completes his / her boarding card with the missing information. Then swap roles.

Extra idea

- Fast finishers could look at the boarding cards, cover the questions and ask the questions from memory.

3C Can you explain the word?

A group card game

Sts practise giving definitions using relative pronouns. Copy and cut up one set of cards per four students.

> **Language**
> *It's a thing which / a person who...*
> *It's a kind of... It's like... You do it when...*

- If necessary, revise language for giving definitions before you start. Put Sts in small groups. Give each group a set of cards face down or in an envelope.
- Demonstrate the activity. Pick up a card and describe the word / phrase until Sts guess it. Insist they say the exact word / phrase on the card with the correct pronunciation before showing them the card.
- Sts play the game, taking turns to take a card and define the word. Tell Sts they *must not use the word on the card*. The first student in the group who says the word correctly gets the card. The winner is the student with the most cards.

Non-cut alternative

- Copy one sheet per pair of SS, and cut in half. Put Sts into pairs and give them one half each. **A** begins by defining one of the words on his / her sheet. If **B** can say the word, then it's **B**'s turn to give a definition.

4A Find the response

A pairwork activity

Sts match sentences with appropriate responses. Copy one sheet per pair (or per student).

> **Language**
> *just / yet / already*
> *They've already gone home.*
> *I haven't met her yet.*
> *I've just spoken to her.*

- Give out the sheets and ask Sts to match 1–16 with responses a–p.
- Check answers.

1 f 2 i 3 a 4 o 5 b 6 m 7 c 8 p 9 l 10 n 11 d
12 k 13 j 14 h 15 g 16 e

- Elicit / teach the meaning of *fold*, and tell Sts that they should fold their sheets vertically.
- Put Sts in pairs. Ask them to look only at the sentences and not to look at the responses. Read out the first one and see who can remember what the response was, e.g. *Do you want to come and see the new Sofia Coppola film?* (I've already seen it.)

- Sts continue in pairs. **A**s read out all the sentences first and **B**s have to remember what the responses were (without looking at the sheet).
- Sts swap roles. Monitor and check pronunciation.

4B Have you ever...?

A group activity

Sts practise making questions from prompts and describe events, contrasting the present perfect and the past simple. Copy and cut up one sheet per group.

Language

Have you ever + past participle...?
Have you ever been to London?
Yes, I have. / No, I haven't.
When did you go there?
Past and present tense follow-up questions
Past tense + and - forms

- Copy the exchange in the Language Box on the board and elicit that this is a typical exchange which begins in the present perfect, and then goes on to the past simple to ask for details.
- Sts take it in turns to take a strip out of the envelope and ask the other Sts in their group the question.
- Demonstrate the activity first by getting a student to ask you the question they've drawn out of the envelope. Answer the question and elicit a follow-up question.
- Encourage the Sts to ask follow-up questions.

Non-cut alternative

- Make one copy per pairand cut in half vertically. Give Sts half each and get them to ask and answer the questions.

4C The same or different?

A pairwork activity

Sts compare information about their lifestyle and practise using *something*, *anything*, *nothing*, etc. They agree with or contradict a series of statements and explain why. Copy one sheet per student.

Language

something, nothing, anything, somebody, someone, anyone, etc.
I don't usually watch anything on TV in the evenings.
I need to go somewhere urgently after class.

- Put Sts into pairs and give out the sheets. Focus on *a*. Demonstrate the activity by eliciting the first answer, *I always have something to eat for breakfast*, and writing it up on the board.
- Ask Sts to complete the sentences individually or in pairs. Give Sts enough time to complete their sheets. Monitor to check that they are making the correct sentences.
- Check answers and write them up on the board if necessary.

1	something	11	nobody / no one
2	anything / everything	12	somewhere
3	anywhere	13	anyone / anybody
4	anything	14	anywhere
5	anything	15	nowhere
6	nobody / no one	16	anything
7	somewhere	17	anywhere
8	anything	18	something
9	something	19	somebody / someone
10	nothing	20	somewhere

- Focus on **b**. Demonstrate the activity by talking to the class about the first statement, e.g. *Sentence 1 isn't true for me because I never eat anything*. Encourage the class to ask for more information, e.g. *What do you drink? When do you have something to eat?*
- Sts talk about each statement and say if it's true / or not true for them and why not. Stop the activity when most pairs seem to have finished and get whole class feedback.

5A Which do you prefer? Why?

A pairwork / group work speaking activity

Sts say which of two things / activities they prefer and why. Personalize the activity by writing local things to compare on the last two cards. Copy and cut up one sheet per four or five Sts.

Language

Comparative forms
I prefer swimming in the sea because it's healthier.

- Put Sts in pairs or groups of four or five and give out a set of cards face down.
- Demonstrate the activity by asking a student to pick a card and ask you. Sts take turns to pick a card and ask the other student(s) *Which do you prefer, ... or ...? Why?*
- Monitor while Sts are talking, correcting any mistakes with comparative forms. When Sts have finished, get feedback from a few pairs or groups.

Non-cut alternative

- Give out one uncut sheet to each pair or group. Get them to discuss the topics on each card saying which they prefer and why.

5B Superlative questions

A pairwork questionnaire

Sts revise superlatives by completing a questionnaire with superlatives and then asking and answering the questions. Copy one sheet per pair and cut into **A** and **B**.

Language

Superlatives
What's the most dangerous sport you've ever done?
What's the latest gadget you've bought?

- Put Sts in pairs **A** and **B** and give out the questionnaires.
- Focus on the adjectives in brackets and tell Sts to complete each question with the superlative of the adjective. Monitor while Sts are working, correcting any mistakes with superlative forms.

- Check answers just by getting students to say the superlative answers.

A 1 the most beautiful 2 the best 3 the most popular 4 the worst 5 the most dangerous 6 the most difficult 7 the easiest 8 the most famous
B 1 worst 2 your earliest 3 the most exciting 4 the best 5 the latest 6 the most boring 7 the best-looking 8 the most interesting

- Now get Sts (sitting face to face if possible) to ask and answer the questions, or **A** can interview **B** and then they swap roles.
- When Sts have finished, get feedback from a few pairs.

5C How old is your body?

A pairwork activity

Sts practise using quantifiers by doing a questionnaire then asking each other about exercise, diet and lifestyle. Copy one sheet per student.

Language
Quantifiers
How much exercise or sport do you do? Quite a lot.
should / shouldn't
I think you should do some more exercise. For example, ...

- Put Sts in pairs and give out the sheets. Get Sts to fold along the line or give out the sheets already folded.
- Give Sts time to read the questions and help with any vocabulary questions.
- Demonstrate the activity by getting a student to ask you the first question. Answer with one of the options given, explain your answer and elicit a follow-up question, e.g.:
  S *How much exercise or sport do you do?*
  T *A lot. I go to the gym every day.*
  S *What do you do there?*
- Sts ask and answer in pairs. Monitor and make sure they are asking follow-up questions and underlining their partner's answers.
- When they have finished, Sts unfold the answers at the bottom of the page and work out their partner's body age. Sts tell their partner his / her body age.
- Focus on **d** and ask Sts to give their partner some advice / recommendations based on their partner's answers to the questionnaire. Remind them to use *should / shouldn't* for giving advice.
- Get whole class feedback and ask a few Sts if their partner has given them good advice.

6A The optimist's phrase book

A pairwork activity

Sts practise making positive predictions. Copy one sheet per pair or per student.

Language
I'm sure you'll pass. You won't fail it next time. Good luck, Cheer up, etc.

- Give out one sheet per pair or per student. Go through sentences 1–12 in **You say** and the responses.
- Focus on **a**. Tell Sts to imagine that they are all optimists. Focus on sentence 1 and elicit a prediction, e.g. *Don't worry. I'm sure you'll find it.*
- Sts continue in pairs, writing positive predictions. Monitor and help / correct. Get feedback, eliciting possible responses.
- When Sts have finished, get them to compare with another pair to see which sounds more positive.
- Focus on **b** and **c**. Get **A** to read out the **You say** sentences. **B** responds from memory. Then they swap roles, with **B** saying the sentences in a different order. Encourage Sts to use positive intonation in their responses.

6B Guess my sentence

A pairwork activity

Sts practise *will* / *shall* sentences by trying to guess the missing part of the sentence. Copy one sheet per pair and cut into **A** and **B**.

Language
will/shall + verb
I think I'll buy them. Shall I call you on your mobile?

- Demonstrate the activity. On a piece of paper, write the sentence, *I'm very tired. I think I'll sit down for half an hour.* Then write on the board the sentence: *I'm very tired. I think I ________ for half an hour.*
- Put Sts in pairs **A** and **B** and give out the sheets. Sit **A** and **B** so that they can't see each other's sheet.
- Tell the class they have to guess the missing phrase, which is a verb or a verb phrase with *'ll*. Elicit a possibility, making sure Sts say the whole sentence. If their guess is not the same as you have on your piece of paper, say 'Try again' until someone says your sentence. Then show them your piece of paper and say 'That's right.'
- Focus on the sheets and explain that half of their sentences have gaps, and their partner has the complete sentences. Sts take turns trying to guess the missing words in their incomplete sentences. Sts continue guessing until they say the exact sentence their partner has. Their partner should help and prompt if necessary.
- Give Sts a minute or so to read their sentences and think of possible completions, but not to write them in the gaps.
- Sts take turns to guess the missing parts of the sentences. Stress that Sts should say the whole sentence each time, not just the missing words. When a student correctly guesses the sentence he / she writes in the missing words.

6C Talk about it

A group board game

Sts revise past, present, and future forms. Make one copy of the board game for every four Sts. You also need one dice per group and one counter per student.

Language
Sentence formation in past and present forms.

- Put Sts in small groups of three or four. Give each group a copy of the board game and a dice.

! If you don't have a dice, give each group a coin. Sts toss the coin for their go and move 1 for heads and 3 for tails.

- Explain the rules of the game. Sts throw a dice and move the corresponding number of circles on the board. When they land on a circle, they must talk for 30 seconds about the topic. Then each of the other Sts in the group must ask them a question about the topic.
- Sts play the game in their groups. The game finishes when someone reaches the finish square.

7A I'm going to tell you about...

A pairwork discussion activity

Sts choose six topics to discuss with a partner. Copy one sheet per student.

> **Language**
> Verbs + to and *-ing*

- Put Sts into pairs and give out sheets.
- Focus on the instructions. Tell Sts to choose six topics they want to talk about with a partner. Tell them to think about what they want to say. Set a time limit.
- Tell Sts to discuss the topics, taking turns to choose the topic. Encourage Sts to ask for and give as much information as possible.
- Monitor and help where necessary, particularly with the verb forms.
- When Sts have finished, get feedback from the class on some of the topics.

7B Find someone who...

A class mingle

Sts ask each other questions to complete a survey. Copy one sheet per student.

> **Language**
> verb + *-ing*
> *Do you enjoy reading in bed?*
> *Are you good at cooking?*

- Give out the sheets and give Sts a few minutes to read 1–15. Help with any vocabulary / comprehension problems.
- Elicit that the answers to the questions *Do you mind…?* are *No, I don't mind it* or *Yes, I hate it*.
- Demonstrate the activity. Ask a student the first question. Elicit *Yes, I do* or *No, I don't*. If a student answers *Yes*, write their name in the column on your sheet, then ask a follow-up question and write the answer under **MORE INFORMATION**. Elicit follow-up questions for 1, e.g. *What time do you usually get up? Have you ever travelled by plane?* etc.
- If the student answers *No*, then say *Thank you* and ask another student until somebody answers *Yes*.
- Tell Sts to write the name of a different student for each question. Sts mingle, asking and answering questions.
- Feedback some answers.

7C In the UK

A pairwork speaking activity

Sts decide if sentences about laws in the UK are true or false, and then talk about the situation in their own country. Copy one sheet per student.

> **Language**
> *You have to... You don't have to...*
> *You mustn't... You must...*

- Put Sts in pairs and give out the sheets.
- Give Sts a few minutes to read all the sentences and make sure Sts understand them. Set a time limit, e.g. ten minutes, for pairs to discuss each sentence one by one, decide if it is true or not true, and tick the appropriate box.
- Focus on **b** and elicit the answers. Find out if any pair identified all the false sentences.

> 1 F 2 F The age limit is 18. 3 T 4 F 5 T 6 F You can ride a 50cc motorbike at 16. 7 T 8 F 9 T 10 F 11 F You have to be 18 12 T 13 F 14 F 15 T 16 T 17 F 18 T

- Focus on **c**. Tell Sts to go through each law and say if the laws are the same or different in their country, and which ones they'd like to have in their country.

8A I need some advice

A group speaking activity

Sts practise giving advice to each other. Copy and cut up one sheet per group of three or four.

> **Language**
> *What should I do? I (don't) think you should... You shouldn't ...*

- Put Sts in groups of four or five. Give one set of cards, face down or in envelopes, to each group.
- Demonstrate the activity first. Pull out a card, dramatically read out our situation and elicit suggestions. Invent excuses for not accepting the first few pieces of advice, however good it is, before finally accepting a suggestion with *That's a good idea. I'll do that.*
- S1 takes out a card and reads out his / her situation. Each student in the group has to give a different piece of advice. S1 gives the card to the person who has given the best advice. Now S2 takes a card and the other Sts offer advice. The student who gives the best advice receives the card.
- When all the cards are finished, the person with the most cards is the winner.
- The student gives the card to whoever he / she thinks has given the best advice.

Non-cut alternative

- Copy one sheet per pair and cut it in half vertically. Put Sts in pairs and give them half each. They should read their problem to each other and ask for advice.

8B On the Trans-Siberian Railway

A pairwork activity

Sts practise using the first conditional by telling a story. Copy one sheet per student.

> **Language**
> First conditional
> *If we start talking, we'll become friends.*

- Give out the sheets and focus on the story. Give Sts one minute to read it. Elicit possible answers to the question in **a**, e.g. *because he wants to read it, because he doesn't like lending things, etc.*
- Ask Sts to look at the pictures and tell them that they show what the man's answer is. Focus on the first picture and sentence *1* (*If I lend you my newspaper, ...*). Tell Sts that this is the beginning of the conversation. Then tell Sts in pairs to number the other sentences 2–9 using the pictures to help them.
- Get feedback and write the answers up on the board.

> 1 If I lend you my newspaper, we'll get talking.
> 2 If we start talking, we'll become friends.
> 3 If we become friends, I'll invite you to my house in Vladivostok.
> 4 If I invite you to my house, you'll meet my beautiful daughter, Olga.
> 5 If you meet Olga, you'll fall in love with her.
> 6 If you fall in love with her, you'll run away together.
> 7 If you run away, I'll find you.
> 8 If I find you, I'll kill you.
> 9 So that's why I won't lend you my newspaper.

- Ask Sts to cover the sentences and look at the pictures. Read out the *if* clause of sentence 1, picture number 1: *If I lend you my newspaper, ...* Elicit the continuation of the sentence: *we'll start talking*. Drill the whole sentence. Do the same with the other sentences 2–9.
- Now model and drill the entire story with the whole class, eliciting it line by line. Make sure that the Sts still have their sentences covered.
- Put Sts in pairs. **A** covers the sentences and retells the story using the pictures. **B** prompts and corrects. Monitor and correct / help with any pronunciation or grammar problems.
- When **A** finishes, they swap roles.

8C Reading questionnaire

A pairwork activity

Sts answer questions about their reading habits. Copy one sheet per student.

> **Language**
> Talking about reading tastes
> *Do you read online?*
> *Are you a fast or a slow reader?*

- Give out the sheets and focus on the pictures. Ask *What / who can you see?*
- Give Sts a time limit, to read the questions. Help with any vocabulary / comprehension problems.
- Get one student to ask you the main question, *Do you like reading books?* Answer the question with *Yes, I do. / No, I don't.* Now get different Sts to ask you the first three corresponding questions (depending on what you said). Answer the questions giving as much information as possible. Encourage Sts to ask some follow-up questions too.
- Put Sts in pairs. **A** asks his / her partner *Do you like reading books?*
- Student **A** asks all the questions first (**B** must have his / her sheet face down) with some follow-up questions if possible.
- When **A** has finished, they should swap roles.
- Get feedback from the whole class to find out, e.g. which magazines Sts read, if any of them have written a blog, etc.

9A I think you'd...

A pairwork activity

Sts practise second conditional sentences by trying to guess the missing half of their partner's sentences. Copy one sheet per pair and cut into **A** and **B**.

> **Language**
> Second conditional:
> *If you bought a new car today, I think you'd buy a ________.*

- Demonstrate the activity by writing on the board: *If somebody offered you a drink now, I think you'd order a ________.*
- Elicit that you need to complete the sentence with a noun. Then tell Sts to guess which pet you'd buy. Elicit answers and then tell the class which pet you really would buy.
- Sit Sts in pairs **A** and **B**, ideally face to face, and give out the sheets. They must not look at what their partner writes. Tell them to complete the sentences, trying to guess how their partner would complete each sentence. Monitor and check that they are using the right words to complete the sentences.
- Now Sts take turns to read their completed sentences to their partner, who tells them if they have guessed correctly or not. Encourage them to react by contradicting what their partner has said, and then giving the real answer if the guess is wrong, e.g. *No, I wouldn't, I don't like cats! But I love dogs.*
- Get feedback from several pairs and find out who in the pair had more correct guesses.

Extra challenge

- If you want to give more practice, get Sts to repeat the activity, but swapping roles **A** and **B**.

9B Famous phobias

A pairwork information gap speaking activity

Sts practise using the present perfect simple + *for* / *since* by reading about famous people and their phobias, some of which are true and some false. They then tell each other about them, and together decide which they think are true. Copy one sheet per pair and cut into **A** and **B**.

> **Language**
> Present perfect simple + *for / since*
> *He's had this phobia for about six years.*

- Put Sts in pairs and give out the sheets. Make sure that Sts can't see each other's sheets.
- Focus on the instructions and go through them. Set a time limit for Sts to read about the famous people and their phobias. Move round the class and help with any vocabulary, comprehension, or pronunciation problems.
- Now get **A** to tell **B** about his / her three people. Encourage Sts to improvise / rephrase this from memory and only to look at their sheet if absolutely necessary. Then **A** and **B** should decide together which two phobias are true.
- Sts swap roles. **B** now tells **A** about his / her three people and together they decide which two phobias are true.
- Get feedback to find out which phobias Sts think are true. You could write the names of the actors / actresses on the board and record which phobias most Sts think are true and which are invented. Finally, tell them which ones are true and which are invented.

> The true phobias are: Jennifer Aniston, Justin Timberlake, Nicole Kidman, and Orlando Bloom.

9C Like mother, like daughter

A pairwork information gap activity

Sts question each other to discover missing biographical information about a mother and daughter using the present perfect simple and past simple. Copy one sheet per pair and cut into **A** and **B**.

> **Language**
> Past simple and present perfect
> *Where was she born?*
> *How long has she been a model?*

- Put Sts in pairs and give out the sheets. Sit **A** and **B** so that they can't see each other's sheets. Explain that they have one complete biography and one with missing information.
- Give Sts time to read both biographies and deal with any vocabulary problems that come up.
- Focus on the questions in **a**. Tell **A** and **B** to read the first biography they have again and to complete questions 1–7. Set a time limit. Monitor and check that Sts are writing the correct questions.
- Quickly check all the questions before starting the activity. Elicit the questions and write them on the board.

> **Jerry Hall**
> 1 What does she do?
> 2 Where was she born?
> 3 Why did she go and live in France?
> 4 Where was she sunbathing (one day)?
> 5 How long has she been a model?
> 6 How many children does she have? / How many children has she got?
> 7 How long have Jerry and Mick been divorced?
>
> **Elizabeth Jagger**
> 1 What does she do?
> 2 Where was she born?
> 3 When did she leave school?
> 4 Why did she leave school?
> 5 When did she start her modelling career?
> 6 Which companies has she worked for since 2000?
> 7 What contract has she just won?

- Focus on **b**. Students **A** and **B** take turns to ask their questions and complete their biographies with the missing information.
- When Sts have completed their biographies, they discuss what the mother and daughter have in common.

> Both of them are models.
> Both were born in the USA.
> They both appeared in a Thierry Mugler fashion show.
> They are both connected to Mick Jagger (ex-wife and daughter).

Extra challenge

- You could get Sts to cover the complete biographies and answer their partner's questions from memory.

10A General knowledge quiz

A pairwork general knowledge quiz

Sts practise using the present simple passive and past simple passive by asking and answering questions. Copy one sheet per pair and cut into **A** and **B**.

> **Language**
> Questions in the present simple passive and past simple passive
> *Which month is named after a Roman emperor?*
> *In which city was the Titanic built?*

- Put Sts in pairs. Get them to sit face to face and make sure that they can't see each other's questions.
- Set a time limit, e.g. 5 minutes, for Sts to read and understand the vocabulary in their questions. Monitor and help with any vocabulary or pronunciation problems they might have.
- Tell **A**s to ask their questions first. Highlight that they should give the three alternatives each time and note down which answers **B** gets right. (The correct answers are in **bold** on the sheet.) Sts swap roles.
- Get feedback to see who got the most right answers.

10B My past

A pairwork speaking activity

Sts complete some boxes and then use the information to talk about past habits using *used to* and *didn't use to*. Copy one sheet per student.

Language
I used to listen to Duran Duran, but I don't now.
I didn't use to like cabbage, but now I love it.

- Put Sts in pairs and give out the sheets. Sit **A** and **B**, so they can't see each other's sheets. Focus on instruction **a**. Go through sentences 1–14 and make sure Sts know what they have to do. Demonstrate by giving some personal examples for sentences 1–3. Make it clear that Sts only have to do this with words / phrases, e.g. *spiders, a Barbie doll, Duran Duran*, and not complete sentences.
- Give Sts time to write something in as many boxes as they can (sometimes they may not be able to think of anything). Monitor and help.
- Focus on **b**. Sts use what they have written in the boxes to tell their partner about their past habits using *I used to / I didn't use to*. Again, demonstrate the activity yourself and give more information, e.g. *I used to have a cat. He was black and his name was Max.* If necessary remind Sts of the pronunciation of *used to / didn't use to*.
- Sts work together, talking about their past habits.
- When they have finished, get some feedback from the class.

10C Match it!

A pairwork activity

Sts practise using *might/might not* by matching sentences. Copy one sheet per student.

Language
He might lose his job.
They might not know the way.

- Put Sts in pairs and give out the sheets. Tell them they have five minutes to match the sentences.
- Monitor and help with any vocabulary problems Sts may have.
- Check answers and write them up on the board.

1 d 2 m 3 i 4 h 5 l 6 j 7 a 8 g 9 k 10 n 11 f
12 b 13 c 14 e

- Focus on **b**. Get Sts to cover the sentences on the right and look only at sentences 1–14. Read out the first one and see who can remember how the sentence finished:
T Keep the receipt for the top.
S She might want to change it.
- Sts continue in pairs. **B** covers the sentences on the right and **A** reads out sentences 1–14. **B** tries to remember how the sentences finished.
- Sts then swap.

11A The race

A pairwork activity

Sts practise giving instructions using prepositions of movement. Copy one sheet per pair and cut into **A** and **B**.

Language
Phrasal verbs
You have to go up the hill and then around the lake.

- Put Sts into pairs **A** and **B**, and give out the sheets. If possible, get Sts to sit opposite each other.
- Focus on the instructions. Make sure that Sts know what a race is and understand what they have to do.
- Give Sts time to plan how to describe the route in **MY RACE**.
- Sts take it in turns to describe their route to their partner, who draws the route on the map headed **A's / B's RACE**. **A** describes his / her route to **B** first. Sts shouldn't look at each other's maps. Monitor and help as Sts do the task.
- When the majority of pairs have finished, get Sts to compare routes to see if they drew them correctly.

11B Phrasal verbs dialogues

A pairwork activity

Sts complete some dialogues using phrasal verbs, practise reading them, then write dialogues themselves. Copy one sheet per student.

Language
take it off   *fill it in*   *try them on*   etc.

- Ask Sts to look at the pictures and to tell you what they can see and what they think is happening.
- Put Sts in pairs and tell them to complete the dialogues with the correct phrasal verbs. Remember to point out that there are two extra phrasal verbs which they don't need.
- Monitor and help with any comprehension problems.
- Get feedback and write the answers on the board.

1 Take it off	4 turn it off
2 look it up	5 pick them up
3 try them on	6 fill it in

- Drill the phrasal verbs once you've got all the answers on the board.
- Focus on **b**. Give Sts a time limit to memorize one of the dialogues and practise it from memory. Monitor and check pronunciation.
- Focus on **c**. In pairs, Sts choose two phrasal verbs from the box and work together to produce two dialogues. You could get some strong confident Sts to perform their dialogues in front of the class.

11C Are we the same?

A pairwork activity

Sts practise agreeing using *So do I.* / *Neither do I.* and disagreeing. Copy one sheet per student.

> **Language**
> *So can I. / Neither do I.*

- Put Sts in pairs preferably face to face. Give them each a sheet and tell them they shouldn't look at each other's.
- Focus on **a** and ask Sts to fill in the gaps with things that are true for them. Demonstrate the activity by doing 1 with the whole class and telling them that this information is true for you. Write on the board: *I went to Madrid last weekend*. Sts complete the rest of the sentences individually.
- Monitor and check Sts are completing the sentences appropriately. Help with any vocabulary and comprehension problems.
- Focus on **b**. Tell Sts that sentences a–l are the responses to 1–12 if you want to say that you are the same. Elicit that the completion for **a** is *So did I.* and write it on the board.
- Sts complete **b–l** individually with auxiliary verbs.
- Check answers.

a did b have c do d am e am f do g can h do
i have j would k do l did

- Focus on **c**. Sts work in pairs. **A** looks at sentences 1–12. **B** looks at the responses a–l. **A** reads out his/her sentences and **B** has to give an appropriate response which is true for him / her.
- Demonstrate with a couple of strong Sts. Get one of them to read out his / her sentence **1**. Then get the other student to say that he / she is the same (*So did I*) or to say where he / she went.
  S1 *I went to the beach last weekend.*
  S2 *So did I or I stayed at home.*
- Sts continue in pairs. First **A** reads his / her sentences and **B** responds, then they swap roles.
- Get feedback to find out any interesting findings and to see which pair is most similar.

Extra challenge

- When Sts have finished, tell them that they are now identical twins and always do the same things. Then tell **B** to turn his / her sheet face down. **A** reads the sentences, and **B** responds from memory *So* ________ *I* or *Neither* ________ *I*. Then they swap roles.

12A Match the sentences

A pairwork activity

Sts practise using the past perfect simple. Copy one sheet per student.

> **Language**
> *I couldn't find my bike because somebody had stolen it.*
> *I didn't want to go to the cinema because I'd already seen the film.*

- Before you give out the copies, elicit / teach the meaning of *fold* and show Sts how they should fold their sheets (or fold them beforehand yourself).
- Put Sts in pairs and give out the sheets. Make sure that Sts fold them correctly. Tell them they have five minutes to think about how the sentences might continue (Sts could do this in pairs or individually orally or writing the continuations on a piece of paper). Monitor and make sure that Sts are using the past perfect.
- Check answers. Correct wrong uses of the past perfect but accept all suggestions that make sense.
- Now get Sts to unfold the sheet and match continuations a–n with the first parts of the sentences.
- Check answers.

1 d 2 a 3 k 4 g 5 c 6 i 7 n 8 b 9 l 10 f 11 h
12 j 13 e 14 m

- Then Sts check how many are the same as what they wrote.
- Get feedback to see which pair got the most identical sentences.
- Now get Sts to fold the sheet again and look only at the beginnings 1–14. Read out the first one and see who can remember how the sentence finished:
  T *I couldn't find my bike because…*
  S *Somebody had stolen it.*
- Sts continue in pairs.

12B Really? How amazing!

A class mingle

Sts practise reported speech by remembering what people said. Copy and cut up 1 set of cards per 16 Sts (or one per pair – see non-cut alternative).

> **Language**
> Reported statements
> *He told me* (that) */ He said* (that) *he went to work by helicopter.*
> *She told me* (that) */ She said* (that) *she only slept three hours a night.*

- Elicit the question we ask when we don't understand what someone has said: *Can you say that again, please?* Drill the pronunciation and intonation. Write it up. Elicit our response when someone gives us information which is interesting or surprising: *Really? How amazing!* Drill the pronunciation and intonation. Write it up.
- Give each student a card with a sentence on it. Ask them to memorize the sentence.
- Get Sts to stand up and say their sentences to the other Sts and listen to their sentences. They can then ask other Sts to repeat their sentences once only.
- Set a time limit, and monitor to check that almost all Sts have said their sentences to each other.

- After the time limit, stop the activity and tell Sts to sit down. Put Sts in pairs and explain that together they have to try and remember what each student in the class said. They then have to write what each student said in reported speech, e.g. *Pepe said that his father was an astronaut.*
- When Sts have written all that they can remember, check answers. Ask one group *What did (Carmen) say?* Then check with (Carmen) that they remembered the sentence correctly. Do the same with the other sentences.

Non-cut alternative

- If you don't want to cut up the cards, or a mingle is not practical in your classroom, you can do the activity in pairs. Copy one sheet per pair and cut it in half so that **A** has the first eight and **B** has the rest. **A** says his / her questions to **B**, and **B** to **A**. They say their sentences alternately.
- When they've finished, they write down from memory in reported speech all the sentences their partner said.
- Finally, they compare lists to see how many sentences they remembered correctly.

12C Hollywood quiz

A pairwork activity about the cinema

Sts practise forming past simple subject and object quiz questions to ask their partner. Copy one sheet per pair and cut into **A** and **B**.

Language

past simple subject and object questions
Which actor appeared in most of Hitchcock's films?

- Give each student a copy of his / her question sheet.
- Divide the class into two groups – the **A**s and the **B**s. As a group or in a pair, Sts complete the questions.
- Monitor and correct the questions for each of the two groups, but don't write the answers on the board.

A 1 lived
2 did an actor say
3 cost
4 did Kate Winslet win
5 does Tom Hanks like
6 did Miranda Kerr marry
7 played
8 did Arnold Schwarzenegger say

B 1 did Peter Jackson film
2 appeared
3 does an Oscar weigh
4 was
5 won
6 played
7 did Audrey Hepburn play
8 does Batmen have

- Put Sts in pairs. Student **A** asks Student **B** his / her first question, without giving the three options for the answer (the option in **bold** is the correct answer). If Student **B** can answer the question correctly, he / she gets two points. If not, Student **A** now gives him / her the three options. If **B** chooses the right answer, he / she gets 1 point.
- Student **A** asks all of his / her questions first. Sts then swap roles.
- Find out who scored the most points in the class.

1A COMMUNICATIVE Student profile

a Complete the questions you need to ask to fill in the form.

STUDENT PROFILE

1	First name	
2	Surname	
3	Nationality	
4	Address	
5	Email address	
6	Occupation	
7	Place of birth	
8	Languages	
9	Interests	
10	Social networking sites	

1 What ______________________________?
2 What ______________________________?
3 Where ______________________________?
4 Where ______________________________?
5 What ______________________________?
6 What ______________________________?
7 Where ______________________________?
8 What languages ______________________________?
9 What ______________________________ in your free time?
10 Which social ______________________________?

b Cover the questions. Interview a partner and complete the form. Ask him / her to spell names and places if necessary.

1B COMMUNICATIVE Ask me a question

What / your mother look like?	How many brothers and sisters / you have?
What / you like to do in your free time?	How often / you go to the cinema?
What / be / your town like?	What / you usually have for breakfast?
What kind of music / you like?	How / you come to class?
What / be / your house like?	Where / your parents live?
How often / you use English?	What / you do to relax in the evenings?
What / be / TV like in your country?	How many languages / you speak?
What sport or exercise / you do?	Where / you work or study?
Who / you get on with best in your family?	Who / you look like in your family?
What apps / your mobile phone have?	What time / this class finish?

1C COMMUNICATIVE At an art gallery

Student A

Describe your picture to **B**. Find and circle the ten differences between your pictures.

Student B

Describe your picture to **A**. Find and circle the ten differences between your pictures.

2A COMMUNICATIVE Bingo!

forget	meet	write	understand	fly	know
think	go	sleep	get	leave	lose
run	come	speak	write	eat	break
wear	do	buy	cost	bring	know
cut	steal	learn	win	shut	catch
become	say	throw	drink	sit	begin
tell	ring	grow	drive	win	have
buy	give	send	make	stand	put
swim	can	fall	lend	teach	catch
learn	meet	feel	fall	say	build
wake up	spend	read	grow	find	hit
take	sell	buy	lose	send	write
lend	choose	put	keep	become	make
bring	hear	fall	sing	break	ring
win	see	find	think	come	let

2B COMMUNICATIVE Fake or real?

A + B

A The helicopter and the shark

A helicopter was flying over the sea. The pilots were looking for a man who was in the sea. It was difficult to find him and they were searching for a long time. Finally, they saw the man and they threw a ladder down for him. But when the man was climbing up the ladder, a shark suddenly came out of the water. The shark began to attack the man. Somebody in a boat took this photo when the shark was attacking the man. In the end, the helicopter rescued the man.

B Nessie

Loch Ness is a big lake in Scotland, which has very dark and deep water. On April 19th 1934, a British doctor, Colonel Robert Wilson, was driving his car around the lake. He was looking at the lake when suddenly he saw something big in the water. He stopped his car and looked at the thing that was moving in the water. It looked like the head of an animal. He took his camera from his car and took a photo. The photo became famous and experts said that it was a kind of sea monster. People called the monster 'Nessie'.

FOLD

FOLD

A Fake or real?

This photo called 'Helicopter Shark' appeared on the internet in 2001 and it became famous all around the world. The text with the photo said that it won first prize in a National Geographic photography competition. It also said that it was a British military helicopter in South Africa. This was impossible because you can see the Golden Gate Bridge in San Francisco. When National Geographic saw the photo, they were very angry because the photo wasn't theirs.
The 'fake' photo was a combination of two photos by two different photographers.
The shark photo was taken in South Africa and the helicopter photo was taken in San Francisco.

B Fake or real?

Sixty years later, one of Dr Wilson's friends, Christian Spurling was dying and decided to tell the truth behind the photo. The 'monster' in the photo wasn't real.
It was really a toy submarine, which was made of wood and plastic. The two men (Wilson and Spurling) made the toy and took a photo of it in the lake. Then they sent the photo to the newspapers! Spurling and Wilson made the toy monster as a joke. But later they were afraid to confess when everybody thought it really was a photo of the Loch Ness monster.

2C COMMUNICATIVE Sentence race

1	I'm a vegetarian, **so**...
2	He didn't study for the exam, **so**...
3	She felt really ill, **so**...
4	The film was really boring, **so**...
5	It was really sunny yesterday, **so**...
6	I'm really happy today **because**...
7	I can't go to the party tonight **because**...
8	Maria didn't buy the jeans **because**...
9	He's a bit overweight **because**...
10	I live with my parents **because**...
11	**Although** she's very attractive,...
12	**Although** my job isn't very well-paid,...
13	It's a great restaurant **although**...
14	**Although** her written English is excellent,...
15	We enjoyed our holiday **although**...
16	They live together, **but**...
17	It's a good film, **but**...
18	My friend invited me to her party, **but**...
19	She didn't like him when they met, **but**...
20	Paul has a lot of money, **but**...

3A COMMUNICATIVE Find a partner

a Read the adverts and choose a holiday for next year. Answer these questions.

1 Where are you going to go? ______________
2 When are you going to go? ______________
3 How long are you going to stay? ______________
4 Where are you going to stay? ______________

ANTARCTICA

Do you like nature? Do you like the cold? If so, then this is the holiday for you! Spend 10 or 15 days at the South Pole walking, fishing, and watching penguins.

Departures: May or July
Accommodation:
in luxury cruise ships

BERMUDA

Spend 7 or 10 nights on this fantastic Caribbean island which is ideal for families and couples. If you like doing nothing except sunbathing, swimming in the turquoise sea, and drinking exotic cocktails, then choose this holiday!

Departures: August or September
Accommodation:
in a villa with a private chef OR
in the ★★★★★ Golden Sands Hotel

AUSTRALIA

Is it possible to see Australia in less than a month? Yes, it is! Come with us and see the best of Australia's beaches, rainforests, and cities. Tours last two or three weeks. Our friendly guides will take you to all the best places and make sure you have a fantastic time.

Departures: December or February
Accommodation:
at local campsites OR
in ★★ hotels

ITALY

If you like cooking and culture, read more! Stay in Florence and learn how to cook fantastic Italian dishes. English speaking teachers and very small groups. Prices all include ingredients, tuition, and an evening meal cooked by the course participants. Courses last three or six days.

Departures: May or June
Accommodation:
in an apartment OR
in a ★★ family-run hotel

b Talk to other students. Try to find someone who is planning to go on exactly the same holiday as you so that you can travel together.

A *Where are you going to go?*
B *I'm going to go to Antarctica.*
A *When are you going to go?*
B *In May.*
A *I'm going to go in July, so we can't go together.*

3B COMMUNICATIVE Come fly with me!

Student A

BOARDING CARD A – MY FLIGHT INFORMATION

1	NAME OF AIRLINE	American Airlines
2	DATE	25/10/
3	ORIGIN	JFK, New York
4	DESTINATION	Paris Orly
5	DEPARTURE TIME	14.30
6	ARRIVAL TIME	01.45

BOARDING CARD B

1	NAME OF AIRLINE	________
2	DATE	________
3	ORIGIN	________
4	DESTINATION	________
5	DEPARTURE TIME	________
6	ARRIVAL TIME	________

a Look at the missing information on boarding card **B**. Write the questions you need to ask **B** to complete boarding card **B**.

1 Who *are you flying* with?
2 When ________________? (leave)
3 Where ________________ from? (fly)
4 Where ________________ to? (fly)
5 What time ________________? (leave)
6 What time ________________? (arrive)

b Ask **B** the questions and complete boarding card **B**.

c Now **B** will ask you for the information on boarding card **A**. Answer his / her questions.

Student B

BOARDING CARD A

1	NAME OF AIRLINE	________
2	DATE	________
3	ORIGIN	________
4	DESTINATION	________
5	DEPARTURE TIME	________
6	ARRIVAL TIME	________

BOARDING CARD B – MY FLIGHT INFORMATION

1	NAME OF AIRLINE	British Airways
2	DATE	16/3
3	ORIGIN	London Heathrow
4	DESTINATION	Schiphol, Amsterdam
5	DEPARTURE TIME	17.25
6	ARRIVAL TIME	18.45

a Look at the missing information on boarding card **A**. Write the questions you need to ask **A** to complete boarding card **A**.

1 Who *are you flying* with?
2 When ________________? (leave)
3 Where ________________ from? (fly)
4 Where ________________ to? (fly)
5 What time ________________? (leave)
6 What time ________________? (arrive)

b **A** will ask you for the information on boarding card **B**. Answer his / her questions.

c Now ask **A** the questions and complete boarding card **A**.

3C COMMUNICATIVE Can you explain the word?

4A COMMUNICATIVE Find the response

a Match the sentences with the responses and then check your answers with your teacher.

1 Do you want to come and see the new Sofia Coppola film? [*f*]	**a** She's already left.
2 Have you done your English homework? [ ]	**b** No, not yet. I'm going to tidy it later.
3 What time's your mother leaving? [ ]	**c** She's fine. I've just spoken to her.
4 Would you like a cup of coffee? [ ]	**d** Thanks. I've just bought them.
5 Have you tidied your room yet? [ ]	**e** You're too late. They've already gone home.
6 Why can't we have chips for dinner? [ ]	~~**f**~~ I've already seen it.
7 Do you know how Sheila is? [ ]	**g** Don't worry! I've already been to the supermarket.
8 What's his new girlfriend like? [ ]	**h** Yes, I know. I've just got up.
9 Have you booked your flight? [ ]	**i** Yes, I've just finished it.
10 What's your English course like? [ ]	**j** I can't. I haven't been to the cashpoint yet.
11 I love your shoes! [ ]	**k** Thanks. I've just washed it.
12 Your hair looks nice. [ ]	**l** No, not yet. I'm going to do it tonight.
13 Can you lend me some money? [ ]	**m** Because you've already had them three times this week.
14 You look really sleepy. [ ]	**n** I haven't started it yet. It starts tomorrow.
15 Don't forget to buy some milk! [ ]	**o** No, thanks. I've just had one.
16 Where are Pete and Andrew? [ ]	**p** I don't know. I haven't met her yet.

FOLD

b Fold the paper vertically. **A** say sentences 1–16. **B** can you remember the responses? Then swap roles.

4B COMMUNICATIVE Have you ever...?

1	/ ever cheat in an exam? Why / cheat?
2	/ ever forget somebody's birthday? Whose birthday / be?
3	/ ever get a present you didn't like? What?
4	/ ever do an extreme sport? Which one / do?
5	/ ever pretend to be ill when you weren't? Why / do it?
6	/ ever study a foreign language apart from English? Which language / study?
7	/ ever live abroad for more than 6 months? Where / live? Why / live there?
8	/ ever do volunteer work? What? How long / do it for?
9	/ ever send an email to the wrong person? Who / send it to? What happened?
10	/ ever run a marathon or a half marathon? When? / finish it?
11	/ ever adopt an animal? Where / get it from?
12	/ ever / lock yourself out of your house or flat? How / get in?
13	/ ever complain in a hotel or restaurant? Why / complain?
14	/ ever have a problem with a phone company? What / the problem about?
15	/ ever lie about your age? Why / lie?
16	/ ever spoken in public? What / speak about? How / feel?

4C COMMUNICATIVE The same or different?

a Complete the sentences with *something*, *anywhere*, *nobody*, etc.

1. I always have ______________ to eat for breakfast.
2. When I watch films in English, I don't usually understand ______________.
3. I never have problems sleeping on buses or planes. I can sleep ______________.
4. I don't usually do ______________ interesting at weekends.
5. I don't usually watch ______________ on TV in the evenings.
6. In my family, ______________ speaks any English except me!
7. I went ______________ really exciting last weekend.
8. I never read ______________ in English apart from my coursebook.
9. There's ______________ I really want to buy at the moment, but I don't have any money.
10. I love doing ______________ on Sunday mornings, just staying in bed late.
11. I hate smoking, and luckily ______________ in my family smokes.
12. I want to go ______________ relax this weekend.
13. I don't know ______________ in this class very well.
14. There isn't ______________ I really want to go on holiday. I think I'll stay at home.
15. In my area, there's ______________ for young people to go at night. It's really boring.
16. I never say ______________ in English in this class. I'm too shy.
17. I'm not going ______________ this weekend. I need to study.
18. I'd really like ______________ to eat right now. I'm really hungry!
19. I met ______________ very interesting last weekend.
20. I always go ______________ quiet when I have to study.

b Talk to a partner. Tell him / her if the sentences are true or not true for you, and why.

5A COMMUNICATIVE Which do you prefer? Why?

swimming in the sea OR swimming in a pool	a holiday with your family OR a holiday with friends
watching a film in your language OR watching a film with subtitles	watching a film at the cinema OR watching a film at home
communicating by email OR communicating by text message	watching sport OR doing sport
doing English homework OR doing housework	reading an e-book OR reading an ordinary book
eating in a restaurant OR eating at home	buying things in a shop OR buying things online
going on holiday in your country OR going on holiday abroad	listening to music with headphones OR listening to music without headphones
going clothes shopping alone OR going clothes shopping with another person	
studying during the day OR studying at night	

5B COMMUNICATIVE Superlative questions

Student A

a Complete the questions with the superlative form of the adjective in brackets.

1 Who do you think is ____________________ (beautiful) actress in your country?

2 What's ____________________ (good) computer game you've ever played?

3 What's ____________________ (popular) festival in your country?

4 What's ____________________ (bad) film you've seen recently?

5 What's ____________________ (dangerous) sport you've ever done?

6 What's ____________________ (difficult) thing about studying English?

7 What do you think is ____________________ (easy) way to get fit?

8 Who's ____________________ (famous) sportsperson in your country?

b Ask **B** the questions. Remember to ask for more information. Answer, and then return the question with *What about you?*

Student B

a Complete the questions with the superlative form of the adjective in brackets.

1 What is / was your ____________________ (bad) subject at school?

2 What's ____________________ (early) memory you have?

3 What's ____________________ (exciting) holiday you've ever had?

4 What's ____________________ (good) concert you've ever been to?

5 What's ____________________ (late) gadget you've bought?

6 What's ____________________ (boring) sport on TV?

7 Who do you think is ____________________ (good-looking) actor in your country?

8 What do you think was ____________________ (interesting) decade for pop music?

b Ask **A** the questions. Remember to ask for more information. Answer, and then return the question with *What about you?*

15 52 45 23 41

What's your body age?

Do the questionnaire and find out!

Exercise

1 How much exercise or sport do you do?
a) a lot **b)** quite a lot **c)** very little **d)** none

Diet

2 How much fast food (processed and pre-prepared) do you eat?
a) I eat too much **b)** I eat quite a lot **c)** I don't eat much **d)** I don't eat any

3 How many portions of fruit and vegetables do you eat per day?
a) 5 or more **b)** 3 or 4 **c)** 2 or less

4 How much water do you drink?
a) a lot **b)** quite a lot **c)** a little

5 What's your worst dietary habit?
a) I eat too much fat **b)** I eat (or drink) too many sweet things
c) I eat (or drink) too much **d)** none of these

Lifestyle

6 How would you describe yourself mentally?
a) I'm a positive person **b)** I'm not positive enough **c)** I'm quite negative

7 How would you describe your stress level?
a) I'm too stressed **b)** I'm stressed but it's under control **c)** I'm quite relaxed

8 How often do you use sunscreen?
a) when it's sunny **b)** only when I'm on holiday **c)** every day

9 How often do you see your close friends?
a) very often **b)** quite often **c)** not enough

10 How much time do you have for yourself?
a) none **b)** not enough **c)** quite a lot

FOLD

Your body age

Start with your calendar age. Add (+) or subtract (–) years according to your answers.

1	a -2	b -1	c 0	d +1	5	a +1	b +1	c +2	d 0	9	a -2	b -1	c +2	
2	a +2	b +1	c 0	d -1	6	a -3	b +1	c +2		10	a +2	b +1	c -2	
3	a -2	b -1	c +1		7	a +3	b 0	c -2						
4	a -2	b -1	c +1		8	a -2	b 0	c +1						

6A COMMUNICATIVE The optimist's phrase book

a In pairs, complete **THE OPTIMIST SAYS** with positive predictions.

	YOU SAY	THE OPTIMIST SAYS
1	I lost my wallet yesterday.	Don't worry. ______
2	I'm getting married in the summer.	Congratulations! I'm sure ______
3	I'm going to a party tonight.	Great! ______
4	I'm running my first marathon on Saturday.	Good luck! I'm sure ______
5	I'm going to start doing yoga.	Fantastic! ______
6	I have to go to the dentist's on Monday.	Don't worry. ______
7	My partner's just left me.	Cheer up! ______
8	I'm taking the First Certificate exam in June.	Mmm. I'm sure ______
9	I'm going to live in the UK for a year.	That's great! ______
10	I've failed my driving test for the third time.	Cheer up! ______
11	I'm going to read an English novel.	That's really good. ______
12	I don't feel very well.	Don't worry. I'm sure ______

b **A** say sentences 1–12. **B** cover the optimist's sentences he / she's written. Respond from memory.

c Swap roles. **B** say sentences 1–12 in a different order. **A** cover the optimist's sentences he / she's written. Respond from memory.

I lost my wallet yesterday. — *Don't worry. I'm sure you'll find it.*

6B COMMUNICATIVE Guess my sentence

Student A

1 I like these shoes. I think I ______________ them.

2 I'll pick you up at eight o'clock. Shall I call you on your mobile before I leave home?

3 Please don't worry, mum. I ______________ you when I get to Paris.

4 Your suitcase looks really heavy. Shall I carry it for you?

5 I ______________ you the money for Maria's present tomorrow.

6 I'll help you with your English homework. I can see you're having problems.

7 It's really hot in here. ______________ I ______________ the air conditioning?

8 The doorbell's ringing. I'll go and see who it is.

9 I ______________ for lunch today. You got it last time.

10 I'll remember to do it. I've got an excellent memory.

11 The phone's ringing. ______________ I ______________ it?

12 Have you forgotten your book? Don't worry. I'll lend you mine.

13 I'm just going to buy some milk. I ______________ in ten minutes.

14 You do the cooking and I'll do the washing up.

Student B

1 I like these shoes. I think I'll buy them.

2 I'll pick you up at eight o'clock. ______________ I ______________ you on your mobile before I leave home?

3 Please don't worry, mum. I'll text you when I get to Paris.

4 Your suitcase looks really heavy. ______________ I ______________ it for you?

5 I'll give you the money for Maria's present tomorrow.

6 I ______________ you with your English homework. I can see you're having problems.

7 It's really hot in here. Shall I turn on the air conditioning?

8 The doorbell's ringing. I ______________ and see who it is.

9 I'll pay for lunch today. You got it last time.

10 I ______________ to do it. I've got an excellent memory.

11 The phone's ringing. Shall I answer it?

12 Have you forgotten your book? Don't worry. I ______________ you mine.

13 I'm just going to buy some milk. I'll be back in ten minutes.

14 You do the cooking and I ______________ the washing up.

6C COMMUNICATIVE Talk about it

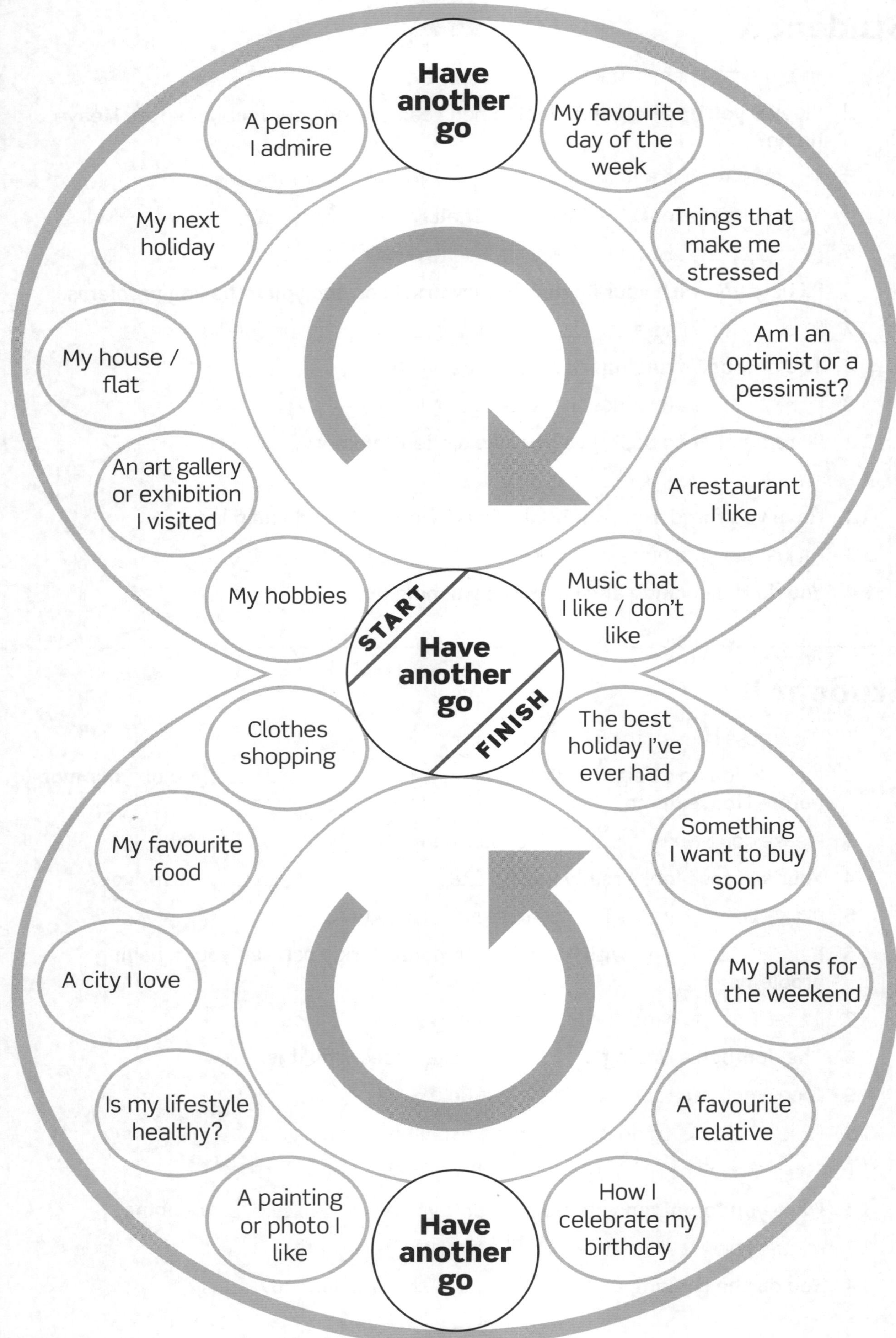

7A COMMUNICATIVE I'm going to tell you about...

Choose six topics and think about what you're going to say. Talk to a partner. Give and ask for more information.

the best way to learn a language

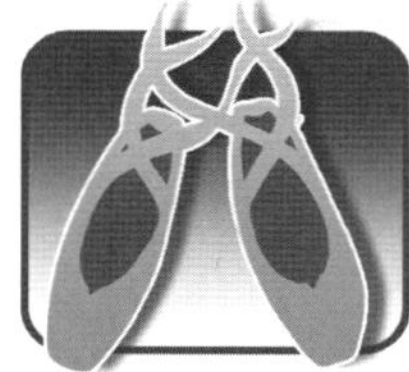

something you learnt to do as a child but can't do now

something you think is important to teach young children

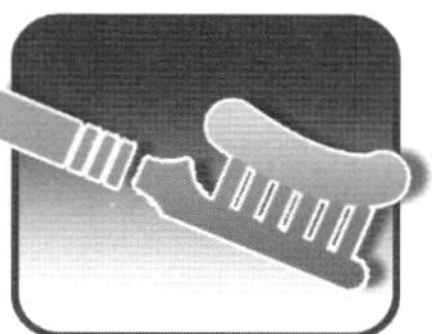

something you sometimes forget to do before you go to bed

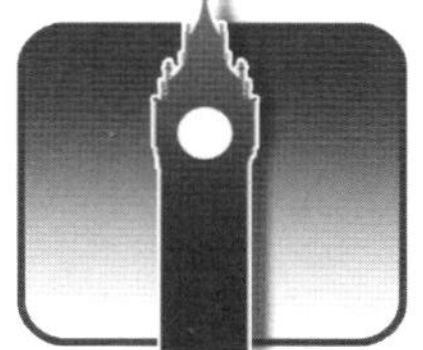

why tourists come to your country

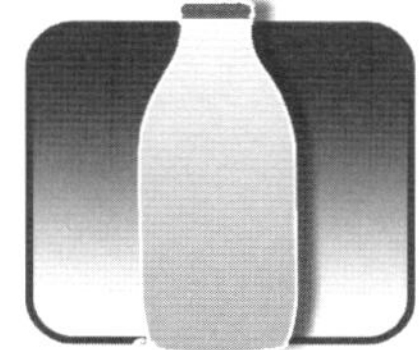

something you need to buy soon

the things you do to relax after a hard day

something you've decided to do in the future

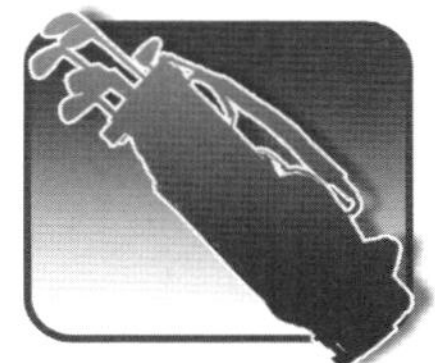

a sport you tried to play but couldn't

something you find difficult to do in English

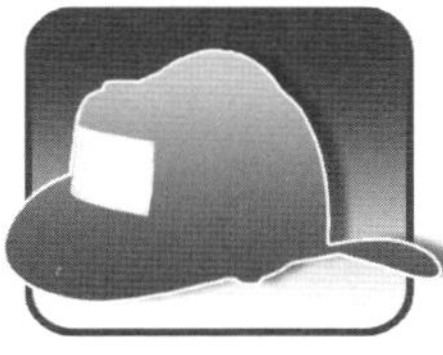

something you wanted to be when you were younger

what you want to do this weekend

somebody you would like to meet

the best way to make new friends

something you started to do but decided to stop doing

things that are important to do if you go for a job interview

the things you think it's important to do for a healthy life

a film that's good to watch when you're feeling sad

7B COMMUNICATIVE Find someone who...

Find someone who answers 'yes' to your questions. Then ask for some more information.

Find someone who...	Student's name	More information
1 likes getting up early.		
2 is afraid of flying.		
3 doesn't mind waiting for people who are late.		
4 hated going to school when they were younger.		
5 enjoys reading in bed.		
6 is good at cooking.		
7 has started doing a new activity recently.		
8 thinks doing exercise is boring.		
9 spends more than an hour walking every day.		
10 has stopped doing an activity recently.		
11 enjoys being alone.		
12 has felt like doing a dangerous sport.		
13 thinks playing computer games teaches you something.		
14 liked eating fruit and vegetables as a child.		
15 is thinking of getting a new haircut soon.		

7C COMMUNICATIVE In the UK

a Work in pairs. Read the sentences about the UK and decide if they are true or false.

		True	False
1	You mustn't cycle in bus lanes.	☐	☐
2	Pubs mustn't sell alcohol to anyone under 21.	☐	☐
3	You don't have to pay to use motorways.	☐	☐
4	All dogs and cats must have a microchip with the name and address of their owner.	☐	☐
5	If you have a TV, you have to buy a TV licence to watch it.	☐	☐
6	You have to be 18 to ride a 50cc motorbike.	☐	☐
7	You don't have to have an ID card.	☐	☐
8	All shops must close on Sundays.	☐	☐
9	You mustn't leave a child under 12 alone at home.	☐	☐
10	You mustn't play loud music in your house after 9.00 p.m.	☐	☐
11	You have to be 17 years old to vote in a general election.	☐	☐
12	If you don't want to vote in a general election, you don't have to.	☐	☐
13	You have to be over 16 to have a Facebook or Twitter account.	☐	☐
14	If you have a dog, you must have a special licence.	☐	☐
15	TV programmes before 9.00p.m. mustn't include bad language.	☐	☐
16	You don't have to study a foreign language at secondary school.	☐	☐
17	You don't have to wear seat belts in the back of the car.	☐	☐
18	Parents don't have to send their children to school. They can educate them at home.	☐	☐

b Check your answers with your teacher.

c Work with a partner. Is it the same or different in your country? Which of these rules would you like to have in your country?

8A COMMUNICATIVE I need some advice

I want to do some exercise but I have a back problem. **What exercise should I do?**	I have a job interview in English next week. I really want the job. **How should I prepare for it?**
I had a big argument with my partner yesterday. It was my fault. **What should I do today?**	My friend's invited me to stay for the weekend but she doesn't like dogs. I have a dog and I don't have anyone to leave it with. **What should I do?**
Some friends are coming to dinner and I can't cook. **What should I do?**	I want to learn to dance. **What kind of dancing should I learn?**
I can't sleep at night. **What should I do?**	I'd like to learn another foreign language. **Which one should I learn?**
I'd like to buy my English teacher a present. **What should I buy?**	I want to spend a romantic evening with my partner. **Where should we go?**
I'm very stressed and I need to relax. **What should I do?**	I'd like to go on holiday somewhere different this year. **Where should I go?**
A company's offered me a fantastic job but I'd have to travel a lot. I'm afraid of flying. **What should I do?**	I'd like to get a new phone. **What phone should I buy?**
I forgot my friend's birthday yesterday and she always remembers mine. **What should I do?**	I want to save money to buy a new laptop. **How should I save the money?**
I don't like my best friend's new partner but he / she is very happy! **What should I do?**	My neighbours are really noisy at night. **What should I do?**

8B COMMUNICATIVE On the Trans-Siberian Railway

a Read the beginning of the story. Why do you think the Russian doesn't want to lend his newspaper to the American?

> A young American was travelling to Vladivostok on the Trans-Siberian Railway, the longest railway in the world. It was a long journey and he was bored. Sitting opposite him was a Russian man. He was about 40 years old. He had an English newspaper on the seat next to him.
>
> 'Excuse me,' the American said. 'Can I borrow your newspaper?'
> 'No,' the Russian said. 'I'm sorry. You can't.'
> 'Why not?' asked the American.
> 'Well,' said the Russian, 'it's quite simple...'

b Look at the pictures. Then number the sentences 1–9.

- [ ] 'If you meet Olga, you'll fall in love with her.'
- [ ] 'If we start talking, we'll become friends.'
- [ ] 'If I invite you to my house, you'll meet my beautiful daughter, Olga.'
- [ ] 'So that's why I won't lend you my newspaper.'
- [ ] 'If I find you, I'll kill you.'
- [ ] 'If you fall in love with her, you'll run away together.'
- [ ] 'If we become friends, I'll invite you to my house in Vladivostok.'
- [1] 'If I lend you my newspaper, we'll start talking.'
- [ ] 'If you run away, I'll find you.'

c Cover sentences 1–9 and look at the pictures. Try to remember the sentences and tell your partner the story.

8C COMMUNICATIVE Reading questionnaire

Interview your partner.

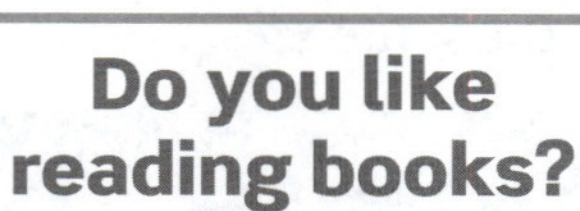
Do you like reading books?

YES

1 Do you have a favourite place or time of day to read? Why do you like it?

2 What kind of books do you like reading?

3 Do you have a favourite author?

4 How many books do you read a month?

5 Do you prefer to read normal books or eBooks? Why?

6 How do you find out about new books and authors?

7 What was the last book you bought? Where did you buy it?

8 Are you a fast reader or a slow reader?

9 Do you sometimes read more than one book at a time?

10 Whose advice on books do you always listen to?

11 Is there a book everyone liked but you hated?

12 Have you ever started reading a book but not finished it? Why not?

13 Have you read a Multimedia eBook? What did you think of it?

14 Do you prefer to read the book or watch the film based on the book? Why?

15 Do you ever read the last page of a novel first?

NO

1 Do you read any magazines or newspapers? Which ones?

2 Do you read online? What do you read?

3 How do you find out about the news? In newspapers? On the internet? On the radio? Why?

4 Did your parents read to you when you were a child? What books did they read?

5 How old were you when you first started to read?

6 Did you read comics when you were a child? Which ones?

7 Is there a book which you can remember reading when you were a child? What was it about?

8 Is there anybody in your family who likes reading? Who?

9 Have you ever written a blog? Do you like reading blogs?

10 Do you think women like reading more than men? Why?

11 Do you think that people today are reading more or less than 20 years ago? Why?

12 If somebody gives you a book as a present, what do you do?

13 Are you following anybody on Twitter?

9A COMMUNICATIVE I think you'd...

Student A

a Complete the sentences about **B**.

1 If you could be anywhere in the world right now, I think you'd choose to be in ______________.
2 If you bought a new car today, I think you'd buy a ______________.
3 If you didn't study English, I think you'd like to study ______________.
4 If we had lunch together, I think you'd take me to ______________.
5 If you could go to a concert tonight, I think you'd go and see ______________.
6 If you could travel to an English-speaking country on holiday, I think you'd go to ______________.
7 If you could meet a famous person, I think you'd like to meet ______________.
8 If you could choose your ideal job, I think you'd like to be a / an ______________.
9 If you did a new sport / hobby, I think you'd like to ______________.
10 If you bought a new flat, I think you'd buy one in ______________.

b Read your sentences to **B**. Were you right?

c Listen to **B**'s sentences about you. Tell him / her if they are right or wrong, and why.

Student B

a Complete the sentences about A.

1 If you got a new pet, I think you'd buy a ______________.
2 If you had a big problem, I think you'd speak to ______________.
3 If you were an animal, I think you'd be a / an ______________.
4 If you went to a karaoke bar, I think you'd sing ______________.
5 If you had more money, I think you'd buy a ______________.
6 If somebody wanted to buy you a present, I think you'd love a / some ______________.
7 If you could change one thing in your house or flat, I think you'd ______________.
8 If you could learn to play a musical instrument well, I think you'd choose ______________.
9 If someone invited you to a very expensive restaurant, I think you'd order ______________.
10 If you could appear on a TV programme, I think you'd appear on ______________.

b Listen to **A**'s sentences about you. Tell him / her if they are right or wrong, and why.

c Read your sentences to **A**. Were you right?

9B COMMUNICATIVE Famous phobias

Student A

Barack Obama Most people recognize the name of this famous politician but not many people know that he suffers from bathophobia which means he is afraid of going up stairs. He's had the phobia for about 40 years because that is when he fell down the stairs in his grandmother's house. The White House is a building which has two floors but the president and his family live on the ground floor. Curiously, bathophobics don't have a problem going down the stairs, only up!

True or false?

Jennifer Aniston This actress has a very common phobia called aviophobia. This means that she's afraid of flying. She's been afraid of flying since 2000, when she was on a small plane which was flying from Toronto to New York City. The plane flew into an electric storm and experienced a lot of turbulence. Since then, she's never caught a plane unless it's been absolutely necessary.

True or false?

Justin Timberlake This singer and actor is from the USA. He has to travel a lot because of his job and sometimes the arachnophobia he suffers from is a problem for him. He's been afraid of spiders for a long time. He thinks his phobia started at the age of seven or eight when he found a spider in his bed. Last year he was staying in a hotel and saw a spider in the bathroom. He couldn't kill it so he asked the receptionist to come and kill it for him!

True or false?

- - - - - - - - - - - - - - - - - - - -

Student B

Nicole Kidman This Australian actress suffers from an unusual phobia called lepidopterophobia. This means that she's a person who doesn't like butterflies. She's had this phobia since she was a child but she can't remember exactly why or how the phobia started. When a butterfly comes near her, she sometimes has a panic attack. This phobia is, of course, a problem when she is making a film, especially if the director is filming outside!

True or false?

Orlando Bloom Have you seen *Pirates of the Caribbean*? If you have, then you'll probably remember this actor who appears in the film. But this 'brave' actor has a serious phobia which is swinophobia. This means that he is afraid of pigs and has been afraid of them since he was a teenager. Although this phobia isn't very common, it's had a direct effect on his career. Recently, a director asked him to be in the film *Animal Farm* but Orlando said no because it meant that he had to work with a pig!

True or false?

Madonna A person who has ataxophobia likes everything in his / her life to be tidy and clean. Madonna has had this phobia for a long time. In her biography, it says she's had it since she was born. For example, in her kitchen, the food and drinks in her fridge are all in a specific order. Her dresses and shoes also have to be separated into colours – black skirts with black jackets, red shoes with red dresses. She hates it when they're not in the right order.

True or false?

9C COMMUNICATIVE Like mother, like daughter

Student A

a Read the biographies. Complete the questions you need to ask **B** to find out the missing information.

Jerry Hall

Jerry Hall is a [1]__________ and an __________ who was born in [2]__________ in 1956. She has four sisters including a non-identical twin sister. In 1974, she had a serious car accident and got a lot of money as compensation. With this money, she left the USA and went to live in France because she [3]__________. One day, she was sunbathing in [4]__________ when an agent from a modelling company saw her. He offered her a modelling contract immediately. Jerry accepted and since [5]__________ she has been a very successful model. Apart from modelling, she has worked as an actress in cinema and the theatre. In 1977, she met Mick Jagger at a party. They got married in 1990 and they have [6]__________ children. Elizabeth Jagger is their oldest daughter. Unfortunately, the marriage broke up and Jerry and Mick have been divorced since [7]__________.

Elizabeth Jagger

Elizabeth Jagger is a model and an actress who was born in New York City in 1984. Her father is the famous singer, Mick Jagger, and her mother is Jerry Hall. Elizabeth decided to leave school when she was 16 because she hated it and because she wanted to become a model. Her father didn't agree with her decision to be a model but her mother was very happy. She began her modelling career in 2000 when she appeared (with her mother) in the Thierry Mugler fashion show. Since 2000, she has worked for Mango, Burberry, and Tommy Hilfiger. She has had several boyfriends including John Lennon's son, Sean. She has just won a big contract to work for the cosmetics company, Lancôme.

1 What ____________________ do?
2 Where ____________________ born?
3 Why ____________________ France?
4 Where ____________________?
5 How long ____________________ a model?
6 How many children ____________________?
7 How long ____________________ divorced?

b Ask **B** the questions and complete Jerry Hall's biography. Answer **B**'s questions about Elizabeth Jagger. What do the mother and daughter have in common?

Student B

a Read the biographies. Complete the questions you need to ask **A** to find out the missing information.

Elizabeth Jagger

Elizabeth Jagger is a [1]__________ and an __________ who was born in [2]__________ in 1984. Her father is the famous singer, Mick Jagger, and her mother is Jerry Hall. Elizabeth decided to leave school when she was [3]__________ because she [4]__________ and because she wanted to __________. Her father didn't agree with her decision to be a model but her mother was very happy. She began her modelling career in [5]__________ when she appeared (with her mother) in the Thierry Mugler fashion show. Since 2000, she has worked for [6]__________, __________, and __________. She has had several boyfriends including John Lennon's son, Sean, but they separated recently. She has just won a big contract to work for [7]__________.

Jerry Hall

Jerry Hall is a model and an actress who was born in Texas in 1956. She has four sisters including a non-identical twin sister. In 1974, she had a serious car accident and got a lot of money as compensation from the insurance company. With this money, she left the USA and went to live in France because she wanted to become a model. One day, she was sunbathing in the French Riviera when an agent from a modelling company saw her. He offered her a modelling contract immediately. Jerry accepted and since 1975 she has been a very successful model. Apart from modelling, she has worked as an actress in cinema and the theatre. In 1977, she met Mick Jagger at a party. They got married in 1990 and they have four children. Elizabeth Jagger is their oldest daughter. Unfortunately, the marriage broke up and Jerry and Mick have been divorced since 1999.

1 What ____________________ do?
2 Where ____________________ born?
3 When ____________________ school?
4 Why ____________________ school?
5 When ____________________ modelling career?
6 Which companies ____________________ since 2000?
7 What contract ____________________?

b Ask **A** the questions and complete Elizabeth Jagger's biography. Answer **A**'s questions about Jerry Hall. What do the mother and daughter have in common?

10A COMMUNICATIVE General knowledge quiz

Student A

1 Which month is named after a Roman emperor?
a) **August** b) July c) January

2 What sport is played at Flushing Meadows, USA?
a) basketball b) baseball c) **tennis**

3 Where are polar bears found?
a) the South Pole b) **Alaska** c) Antarctica

4 What is the Greek goddess of victory called?
a) Adidas b) Reebok c) **Nike**

5 On a computer keyboard, which letter is found between Z and C?
a) V b) P c) **X**

6 What was the first song sung in space?
a) **Happy Birthday to You** b) We Wish You a Merry Christmas c) We Are the Champions

7 In which European city is the Nobel Peace Prize given?
a) London b) Paris c) **Oslo**

8 What is *tofu* made of?
a) water b) **soya milk** c) cow's milk

9 What drink was created by The Coca-Cola Company in Germany during World War II?
a) Coca-Cola b) Dr Pepper c) **Fanta**

10 In which country was golf first played?
a) England b) **Scotland** c) Spain

Student B

1 In which city was the Titanic built?
a) **Belfast** b) New York c) Portsmouth

2 Who was the ball point pen invented by?
a) Mr Bic b) **Mr Biro** c) Mr Parker

3 On which day is Thanksgiving celebrated in the USA?
a) **the fourth Thursday in November** b) the second Thursday in July
c) the first Thursday in December

4 In which decade was Greenpeace founded?
a) the 1960s b) the 1980s c) **the 1970s**

5 Which style of music was created by Antonio Carlos Jobim and João Gilberto in Brazil?
a) heavy metal b) **bossa nova** c) samba

6 In which film was the word 'supercalifragilisticexpialidocious' used?
a) ***Mary Poppins*** b) *Harry Potter* c) *E.T.*

7 Who was the Sistine Chapel painted by?
a) Tintoretto b) da Vinci c) **Michelangelo**

8 The Canary Islands are named after which animal?
a) a canary b) a cat c) **a dog**

9 How many squares are there on a chess board?
a) 144 b) 96 c) **64**

10 Which is the most visited paying monument in the world?
a) the Taj Mahal b) **the Eiffel Tower** c) the Empire State Building

10B COMMUNICATIVE My past

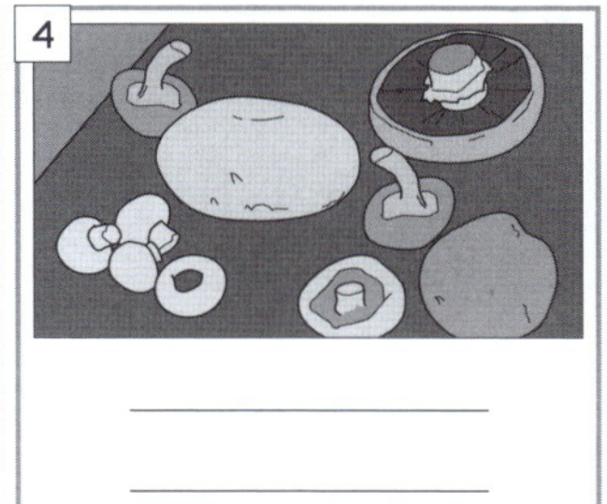

a How have you changed? Write a name or phrase in as many boxes as you can.

1 Something you used to be afraid of but aren't now.
2 A favourite toy you used to have but don't have now.
3 A singer or band you used to listen to but don't now.
4 A kind of food or drink you didn't use to like but do now.
5 Something you used to collect but don't now.
6 A game you used to play a lot but don't play now.
7 A pet you used to have but don't have now.
8 A place where you used to go to on holiday with your family but don't now.
9 A friend you used to have at school but don't have now.
10 A bad habit you used to have but don't now.
11 A TV programme you used to watch a lot but don't now.
12 Something you didn't use to do at weekends but do now.
13 A house you used to live in but don't now.
14 An instrument you used to play but don't now.

b Compare your boxes with a partner's. Ask for / give more information about how and why you've changed.

10C COMMUNICATIVE Match it!

a Match the sentences.

		FOLD		
1 Keep the receipt for the top.	*d*		**a**	He might lose his job.
2 There are some good films on,			**b**	If I don't, I might forget it.
3 I need to improve English,			**c**	The dress might be cheaper then.
4 I'm not sure which one to buy.			~~**d**~~	You might want to change it.
5 They've never been to my house before.			**e**	I think I might have flu.
6 She's not answering her phone.			**f**	She might not be at the party tonight.
7 His company isn't doing very well.			**g**	She might not pay you back.
8 I wouldn't lend her the money if I were you.			**h**	I might get the blue one or the red one.
9 Take an umbrella with you.			**i**	I might do a sumer course in the UK.
10 It's quite early.			**j**	She might be driving.
11 She told me she was very tired.			**k**	I heard that it might rain later.
12 I must write down the date of my doctor's appointment.			**l**	They might not know the way.
13 Why don't you wait for the Christmas sales?			**m**	We might go to the cinema.
14 I have a cough and a cold.			**n**	The children might not be in bed yet.

b Work with a partner. Cover the sentences on the right. Take turns to test your partner. How many of the sentences can he / she remember?

11A COMMUNICATIVE The race

Student A

MY RACE

B's RACE

a Describe the route marked **MY RACE** to **B**.

b Then draw the route which **B** describes on the map marked **B's RACE**.

c Compare the two routes. Are they the same as the original?

Student B

A's RACE

MY RACE

a Draw the route which **A** describes on the map marked **A's RACE**.

b Describe the route marked **MY RACE** to **A**.

c Compare the two routes. Are they the same as the original?

11B COMMUNICATIVE Phrasal verbs dialogues

a Complete each dialogue with one of the phrasal verbs in the list. There are two you don't need.

fill it in   look it up   pick them up   take it off   throw them away
try them on   turn it off   write it down

1 **A** Is that my shirt you're wearing?
B Yes, it is.
A Did I say you could borrow it?
B Erm, no.
A ______________ and next time, ask me first!

2 **A** Excuse me, Ms Smythe. I don't understand this word.
B Have you brought your dictionary to class today?
A Yes, here it is.
B Well, if you don't know what the word means, ______________!

3 **A** Do you think I should buy these jeans?
B Yes, they look great. Have they got your size?
A I'm not sure.
B Ask the shop assistant, and then go and ______________.

4 **A** It's really cold in here. Is the air conditioning on?
B I'll go and have a look.
A OK. Thanks.
B Yes, it is. Shall I ______________?
A Yes, please!

5 **A** How many times do I have to tell you?
B What is it now?
A Your clothes are all over the floor.
B So? It's my bedroom.
A ______________ immediately!

6 **A** Hello. Can I help you?
B Yes, please. How do I become a member of this gym?
A First we need your personal and bank details. Here's the form.
B Could you help me ______________, please? I've left my glasses at home and I can't read it!

b Work with a partner. Memorize one of the dialogues and act it out from memory.

c Work with a partner. Choose two phrasal verbs from the list and write two short dialogues using a phrasal verb in each of them.

11C COMMUNICATIVE Are we the same?

a Complete the sentences so that they are true for you.

b Complete the phrases in the second columnwith the correct auxiliary verb.

1	I went to ____________ (a place) last weekend.	a	So ____________ I.
2	I've seen ____________ (the name of a film) more than once.	b	So ____________ I.
3	I really don't like ____________ (a sport).	c	Neither ____________ I.
4	I'm afraid of ____________ (an animal / insect).	d	So ____________ I.
5	When I get home tonight, I'm going to ____________ (an activity).	e	So ____________ I.
6	I feel very ____________ (an adjective) at the moment.	f	So ____________ I.
7	I can't play the ____________ (an instrument).	g	Neither ____________ I.
8	I usually have ____________ (a type of food) for breakfast.	h	So ____________ I.
9	I've been to ____________ (a city).	i	So ____________ I.
10	I'd like to go to ____________ (a country) for my next holiday.	j	So ____________ I.
11	I don't like ____________ (a kind of housework).	k	Neither ____________ I.
12	I didn't like ____________ (a food or drink) when I was a child.	l	Neither ____________ I.

c Work with a partner. **A** read sentences 1–12 to **B**. **B**, if you are the same, respond with *So ____________ I.* | *Neither ____________ I.* If you aren't the same, say why.

I went to a restaurant last weekend.

So did I. **OR** *I went to the cinema.*

12A COMMUNICATIVE Match the sentences

a Fold the sheet. Read the first halves of sentences 1–14. With a partner, think about how the sentences might continue. Use the past perfect.

		FOLD		
1	I couldn't find my bike because... ☐		**a**	I'd already seen the film.
2	I didn't want to go to the cinema because... ☐		**b**	I'd left my towel at home.
3	I didn't recognize Jack at first because... ☐		**c**	I'd already rung her three times.
4	I couldn't catch the flight because... ☐		**d**	somebody had stolen it.
5	I didn't want to call Jane again because... ☐		**e**	I hadn't brought my glasses.
6	I bought the book because... ☐		**f**	he'd cut my hair much too short.
7	My phone didn't work because... ☐		**g**	I'd left my passport at home.
8	I couldn't go swimming because... ☐		**h**	I'd drunk too much coffee.
9	I had a big argument with my husband last night because... ☐		**i**	my sister had recommended it.
10	I nearly cried when I came out of the hairdresser's because... ☐		**j**	I hadn't studied enough.
11	I couldn't sleep because... ☐		**k**	I hadn't seen him for 30 years.
12	I failed the exam because... ☐		**l**	he'd forgotten our wedding anniversary.
13	I had problems reading the menu because... ☐		**m**	the chef hadn't cooked it enough.
14	I couldn't eat the fish because... ☐		**n**	I'd forgotten to charge it.

b Match the sentence halves.

c Fold the paper vertically and try to remember the second halves of the sentences.

12B COMMUNICATIVE Really? How amazing!

I go to work by helicopter.

I spoke to the British Prime Minister on Monday.

I'm going to have a baby.

I'm scared of sheep.

I don't have a mobile phone.

I've met Brad Pitt.

I flew to London and back yesterday.

I have a pet crocodile.

My father is an astronaut.

I've been to Australia three times.

I can speak Chinese, Russian, and Arabic.

I have 13 brothers and sisters.

I've never eaten pizza.

I only sleep three hours a night.

I'm going on holiday to Hawaii.

12C COMMUNICATIVE Hollywood quiz

Student A

1 Which fictional family __________ at 742 Evergreen Terrace? (live)
a) The Simpsons b) The Griffins c) The Potters

2 In which film __________ 'May the force be with you'? (an actor / say)
a) *Star Trek* b) *Back to the Future* c) *Star Wars*

3 Which film __________ the most to make in all of Hollywood's history? (cost)
a) *King Kong* b) *Pirates of the Caribbean (at the World's End)*
c) *Avatar*

4 For which film __________ her only Oscar? (Kate Winslet / win)
a) *Titanic* b) *The Reader* c) *Lost in Translation*

5 What __________ collecting? (Tom Hanks / like)
a) old cars b) old radios c) old typewriters

6 Who __________ in July 2010? (Miranda Kerr / marry)
a) Johnny Depp b) Orlando Bloom c) Daniel Craig

7 Who __________ Harrison Ford's father in *Indiana Jones and the Last Crusade*? (play)
a) Michael Caine b) Michael Douglas c) Sean Connery

8 In which film __________ 'I'm back'? (Arnold Schwarzenegger / say)
a) *Terminator 1* b) *Terminator 2* c) *Terminator 3*

Student B

1 In which country __________ *The Lord of the Rings* trilogy? (Peter Jackson / film)
a) England b) Australia c) New Zealand

2 Which actor __________ in most of Hitchcock's films? (appear)
a) Alfred Hitchcock b) James Stewart c) Cary Grant

3 How much __________? (an Oscar / weigh)
a) 2.5 kilos b) 4 kilos c) 7 kilos

4 Which Harry Potter actor __________ in a Halloween episode of *The Simpsons*? (be)
a) Daniel Radcliffe b) Rupert Grint c) Alan Rickman

5 Which film __________ the Oscar for Best Picture in 2011? (win)
a) *Precious* b) *The King's Speech* c) *Toy Story 3*

6 Which actor __________ the part of Donkey in the *Shrek* films? (play)
a) Antonio Banderas b) Mike Myers c) Eddie Murphy

7 In which film __________ the part of a chauffeur's daughter? (Audrey Hepburn / play)
a) *Sabrina* b) *Breakfast at Tiffany's* c) *Roman Holiday*

8 What superpower __________? (Batman / have)
a) superintelligence b) none c) X-ray vision

Vocabulary activity instructions

1B Describing people

A pairwork vocabulary race

Sts look at pictures and definitions and complete the missing words. Copy one sheet per pair or one sheet per student.

Vocabulary
person / physical appearance adjectives

- Put Sts in pairs and give out the sheets. Focus on **a** and set a time limit.
- Tell Sts that they have to read the definitions and look at the pictures and write as many words as they can within the time limit. The lines indicate how many letters are necessary for each word.
- The first pair to complete all the words correctly is the winner. Check answers.

1 moustache 2 curly 3 slim 4 bald 5 mean 6 medium-height 7 blonde 8 beard 9 clever 10 hard-working 11 overweight 12 funny 13 heavy 14 quiet 15 nice

- Focus on **b**. Give Sts time to revise and then test themselves.

1C Things you wear

A pairwork brainstorm activity

Sts think of 1, 2, or 3 words connected to clothes. Copy one sheet per pair or one sheet per student.

Vocabulary
clothes

- Put Sts in pairs and give out the sheets. Don't go through all the questions but demonstrate the activity, eliciting answers to the first question, e.g. *gloves*.
- Set a time limit, and tell Sts to start. Give more time if you can see that Sts need it. When the time limit is up, check answers and find out which pair has the most correct answers.

1 gloves 2 jumper 3 hat, cap 4 sandals, boots, shoes, socks 5 leggings, tights 6 scarf, tie 7 trousers, jeans 8 necklace, bracelet, ring 9 trainers, shorts, T-shirt 10 sweater, cardigan, coat

2A Holidays

A gap fill activity

Sts complete three texts connected to holidays. Copy one sheet per student.

Vocabulary
holiday verbs

- Give out the sheets. Tell Sts they have to complete the texts with an appropriate verb in the correct form. Point out that the first letter is given to help them.
- Set a time limit. Sts compare answers in pairs. Check answers.

Story 1 1 away 2 go 3 stay 4 book 5 camping
Story 2 1 skiing 2 hired 3 rent 4 had
Story 3 1 sightseeing 2 swimming 3 sunbathe 4 spend 5 take

2B Prepositions *in, at, on*

A preposition gap fill activity

Sts complete sentences which have missing prepositions. Copy one sheet per student.

Vocabulary
prepositions of time and place

- Give out the sheets. Focus on **a**. Set a time limit. Tell Sts that they have to write in the PREPOSITIONS column and complete as many sentences as they can.
- Check answers.

1 in 2 in 3 at 4 at 5 on 6 in 7 in 8 on 9 at 10 in 11 at 12 in 13 on 14 at 15 at 16 on 17 at 18 in 19 at 20 in

- Focus on **b**. Give Sts time to revise and then test themselves.

3B What's the preposition?

An error correction activity

Sts correct prepositions mistakes. Copy one sheet per student.

Vocabulary
prepositions

- Put Sts in pairs and give out the sheets. Focus on **a** and elicit that 2 is wrong, as the preposition should be *at*.
- Sts continue in pairs. Check answers.

1 ✓
3 ✗ He depends **on**...
4 ✓
5 ✗ Can you ask the teacher **for** a...
6 ✗ I'll pay **for** the dinner...
7 ✓
8 ✓
9 ✗ My husband's worried **about**...
10 ✗ What do you think **of**...
11 ✓
12 ✗ How often do you speak **to**...
13 ✗ Maria's invited me **to**...
14 ✗ She's fallen in love **with**...
15 ✓

4A Housework, *make* and *do*

A gap fill revision activity

Sts complete sentences with the correct form of the verb. Copy one sheet per student.

> **Vocabulary**
> *make, do, put, lay, have*

- Put Sts in pairs and give out the sheets. Focus on **a** and elicit that the answer to number 1 is *doing*.
- Tell Sts that they have to complete as many sentences as they can. Point out that they have to use the right form of the verb.
- Check answers.

> 1 doing 2 puts 3 make 4 does 5 made 6 do 7 lay
> 8 do 9 made 10 doing 11 made 12 making 13 do / tidy
> 14 put / take 15 did 16 pick 17 make 18 do
> 19 do 20 make

- Focus on **b**. Give Sts time to revise and test themselves.

4B Shopping

A gap fill activity

Sts read the definitions and write down the correct word. Copy one sheet per student.

> **Vocabulary**
> shopping

- Give out the sheets, either to individual Sts or pairs. Focus on the instructions. Set a time limit.
- If Sts did the exercise individually, get them to compare with a partner before you check answers.

> 1 changing room 2 take (it) back 3 credit card 4 receipt
> 5 shop assistant 6 check out 7 item 8 trolley 9 fit
> 10 (shopping) basket / cart 11 postal 12 size 13 suit
> 14 auction

5B Describing a town or city

A pairwork vocabulary activity

Sts read the sentences and complete the missing words. Copy one sheet per student or one sheet per pair.

> **Vocabulary**
> adjectives and nouns connected to towns and cities

- Put Sts in pairs and give out the sheets. Tell Sts that they have to complete the sentences with the correct word. The first letter is given for each missing word. Set a time limit.
- Check answers.

> 1 museum 2 crowded 3 coast 4 empty 5 Castle
> 6 centre 7 dangerous 8 Cathedral 9 medium-sized
> 10 modern 11 town hall 12 polluted 13 noisy 14 east
> 15 department store

6A Opposite verbs

A memory activity

Sts read the sentences and write the opposite of the verb in bold. Copy one sheet per student or one sheet per pair.

> **Vocabulary**
> high frequency verbs and their opposites

- Give out the sheets and focus on **a**. Elicit the answer to 1 (*failed*) and highlight that the verb must be in the correct form. Sts continue.
- Check answers.

> 1 failed 2 lent ... to 3 lose 4 pull 5 forgets
> 6 got / received ... from 7 arrive 8 finishes 9 taught
> 10 sell 11 Turn on 12 found 13 repairing / mending
> 14 miss

- Focus on **b**. Sts do this individually and test themselves. This could also be done in pairs, where **A**s test **B**s, and then swap roles.

7B Verb forms: infinitive or gerund?

A sentence completion activity

Sts complete sentences with the right form of the verb. Copy one sheet per student.

> **Vocabulary**
> Verbs + *to* and *–ing*: *like, decide*

- Put Sts into pairs and give out the sheets. Focus on **a** and elicit that the answer to sentence 1 is *feel*.
- Tell Sts that they have to complete as many verbs as possible. Point out that these verbs are followed by to or *–ing* forms.
- Check answers.

> 2 want 3 planning 4 like 5 forget 6 pretended
> 7 finished 8 mind 9 Would...like 10 forget 11 decided
> 12 tried 13 go on 14 promised 15 start

- Focus on **b**. Give Sts time to revise and test themselves.

8A *get*

A sentence completion activity

Sts choose the correct word to complete the sentences. Copy one sheet per student or one sheet per pair.

> **Vocabulary**
> *get* + its different collocates, *e.g. get divorced, get colder, get a job, get up, get home, get a text message*

- Give out the sheets and focus on the instructions. In pairs or individually, Sts choose the correct word from the list to complete the sentences.
- If Sts did the activity individually, get them to compare their answers before you check.

> 1 on 2 divorced 3 present 4 home 5 up 6 ticket
> 7 lost 8 married 9 fit 10 nervous 11 better
> 12 newspaper 13 colder 14 stressed 15 worse
> 16 job 17 message 18 angry

8B Confusing verbs

A vocabulary discrimination activity

Sts circle the correct word. Copy one sheet per student or one sheet per pair.

Vocabulary
verbs with similar meanings

- Give out the sheets to individual Sts or to pairs and set a time limit. Focus on the instructions. Give Sts time to circle the words.
- If they did the activity individually, get them to compare with a partner before you check.

1 wearing 2 won 3 met 4 watching 5 looks like 6 bring 7 found 8 telling 9 missed 10 lend 11 hope 12 carrying 13 known 14 looking at 15 earn 16 look 17 look for 18 take 19 said 20 waiting 21 borrow 22 losing

9A Animal quiz

A pairwork vocabulary quiz

Sts read a series of definitions and write the words. Copy one sheet per student or one sheet per pair.

Vocabulary
animals

- Put Sts in pairs and give out the sheets. Set a time limit. Tell Sts that they have to write as many words as they can within the time limit.
- Check answers.

1 kangaroo 2 bee 3 dolphin 4 camel 5 rabbit 6 jelly fishs 7 giraffe 8 cows 9 sheep 10 mosquito 11 mouse 12 crocodile 13 elephant 14 snake 15 horse 16 lion 17 tiger 18 pig 19 bull 20 bat

- Focus on **b**. Put Sts in pairs to test each other. Another option is to do this individually.

11A Expressing movement

A pairwork vocabulary race

Sts race to think of 1, 2, or 3 answers to questions containing a preposition of movement. Copy one sheet per student or one sheet per pair.

Vocabulary
prepositions of movement

- Put Sts in pairs and give out the sheets. Set a time limit, but give Sts more time if you can see that they need it. Tell Sts that they have to read the questions and write down the answers.
- Check answers. Accept any answers which may not be in the list below, but which are correct.

Possible answers
1 river, swimming pool
2 stairs, hill, mountain
3 a road, a room
4 tennis, badminton, volleyball
5 a lipstick, keys, mobile phone
6 a (white) rabbit
7 cinema, theatre
8 bus, plane
9 marathon
10 tree, parasol
11 The London Eye, St Paul's Cathederal
12 waiter, lorry driver
13 Formula 1, athletics
14 monkey, cat, bear
15 chess

11B Phrasal verbs

A sentence completion activity

Sts read the sentences and complete them with a word from the list. Copy one sheet per student.

Vocabulary
phrasal verbs

- Give out the sheets to individual Sts and ask them to complete the sentences with the correct word from the list. Sts compare with a partner when they have finished.
- Check answers.

1 after 2 over 3 up 4 away 5 down 6 in 7 on 8 back 9 down 10 out 11 up 12 on 13 off 14 forward to 15 up 16 for 17 down 18 up 19 on 20 up

1B VOCABULARY Describing people

a Work with a partner. Look at the pictures and the definitions. Write the words.

1 ____ ____ ____ ____ ____ ____ ____ ____ ____ ____

2 It's the opposite of **straight** (hair). _ _ _ _ _

3 **thin** in an attractive way _ _ _ _

4 _ _ _ _

5 an **adjective** to describe **someone who doesn't like spending money** _ _ _ _

6 **not tall, not short** _ _ _ _ _ _-_ _ _ _ _ _

7 another word for **fair** (for a woman) _ _ _ _ _ _

8 _ _ _ _ _

9 a synonym of **intelligent** _ _ _ _ _ _

10 the opposite of **lazy** _ _ _ _-_ _ _ _ _ _ _

11 a polite way of saying **fat** _ _ _ _ _ _ _ _ _ _

12 **a person who can make other people laugh** is this _ _ _ _ _

13 the opposite of **light** _ _ _ _ _

14 **somebody who doesn't talk a lot** _ _ _ _ _

15 one word to describe **a person who's friendly and kind** _ _ _ _

activation

b Cover the words on the right and look at the pictures and the definitions. How many words can you remember?

Can you think of...?

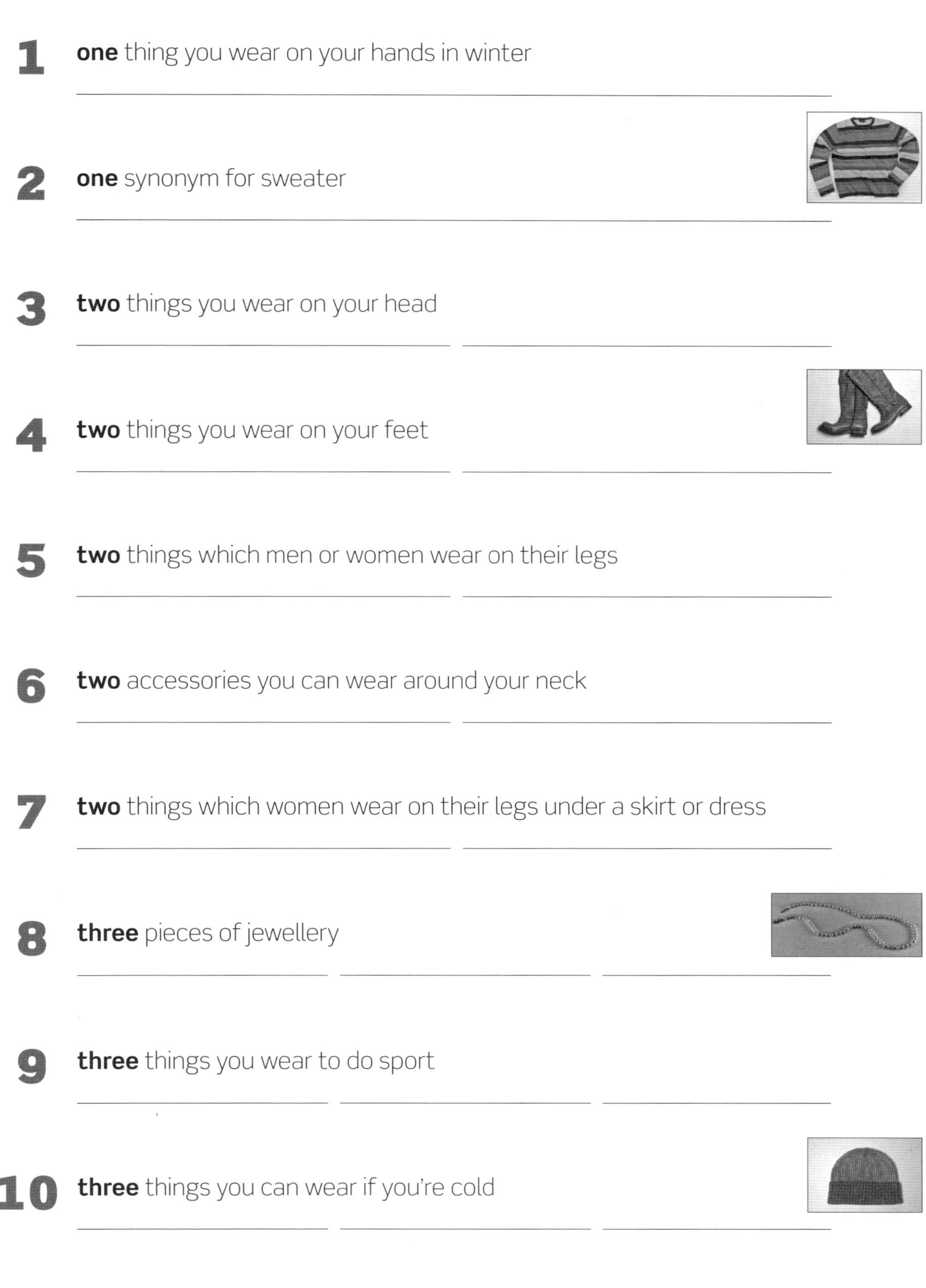

1 **one** thing you wear on your hands in winter

____

2 **one** synonym for sweater

____

3 **two** things you wear on your head

______________ ______________

4 **two** things you wear on your feet

______________ ______________

5 **two** things which men or women wear on their legs

______________ ______________

6 **two** accessories you can wear around your neck

______________ ______________

7 **two** things which women wear on their legs under a skirt or dress

______________ ______________

8 **three** pieces of jewellery

__________ __________ __________

9 **three** things you wear to do sport

__________ __________ __________

10 **three** things you can wear if you're cold

__________ __________ __________

2A VOCABULARY Holidays

Complete the texts. Put one word in each gap. The first letter is given.

1

I love going [1]a________________ for the weekend with my friends. We usually [2]g________________ by car to a town or village and [3]s________________ in a hotel.

We don't have much money, so we always [4]b________________ the hotel online as it's cheaper that way. We never go [5]c________________ because we want to be comfortable and we don't like sleeping in tents.

2

Last winter, my best friend and I decided to go [1]s________________ in the Alps. I didn't have any skis, so I [2]h________________ a pair when I got there. We decided to [3]r________________ a small apartment near the ski slopes and we [4]h________________ a very good time there. We'll definitely go back there next year.

3

If you like the beach and big cities, you should go to Barcelona! In the mornings, you can go [1]s________________ and see all the museums and monuments. In the afternoons, you can go [2]s________________ in the sea or simply [3]s________________ on the beach. You don't have to [4]s________________ a lot of money as everything is very cheap. Don't forget your camera so that you can [5]t________________ lots of photos!

2B VOCABULARY Prepositions *in*, *at*, *on*

a Complete each sentence with the correct preposition. Write your answers in the **PREPOSITIONS** column.

		PREPOSITIONS
1	The children are playing ▬ the park.	________
2	I love sunbathing ▬ the garden.	________
3	He's studying physics ▬ university.	________
4	Let's meet ▬ the bus stop.	________
5	Look! That's a Picasso ▬ the wall.	________
6	The course starts ▬ May.	________
7	My grandfather died ▬ 1984.	________
8	I was born ▬ 25th October.	________
9	We have a coffee machine ▬ work.	________
10	Do you like skiing ▬ winter?	________
11	What time will you be ▬ home tonight?	________
12	Do you eat a lot ▬ the evenings?	________
13	My English classes are ▬ Tuesdays and Thursdays.	________
14	He usually does his homework ▬ night.	________
15	The flight's ▬ 7.00 a.m.	________
16	It's so romantic! They got married ▬ St Valentine's Day.	________
17	We usually go away ▬ Christmas.	________
18	I think you left your bag ▬ the bedroom.	________
19	Do you usually go away ▬ the weekend?	________
20	I live ▬ the centre of London.	________

activation

b Cover the **PREPOSITIONS** column and look at the sentences. Say them with the right preposition.

3B VOCABULARY What's the preposition?

Are the prepositions in **bold** right (✓) or wrong (✗)? Correct the wrong ones.

1	What time does your plane arrive **in** Madrid? ✓
2	When I arrived ~~**to**~~ *at* the museum, it was closed.
3	He depends **of** his parents to give him money.
4	I completely agree **with** you.
5	Can you ask the teacher **to** a photocopy?
6	It's your birthday. I'll pay **back** the dinner tonight.
7	Do you spend a lot of money **on** clothes?
8	She writes **to** him every day.
9	My husband's worried **with** his job at the moment.
10	What do you think **about** my new shoes?
11	I can't think **about** anybody except Pete at the moment!
12	How often do you speak **at** your sister on *Skype*?
13	Maria's invited me **for** a concert, but I don't want to go.
14	She's fallen **in** love **to** her sister's boyfriend!
15	Sally waited 30 minutes **for** the bus.

4A VOCABULARY Housework, *make* and *do*

a Complete each sentence with a verb in the correct form. Write your answers in the **VERBS** column.

		VERBS
1	I don't like ▬ the ironing.	________
2	She's very untidy. She never ▬ away her clothes.	________
3	Shhh, don't ▬ a noise. The baby's asleep.	________
4	My mother ▬ the washing on Mondays.	________
5	When I was little, I always ▬ my bed before I went to school.	________
6	Can you ▬ the shopping for me, please?	________
7	Please ▬ the table! We're eating in five minutes.	________
8	How often do you ▬ exercise?	________
9	My children have ▬ a lot of friends at their new school.	________
10	I broke a glass while I was ▬ the washing-up.	________
11	I ▬ the mistake of telling her my secret.	________
12	Do you like ▬ plans for the future?	________
13	Please ▬ your room. There are books and clothes all over the floor.	________
14	It's my job to ▬ out the rubbish at night.	________
15	When was the last time you ▬ an exam?	________
16	You've left your towel on the floor. Please ▬ it up.	________
17	I don't have time to ▬ lunch. Let's eat out.	________
18	Did you ▬ anything exciting at the weekend?	________
19	Please can you ▬ exercise 1 on page 46?	________
20	Can I borrow your phone. I need to ▬ a call.	________

activation

b Cover the **VERBS** column and look at the sentences. Say the sentences with the right verbs.

4B VOCABULARY Shopping

Read the definitions and write the words in the column on the right.

1 The place where you try on clothes before buying them. __________ __________

2 **If you're not happy with something you've bought, you can _____ it _____.** __________ it __________

3 Some people call it 'plastic money'. __________ __________

4 **The piece of paper which they give you in a shop after you pay for something.** __________

5 A person who works, for example, in a boutique. __________ __________

6 **It's the place in a supermarket where you pay for the things you buy.** __________ __________

7 Another word for 'a thing' you buy. __________

8 **It has four wheels and you push it in the supermarket.** __________

9 The verb we use to say that something isn't too big or too small for you. __________

10 **When you buy something on a website, the thing you have bought goes into your _____.** __________ __________

11 If you want something sent to your house, you need to give a _____ address. __________

12 **If a pair of jeans is too big or too small for you, they're not your _____.** __________

13 It's a verb which we use when clothes look good on you. __________

14 **eBay is an _____ website.** __________

5B VOCABULARY Describing a town or city

Complete the missing words in the sentences. The first letter is given.

1 The Louvre is a famous m *u s e u m* in Paris.

2 Venice is very c_ _ _ _ _ _ in the tourist season. Thousands of people go there.

3 Brighton is on the south c_ _ _ _ of England.

4 The city centre is e_ _ _ _ in the summer because everyone goes to the beach.

5 The first king to live in Windsor C_ _ _ _ _ was Henry I.

6 There's a really good shopping c_ _ _ _ _ near here. It has lots of shops and restaurants.

7 Don't go to that part of the city! There's a lot of crime and it's very d_ _ _ _ _ _ _ _.

8 St Paul's C_ _ _ _ _ _ _ _ is in the centre of London.

9 Bordeaux's not big and it's not small. It's a m_ _ _ _ _-s_ _ _ _ city.

10 Do you prefer old or m_ _ _ _ _ houses?

11 Local government officials usually have meetings in the t_ _ _ h_ _ _.

12 Some cities are very p_ _ _ _ _ _ _ because there are a lot of cars and factories.

13 We have a nightclub under our flat. It's very n_ _ _ _ and we can hear the music at night.

14 Liège is 100 kilometres to the e_ _ _ of Brussels.

15 You can buy everything you need in a d_ _ _ _ _ _ _ _ _ s_ _ _ _.

6A VOCABULARY Opposite verbs

a In each sentence, change the verb in **bold** to the opposite verb in the same form. Write your answers in the **OPPOSITES** column.

		OPPOSITES
1	I **passed** my exams last week.	________
2	Have you ever **borrowed** money **from** a friend?	________
3	Do you think they're going to **win** the league?	________
4	You need to **push** the door to open it.	________
5	She always **remembers** people's names.	________
6	I **sent** an email **to** my sister yesterday.	________
7	What time does the plane **leave**?	________
8	The match **starts** at 5.30p.m.	________
9	He's never **learnt** English.	________
10	eBay's a good website if you want to **buy** something second-hand.	________
11	**Turn off** your computer!	________
12	I **lost** my car keys in the garden.	________
13	Maria's very good at **breaking** things.	________
14	I'll probably **catch** the train tonight.	________

activation

b Cover the sentences and look at the **OPPOSITES** column. How many verbs can you remember from the sentences?

7B VOCABULARY Verb form: infinitive or gerund?

a Complete each sentence with a verb from the list in the correct form. Write your answers in the **VERBS** column.

decide feel finish forget go on like mind plan
pretend promise remember start try want would like

		VERBS
1	I really don't ▬ like going to the party tonight. I'm really tired.	________
2	If you ▬ to learn to play tennis better, you should have lessons.	________
3	I'm ▬ to have a big party for my 60th birthday.	________
4	Do you ▬ sunbathing on the beach in summer? I love it!	________
5	Please ▬ to turn off the lights before you leave.	________
6	He ▬ to like the present although he actually hated it.	________
7	Have you ▬ eating dinner or shall I call you back later?	________
8	My students don't ▬ doing their homework because they know it's good practice.	________
9	▬ you ▬ a coffee after work?	________
10	Don't ▬ to call me tonight. You know you never remember!	________
11	Have you ▬ where to go on holiday this summer, or are you still thinking about it?	________
12	I ▬ learning Chinese last year, but I found it very difficult, so I stopped going to class.	________
13	Do you think you'll ▬ living here, or do you think you'll move somewhere else in the future?	________
14	He ▬ to call me when he got there. He always does what he says.	________
15	At least ▬ to do the exercise. If you can't, I'll help you with it.	________

activation

b Cover the **VERBS** column and look at the sentences. How many verbs can you remember?

8A VOCABULARY *get*

Complete the sentences with a word from the list.

angry better colder divorced fit home job lost married message nervous newspaper on present tickets to up worse

1 Do you get __________ well with your parents?

2 They were married for 20 years, but they got __________ last year.

3 It's Diana's birthday next week. Shall we get her a __________?

4 How long does it take you to get __________ after work?

5 I don't like getting __________ early on Sunday mornings.

6 You need to get __________ for the concert soon. They say it's going to sell out quickly.

7 We've been to your house before, so we won't get __________.

8 In the UK, you can get __________ in a church or in a registry office.

9 What's the best way to get __________? Yoga or aerobics?

10 Most people get really __________ before doing an exam.

11 Get __________ soon! And don't come back to work till you feel 100%.

12 I didn't get a __________ yesterday, because I read the news online.

13 It gets __________ after 6 p.m. Temperatures go down to -10°C.

14 What time do you usually get __________ school?

15 I think the unemployment situation in my country is getting __________ and not better.

16 How did the interview go? Did you get the __________?

17 I got a __________ from Pete to say he would be late.

18 She gets very __________ when she doesn't get her own way.

8B VOCABULARY Confusing verbs

Circle the correct verb to complete each sentence.

1 I love those shoes you're **wearing** / **carrying**.

2 Have you ever **won** / **earned** a prize?

3 They **met** / **knew** at a party last year.

4 Can you help me, or are you **watching** / **looking at** the news on TV?

5 She **looks** / **looks like** her mother. They have the same eyes.

6 Did you **bring** / **take** me anything back from New York?

7 Alba's **looked for** / **found**, a new job which starts next week.

8 Are people from your country good at **saying** / **telling** jokes?

9 We got to the airport late, so we **missed** / **lost** the plane.

10 Would you **lend** / **borrow** money to a good friend?

11 I **hope** / **wait** that I pass my end-of-year exams.

12 She's **wearing** / **carrying** a really heavy bag.

13 I've **known** / **met** my best friend for ten years.

14 Do you like **watching** / **looking at** photos of yourself?

15 How much money do you **win** / **earn** a month?

16 You **look** / **look like** really sad. What's wrong?

17 If you need the answer, you can **look for** / **find** it on the internet.

18 It's going to rain later, so don't forget to **bring** / **take** an umbrella with you.

19 She **said** / **told** that she was sorry.

20 Do you mind **hoping** / **waiting** for a few minutes?

21 We had to **lend** / **borrow** money from the bank to buy a car.

22 I'm always **missing** / **losing** my glasses.

9A VOCABULARY Animal quiz

a Read the definitions and write the animals in the column on the right.

1 This animal lives in Australia and carries its baby in a pocket. ____________
2 It's an insect which makes honey. It's yellow and black. ____________
3 This animal lives in the sea and is very clever. ____________
4 It's an animal which can live for two weeks with no water. ____________
5 The cartoon character *Bugs Bunny* is one of these. ____________
6 They're sea animals and swim slowly. If one touches you, it really hurts! ____________
7 This animal has a very long neck and lives in Africa. ____________
8 These animals give milk which people drink. ____________
9 This animal has a very warm, white coat. ____________
10 It's a very small insect which bites people at night. ____________
11 The plural of this animal is *mice*. ____________
12 This animal lives in rivers. It's green or grey and has a lot of teeth. ____________
13 It's a very big, grey animal from Africa or India. ____________
14 This animal is a long, thin reptile, and many people are scared of them. ____________
15 People rode this animal before they had cars. ____________
16 This animal is 'the king of the jungle'. ____________
17 It's a very big, orange and black cat. ____________
18 This pink animal lives on a farm and isn't very clean. ____________
19 People say this animal will attack you if you're wearing something red. ____________
20 This animal doesn't come out during the day. It can fly, but it can't see. ____________

activation

b Cover the animals and look at sentences 1–20. Can you remember the animals?

Can you think of...?

1 two places that you can **swim across**

______________ ______________

2 two things you can **go up**

______________ ______________

3 two places you can **walk across**

______________ ______________

4 three sports where you **hit** something **over** a net

______________ ______________ ______________

5 three objects you sometimes **put into** your pocket

______________ ______________ ______________

6 something a magician **takes out of** a hat

____

7 two places you can't **go into** without a ticket

______________ ______________

8 two forms of transport you can **get on** or **get off**

______________ ______________

9 one Olympic sport where you **run around** a city

____

10 two things you can **sit under** if it's hot and sunny

______________ ______________

11 two things you might see if you **fly over** London

______________ ______________

12 two jobs where people **take** things **from** one place **to** another

______________ ______________

13 two sports where you **go round and round** a track

______________ ______________

14 two animals which can **climb up** trees

______________ ______________

15 two games where you **move** pieces **across** a board

______________ ______________

11B VOCABULARY Phrasal verbs

Complete the phrasal verbs with a word from the list.

after away back down (x3) for forward to in off on (x3) out over up (x5)

1 I had to look ______________ my sister last week because she was ill.

2 He'll be really happy when all of his exams are ______________.

3 If you don't know what the word means, look it ______________ in a dictionary.

4 Don't throw that sandwich ______________! I'll eat it.

5 Could you turn the music ______________ a bit? I'm trying to study.

6 To get a passport, you need to fill ______________ two forms.

7 You should try ______________ the trousers before you buy them.

8 She's not here at the moment. Can you call ______________ later?

9 Our teacher always tells us to write ______________ any new vocabulary.

10 We have to look on the internet to find ______________ what time the film starts tonight.

11 What time do you usually get ______________ in the mornings?

12 They don't get ______________ very well. They're always arguing!

13 You need to take ______________ your shoes before you go into the temple.

14 I'm really looking ______________ ______________ my birthday this year.

15 **A** Why are you turning ______________ the volume?
B Because I'm trying to watch the film, and you keep talking.

16 She's looking ______________ a new job. She's not happy with the one she has.

17 Tim sat ______________ on the sofa and turned on the TV.

18 Your room's very untidy. Please pick ______________ the clothes which are on the floor.

19 Do you always put ______________ sunscreen before you sunbathe?

20 My brother is trying to give ______________ sweets and chocolate – he's a bit overweight.

Song activity instructions

1B Ugly

Listening for missing words 1 18

Language
Personality and appearance

- Give each student a sheet. Ask Sts what they think the picture shows.
- Focus on the task. Sts have to complete the song with an adjective or a noun from the list. Go through the list to check that Sts understand all of the words.
- Now play the song once all the way through for Sts to try and complete some of the gaps on a first listen. Tell them that they you will replay the song.
- Then play the song again, pausing after each verse to give Sts time to write in the words. Replay any sections as necessary.
- Check answers.

2 eyes 3 hair 4 beautiful 5 smile 6 comfortable 7 jealous 8 Personality 9 ugly 10 shorter 11 life 12 body 13 taller 14 great 15 bad

- Focus on **b**. Give Sts time to read the song again with the glossary. Help with any other vocabulary problems. Try to help your Sts get the gist of what the song is about even if they can't understand everything.

Extra support

If you know your Sts language you could go through the song line by line.

- Now focus on the summary and give Sts time to choose the correct words to complete the summary. Get them to compare with a partner before checking answers.

1 worried 2 appearance 3 different from 4 unkind 5 older 6 confident

- Read **Song facts** to the class.
- Finally, if you think your Sts would like to hear the song again, play it to them one more time. If your class likes singing, they can sing along.

2C Blue As Your Eyes

Listening for extra words 1 52

Language
Language expressing emotions

- Give each student a sheet. Ask Sts what they think the picture shows.
- Focus on **a**. Explain that an extra word has been added to some of the bold lines of the song. The extra word makes sense, but is not sung. Sts have to listen carefully, cross out the extra words and tick the lines which are correct.
- Demonstrate by playing the first two lines and so Sts can see why *completely* is crossed and the second line has been ticked.
- Now play the rest of the song once all through and tell Sts to try and tick the correct lines and to cross out as many extra ones as they can on a first listen. Tell them that you will replay the song.
- Then play the song again, pausing after each verse to give Sts time to write in the words. Replay any lines as necessary.
- Check answers.

2 ✓ 3 little 4 ✓ 5 great 6 old 7 forever 8 ✓ 9 only 10 now 11 that 12 ✓

- Focus on **b**. Give Sts time to read the song with the glossary and help with any other vocabulary problems. Check answers asking the class to tell you which parts of the song make them think that their answers are correct.

b confused (*Am I going insane? You turn me away, you beg me to stay/You want it to change, you want it the same etc*)

Extra support

If you know your Sts language you could go through the song line by line.

- Read **Song facts** to the class.
- Finally, if you think your Sts would like to hear the song again, play it to them one more time. If your class likes singing, they can sing along.

3A This is the Life

Listening to choose the correct words 

Language
Present continuous

- Give each student a sheet. Ask Sts what they think the picture shows.
- Focus on **a**. Sts have to listen and choose which word they hear for each gap.
- Play the song once the whole way through and tell Sts to try to circle some of the correct words on a first listen. Tell them that you will replay the song.
- Focus on **b** and play the song again pausing after each verse to give Sts time to circle the correct words. Replay any lines as necessary.

- Check answers and get Sts to write the correct words in the gaps.

2 dancing 3 boys 4 better 5 thinking 6 wake 7 sleep 8 road 9 waiting 10 sitting

- Give Sts time to read the song with the glossary and help with any other vocabulary problems. Try to help your Sts get the gist of what the song is about even if they can't understand everything. Note: It isn't clear from the context who 'Robert Riger' is although he might be a friend who they are chatting about.

Extra support

If you know your Sts language you could go through the song line by line.

- Read **Song facts** to the class.
- Finally, if you think your Sts would like to hear the song again, play it to them one more time. If your class likes singing, they can sing along.

4C If you Love Somebody, Set Them Free

Listening to choose the correct verbs 2 38

Language

Common verbs

- Give each student a sheet. Ask Sts what they think the picture shows.
- Focus on **a**. Sts must listen and choose the correct verb for each gap. Go through the verbs which have been taken out of the song and make sure Sts know their meaning.
- Focus on **b** and play the song once all the way through and tell Sts to try to complete some of the gaps on a first listen. Tell them that you will replay the song.
- Then play the song again, pausing after each verse to give Sts time to write in the words. Replay any lines as necessary.

Extra challenge

Alternatively, with a strong class you could ask them to read the song and try to fill some of the gaps *before* listening to the song.

- Check answers.

2 do 3 keep 4 throw 5 want 6 think 7 look 8 see 9 want 10 control 11 love 12 believe 13 live 14 want

- Give Sts time to read the song with the glossary and help with any other vocabulary problems. Try to help your Sts get the gist of what the song is about even if they can't understand everything.

Extra support

If you know your Sts language you could go through the song line by line.

- Read **Song facts** to the class.
- Finally, if you think your Sts would like to hear the song again, play it to them one more time. If your class likes singing, they can sing along.

5B Nobody Does It Better

Listening for missing words 2 49

Language

Vowel sounds; Ways of comparing

- Give each student a sheet. Ask them what they think the picture shows.
- Focus on **a** and make sure Sts under the word *rhyme*. Sts must match words in **A** with words in **B** which contain the same vowel sounds.
- Check answers. Point out to Sts how the same sounds are sometimes spelt differently.

A	B
rest	best
above	loved
you	do
could	good
tried	hide

- Focus on **b**. Sts have to complete the gaps in the song with the words in **a**.
- Play the song once all the way through for Sts to complete as many gaps as they can on a first listen. Tell them that you will replay the song.
- Then play the song again for Sts to complete any missing gaps.
- Check answers.

1 rest 2 best 3 tried 4 hide 5 above 6 loved 7 could 8 good 9 you 10 do

- Give Sts time to read the song with the glossary and help with any other vocabulary problems. Help with any other vocabulary problems. Try to help your Sts get the gist of what the song is about even if they can't understand everything.

Extra support

If you know your Sts language you could go through the song line by line.

- Read **Song facts** to the class.
- Finally, if you think your Sts would like to hear the song again, play it to them one more time. If your class likes singing, they can sing along.

6B Reach Out, I'll Be There

Listening for wrong words 3 15

Language

will for offers

- Give each student a sheet. Ask them what they think the picture shows.
- Focus on the task in **a**. Explain that Sts have to listen and decide if the **bold** word in each line are right (what the singer sings) or wrong (different from what the singer sings).
- Demonstrate by playing the first two lines and so Sts can see that the first bolded word in the song is wrong and has been corrected and that the second line is correct and has been ticked.

- Play the song once, verse by verse and tell Sts to just try to hear if the lines are right or wrong and put a tick or a cross. They shouldn't try to correct the wrong words at this stage.

Extra support

As the song is quite fast you may need to play some or all verses twice for Sts to hear if the words are right or wrong.

- Check answers but tell Sts not to call out the right words.

2✓ 3✗ 4✗ 5✓ 6✗ 7✗ 8✗ 9✗ 10✗ 11✓
12✗ 13✗ 14✓ 15✗

- Focus on **b**. Play the audio again and this time Sts have to try and correct the wrong words. Replay individual lines or verses as necessary.
- Get Sts to compare with a partner, and then check answers.

1 can't 3 life 4 darling 6 feel 7 best 8 hand
9 love 10 for 12 look 13 thinking 15 need

- Give Sts time to read the song with the glossary and help with any other vocabulary problems. Try to help your Sts get the gist of what the song is about even if they can't understand everything.

Extra support

If you know your Sts language you could go through the song line by line.

- Read **Song facts** to the class.
- Finally, if you think your Sts would like to hear the song again, play it to them one more time. If your class likes singing, they can sing along.

7B Don't Stop Me Now

Listening to choose the correct words 3 33

Language
Vowel sounds: /ɪ/ and /aɪ/

- Give each student a sheet.
- Focus on **a** and give Sts time to to match the words and pictures.
- Get Sts to compare with a partner, and then check answers. Make sure Sts understand the lexis. Model and drill pronunciation of any tricky words.

1 the speed of light 2 the laws of gravity
3 Two hundred degrees 4 a shooting star
5 a rocket ship 6 a racing car 7 a satellite
8 a tiger

- Focus on **b**. Sts listen and choose the correct phrases from **a** to complete the gaps. Highlight that some phrases are used more than once.
- Play the song all the way through once for Sts to try to complete some of the the gaps on a first listn. Tell them that you will replay the song.
- Then play the song again, pausing every few lines to give Sts time to write in the missing phrases.

Extra challenge

Alternatively with a good class you could give Sts time to read the lyrics and to try to complete some of the gaps before they listen.

- Check answers.

1 shooting star 2 a tiger 3 the laws of gravity
4 a racing car 5 Two hundred degrees
6 the speed of light 7 a rocket ship 8 a satellite
9 Two hundred degrees 10 Two hundred degrees
11 the speed of light

- Focus on **c** and elicit opinons. Then tell Sts the answer.

It was voted the most popular driving song by the TV programme *Top Gear*.

- Give Sts time to read the song again with the glossary. Help with any other vocabulary problems. Try to help your Sts get the gist of what the song is about even if they can't understand everything.

Extra support

If you know your Sts language you could go through the song line by line.

- Read **Song facts** to the class.
- Finally, if you think your Sts would like to hear the song again, play it to them one more time. If your class likes singing, they can sing along.

8A Why Do I Feel So Sad?

Listening for extra words 3 56

Language
Feelings and emotions

- Give each student a sheet. Ask Sts what they think the picture shows.
- Focus on **a**. Explain that an extra word has been added to every line of the song. The extra word makes sense, but is not sung. Sts must listen carefully and cross out this extra word.
- To demonstrate play the first line of the song so that Sts can see that *your* is not sung and has been crossed out.
- Now play the rest of the song once all through and tell students to try and cross out as many extra words as they can on a first listen. Tell them that you will replay the song.
- Then play the song again, pausing after each verse to give Sts time to cross out the extra words. Replay any lines as necessary.
- Check answers.

2 again 3 all 4 now 5 these 6 very 7 longer 8 now
9 always 10 any 11 really 12 me 13 today 14 please

- Focus on **b** and on the example and give Sts time to match the words and phrases from the song (1–8) with meanings a–h. Tell Sts to look a the phrases in context in the song to help them.
- Get Sts to compare with a partner, and then check answers.

1 e 2 h 3 f 4 g 5 c 6 b 7 d 8 a

- Give Sts time to read the song again with the glossary. Help with any other vocabulary problems. Try to help your Sts get the gist of what the song is about even if they can't understand everything.

Extra support

If you know your Sts language you could go through the song line by line.

- Read **Song facts** to the class.
- Finally, if you think your Sts would like to hear the song again, play it to them one more time. If your class likes singing, they can sing along.

9C You're My #1

Listening to choose the correct words 

Language

Present perfect

- Give each student a sheet.
- Focus on **a**. Get Sts to match the words and pictures.
- Check answers. Model and drill pronunciation of any tricky words.

1 the moon 2 angels 3 a fountain 4 lips 5 a butterfly
6 a tear 7 a sunset 8 the sky

- Focus on **b**. Sts have to listen and choose which word they hear for each gap.
- Play the song once the whole way through and tell Sts to try to circle some of the correct words on a first listen. Tell them that you will replay the song.
- Focus on c and play the song again for Sts to check their answers. pausing after each verse to give Sts time to circle the correct words. Replay any lines as necessary.
- Check answers, getting Sts to write the correct word in each gap.

1 a million 2 summertime 3 highest 4 a hundred
5 seen 6 haven't seen 7 amazes 8 I'm feeling
9 right 10 done 11 baby 12 sailed 13 Danced

- Give Sts time to read the song with the glossary and help with any other vocabulary problems. Try to help your Sts get the gist of what the song is about even if they can't understand everything.

Extra support

If you know your Sts language you could go through the song line by line.

- Read **Song facts** to the class.
- Finally, if you think your Sts would like to hear the song again, play it to them one more time. If your class likes singing, they can sing along.

10B ABC

Listening to choose the correct verb 4 47

Language

Verbs; Classroom language

- Give each student a sheet. Ask Sts what the pictures show.
- Focus on **a**. Sts have to listen to the song and complete the gaps with the verbs in the box.
- Play the song verse by verse, pausing at the end of each verse to give Sts time to complete the gaps. Replay as necessary.

Extra challenge

Alternatively, with a strong class you could ask them to read the song and try to fill some of the gaps *before* listening to the song.

- Check answers.

2 teach 3 take 4 repeat 5 Come 6 love 7 show
8 listen 9 show 10 spell 11 Listen

- Focus on **b**. Get Sts to match meanings 1-6 with the **bold** words and phrases in the song.
- Check answers. Explain the spelling rule (6) to Sts by giving them some words with i and e in them, e.g. *friend* and *receive*.

1 do re mi 2 A B C 3 two plus two makes four
4 1 2 3 e take a seat 5 reading, writing, arithmetic
6 I before E except after C

- Give Sts time to read the song again with the glossary. Help with any other vocabulary problems. Try to help your Sts get the gist of what the song is about even if they can't understand everything.

Extra support

If you know your Sts language you could go through the song line by line.

- Read **Song facts** to the class.
- Finally, if you think your Sts would like to hear the song again, play it to them one more time. If your class likes singing, they can sing along.

11A The Final Countdown

Listening to match sentence halves 4 59

Language

Vowel sounds

- Give each student a sheet. Ask Sts what the picture shows.
- Focus on **a** and tell Sts they must match the halves of the sentences. Focus on the example which has been done (1h).
- Play the song once the whole way through and tell Sts to try and match as many as the lines as they can on a first listen. Tell them that you will replay the song.
- Then play the song again for Sts to check and complete the task.
- Check answers.

2 i 3 d 4 e 5 a 6 f 7 g 8 c 9 b

- Focus on **b**. In pairs, get Sts to decide if the pair of words have the same vowel sounds or not.
- Check answers. Point out how the sounds are spelt many different ways.

1 different: *leaving* /iː/ and *heading* /e/
2 ✓ /e/
3 different: *guess* /e/ and *be* /iː/
4 ✓ /iː/
5 ✓ /e/
6 different: *seen* /iː/ and *welcome* /e/

- Give Sts time to read the song with the glossary and help with any other vocabulary. Try to help your Sts get the gist of what the song is about even if they can't understand everything.

Extra support

If you know your Sts language you could go through the song line by line.

- Read **Song facts** to the class.
- Finally, if you think your Sts would like to hear the song again, play it to them one more time. If your class likes singing, they can sing along.

12B I Heard It Through the Grapevine

Listening for missing words 5 26

Language

Tenses; Verb forms;
Informal language, idioms, and collocations

- Give each student a sheet. Ask them what they think the picture shows.
- Focus on the song title and elicit / explain that *to hear something on the grapevine* is to find out about something by hearing a rumour or gossip which is spread from person to person.
- Focus on **a**. Sts have to listen and complete the numbered words which rhyme with the previous **bolded** word.
- Play the song once for Sts to try to complete some of gapped words on a first listen. Tell them that you will play the song again.
- Then play the song again for Sts to complete the task.
- Check answers.

2 more 3 yesterday 4 mine 5 inside 6 me 7 dear 8 know

Extra challenge

Alternatively with a good class you could get Sts to try and guess some or all of the missing words before they listen using the rhyme scheme to help them.

- Focus on **b** and on the example and get Sts to match the words and phrases (1–10) with their meanings (a–j). Tell Sts to look at the words in context in the song to help them do the task.
- Get Sts to compare with a partner, and then check answers.

1 i 2 d 3 j 4 h 5 b 6 e 7 c 8 a 9 g 10 f

- Give Sts time to read the song and help with any other new vocabulary. Try to help your Sts get the gist of what the song is about even if they can't understand everything.

Extra support

If you know your Sts language you could go through the song line by line.

- Read **Song facts** to the class.
- Finally, if you think your Sts would like to hear the song again, play it to them one more time. If your class likes singing, they can sing along.

1B SONG Ugly

a Look at the song and the words in the list. Then listen to the song and complete the gaps with an adjective or noun.

Adjectives: bad beautiful comfortable jealous shorter ~~strange~~ taller ugly

Nouns: body eyes hair life personality smile

Ugly

When I was seven they said I was [1] *strange*
I noticed that my [2]__________ and
[3]__________ weren't the same.
I asked my parents if I was OK
They said you're more [4]__________ and that's the way
They show that they wish that they had your
[5]__________
So my confidence was up for a while,
I got real [6]__________ with my own style
I knew that they were only [7]__________ 'cause

Chorus
People are all the same
And we only get judged by what we do
[8]__________ reflects name
And if I'm [9]__________ then so are you,
so are you

There was a time when I felt like I cared
That I was [10]__________ than everyone there
People made me feel like [11]__________ was unfair
And I did things that made me ashamed
'Cause I didn't know my [12]__________ would change
I grew [13]__________ than them in more ways
But there will always be the one who will say
Something bad to make them feel great.

Chorus (x2)

Everybody talks [14]__________ about somebody and
Never realizes how it affects somebody and
You bet it won't be forgotten
Envy is the only thing it could be

Chorus

b Listen again and read the lyrics. Use the glossary to help you. Then choose the correct alternatives to make a summary of the song.

Ugly is about a girl who grows up feeling [1] **happy / worried** about her [2] **appearance / parents**. She feels [3] **different from / the same as** people around her. Some people say [4] **kind / unkind** things about her. As she becomes [5] **older / richer**, she feels a lot more [6] **confident / jealous** about herself and her life.

SONG FACTS

Ugly was a hit single for the Sugababes in many countries in 2005 and 2006. The band recorded the song after negative comments about them in British newspapers. Sugababes used a line from this song as the name of their fourth album, *Taller in More Ways*.

GLOSSARY

my confidence was up = I felt good about myself
comfortable with my own style = I liked the way I looked
we get judged by what we do = our actions are important, not our appearance
So are you = you are too.
unfair = not treating people equally
ashamed = feeling bad about things you have done
grew taller ... in more ways = a better person
realize how it affects somebody = see the results of your actions
you bet = you can be sure
envy = feeling jealous of another person

2C SONG Blue As Your Eyes

a Some of the **bold** lines in the lyrics have an extra word. Listen to the song. Tick (✓) the correct lines or cross out the extra word.

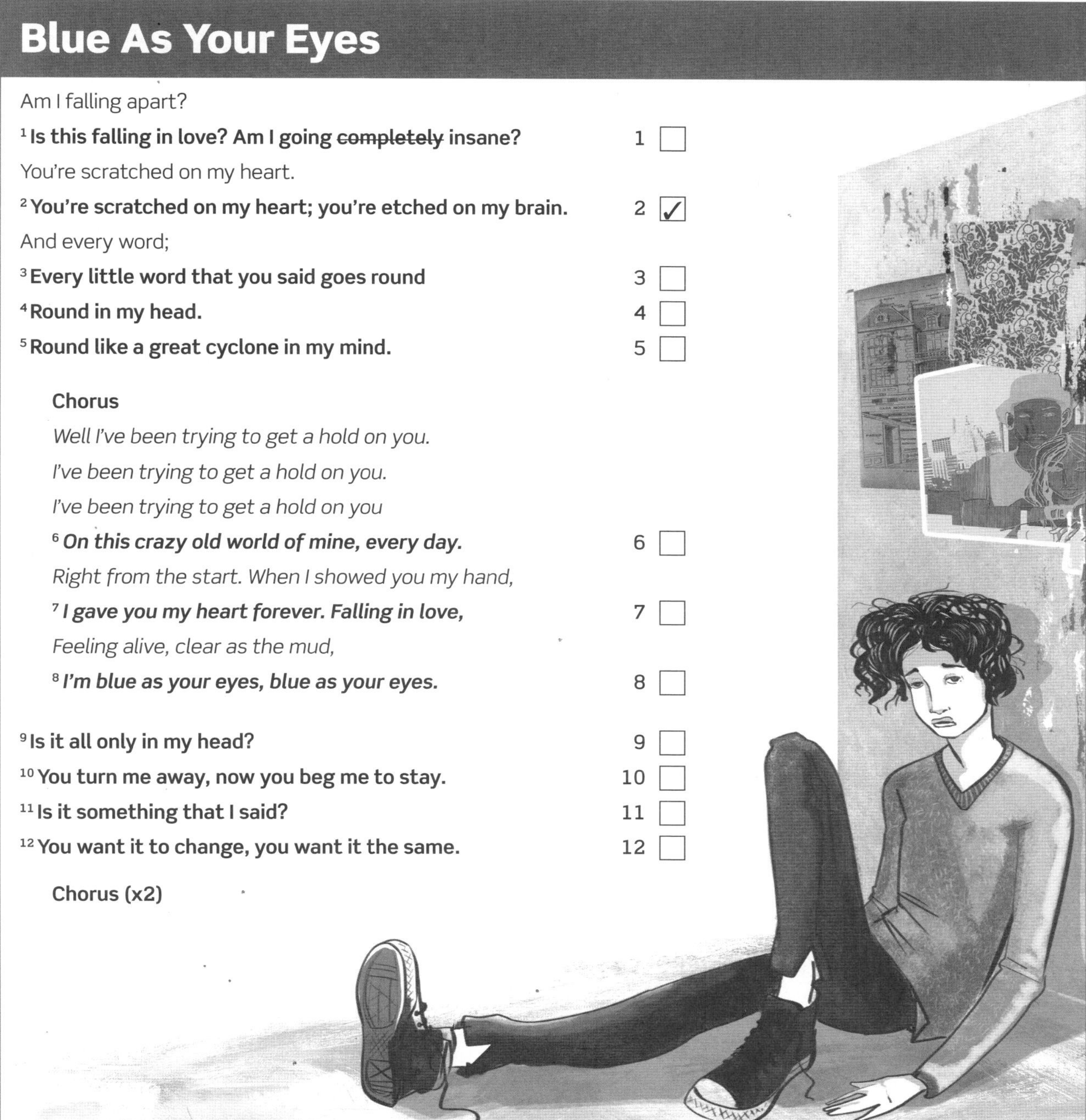

Blue As Your Eyes

Am I falling apart?
[1] Is this falling in love? Am I going ~~completely~~ insane? 1 ☐
You're scratched on my heart.
[2] You're scratched on my heart; you're etched on my brain. 2 ☑
And every word;
[3] Every little word that you said goes round 3 ☐
[4] Round in my head. 4 ☐
[5] Round like a great cyclone in my mind. 5 ☐

Chorus
Well I've been trying to get a hold on you.
I've been trying to get a hold on you.
I've been trying to get a hold on you
[6] On this crazy old world of mine, every day. 6 ☐
Right from the start. When I showed you my hand,
[7] I gave you my heart forever. Falling in love, 7 ☐
Feeling alive, clear as the mud,
[8] I'm blue as your eyes, blue as your eyes. 8 ☐

[9] Is it all only in my head? 9 ☐
[10] You turn me away, now you beg me to stay. 10 ☐
[11] Is it something that I said? 11 ☐
[12] You want it to change, you want it the same. 12 ☐

Chorus (x2)

b Listen to the song again and read the lyrics. Use the glossary to help you. How is the boy feeling?

a jealous   b confused   c depressed

SONG FACTS

This song was originally recorded by the UK band Scouting For Girls. The band's name comes from the fact that two of them met when they were in The Scouts, a national club where young boys learn things like camping, climbing, and outdoor sports. *Blue As Your Eyes* is a song from their 2010 album *Everybody Wants To Be on TV*.

GLOSSARY

falling apart = breaking
insane = crazy, mad
You're scratched on my heart = It's impossible to stop loving you
You're etched on my brain = It's impossible to stop thinking about you
get a hold on you = understand you
showed you my hand = told you my feelings
clear as the mud = unclear
beg me = ask me

3A SONG This is the Life

a Listen to the song. Circle the correct word for each gap.

This is the Life

Oh the wind whistles down	
The cold [1] ________________ street tonight	dark / hard
And the people they were [2] ________________	asking / dancing
To the music vibe	
And the [3] ________________ chase the girls with the curls in their hair	men / boys
While the shy tormented youth sit way over there	
And the songs they get louder, each one [4] ________________ than before	better / louder
Chorus	
And you're singing the songs, [5] ________________ this is the life	*singing / thinking*
And you [6] ________________ in the morning and your head feels twice the size	*wake up / get up*
Where you gonna go? Where you gonna go? Where you gonna [7] ________________ tonight?	*sleep / stay*
(repeat)	
So you're heading down the [8] ________________ in your taxi for four	road / street
And you're [9] ________________ outside Jimmy's front door	standing / waiting
But nobody's in and nobody's home till four	
So you're [10] ________________ there with nothing to do	sitting / singing
Talking about Robert Riger and his motley crew	
And where you're gonna go and where you're gonna sleep tonight	
Chorus	

b Listen again to check and write the correct word in the gaps.

SONG FACTS

This song was originally recorded by Amy Macdonald, a Scottish singer and songwriter. At the age of just 20, she had a top-ten hit with *This is the Life* in 17 countries and the song was used for a Fiat advertisement in Europe in 2010. *This is the Life* was also the name of her first album.

GLOSSARY

whistles = makes a high sound
vibe = strong positive feeling from a place, or from music
chase = run after, try to catch
shy tormented youth = emotional young people
this is the life = this is fantastic
your head feels twice the size = you feel terrible
you gonna = are you going to
heading = going
motley crew = group of friends

4C SONG If You Love Somebody, Set Them Free

a Read the song lyrics. The listen to the song and complete each verse with the correct verbs.

If You Love Somebody, Set Them Free

(Free free, set them free)

VERSE 1 ~~call~~ do keep think throw want

If you need somebody, [1]*call* my name
If you want someone, you can [2]__________ the same
If you want to [3]__________ something precious
You got to lock it up and [4]__________ away the key
If you [5]__________ to hold on to your possessions
Don't even [6]__________ about me.

Chorus
If you love somebody
If you love someone
Set them free. (Free free, set them free)

VERSE 2 look see want

If it's a mirror you want, just [7]__________ into my eyes
Or a whipping boy, someone to despise
Or a prisoner in the dark tied up in chains
You just can't [8]__________;
Or a beast in a gilded cage
That's all some people ever [9]__________ to be

Chorus

VERSE 3 believe control live love want

You can't [10]__________ an independent heart
Can't tear the one you [11]__________ apart
Forever conditioned to [12]__________ that we can't live,
We can't [13]__________ here and be happy with less
So many riches, so many souls
Everything we see that we [14]__________ to possess

Verse 1 repeated

Chorus

GLOSSARY
precious = special or expensive
got to = have to
whipping boy = a person that you are bad to
despise = hate
beast = animal
gilded = made of gold
tear…apart = break completely
conditioned to believe = always told to think something is true
riches = money

SONG FACTS

This song was originally recorded by Sting, the singer and songwriter, who first became famous as part of the group The Police. *If You Love Somebody, Set Them Free* was one of his first hits as a solo artist, in 1985.

5B SONG Nobody Does It Better

a Match a word in A with a rhyming word in B.

A

1 rest ☐ 2 above ☐
3 tried ☐ 4 you ☐
5 could ☐

B

a good b best
c hide d do
e loved

b Listen to the song and write the words in the gaps.

Nobody Does It Better

Nobody does it better
Makes me feel sad for the [1] *rest*
Nobody does it half as good as you
Baby, you're the [2] ________

I wasn't looking but somehow you found me
I [3] ________ to [4] ________
from your love light
But like heaven [5] ________ me, the spy
who [6] ________ me
Is keeping all my secrets safe tonight
And nobody does it better
Though sometimes I wish someone [7] ________
Nobody does it quite the way you do
Why do you have to be so [8] ________?

The way that you hold me
Whenever you hold me
There's some kind of magic inside [9] ________
That keeps me from running, but just keep it coming
How'd you learn to do the things you [10] ________?

And nobody does it better, etc.

Baby, you're the best
Darling, you're the best
Sweet thing, you're the best

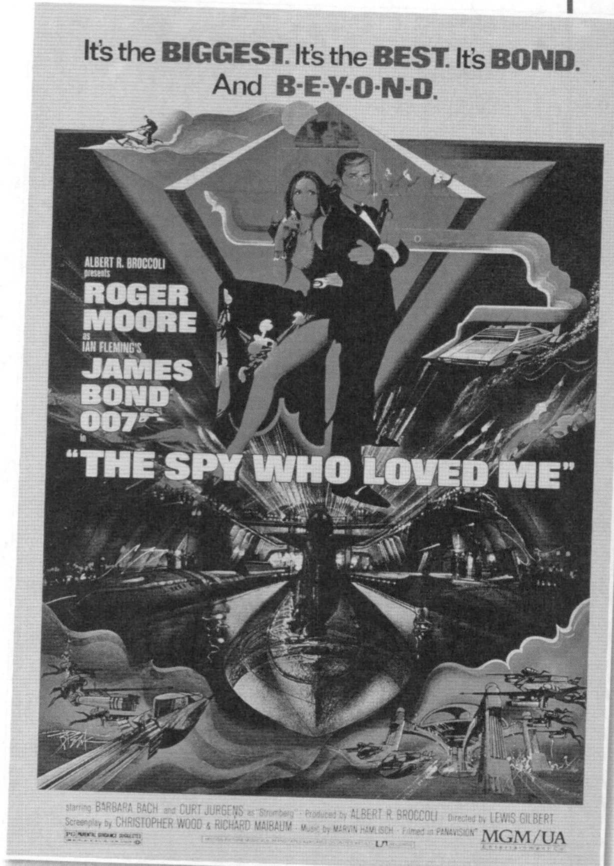

SONG FACTS

Nobody Does It Better was the theme tune for the James Bond film, *The Spy Who Loved Me*. Carly Simon had a hit with the song in 1977. The song has appeared in many films since then, and it has been a hit for several different bands.

GLOSSARY

somehow = I don't know how
hide = go to a place where nobody can find you
heaven = the sky and the stars
spy = a person who does secret work
whenever = every time
keeps me from running = stops me leaving
keep it coming = don't stop
how'd you = how did you

6B SONG Reach Out, I'll Be There

a Listen to the song. Some of the **bold** words are right, and some are wrong. Tick (✓) the right words, and cross (✗) the wrong ones.

Reach Out, I'll Be There

Now if you feel that you [1]**won't** go on	1	✗	*can't*
Because all of your hope is [2]**gone**	2	☐	______
And your day is filled with much [3]**confusion**	3	☐	______
Until happiness is just an illusion			
And your world around is tumbling down, [4]**baby**	4	☐	______
Reach out! Come on, girl! Reach on out for me!			
Reach out! Reach out, for me.			
Chorus			
I'll be there with a [5]**house** that will shelter you	5	☐	______
I'll be there with a love that will see you through			
When you are [6]**sad** and about to give up	6	☐	______
'Cause your life just ain't [7]**good** enough	7	☐	______
And you feel the world has grown cold			
And you're drifting out all on your own			
And you need a [8]**person** to hold, darling	8	☐	______
Reach out! Come on, girl! Reach out for me!			
Reach out! Reach out, for me!			
Chorus			
I'll be there to [9]**hold** and comfort you	9	☐	______
And I'll be there, to cherish and care about you			
(I'll be there to [10]**often** see you through)	10	☐	______
(I'll be there to love and comfort you)			
I can tell the way you hang your head			
You're without love now, now you're [11]**afraid**	11	☐	______
And through your tears you [12] **turn** around	12	☐	______
But there's no peace of mind to be found			
I know what you're [13]**saying**, you're alone now	13	☐	______
No love of your own, but darling			
Reach out! Come on, girl! Reach out for me!			
Reach out! Reach out!			
Just [14]**look** over your shoulder	14	☐	______
I'll be there to give you all the love you [15]**want**.	15	☐	______
And I'll be there, you can always depend on me.			

b Listen again. Try to correct the wrong words.

GLOSSARY

tumbling = falling
reach out = hold out your arms towards me
shelter = look after
cherish = love
see you through = stay with you
about to = going
drifting = unsure which way you are going
hang your head = feel sad
over your shoulder = behind you

SONG FACTS

Reach Out, I'll Be There was an international number one hit for The Four Tops in 1966. Today, it is still one of the most popular songs of the 1960s.

7B SONG Don't Stop Me Now

a Match the phrases and pictures.

a shooting star ☐ a racing car ☐ the laws of gravity ☐ the speed of light ☐
a rocket ship ☐ a satellite ☐ Two hundred degrees ☐ a tiger ☐

1 299 792 458 MILES PER SECOND 2 $F = G\frac{m_1 m_2}{r^2}$ 3 200° 4 5 6 7 8

Don't Stop Me Now

Tonight I'm gonna have myself a real good time
I feel alive
And the world is turning inside out, yeah!
I'm floating around in ecstasy, so
(Don't stop me now)
(Don't stop me) 'cause I'm having a good time, having a good time

I'm [1]*a shooting star* leaping through the sky like [2]__________
Defying [3]__________
I'm [4]__________ passing by like Lady Godiva*
I'm gonna go, go, go, there's no stopping me
I'm burning through the sky, yeah!
[5]__________, that's why they call me Mister Fahrenheit
I'm travelling at [6]__________, I wanna make a
Supersonic man out of you

Chorus
(Don't stop me now)
I'm having such a good time, I'm having a ball
If you wanna have a good time, just give me a call
'Cause I'm having a good time
Yes I'm having a good time, I don't want to stop at all

I'm [7]__________ on my way to Mars on a collision course
I am [8]__________, I'm out of control
I am a machine, ready to reload
Like an atome bomb, about to explode
I'm burning through the sky, yeah!
[9]__________, that's why they call me Mister Fahrenheit
I'm travelling at the speed of light, I wanna make a
Supersonic woman of you

(Don't stop me, don't stop me, don't stop me)
Hey hey hey! (Don't stop me, don't stop me, Ooh ooh ooh)
I like it (Don't stop me, don't stop me)
Have a good time, good time
(Don't stop me, don't stop me)
Ooh ooh, alright

Oh, burning through the sky, yeah!
[10]__________, that's why they call me *Mister Fahrenheit*
Travelling at [11]__________, I wanna make a
Supersonic man out of you

Chorus

b Listen to the song, verse by verse, and complete the gaps with a phrase from **a**. Some of them are used more than once.

c What do you think this song was voted in the UK?

a The greatest dancing song ever
b The greatest driving song ever
c The greatest karaoke song ever

GLOSSARY

gonna = going to
defy = go against
wanna = want to
turning inside out = completely different from normal
floating = moving slowly in the air
in ecstasy = very happily
burning through the sky = going very fast, like a rocket
supersonic = travelling at the speed of sound
having a ball = having a good time
on a collision course = going to crash into something

*Lady Godiva is famous in English history. She rode a horse in public while wearing no clothes. The singer means that everyone will notice him.

SONG FACTS

Don't Stop Me Now was a hit for the UK group Queen in 1978. Many other bands have recorded versions of the song, and it has been used in films and adverts.

8A SONG Why Do I Feel So Sad?

a Listen to the song and cross out the extra word in each line.

Why Do I Feel So Sad?

1 Friends we've been for so long, now ~~your~~ true colours are showing
2 Makes me wanna cry, oh yes it does, 'Cause I had to say goodbye again

Chorus
3 By now I should know, that in time all things must change,
4 So it shouldn't be so bad, so why do I feel so sad now?

5 How can I adjust, to the way that these things are going?
6 It's killing me very slowly. Oh I just want it to be how it used to be
7 'Cause I wish that I could stay longer, but in time things must change
8 So it shouldn't be so bad, so why do I feel so sad now?

9 You cannot always hide the way you feel inside I realize
10 Your actions speak much louder than any words, so tell me why, oh

Chorus (x2)

11 By now, by now I should really know, that in time things must grow
12 And I had to leave you behind me,
13 So why do I feel so sad today, if it couldn't be that bad
14 Please tell me why

Chorus

b Read the lyrics and match the words and phrases.

1	true colours are showing	*e*	a	walk away from
2	makes me wanna cry	___	b	know something is true
3	adjust	___	c	want to
4	used to be	___	d	the things you do are more important than what you say
5	wish that I could	___	~~e~~	I can see your real personality
6	realize	___	f	change yourself, when life changes
7	actions speak louder than words	___	g	was in the past
8	leave…behind	___	h	makes me sad

SONG FACTS

Why Do I Feel So Sad? was a song from Alicia Keys' 2001 album, *Songs in A Minor.*

9C SONG You're My #1

a Match the words and the pictures.

angels	☐	the moon	☐
a butterfly	☐	the sky	☐
a fountain	☐	a sunset	☐
lips	☐	a tear	☐

1 2 3 4 5 6 7 8

b Listen to the song and circle the right word or phrase from each pair.

You're My #1

I've kissed the moon ¹__________ times	a thousand / a million
Danced with angels in the sky	
I've seen snowfall in the ²__________	summertime / winter
Felt the healing of the powers up above	
I've seen the world from the ³__________ mountain	highest / tallest
Tasted love from the purest fountain	
I've seen lips that spark desire	
Felt the butterflies ⁴__________ times	a hundred / a thousand
I've even ⁵__________ miracles	known / seen
I've felt the pain disappear	
But still ⁶__________ anything	haven't seen / didn't see
That ⁷__________ me quite like you do	amazes / surprises
Chorus	
You bring me up when ⁸__________ down	I feel / I'm feeling
You touch me deep you touch me ⁹__________	again / right
You do the things I've never ¹⁰__________	done / known
You make me wicked you make me wild	
'Cause ¹¹__________, you're my number one	baby / darling
I've ¹²__________ in a perfect dream	flown / sailed
I've seen the sun make love to the sea	
I've kissed the moon a million times	
¹³__________ with angels in the sky	Talked / Danced

I've even seen miracles
I've seen the tears disappear
But still haven't seen anything
That amazes me quite like you do

Chorus

GLOSSARY

Felt the healing of the powers up above = felt better because of God
purest = cleanest
spark desire = make me want them
felt the butterflies = felt scared or nervous ('have butterflies in your stomach')
miracles = wonderful and surprising things
disappear = go away
amazes = surprises very much
bring me up = make me happy
feel down = feel sad
touch me deep = change me a lot
wicked = wanting to do bad things
wild = excited

c Listen to the song again to check and read the lyrics. Write the missing word or phrase in the gap.

SONG FACTS

Enrique Iglesias is one of the most successful Latin singers of all time. His father Julio Iglesias is also a famous singer in Spanish and English. *You're My #1* was a single on his first English-speaking album, *Enrique*, in 1999.

10B SONG ABC

a Listen to the song, verse by verse, and complete gaps 1–10 with a verb from the list.

ABC

VERSE 1 ~~make~~ repeat take teach

You went to school to learn, girl
Things you never, never knew before
Like **I before E except after C**
And why **two plus two** 1*makes* **four**, now now now,
I'm gonna 2__________ you Teach you, teach you
All about love, dear All about love
Sit yourself down, 3__________ a seat
All you gotta do is 4__________ after me.

Chorus
***A B C**, Easy as*
One, two, three, Or simple as
***Do re mi**, A B C,*
One, two, three, baby, you and me girl!
A B C, Easy as
***One, two, three**, Or simple as*
Do re mi, A B C,
One, two, three, baby, you and me, girl!

VERSE 2 listen (x2) love show(x2) spell

Come on, let me 5__________ you just a little bit
I'm going to teach you how to sing it out!
Come on, come on, let me 6__________ you what it's all about
Reading, writing arithmetic are the
Branches of the learning tree
But 7__________! Without the roots of love every day girl,
Your education ain't complete
Teacher's gonna 8__________ you
How to get an A
9__________ "me" "you", add the two
10__________ to me baby, that's all you gotta do

Chorus (x2)

That's how easy love can be (x2)
Sing a simple melody
One two three, you and me

b Read the lyrics and match the highlighted phrases in the song to their meanings.

1 __________ the first three musical notes
2 __________ the first three letters of the alphabet
3 __________ a maths sum
4 __________ the first three numbers
5 __________ three school subjects
6 __________ a rule about spelling

SONG FACTS

ABC was a big hit for The Jackson Five in 1970. Michael Jackson sang the lead vocals on the song, at the age of just 11 years old. The song was more recently recorded by the cast of *Glee* in the American musical comedy series.

GLOSSARY
gotta = have got to (= have to, must)
branches, roots = parts of a tree
ain't = isn't
get an 'A' = get top marks in a test or exam

11A SONG The Final Countdown

a Listen to the song and match lines 1–8 with lines a–h.

The Final Countdown

1 We're leaving together, [g]
2 And maybe we'll come back [ ]
3 I guess there is [ ]
4 We're leaving ground [ ]

Chorus
It's the final countdown
the final countdown

5 We're heading for Venus, Venus, [ ]
6 Cause maybe they've seen us [ ]
7 With so many light years to go [ ]
8 I'm sure that [ ]

Chorus

a be the same again?
b we all miss her so
c and things to be found
d no one to blame
e and still we stand tall
f and welcome us all
g but still it's farewell
h to earth, who can tell

b Tick (✓) the pairs of words from the song which have the same sound.

1	leaving	heading	[ ]
2	together	farewell	[ ]
3	guess	be	[ ]
4	we	maybe	[ ]
5	again	tell	[ ]
6	seen	welcome	[ ]

SONG FACTS

The 1986 song *The Final Countdown* was a number one hit in 25 countries for Swedish band Europe. They originally wrote the song just to open their concerts with an exciting 'countdown' to the start of the show, and were surprised when it was so successful. It is often played around the world at sports events.

GLOSSARY

miss = feel sad because you are far from something or somebody
I guess = I think
no one to blame = nobody did anything wrong
leaving ground = leaving the earth (in a rocket)
final countdown = counting from ten to zero before a rocket leaves the ground
stand tall = feel proud and brave
heading for = travelling to
farewell = goodbye
light years = a very long distance
who can tell = nobody knows

12B SONG I Heard It Through the Grapevine

a Read the song lyrics and try to guess some of the missing words (1–8) They contain the same sound as the previous word in **bold**. Then listen and complete the gaps.

I Heard It Through the Grapevine

Ooh, I bet you're wondering how I **knew**
'Bout your plans to make me [1]**bl***ue*
With some other guy you knew **before,**
Between the two of us guys you know I love you [2]**m**__________.
It took me by surprise I must **say**,
When I found out [3]**y**__________. Don't you know that ...

Chorus
I heard it through the **grapevine**
Not much longer would you be [4]**m**__________. Oh,
I heard it through the grapevine, Oh
I'm just about to lose my mind.
Honey, honey yeah.
(Heard it through the grapevine, not much longer would you be mine baby, ooh)

I know that a man ain't supposed to **cry**,
But these tears I can't hold [5]**in**__________.
Losing you would end my life, you **see**,
'Cause you mean that much to [6]**m**__________.
You could have told me yourself
That you loved someone else. Instead...

Chorus

People say 'Believe half of what you see,
Son, and none of what you **hear**.'
But I can't help being confused
If it's true please tell me, [7]**d**__________?
Do you plan to let me **go,**
For the other guy you loved before? Don't you [8]**kn**__________ that ...

Chorus

b Match the words and phrases with their meanings.

1	I bet *i*	a	are important /special
2	blue ____	b	from other people's conversation
3	guy ____	c	become crazy
4	found out ____	d	sad
5	through the grapevine ____	e	shouldn't
6	ain't supposed to ____	f	unsure
7	lose my mind ____	g	It was wrong that you didn't tell me.
8	mean that much ____	h	heard / discovered
9	you could have told me ____	~~i~~	I'm sure
10	confused ____	j	man

SONG FACTS

I Heard It Through the Grapevine was written in 1966, and has been a hit for many different artists. Marvin Gaye's 1968 version of the song was the most successful of all, and is one of the most popular soul songs of all time.